CLASSICAL
APOLOGETICS

CLASSICAL APOLOGETICS

A Rational Defense
of the Christian Faith and
a Critique of Presuppositional
Apologetics

R. C. SPROUL   JOHN GERSTNER

ARTHUR LINDSLEY

ZondervanPublishingHouse
Grand Rapids, Michigan

A Division of HarperCollins*Publishers*

CLASSICAL APOLOGETICS
Copyright © 1984 by The Zondervan Corporation
Grand Rapids, Michigan

Request for information should be addressed to:
  Zondervan Publishing House
  Grand Rapids, Michigan 49530

Library of Congress Cataloging in Publication Data
Sproul, R. C. (Robert Charles), 1939–
  Classical apologetics.

  Includes bibliographical references.
  1. Apologetics. 2. Natural theology. I. Gerstner,
John H. II. Lindsley, Arthur. III. Title.
BT1102.S586 1984   239   83-26020
ISBN 0-310-44951-0

Edited by Jack Stewart
Designed by Louise Bauer

Printed in the United States of America

99 00 01 02 /DC/28 27 26 25 24 23 22 21 20 19 18

To

Cornelius Van Til

*who has taught a generation
that Christ is the Alpha
and Omega of thought and life*

Contents

CONTENTS

Preface

Christianity is rational. But because it provokes passion, devotion, prayer, worship, and aspirations to obedience, its purely rational element can easily be submerged or concealed from view. It has been called variously a "religion," a "way of life," an "experience," a "faith," and an "ideology." That Christianity involves more, much more than rationality, is evident. That it is eminently rational is not always evident.

Throughout this work, the authors, John Gerstner, Arthur Lindsley, and R. C. Sproul, affirm the *primacy of the mind* in the Christian faith. To suggest the primacy of the mind is outrageous to some, particularly to those who equate rationality with rationalism. We also affirm the *primacy of the heart*. The scope of this volume focuses primarily on the rational aspect of Christianity. Our emphasis on this part, however, must not be misconstrued as a summary of the whole.

But how can we speak of two primacies? Must not the one hold ultimate primacy over the other or at least be considered the *primus inter pares?* We take no refuge in dialectics but speak of two different kinds of primacies. The mind has a primacy of *order,* while the heart has a primacy of *importance.* By this we mean that one can have no meaningful love or passion for that which is utterly unintelligible to the mind. Man is so constituted that his heart is to follow his head, just as love blossoms in the fertile ground of understanding. Though the mind is first in temporal and logical order, it does not settle our standing before God. Christianity recognizes the real possibility of a cognitive understanding of doctrine and philosophy which is held captive by a cold and recalcitrant heart. To have a lucid understanding of the things of God without a heart burning with affection toward Him is to be exposed all the more to His judgment. It betrays the most deadly form of schizophrenia. On the other hand, to be flowing with love toward Him, even when confused or less than precise about doctrine, is to be numbered among His children. Were we to be forced to choose between mind and heart, between reason and faith we would say, "to the gallows with reason," that we not miss the kingdom. But such would be a false dilemma, an illegitimate rupture of that which God has joined together, each enjoying its particular kind of primacy.

We affirm reason without rationalism, personal love without personalism, faith without fideism. It is because we believe that the capacity of the heart to increase its passion for God is inseparably bound up with the increase of the understanding of the character of God that we care so much for the intellectual dimension of faith. The more we know of God the greater is our capacity to love Him.

This book is divided into three parts. Section I is a prolegomenon dealing with the problems and method of apologetics. Section II develops the theistic proofs and the authority of Scripture. Section III is given over to a critique of presuppositionalism in apologetics, particularly with reference to the thought of Cornelius Van Til.

We want to acknowledge the help of those who have given valuable assistance to the project. We are particularly indebted to Bob and Lillian Love and to Eastminster Presbyterian Church in Wichita, Kansas, for providing multiple resources, including a place to work and secretarial assistance for the authors. Dr. Gerstner is particularly grateful for services rendered by the excellent staffs of the Speer Library of Princeton Theological Seminary, the Roberts Library of Southwestern Baptist Theological Seminary, and the Sterling Library of Yale University. Thanks also to Esther DiQuattro, Kathy Wallace, Patricia Monticue, David Coffin, and Mary Semack for typing the manuscript, and to Vesta Sproul for her help in documentation research. Thanks also to Stanley N. Gundry for his editorial patience and magic, to Wynn Kenyon for suggested revisions, and to Jack Stewart for his masterly editorial assistance.

During the preparation of this volume, the authors have been in dialogue with representatives of persons from various apologetic traditions. We owe an especially heavy debt to Professor John Frame for his prolonged dialogue over several months which significantly sharpened our understanding of Vantillian apologetics.

The Ligonier Valley
Advent—1982

SECTION I

CLASSICAL NATURAL THEOLOGY:
An Overview of Problem and Method

CHAPTER 1

The Crisis of Secularism

WESTERN CULTURE IS not pagan; nor is it Christian. It has been secularized. Western man has "come of age," passing through the stages of mythology, theology, and metaphysics, reaching the maturity of science. The totem pole has yielded to the temple which in turn has given way to the acme of human progress, the laboratory. The contest between Elijah and the prophets of Baal would not merit a press notice in the media, save possibly for a headline in a supermarket tabloid. Resistance to Christianity comes not from the deposed priests of Isis but from the guns of secularism. The Christian task (more specifically, the rational apologetic task) in the modern epoch is not so much to produce a new *Summa Contra Gentiles* as it is to produce a *Summa Contra Secularisma*.

Paganism is a *pre*-Christian phenomenon building on the foundation of mythology and the sacralization of the realm of nature. It is at once prescientific and extrabiblical in its orientation, representing the creative imagination of primitive humanity. Some view paganism as the creeping stage of the civilized infant, a necessary starting point in the evolutionary progress of the race. Others see it as a crude, yet noble genesis of man's quest for ultimate reality. The biblical judgment is less sanguine, regarding paganism as a devolution; a contrived and fanciful flight from God's revelation of Himself in nature. Paganism reflects the deep-rooted enmity of Adam's seed who prefer gods fashioned by their own hands to the God who fashions men by His own hand. It betrays the proclivity of man to be a *fabricum idolarum* (makers of idols or "idol-factory") as Calvin maintained. The pagan is aware of nature. Eschewing the God nature displays, the pagan worships the creature instead of the Creator, trading the transcendent for the immanent, the eternal for the temporal, the majestic for the mundane.

Secularism, on the other hand, is a *post*-Christian phenomenon carrying in its baggage, a *conscious* rejection of the Christian world view. It supplants the Christian consensus with its own structured view of reality. Less barbaric on the surface than paganism, secularism adopts a benevolent paternalism toward the not yet enlightened Christian who continues the practice of an anachronistic faith. Wearing a benign mask, the secularist loudly proclaims his commitment to religious tolerance on behalf of those weak-minded souls who still cannot bear to face a hostile or, worse, an indifferent universe, without the narcotic effect of ecclesiastical opium. The church is safe from vicious persecution at the hands of the secularist, as educated people have finished with stake-burning circuses and torture racks. No martyr's blood is shed in the secularist West—so long as the church knows her place and remains quietly at peace on her modern reservation. Let the babes pray and sing and read their Bibles, continuing steadfast in their intellectual retardation; the church's extinction will come not by sword or pillory, but by the quiet death of irrelevance. It will pass away with a whimper not a bang. But let the church step off the reservation, let her penetrate once more the culture of the day and the Janus-face of secularism will change from benign smile to savage snarl.

It was Harvey Cox who best defined the modern *Weltanschauung* of secularism. In 1965 Cox published *The Secular City*, his reply to Augustine's classic, *The City of God*. Viewing contemporary America from sociological and theological perspectives, he acutely described the distinction between the process of secularization and that of secularism:

> The English word *secular* derives from the Latin word *saeculum*, meaning "the age." Basically saeculum is one of the two Latin words denoting "world" (the other being *mundus*). . . . The relationship between the two words is a complex one. Saeculum is a time word, used frequently to translate the Greek word *aeon*, which also means age or epoch. Mundus, on the other hand, is a space-word, used most frequently to translate the Greek word *cosmos*, meaning the universe or the created order.
>
> In its first wide spread usage, our word secularization had a very narrow and specialized meaning. It designated the process by which a "religious" priest was transferred to a parish responsibil-

ity. He was secularized. Gradually the meaning of the term was widened. When the separation of Pope and emperor became a fact of life in Christendom, the division between the spiritual and the secular assumed institutional embodiment. . . . Secularization as a descriptive term has a wide and inclusive significance. It appears in many different guises, depending on the religious and political history of the area concerned. But wherever it appears, it should be carefully distinguished from secularism. Secularization implies a historical process, almost certainly irreversible, in which society and culture are delivered from tutelage to religious control and a closed metaphysical world-view. . . . Secularism, on the other hand, is the name for an ideology, a new closed world-view which functions very much like a new religion.[1]

The distinction Cox traces in the Latin words for "world" (*saeculum* and *mundus*) penetrates the core of what is meant by secularism. The difference is between the temporal and the spatial, between time and space.

A second, equally important distinction between the words *secular* and *secularism* is that they signal the difference between the descriptive and the normative, between a philosophically neutral word and an ideology. Just as a vast difference exists between reason and rationalism, nature and naturalism, existence and existentialism, so a huge chasm is crossed from the secular to secularism.

TIME AND SPACE

The word *secular* refers simply to the world as it moves in the flux of time. It is the sphere of activity or theater of operations of the present age, the here and now as distinguished from eternity. The church is always called to be actively involved with the secular; we have no other arena in which to work. Though the significance of Christian ministry transcends the temporal, the locus of it is in the here and now. The realm of redemption is history, with all of its temporal considerations. Christianity may distinguish time from eternity, but it never divorces them. This age may indeed be wicked or paltry, but such negative evaluations only underscore the fact that here is where redemption is needed and is to be applied. In this sense Christianity is passionately concerned with the secular and the mundane. Other religions may choose a radical denial of this world, seeking asylum in a supratemporal sphere of mystical other-worldliness; but Christianity enjoys no such luxurious option. Attempts by Christians, past or present, to quit this world in ascetic retreat betray a tacit denial of the most elemental principles of the Christian view of creation and redemption. Neither Gnostics nor Manicheans are we, to abandon our Father's world.

It is this world, this time, this secular *mundus* over which God is sovereign and Christ is King. It is this world God entered as the incarnate Lord of history. It is precisely because Christianity is so secular that secularism hates it. It is the secular thrust of redemption that makes confinement to a reservation intolerable to the Christian. Thus the process of secularization, as here defined by Cox, is a positive move if it means that the church is carrying out her mandate in the world.

Taken in its pejorative sense, secularization may mean the capitulation of the church to secularism, the surrender of her redemptive mission to the spirit of this world. In this sense the church would cease to be the church; its identity would be lost, its message but an echo of secularism. The fear of such an amalgamation moves some to embrace the reservation as a place where the pristine purity of the faith may be jealously guarded (while it dies in peace). But the church must be profane if it is to be the church; profane not in the vulgar sense but in the sense in which Luther used it—that the church must come outside of the temple (*pro fanus*) and into the world. It is not the profanity of blasphemy but the profanity Christ inaugurated by the Great Commission. The process of secularization in the meliorative sense, began the moment Christ intruded into the Upper Room where the disciples had withdrawn into hiding because of their fear: Pentecost impelled the church into the here and now. The power was from on high but its focus was on the here and now.

THE MEANING OF SECULARISM

A word can be quite harmless until someone attaches a suffix to it. As soon as the letters *ism* augment a term it becomes an ideology. One can work with capital, for example, without embracing capitalism, or be practical without endorsing pragmatism. One can have an ego while rejecting egoism, and be human while opposing humanism.

A plethora of isms and even a hierarchy of isms may be found side by side or in intense competition in a culture. In the Western world many such isms vie for intellectual dominance. Some are utterly dissimiliar, being mutually exclusive and antithetical while others coexist peacefully in facile compatibility. The twentieth century has witnessed a wide assortment of isms including positivism, humanism, relativism, pragmatism, pluralism, and existentialism. Though fierce debate and internecine rivalry have developed between advocates of these various schools (such as that between logical positivism and existentialism), yet a common thread is woven through them all. Each of these isms may be subsumed under a generic category without doing violence to a single one of them. Each is a particular species of the genus secularism. Secularism is the umbrella under which they all converge. Each of them shares the central axiomatic thesis of secularism, the leitmotif that defines secularism: *All possible knowledge is restricted to the temporal.* The temporal is all there is or all that can be known. The metaphysical quest is dead, consigned to the junkyard of skepticism. There is no transcendent, no eternal—only the phenomenal bounded by the steel doors of time and space. What you see is what you get; the gateway to eternity is sealed by Kant's impregnable agnostic wall and surrounded by the unbridgeable moat of Lessing's ditch. All of life is to be understood and lived on "this side" (*diesseitig*). There is no "other side" (*jenseits*) to reality. The classical Greek quest for the *meta* of physics, the *supra* of nature, the unity of diversity, has been abandoned. Cut off from any transcendent, the particulars of the present are no more than hideously dangling participles.

The working assumption of secularism is that there is no transcendent eternal God who is the basis for the origin of all things and in whose hands is the destiny of all things. Or, if such a Being does exist, He remains unknown and unknowable, a *Deus Absconditus* whose nature remains wholly other and incommunicado. This life in this time is all there is. "You only go around once." All truth, all value, all beauty must be measured without appeal or recourse to eternal verities or absolute standards. Nothing can be measured *sub species aeternitatis* because the species of the eternal is eliminated. It is only the here and now which counts because the here and now is all there is. For the Christian the now counts forever. For the secularist the now counts for now.

The philosophical schools mentioned are complex; and each includes erudite scholars among its chief proponents. We oversimplify if we reduce the whole of their thought to their points of contact with each other. We have risked oversimplification in order to draw the big picture of secularism. We will now look more closely at each school, isolating its distinctive strands which, when woven together with others, comprise the larger cable of secularism.

Positivism restricts knowledge to the necessary truths of mathematics, logic, and empirical verification, eliminating metaphysics and theology at the outset. Only two types of statements—analytic and synthetic—are capable of being true. Analytic statements may be true by definition ("A square has four sides") but offer no factual information about real states of affairs. Synthetic statements must be capable of being tested by empirical means to be either verified or falsified. Assertions about a transcendent God may be granted "emotive" meaning, but are judged to be psuedo-synthetic (not capable of empirical verification) and consequently factually meaningless. Here the secular—temporal and spatial—forms the boundaries for knowledge.

Humanism makes humanity the norm of all knowledge of truth, value, and being. Protagoras proffered the first and abiding creed of the humanist: *Homo mensura*—"man is the measure of all things, of the existence of the things that are and the nonexistence of the things that are."[2] Humanism has manifested itself in various forms and stages ranging from the naive to the nihilistic; but in each stage it denys a transcendent God. Human values must be hammered out in the sphere of the temporal because our origin and destiny are irrevocably bound to the secular.

Relativism eschews the discovering of absolute or transcendent norms. For the relativist there may be truths, but not truth; purposes, but no purpose; values, but no value. All must be relative because knowledge is limited to the phenomenal with no access to the noumenal, limited to the particulars with no access to the universal.

Pragmatism, especially that of Charles S. Pierce and William James, restricts the meaning of a proposition or the value of an action to that which lies in observable consequences. Pragmatism is temporally bound, its judgment of the good and useful determined by the observable. Considerations of eternal utility are ruled out as pragmatism functions in a framework of metaphysical skepticism.

Pluralism is a term capable of more than one definition. Used in a cultural sense it may refer to the coexistence of a variety of ideologies, religions, ethnic groups or other forms of diversity within a broad unified structure. The motto of the United States reflects the idea: *E Pluribus Unum*. The concept of America as a cultural melting pot was built on a quest for unity out of diversity, a unified plurality. Pluralism, in the philosophical sense, goes beyond the mere awareness of diverse factors within a unified whole to despair of any possibility of ultimate unity. The plural itself is ultimate with no unifying factors of coherence. No symphony results from dissonant sounds. The new motto of pluralism is *E Pluribus Plurus.*

More clearly than the others, existentialism embodies and advances the principles of secularism. Sartre's formula "existence precedes essence" captures the kernel of the philosophy. The realm of essence is banished to the unreal, unknowable, or unimportant level. The human predicament must be worked out within the limits of finite existence bound by the temporal. Twentieth-century existential philosophy has been preoccupied with the problem of time as evidenced by Sartre's *Being and Nothingness* and Heidegger's *Being and Time.* Heidegger sees the being (*Dasein*) of humanity as determined by the here and now of existence. The human experiences the dread of being "thrown" into existence (*Geworfenheit*) where there is no bridge to the eternal and the permanent. This is at the root of human concern (*Besorgen*) and anxiety (*Angst*).

THE IMPACT OF SECULARISM

No philosophical system is without impact. The impact may be isolated to a small segment of society and be of short duration, suffering the swift demise of a passing fad. The impact of secularism, however, has been pervasive and cataclysmic, shaking the foundations of the value structures of Western civilization. The Judeo-Christian consensus is no more; it has lost its place as the dominant shaping force of cultural ethics. The sons and daughters of the church have ceased being the pace-setters in the fields of art, literature, and science. The Michelangelos and Rembrandts have yielded to the Picassos and the Andy Warhols; it is a long way from the Sistine Chapel to the soup can. The Dantes and the Miltons have been displaced by the Hemingways and the Vidals. Where are the Mendelssohns, the Handels, and the Bachs? Where are the Newtons who in their scientific research are seeking to "think God's thoughts after Him"?

Where once the church was the avant-garde of higher education, her influence has declined to that of the subcultural pedagogue. The medieval university was established on the premise that all knowledge is ultimately coherent and unified. The very word *university* was borrowed from the word *universe,* which derives from two different and opposite words, *unity* and *diversity.* A universe is a place where the many (diversity) come together into the unified whole (unity). The working assumption was that all diverse particulars of knowledge discovered and analyzed in the specialized academic disciplines, found their coherency in God. It was the unifying power of theology that elevated her to the queen of the sciences, being assisted by her metaphysical handmaiden philosophy. The queen alone was able to integrate knowledge.

With the rejection of theology as a valid scientific discipline, the queen was deposed and the whole concept of university fell with her. To be sure, her demise was slow; but when it came it left an abhorrent emptiness in the school. Attempts were made to fill the void with philosophical alternatives but the handmaiden was treated as rudely as the monarch. Rather than abhoring the vacuum, the West has acted against nature and preferred to leave it vacant. But the price tag for the vacancy is exorbitant. Sooner or later the vacuum will be filled, and if it cannot be filled by the transcendent, then it will be filled by the immanent. The force that floods into such vacuums is statism, the inevitable omega point of secularism.

The university has become the multiversity and students feel the impact of the disintegration of higher education. The students' schedules are filled with liberal arts courses which expose them to a wide variety of academic disciplines. But these disciplines have no apparent cohesion with each other. Students move from lecture to lecture, absorbing differing and often mutually exclusive views. The information they glean about their own humanity incites painful confusion. In psychology, one view; in biology, another; in philosophy, a *tertium quid* is thrown into the jumble. The specific sciences do not merely accent a particular nuance of the whole by focusing here on the ontic, there on the noetic, or elsewhere on the sociological. The sciences can vastly increase our knowledge of various disciplines via specialization, but the problem of integrating knowledge remains. The classical theory of the *university,* where the diversity of human experience sought its unity in synthesis, was acutely aware of the multiplicity of nuances which together comprise what is human. Anthropology was not monistic then. Instead, the rich human diversities were explored to gain a broad and deep understanding of the multi-faceted character of human life. The intricacies of the facets called attention to the significance and dignity of a creature fearfully and wonderfully made in the image of God, whose transcendent being incorporates ultimate unity and diversity. Secularism has rudely snatched this unifying basis from

Western life. The secularist views existence as a cacophony of sounds, a chaos of incoherence. The human being, in Sartre's verdict, is a "useless passion."

The chaos of secularistic education is keenly felt by the students enduring it. Some are driven to despair as the message of nihilism gets through. Some seek to quiet the haunting questions of the mind by indulging in forms of escapism. Others seek solace in the acceptable practice of specialization in which the conflict of the disciplines can be avoided by preoccupation with a highly specialized, singular field of endeavor. The poles of the dialectic are not harmonized but kept at a safe distance from each other through intellectual avoidance. This absorption of life under one pole produces a kind of personal reductionism which yields the one-dimensional personality. With the death of God must come the death of the "Renaissance man." Within the nonframework of pluralistic secularism, if the Renaissance man is to survive, he must subsist as an intellectual schizophrenic.

The capitulation of the academic world to secularism can occur without people realizing it. During a recent visit to a Christian college noted for its high standard of scholarship, we witnessed this silent surrender. The faculty had requested an address on the subject of integrating the Christian faith with their academic curriculum. They wanted to know what makes a Christian institution of higher education uniquely Christian.

A tour of the campus preceded the formal address. The escort pointed out the various buildings and offices, noting in passing one wing which displayed the sign—RELIGION DEPARTMENT. In the faculty meeting later the question had to be raised: "How long has the Religion department been called the Religion department?"

An elder member of the faculty recalled that the name of the department had been changed about twenty-five years earlier from its original designation, Theology department. The next question was mandatory: "Why did you change it?" Blank faces. Again it was a veteran of the faculty who explained that the change was made to facilitate the transfer of credits from their school to other schools, primarily to accommodate state universities.

Most of the faculty understood that there is a profound difference between the study of theology and the study of religion. Theology's primary foci are the being and activity of God. Religion, on the other hand, is a study of human activity, often subsumed under the broader headings of anthropology or sociology. Religion concerns human actions of devotion, liturgical practices, cultic structures, and the like. It focuses on this world, the world of knowable phenomena. Within the philosophical framework of secularism, the study of religion is a possible and legitimate enterprise; the study of the nature of God is not. The secularist regards the study of God as a fool's errand, yielding no viable scientific knowledge.

The study of religious behavior is a valuable exercise. However, when a Christian institution supplants the study of theology with the study of religion, exclusively, it ceases to be a Christian institution. At some institutions, it is still *theology* that is studied, albeit under the rubric of religion; the change is merely one of nomenclature. But when the name is changed without an awareness of the significance of this change, the tail is well on the way to wagging the dog.

Secularism did not spring fully grown from the head of Zeus. Historical patterns had to be reshaped before its rise to prominence could occur. The classical synthesis of traditional apologetics had to be displaced before secularism could move to center stage. Traditional apologetics is far from dead, but there is no denying that it is sick and ailing. It is by no means completely broken down, but it has been severely crippled by the blow dealt it by the Enlightenment.

Ours is perhaps the most anti-intellectual era of Christian history despite our positive support for scholarship, research, and technology. For the intellect is suspect: the mind and its primary tool—rationality—are seen as a pagan intrusion into the pristine domain of faith. In our day not only Christians in general and neo-orthodox ones in particular are anti-apologetics, but even evangelical orthodox Christians tend to be so. The possibility and the desirability of apologetics are both under attack. We have seen in this chapter that secularism has called the entire enterprise into question. But before we can embark safely on the journey of apologetics we have one more preliminary task: we must define positively what apologetics is and what role it should have in the life of the church.

CHAPTER 2

The Task of Apologetics

WHAT IS APOLOGETICS? Apologetics is the reasoned defense of the Christian religion. Christianity is a faith, to be sure; but there are reasons for this faith. Faith is not to be confused with reason; but neither is it to be separated from it.

IRRATIONAL "APOLOGETICS"

But some would say that if there are reasons, there is no room for faith; if there is faith, reasons are an impertinence. One must choose, some say, between a religion of faith and a religion of reason; one cannot have both. Henry Dodwell, Jr., expressed this anti-apologetic view in 1740 in his book *Christianity Not Founded On Argument.*[1] Although this position is more common in the twentieth century than it was in the eighteenth, Dodwell pretty well exhausted the contrasts between a rational and an antirational religion. The former was cool, slow, and detached, while antirational religion called for immediate, warm commitment.[2]

Alan Richardson is something of a contemporary Dodwell. His *Christian Apologetics*[3] is virtually designed to prove that there is no reasoned defense of the Christian religion. That is, his apologetics is an apologetic to end all apologetics. The title of his book thus raises false expectations, and is as appropriate as Karl Barth's giving the Gifford Lectures, which were founded to defend natural theology.

Barth is another twentieth-century defender of no-defense Christianity. Already in the early pages of his massive *Church Dogmatics,* the longest theology ever written, he repudiated any argument for divine revelation (which he professes to believe nonetheless). "In faith and only in faith is human action related to the essence of the Church, to the revealing and reconciling action of God. Thus dogmatics is only possible as an act of faith. Without faith it would lack object and meaning."[4] Earlier, Barth had declared that what is philosophical is not Christian and what is Christian is not philosophical.

William Barrett has described the era through which we have just passed as the age of the "irrational man."[5] Many have echoed his sentiments. The "reverend agnosticism"[6] of Barth took the form of paradox which is the banner of irrationality and the antithesis of rational coherence. It has been called our "declaration of independence"[7] from the claims of our minds. Reinhold Niebuhr thought that revelation was absurd;[8] and his mentor, Sören Kierkegaard, saw the Incarnation as the ultimate absurdity, teaching that the eternal God was transformed into temporal man.[9] Emil Brunner went so far as to say that the Incarnation is not only unintelligible, but that the feature of unintelligibility proves it true.[10]

While theology was going irrational, positivist philosophy was questioning all knowledge. C. I. Lewis, for example, the positivist philosopher of Harvard, once wrote that "not even the law of non-contradiction is necessarily true of the real world."[11] Of course, apart from the law of non-contradiction, Lewis cannot even think that, much less say it. Even to make the charge, one must make use of the law. An intelligible objection to the law of non-contradiction cannot be made without it. To conceive of a real world in which the law does not obtain requires the law in order to conceive of a world where it does not obtain. We cannot even imagine such a world without this law because it would be utterly dissimilar from a world with it. Philosophers such as Lewis say as little as necessary and possible; they live in fear of being loquacious. But in the above remark he has uttered the unutterable, the unthinkable, the ultimate rhetorical extravagance.

Things have gotten worse in many ways in the third quarter of our century. For one thing, there is the "new hermeneutic" which reduces exegesis to existential experience. The word is dead on the page according to Ernst Fuchs, Gerhard Ebeling, Herbert Braun, and others. Only as it comes alive somehow in the experience of the contemporary reader does it have meaning—existential meaning. What meaning it had for the original writer can never be known (as earlier scholars had though it could). Even Bultmann thought it could be approximated. By opening ourselves to the words of revelation which we cannot understand but which may understand or interpret us, we may have a meaningful contemporary experience.

Building on Bultmann's foundation, Herbert Braun, for example, claims that "we cannot . . . set aside our pre-understanding [*Vorverstandnis*], and *we should not desire to do so*. We can, however, have an open mind."[12] If we are going to allow and even encourage our pre-understanding, how can this allow for an open mind? An open mind could conceivably require a repudiation or a modification of our pre-understanding. To allow it at the outset calls for a closed mind on that subject. Given this pattern of reasoning, it is not surprising that, for Braun, Jesus of Nazareth ends up as a quality of human experience.[13]

Nor is it surprising, given this openness to our "pre-understanding," that redaction criticism has become the new kid on the critical block,[14] for it gives subjectivism almost a carte blanche. The original literary criticism had a degree of speculation but preserved essential objectivity. Form criticism, because it attempts to locate the life setting (*Sitz im Ieben*) of biblical documents, is more subjective. Now comes redaction criticism which tries to discover why and how the parts were woven together. If it could be said of some earlier critics that they thought they could hear the grass grow, some redaction critics aspire to recreate the sod.

A RETURN TO RATIONAL APOLOGETICS

There are signs today of a retreat from this anti-intellectual binge. This is what led I. T. Ramsey to republish John Locke's *Reasonableness of Christianity* going back to 1695 for a guide to inebriated thinkers on the intellectual morning after the night before. As Ramsey understates, "For many years it has not been fashionable to talk of the reasonableness of Christianity."[15] Today, even the philosophers are talking again about proofs, the theistic proofs at that, including the ontological argument for the existence of God.[16]

Apologetics, of course, survived the era of irrationality. To do so, however, it had to justify its justifications. It had to apologize for its apologetics. Before it could present its reasoned defense of the Christian religion, it had first to prove its own excuse for existence. That is, it had to prove that it was important to prove anything. It had to prove the possibility and even the advisability of proving. Paul Tillich argued that a God who could be proved would be no God. If God did exist, one could not prove His existence.[17] If apologetics succeeded, it failed.

We will endeavor to show that not only neo-orthodox thinkers, but many orthodox thinkers were saying, in their own idiom, essentially the same thing Tillich said. In a sense, presuppositionalism is orthodoxy's defense of no-reasoned defense for Christianity. As the secular world is waking up from its anti-intellectual binge, we hope that orthodoxy today may do the same. That is, we hope presuppositionalism will be giving way more and more to classical apologetics as a reasonable modern response to reasonable modern people who want a reason why they should believe.

Apologetics, the reasoned defense of the Christian religion, is the job of every Christian, always "ready to make defense to everyone who asks you to give an account for the hope that is in you" (1 Peter 3:15 NASB). As a science, it is a putting together of the data common to all Christians in a consistent and scientific whole. It explains why Christians are Christians and why non-Christians should be Christians. If theology is the queen of the sciences, apologetics is her handmaid. It introduces people to the queen and demonstrates her majesty.

Scholarship must defend the faith of the non-scholar. It must be articulate for the one who is unable to articulate his hope, although he quite well understands it. Bob Jones, Sr., once said, "I would rather hear a man say 'I *seen* something' when he really *saw* something, than hear a man say 'I have seen something' when he has never seen anything." Apologetics teaches the man who "seen something" to say "I have seen something." It shows the man who knows the King's gospel how to express it in the King's English, rationally speaking.

But some very commonly still ask, *Why* apologetics? Does a person have to understand in order to believe? Is it not, rather, that he believes in order to understand? To put it another way: Does not apologetics derive from a new heart, rather than a new heart from apologetics? Who was ever saved, it has often been cynically asked, by apologetics? Many testify that they never questioned their Christianity until they heard somebody try to prove it. So why apologetics?

Why oxygen? Because we humans are oxygen-breathing, oxygen-needing animals. Why apologetics? Because we are rational creatures. Because we are by nature rational, we must be approached with reasons. Because, as creatures, it is essential that we know about our Creator. Because we are rational animals who need religion, we must be given reasons for believing the true religion.

If this were all there is to it, apologetics would be a very simple science. But it is not that simple. There are many alleged gods and a variety of religious claimants. This very confusion about things known and ways of knowing them makes it evident that though the Creator is in His heaven, all is not well with His world. As a solution to this "sin" or "evil," many of these religions call for a crucifixion of the intellect rather than a use of it. Their advocates even use their own intellects to justify the non-use of the intellect. Sin complicates both the knowing and the object known, adding clarification to the already heavy responsibility of apologetics.

Any religion has problems. Christianity has some that are unique. It teaches that the Creator is angry with His creatures and calls upon them to repent, though they are so hostile to God that they are indisposed to do so. Since Christianity's God requires an unpalatable response the person the apologist approaches is inclined toward a negative bias. He does not welcome this religion. Since he is a rational creature he is going to be using his brain to combat every argument the apologist can offer. He has a vested interest in not believing. Since belief or unbelief has to be justified, he works to prove that the apologist cannot prove his case.

Under such adverse circumstance why does the apologist persist? Why not resort to fideism? Why not scrap apologetics in favor of sheer proclamation, offering no argument, only a choice? Let testimony supplant debate. This is the way Bultmann commonly speaks. Why not spare ourselves the burden of proof which the person will not admit in any case, no matter how convincing? Why pursue the thankless, resented task when no one is going to be won by it? There could conceivably be an argument for some other type of religion. But what possible justification is there for arguing Christianity?

It is no wonder that the overwhelming number of Christian thinkers today (liberal, conservative, orthodox, neo-orthodox), thus persuaded, are not apologists. Most are anti-apologists. If one is going to reason with people who will never admit, or even appreciate, your reasoning, it seems reasonable to abandon reasoning.

But there *is* a very good reason for reasoning with people who will not accept reasons, who will use all their intellectual energy to refute reasons, and who will only spurn reasons they fail to refute. That very good reason is this: God commands Christians to give a reasoned defense of the Christian religion. That is enough for any reasonable person. If the all-wise God says that we should reason with anti-rationalists (though they will only use their own reason to justify their resistance to true reason), then we know for certain it *is* reasonable to reason with the unreasonable. The God who knows all, knows why we should reason when it seems not to be reasonable. Indeed, it would be *un*reasonable for us to stop reasoning if God commands that we continue reasoning.

It is precisely this point—whether God commands Christians to reason with unbelievers—which is debated among Christians. No monolithic view of the obligation to provide a reasoned defense of Christianity has emerged. We maintain, in spite of the confusion and lack of agreement on this point, that there is abundant, clear biblical warrant for such activity. The warrant comes from God's *example* and His *command*.

APOLOGETICS: GOD'S EXAMPLE AND COMMAND

God Himself provides evidence for the claim that He is the true God, displaying His divine credentials openly. Elijah stood on Mount Carmel and put the question before the people: "How long will you go limping with two different opinions? If the LORD is God, follow him; but if Baal, then follow him" (1 Kings 18:21 RSV). Elijah stood in the breach between two mutually exclusive truth claims. He did not ask for an arbitrary decision or an existential leap into the abyss of subjectivity. He called for a decision based on evidence, pleading with his God to provide it. He asked that God reveal Himself and certify that Elijah was truly His prophet. The fire that fell from heaven not only consumed the altars of Baal, but reduced the false claims of Baal to ashes.

Isaiah records the challenge of God to other "gods" to present evidence of their authenticity: .

> "Present your case," the LORD says. "Bring forward your strong arguments," the King of Jacob says. Let them bring forth and declare to us what is going to take place; as for the former events, declare what they were, that we may consider them, and know their outcome; or announce to us what is coming. Declare the things that are going to come afterward, that we may know that you are gods." (Isa. 41:21–23 NASB)

The evidence of the "gods" is vacuous, their works "amount to nothing" (v. 24) and are deemed "worthless" (v. 29).

The God of Israel, on the other hand, presents His case, providing myriads of demonstrative evidential works and future prophecies which vindicate His claim as a truth-teller. He gave a sign to Gideon on the fleece (Judg. 6:30–40), and a sign to Moses and the court magicians by a staff (Exod. 4). Moses saw the leprous hand and the burning bush, both attesting to the divine claim. To Pharaoh and the people of Egypt were given the plagues, culminating in the Nile's becoming a river of blood and the firstborn children a sign of judgment.

What the Old Testament employs as evidence is carried throughout the New Testament as well. Jesus heals the paralytic and says, "But in order that you may know that the Son of Man has authority on earth to forgive sins . . . I say to you, rise, take up your pallet and go home" (Mark 2:10–11 NASB). Here Jesus uses the subjunctive of purpose to communicate cognitive awareness of His authority. He responds to the inquiry from John the Baptist whether Jesus is the expected Messiah by pointing to His own miracles and their fulfillment of the messianic prophecy of Isaiah 61.

In John's Gospel Jesus sets forth an apologetic principle which is critical to the discussion:

> If I alone bear witness of Myself, My testimony is not true. There is another who bears witness of Me; and I know that the testimony which He bears of Me is true. . . . But the witness which I have is greater than that of John; for the works which the Father has given Me to accomplish, the very works that I do, bear witness of Me, that the Father has sent Me. (John 5:31–36 NASB)

At this state in His public ministry, Jesus follows the Old Testament rule of the corroboration of testimony by at least two witnesses, and shrinks from any claim of self-attestation. The principle is clear: "If I alone bear witness of Myself, My testimony is not true." Far from verification, Jesus declares that singular self-attestation does not verify, it falsifies.

Jesus appeals to His "works" to give credence to His claims. The word *works* from the Greek *ergon,* though not always identified with miracles, often is used to designate them:

> The concept of God's saving acts through Christ is common in John's Gospel: 5:20, 36; 7:3, 21; 9:3, 4; 10:25, 32, 37, 38; 14:10, 11, 12; 15:24. These statements relate to individual works done by Jesus. As miracles they bear witness to Jesus and to the salvation which He brings.[18]

Elsewhere Jesus provides a "calculus" of the judgment of culpability based on the level of evidence available to recipients. The cities of Chorazin, Bethsaida, and Capernaum are warned of a more severe judgment than that which will befall Tyre, Sidon, and Sodom. Judgment will be more tolerable for those who received lesser evidence (Matt. 11:20–24).

Paul's reasoned defense of the Resurrection (I Cor. 15, which Bultmann dismissed as an exercise in natural theology) stands as a clear example of apostolic appeals to reason and to empirical data to support a truth claim. At Mars Hill the apostle cites the resurrection as "proof" of Christ's identity (Acts 17:31). Luke records that it was Paul's custom at Ephesus to be engaged in "reasoning daily in the school of Tyrannus" (Acts 19:8–10 NASB). The Greek word translated "reasoning" is *dialegomenos* (διαλεγόμενος). Arndt and Gingrich assign the meaning "1. discuss, conduct a discussion of lectures which were likely to end in disputations."[19] Here the word is conjoined with *peithon* (πείθων) which carries the force of "to convince."[20]

The word as well as the concept of apologetics is rooted in Scripture. J. K. S. Reid points out:

> The word apology and its cognate Apologetics are of Greek origin. *Apologia* (in general, meaning defense) and its verbal form *apologoumai* (make a defense) are words used in classical Greek, in New Testament Greek, and also in the Patristic writings. Their meaning in these three linguistic forms does not differ significantly. But it is with their employment in the New Testament that we are concerned. The words appear with some frequency. The lexicons show that *apologia* occurs about eight times and the verbal form about eleven. This is evidence enough to show pretty accurately what their meaning is. It appears that the verbal form always, and the nominal form usually, denote an answer given in reply to a charge levelled against an individual, or an argument justifying a claim advanced by an individual.[21]

The word *apologia* occurs in the *locus classicus* for apologetics, 1 Peter 3:15:

> But sanctify the Lord God in your hearts: and be ready always to give an answer to every man that asketh you a reason of the hope that is in you with meekness and fear. (KJV)

By divine example and divine command apologetics is a mandate God gives to His people. If God Himself provides evidence for what He declares to be truth it is calumnous to repudiate the value of evidence. If God commands us to do the work of apologetics it is disobedience to refuse the task.

APOLOGETICS AND FAITH

The most frequent objection to apologetics is that it is an exercise in futility, given the fact that no one is ever argued into the kingdom of God. The work of regeneration is the work of the Holy Spirit and cannot be achieved by apologetics, no matter how cogent. This objection is most keenly felt by Calvinists who regard the working of faith in the human heart as the monergistic work of God.

The character or nature of faith, particularly justifying faith, was a cardinal issue of the Protestant Reformation. Building upon Augustine's understanding of the multi-faceted character of faith, the Reformers isolated three key elements in authentic faith: *notitia, assensus,* and *fiducia. Notitia* refers to the data (*notae*) or content of the Christian faith. New Testament faith is not empty of content nor is it a faith-in-general. The gospel has a content which is to be recognized, understood, and affirmed. Here we see the primacy of the intellect, for one cannot worship a God with his heart if he has no prior mental awareness of Him. The motif of clarification as part of apologetics is important here. The first aspect of faith is cognitive.

The second aspect of faith which follows upon *notitia* is *assensus.* As the Latin suggests, *assensus* refers to the element of faith which involves the assent of the intellect to the truth of the data. It is axiomatic that the heart cannot truly embrace what the mind repudiates. It is possible to have a lucid understanding of the data (*notitia*) and even give intellectual assent (*assensus*) to its truth without having saving faith. James verifies this in his caustic statement, "You believe that God is one; you do well. Even the demons believe—and shudder" (James 2:19). To achieve *notitia* and *assensus* gives us no more qualifications than devils. Yet these two elements are integral ingredients of the full measure of redemptive faith and are not dispensable. In and of themselves they are insufficient, but redemptive faith does not flow without them. Apologetics is indispensable for the establishing of these two aspects. Though apologetics may not be evangelism, it is a vital part of pre-evangelism.

The third aspect of faith is most crucial. It is on *fiducia* that one's personal redemption stands or falls. *Fiducia* refers to the personal trust dimension of faith. The English derivative is the word *fiduciary* which places the emphasis on trust. Saving faith, or what Luther termed a *fides viva,* involves placing one's personal trust in Christ, resting on Him and on Him alone for redemption. This aspect involves the mind but goes beyond the intellect to the heart, the will, the affections—to one's personal inclination toward Christ. This is the element no apologist can produce; this is the monergistic work of God the Holy Spirit. But the Spirit does not work in a vacuum, persuading irrationally against evidence, but, as Calvin pointed out, inclines the person to acquiesce in the evidence.

Often apologetics is deemed fruitless or valueless because it is restricted to evangelism. Though it does relate to evangelism and thereby to the sphere of special grace, as we have seen, its application goes beyond that sphere to the arena of common grace. Apologetics acts as a bulwark against unbridled antitheistic ideologies and their cultural impact. Man's general welfare is enhanced by a cultural consensus in which Christianity and its values are deemed credible. Apologetics is a useful tool to shut the mouths of the obstreperous.

Moreover, the sphere of special grace includes more than a concern for justification. Sanctification is also vital to the life of the church. Saving faith is often mixed with an alloy of doubt which can be an intimidating and paralyzing force which stunts the growth and development of the Christian life. The pervasive contemporary skepticism is not without its deleterious effect on Christian faith. Apologetics can be used by God as a liberating force in the life of the Christian plagued by the darts of doubt.

APOLOGETICS AND THE LAITY

It is a frequent complaint among the laity that apologetics is an unnecessary and undesirable complication of the simple Christian life. Many declare that they are unable to articulate the reasons for their faith, and resort to a simple testimony of their experience. Like the man born blind their apologetic is restricted to, "All I know is that once I was blind but now I see" (cf. John 9:25). They often overlook the fact that their testimony is itself an apologetic and that the inability to articulate all the reasons for their faith is not an indication that there are no reasons for their faith. If it were true that they believed for absolutely no reason, they would not be believing at all, but acting on superstition.

We once heard a radio debate among scholars concerning the existence of God. When the phone lines were opened to the public, an irate woman called in who obviously lacked academic sophistication.

She was thoroughly frustrated by the scholarly debate and, though she probably never had heard of the cosmological argument, she complained, "Ain't you guys got your eyes open? Look out the window. Where do yins think all that come from?" She had a reason for her faith.

CHAPTER 3

Natural Theology and Fideism

THE QUESTION OF the relation between faith and reason has vexed the Christian church from its inception to the present day. G. C. Berkouwer puts the question this way:

> Is faith an irrational and esoteric mystery that has no point of contact with the other person? Can we only *witness* to our faith? Or is there within human thought a possibility for real and mutually understood dialogue?[1]

The issue of which Berkouwer writes is the perennial debate of the relation between some form of natural theology and fideism. The problem crosses ecclesiastical borders, inciting skirmishes not only among Protestant thinkers but among Roman Catholic scholars as well.

This question precipitated a crisis in the Roman Catholic Church in the nineteenth century. Despite a strong, indeed almost an undeviating Roman Catholic tradition of natural theology, the relationship of rationalism and fideism arose and was placed on the agenda at Vatican Council I. Hans Kung notes the Council's definitions which marked a *via media* between rationalism and fideism. Citing Denzinger (the official collection of conciliar decrees, canons, and Papal Encyclicals), Kung points to a middle road between two orders of knowledge:

> Above the natural sphere of natural truths (including the knowledge of the existence of God), which are known by natural reason, there is a supernatural sphere of revealed divine truths, which are mysteries of faith and are known only by divine faith.

Reason and faith do not contradict one another . . . but can provide mutual aid. Reason establishes the foundations of faith and—enlightened by faith—works out the science of theology. Man can know the one true God and Creator with certainty by the natural light of human reason. On the other hand, faith frees reason from errors, protects it, and equips it with manifold knowledge.[2]

The significance of the Council's guidelines, according to Kung, is that they demarcate two main fronts, rationalism and fideism, placing the Council between the two:

There must be no reduction of faith to reason. This is what radical rationalism did, upholding a reason without faith and rejecting everything supernatural.
There must be no reduction of reason to faith. This in fact is what radical fideism did, upholding in practice an irrational faith—a faith without reason—and rejecting any natural knowledge of God.[3]

Before proceeding any further in the examination of natural theology and fideism, we must define the concepts. Simply stated, natural theology refers to knowledge of God acquired through nature. Classically, natural theology does not stand in contradiction to divine revelation nor does it exclude such revelation. In fact, natural theology is *dependent* upon divine revelation for its content. To be sure, there have been philosophical attempts to achieve a natural theology in isolation from and as a substitute for natural revelation. That we call naturalism. Contrary to naturalism, Christian approaches to natural theology are established upon the foundation of a prior divine revelation. For the Christian, natural theology does not mean that humans, in their natural state, have the intrinsic ability to rise to a knowledge of God by the sheer force of intellect unaided by divine revelation. Such a view is repudiated by Protestants and Roman Catholics alike, including St. Thomas Aquinas:

It seems that a man cannot know any truth without grace. . . . Now however pure it be, bodily sense cannot see any visible thing without the light of the sun. Hence however perfect be the human mind, it cannot by reasoning know any truth without the light of God, which belongs to the aid of grace. . . . The natural light bestowed on the mind is God's light, by which we are enlightened to know such things as belong to natural knowledge.[4]

Natural theology, then, is dependent upon a prior revelation or self-disclosure from God. This prior revelation is a revelation in nature. Natural theology refers to a knowledge of God acquired from God's revelation of Himself in nature. This revelation is sometimes called *natural revelation,* but is more frequently referred to as *general revelation.* There is a crucial difference between natural (general) *revelation* and natural *theology.* Natural revelation refers to an activity of God. Natural theology refers to a human activity. Natural revelation is *objective* in the sense that it exists independent of human activity. Natural theology is *subjective* (though not subjectivistic), in the sense that it involves the human subject's apprehension and appropriation of natural revelation. Thus, natural theology may be defined as human knowledge of God derived from God's natural revelation.

Though natural revelation and natural theology may be and must be *distinguished,* they must never be *separated.* This distinction is critical to our evaluation of natural theology. They must not be separated precisely because natural theology is dependent upon natural revelation. To separate them is to move from rationality to rationalism, from natural theology to naturalism, from Christianity to secularism.

NATURAL THEOLOGY AND GENERAL REVELATION

Natural revelation is more frequently called general revelation for two reasons. The adjective *general* has reference both to *content* and *audience.* The content of natural revelation is general in the sense that the knowledge of God it yields is of a general sort. Many specific aspects and activities of God are not included in the content of natural revelation. The notion of Trinity, for example, cannot validly be deduced from a study of biology, physics, or astronomy (though some, of course, have sought to construct speculative theories of Trinity in this manner). Nor is the Incarnation of Christ discernible from a study of, say, botany. God's redemptive activity in history, such as the Atonement, cannot be discovered by analyzing the circulatory system of the human body. The content of natural revelation yields a knowledge of God-in-general.

Natural revelation is called general, secondly, because of the scope of the audience that has received it. General revelation has been made manifest to all mankind; its audience is universal. The audience or recipient of natural revelation has never been limited to those groups which have been privy to special revelation, such as the ancient Hebrews and the Christian community. It includes all people of all times and places. Unlike special revelation which requires the involvement of human messengers, general revelation penetrates every nook and cranny of the earth and is accessible to all people.

Special revelation, on the other hand, though *fitted* for all, does not in fact reach all. Special revelation goes beyond the scope of the content of general revelation. It provides a vast body of knowledge of the nature, character, and activity of God. It does not negate, contradict, or supplant the content of general revelation, but goes beyond it, providing a crucial supplement to it. The Bible is the exemplar of special revelation. The Bible provides an enormous quantity of information about God which cannot be known from the study of nature alone.

Natural theology, which is derived from general revelation, stands as a polar opposite to fideism in matters of philosophy and theology. Where natural theology asserts that people can and do gain valid knowledge of God by means of natural reason reflecting upon natural revelation, fideism asserts that God can be known only by faith. Fideism as an ism does not merely assert that faith is crucial to Christianity. The *ism* of fideism negates a knowledge of God via natural theology. It denies man's ability to know God except by faith.

As an alternative to natural theology and apologetics, fideism received a boost from Immanuel Kant's critique of the theistic proofs. Some rejoiced in Kant's work of demolition, saying that, by attacking reason, he "made room for faith." But fideism is not merely a post-Kantian phenomenon. Though some form of natural theology has been the majority report of historic Christianity, there has always been a minority report as well.

Tertullian did not entirely repudiate natural theology, but he gave voice to the initial formulation of the spirit of fideism:

> What is there in common between Athens and Jerusalem? What between the Academy and the Church . . . ? away with all projects for a "Stoic," a "Platonic," or a "Realistic" Christianity—*Credo quia absurdum.*[5]

Fideism of sorts co-existed with natural theology until the fourteenth century. Then, fideists, fearing that the pure biblical faith might be contaminated by a synthesis between theology and philosophy, fired in earnest at their chief target—the classical synthesis of Thomas

Aquinas. John Duns Scotus provided some ammunition, but the main volley was fired by William of Ockham. Ockham's nominalism offered a thorough-going critique of Aquinas. At issue was the Thomistic insistence that natural arguments for the existence of God "belong to the *preambula fidei,* in the sense that the acceptance of divine revelation logically presupposes the knowledge that a God exists who is capable of revealing Himself, a knowledge which is gained in abstraction from theology."[6]

Against Aquinas, the nominalists maintained that no cogent proof for God's existence could be given; the question of the existence of God had to be relegated to the sphere of faith. Frederick Copleston says of Ockham:

> By assigning to the sphere of faith the truth that there exists an absolutely supreme, infinite, free, omniscient and omnipotent being, he snapped the link between metaphysics and theology which had been provided by Aquinas' doctrine of the provable *preambula fidei.*[7]

Fideism continued in the fifteenth century in the work of Nicolas of Cusa. "Cusanus" anticipated Kant's later critique of the ability of theoretical thought to move from the created order to a knowledge of God. He argued that the senses and reason are essentially bound to finite objects and cannot make the inference to the infinite being of God.

The sixteenth century which featured the Protestant Reformation also witnessed a revival of fideism in the writings of Francisco Sanche,[8] Michel de Montaigne and Pierre Charron. And the Paduan school of Pietro Pomponazzi revived a refined form of Aristotelianism in which a distinction was made between what philosophy demonstrates and what can be learned by faith.

Many Christians reacted to this schizoid separation of philosophy and theology by attacking reason in general and Aristotle in particular. James Collins observes:

> Skepticism about philosophical matters thus appeared to be the safest way of safeguarding the orthodox faith. This was the motivation behind the fideistic skeptics, who sought to join doubt about the mind's natural powers with faith in supernatural revelation.[9]

Collins's point is perceptive and could be applied to a variety of fideists. The desire is for safety—to free religion from philosophical attack by removing it from the range of the critics' guns. If religion is relegated exclusively to the realm of "faith," then it can live safely in its isolated environment.

The French essayist Michel de Montaigne was influenced by Sextus Empiricus who had championed the revival of classical Pyrrhonian skepticism. Like Pyrrho of Elis, Sextus employed the principle of *equipollence*. Equipollence was that method by which any given proposition was balanced against its contradictory opposite. This dialectical method resulted in all propositions being treated as equally probable and improbable. In matters of metaphysics, anticipating Kant's critique, equal evidence for and against God, essences, and the self could be given. Since philosophical investigation leads to a logical impasse, room is made for faith.

Following Sextus, in making room for faith, Montaigne described man as a "mass of weakness and corruption. . . . We must strip him to his shirt."[10] Natural reason is incompetent to attain knowledge of being. All knowledge of reality is dependent upon the senses and the senses always distort the data they receive from the external world. Neither sense nor reason can establish anything whatsoever about God. God's existence is known only via a gift of faith.

The French priest Pierre Charron came to the same skepticism. Against Aquinas he maintained that it is not natural theory, but skepticism which is the true *preambula fidei*. The missionary should approach the unbeliever with the Bible in one hand and Sextus Empiricus in the other.[11]

Fideism continued to flourish in the seventeenth century with the aid of Pierre Gassendi who held high the banner of skepticism: "I know nothing Aristotelianwise."[12] In Gassendi's wind, the classical synthesis of theology and philosophy was inexorably tied to Aristotle, therefore, to reject Aristotle was to be a skeptic.

KANT'S COPERNICAN REVOLUTION

With the advent of the Enlightenment (the thorough-going skepticism of Hume and the agnosticism of Kant), fideism was catapulted to center stage of Christian theology.

The pivotal figure contributing to the breakdown of classical apologetics was the philosopher from Königsberg, Immanuel Kant. Though Kant has been dead for a century and a half, he still dominates the intellectual scene. He claimed that in the realm of mind, he effected a Copernican revolution. In retrospect the claim was a modest one. Kant banished God from the world of pure reason and God remains an exile from His own land. *The Critique of Pure Reason* was published in 1781, five years after the American revolution. In comparison the American revolution was a trifle. The United States declared political independence of Great Britain; Kant declared intellectual independence of God.

Kant went beyond all previous refutations by laying his ax at the root of the tree of the knowledge of God. He tried to demonstrate (satisfying most of the scholarly world) that it is impossible to know God intellectually or to prove His being. While it has always been realized that humankind could not comprehend God fully (*finitum non capax infinitum*), Kant was saying that humans cannot know Him even partially.

Kant attempted to establish his agnostic or metaphysical skepticism in three ways. First, he argued that human knowledge only extends to the world's phenomena and not to the noumenal realm of God. Second, he made a direct assault on the traditional proofs. Third, he argued that theistic reasoning ended in antinomies. His *Critique of Pure Reason* was designed to show that knowledge of God was impossible; but if we do not accept his epistemology, he will show us that, on our own principles, God cannot be proven to exist. It has been said of some debaters that they not only annihilated their opponents, but dusted off the spot where they stood. Kant's critique is said to annihilate all theistic arguments and, by the specific attack on the proofs plus showing the antinomies, to dust off the spot where they stood.

Kant's Epistemology

In the first argument, Kant erects a theory of knowledge that precludes any theoretical knowledge of God. His epistemology is well known and may briefly be recapitulated. The knowing process begins when something comes to our minds from out-there (the sense manifold), entering our minds through our senses. This something is experienced with intuitions (*Anchauungen*) of space and time which are not out-there but in-here, in our sensibility. We could never apprehend the out-there without this in-here element. The external must flow through the internal, pure intuitions of space and time. But we are not yet able to form a rational judgment without the involvement of certain categories (quantity, quality, relation, modality) which also are not out-there but in-here, in our understanding (*Verstand*). The final step in knowledge is the schematism of the reason proper (*Vernunft*) which combines these judgments into a cosmology, psychology, and theology.

According to Kant, our knowledge is largely what we would call subjective (in-here). If this is so, any knowledge of a divine being existing in and of himself is beyond the reach of our minds.

Kant's Attack on Theistic Proofs

Kant directly attacked the ontological, cosmological, and teleological arguments. He rejected the ontological argument on the ground that we cannot conclude that the perfect being exists merely because the idea of the perfect being entails the *idea* of existence. Existence, he argued, is not a predicate. The cosmological argument loses its validity because it rests on the ontological argument. But even if it does not, it is still invalid because, in fact, we do not know things as they are but only as they appear. For the teleological argument, Kant has the greatest respect short of acceptance. But it proves at most, he said, an architect trying to shape the world and not a creator dominating it. Moreover, purpose is a highly subjective thing which we tend to read into nature and history.[13]

Kant's Antinomies

Kant's third basic line of argument, dusting off the spot where the theistic proofs stood, is his antinomies. Briefly, these are attempts to show that one line of traditional argumentation for a particular theistic proof can be countered by another line of reasoning proving the opposite, thereby neutralizing or canceling each other, leaving no argument standing.

We will set forth these antinomies briefly, asking the reader to remember that they are supposed to proceed *ad hominem*. That is, Kant is claiming to take non-Kantian assumptions to show that theistic argumentation, on its own principles, is self-contradictory. He has already shown that on the ground of his epistemological analysis there is no possibility whatever of any rational argument for God. He now moves over to theistic ground to show that even here there is no sound argument.

Four sets of antinomies are advanced:

(1) One can argue that the world has no beginning in unlimited space and time (else the cause would be in the series, itself needing explanation). On the other hand, the world had a beginning in space and time (else there would have been a void from which nothing would have come).

(2) Everything existing must be simple, not complex. But on the other hand, they must consist of parts and cannot be simple substances.

(3) The freedom–causality antinomy: if every effect must have a cause, nothing is free; but free agency must exist to will the effects.

(4) There must be a necessary being on which the contingent temporalities depend; but there cannot be, because such a being would have no relation to the contingent.

We will later examine a number of contemporary evangelical scholars who, contrary to the classic Christian tradition, have abandoned the theistic arguments. There must be some explanation. When a planet moves contrary to its proper orbit, an astronomer, convinced some unknown body must be deflecting it, trains his telescope on the calculated spot and discovers a new planet. In Kant, we discover the cause of this deviation from the classic theological pattern, very apparent in neo-orthodox theologians, but almost as clear in the orthodox. The only difference between evangelicals and neo-orthodox on this point, is the greater enthusiasm of the latter. Jaroslav Pelikan, for example, will go so far as to say that Kant's removal of theistic reasoning from Christianity makes it easier to accept justification by faith alone.[14] Evangelicals could never say anything that "far-out," of course, but many do feel greatly relieved that, thanks to Kant, they no longer have to try to prove the existence of God.

NATURAL THEOLOGY AFTER KANT

The idealism of Friedrich Hegel, an important reaction to Kant, enjoyed a brief but vitally important interlude of dominance in nineteenth-century thought. Some view Hegel's effort as the ultimate form of natural theology; but others, such as John Cobb, do not regard it as a type of natural theology at all. According to Hegel, the Kantian antinomies were resolved by a dialectical process through history; in this resolution, new theses were formed as the contradictions were surpassed (*aufgehoben*). Scruton observes:

> The Kantian contradictions, Hegel thought, were only contradictions from the limited point of view of the understanding. They therefore provided a kind of logical impetus to transcend that point of view into the world of pure reason itself, from the perspective of which these and many other contradictions could be resolved.[15]

The massive response to Hegelian philosophy, both within and without the church, proved to be a blessing in disguise for fideists. In the realm of theology, a strong negative reaction set in against natural theology. Cobb notes, "After the abortive attempt to employ Hegelian philosophy as a natural theology, Continental Protestant theologians turned against natural theology as a whole."[16] The works of Schopenhauer, Nietzsche, and Kierkegaard (not to mention Marx) are not intelligible apart from their reactions to Hegel.

From Kant onward the dominant motif in Protestant theology has been fideistic. This is evident in Schleiermacher's emphasis on the experience of a feeling of dependence, in Kierkegaard's view of truth as subjectivity, and in Albrecht Ritschl's desire to exclude metaphysics from theology, focusing instead on nominalistic-phenomenalistic ethical values.[17]

In the twentieth century, theology found its grand master fideist in the person of Karl Barth. Barth consciously wanted a radical rejection of natural theology. He criticized both Roman Catholic and Protestant views of revelation, going as far as to deny general revelation along with natural theology, thereby provoking outcries from his early comrades Emil Brunner and Paul Althaus.[18]

When Brunner attempted to construct a "true" form of natural theology, keeping general revelation intact as the basis for human guilt, he elicited a resounding NO! from Barth. *Natur und Gnade* (1934), Brunner's attempt to reconstruct natural theology, provoked Barth's famous response—*Nein! Antwort an Emil Brunner*.[19]

In his *Epistle to the Romans*, Barth wrote the magna charta of twentieth-century fideism:

> The Gospel requires—*faith*. Only for those who believe is it the *power of God unto salvation*. It can therefore be neither directly communicated nor directly apprehended. . . . "If Christ be very God, He must be unknown, for to be known directly is the charac-

teristic mark of an idol" (Kierkegaard). So new, so unheard of, so unexpected in this world is the power of God unto salvation, that it can appear among us, be received and understood by us, only as contradiction. The Gospel does not expound or recommend itself. It does not negotiate or plead, threaten, or make promises. It withdraws itself always when it is not listened to for its own sake. . . . The Gospel of salvation can only be believed in; it is a matter of faith only. It demands choice. This is its seriousness. To him that is not sufficiently mature to accept a contradiction and to rest in it, it becomes a scandal—to him that is unable to escape the necessity of contradiction, it becomes a matter for faith. . . . He who finally makes open confession of the contradiction and determines to base his life upon it—he it is that believes.[20]

Here is unalloyed fideism, fideism in its pure state. Faith is a decision—it requires resting in contradiction. Faith is more a matter of will (choice) than of mind. This is the leap-of-faith syndrome which refuses to ground faith in any rational proof or evidence. Not only is rational evidence unnecessary to the fideist, it is undesirable as well, signaling a kind of intrusion of pagan categories of thought into the pristine purity of faith.

It is Barth's type of fideism that provoked Wolfhart Pannenberg's critique in his *Wissenschaftstheorie und Theologie*. Pannenberg sees in Barth's approach nothing but an irrational and uncertain risk, a gamble, a dangerous experiment, a leap. Faith is an act of "subjective arbitrariness." To begin with revelation (rather than with reason), Pannenberg argues, involves one in a "rootless postulation of theological consciousness . . . a naked existentialistic certainty that allows no ground or argument to support it."[21]

Fideism makes for strange theological bedfellows. Though crass forms of fundamentalism and dialectical thinkers like Barth and Bultmann are worlds apart with respect to their understanding of the content of Christianity, their method of faith is essentially the same. Fideism is no respecter of persons, finding advocates among liberals and conservatives, as well as virtually every other stripe of theology. The common denominator is the conviction that faith does not rest upon reason but functions prior to and independent of rational evidence.

We have seen in our survey that traditional apologetics is far from dead, but there can be no denying that it is sick and ailing. The Enlightenment dealt it a blow from which it has not yet fully recovered.

If the classical Christian view has been built upon theistic proofs, one would hardly guess it today. It is not merely that we are living in a predominantly fideistic Christian era; we have become *so* fideistic that we tend to assume that Christianity obviously is and always has been so. We are so sure of this that we cannot hear history speaking differently—how could any Christian ever think otherwise?

Clyde Manschreck, for example, a historian of Christianity and specialist on Melanchthon, sees history through a fideistic filter. Consider his treatment of William Chillingworth (1602–1644). Manschreck notes approvingly that Chillingworth is "sometimes called the father of the rationalists in religion."[22] Why? Because in his book *The Religion of Protestants* (1638) Chillingworth wrote: "For my part, I am certain that God hath given us our reason to discern between truth and falsehood, and he that makes not this use of it but believes things he knows not why, I say, it is by chance that he believes the truth and not by choice; and that I cannot but fear, that God will not accept this sacrifice of fools."[23] Manschreck remarks that neither Geneva, Canterbury, nor Rome liked this view. But what is wrong with a view which says, once the authority of the Bible has been established: "Propose me anything out of this book, and require whether I believe it or no, and seem it never so incomprehensible to human reason, I will subscribe it with hand and heart, as knowing no demonstration can be stronger than this; God hath said so, therefore, it is true."[24] Chillingworth was not the soundest of theologians, but at this point he is classically Christian and it is the modern commentator who is out of step with Christian history.

Today, not only are Christians in general (and neo-orthodox ones especially) fideistic, but even Evangelical, orthodox Christians tend to be so. At least many, indeed, most Evangelical scholars reject the theistic proofs, and it is very difficult, if not logically impossible, to avoid fideism without them (although some Evangelicals are attempting to do so).

Historically, Christians have appealed to special revelation as corroboration of the validity of natural theology. From the Bible itself we learn that there is general revelation and natural theology. Though natural theology has been the subject of rigorous and persistent controversy, the idea of general revelation, based on the clear teaching of the Bible, has been virtually axiomatic, Karl Barth being its most notable detractor.

THE "BACK OF THE BOOK" METHOD

General revelation of some sort is widely affirmed, as we said, because special revelation so clearly affirms it. But the question remains: do we move from general revelation to special revelation or from special revelation to general revelation? In Section 3 of this volume we will endeavor to show in detail that moving from special revelation to general revelation involves the invalid method of circular reasoning and that the proper procedure is to move from general revelation to special revelation.

Thomas Aquinas has been charged with such circularity for working "backwards" to formulate his natural theology. Like a student who looks up the answers in the back of the book so that he knows the answer he is searching for before the problem-solving activity even begins, Aquinas has been accused of philosophical "cheating." To be sure, Aquinas does mention the biblical teaching of natural theology in passing, but he does not build his case for natural theology by a simple appeal to the New Testament:

> The existence of God and similar things which can be known by natural reason as Romans, Chapter I affirms, are not articles of faith, but preambles to the articles. Faith presupposes natural knowledge as grace presupposes nature.[25]

Aquinas and other advocates of natural theology were aware of what the Bible says about the matter. Special revelation confirms natural theology. This fact is important to the debate over natural theology for two reasons. The first is that the Bible makes a claim for the validity of natural theology which claim must be tested and seen to be valid or invalid. The second is that once the Bible is established as special revelation its teaching on the question of natural theology is normative. This is crucial to those scholars who affirm special revelation and general revelation but deny natural theology. For if the special revelation which they affirm teaches natural theology, then their position is exposed as inconsistent.

We are not here basing the validity of natural theology upon the Bible. We have not yet either demonstrated that the Bible is in fact special revelation or that the Bible teaches natural theology. What we are doing at the moment is pointing out that *if* the Bible is special revelation and *if* it teaches natural theology then, of course, by irresistible logic we must conclude that natural theology is valid.

The authors of this volume *do* believe the Bible is special revelation and that it does teach natural theology. We do not cease believing those things while we seek to demonstrate them. By our use of the conditional word *if* in the premises above we merely acknowledge that thus far we have not *demonstrated* the truth of what we are *affirming*. This, we think, is what Aquinas was doing when he mentioned Romans 1 and 2. He was not arguing in circular fashion from special revelation to natural theology.

As we approach the historical debate between natural theology and fideism, we notice that some fideists accept special revelation while others deny it. (Kant, for example, in criticizing the theistic proofs did not fall back on special revelation as an alternative, whereas Barth, while criticizing natural theology, *did* fall back on special revelation, though of a modified and unorthodox sort. Still others who advocate an orthodox view of special revelation, also reject natural theology.)

Those theologians who accept special revelation *and* affirm that natural theology is confirmed by special revelation face a philosophical dilemma. For Kant argued that God *cannot* be known by natural theology and the apostle Paul taught that God *is* known by natural theology. Both cannot be right.

The competing propositions "God can be known by natural theology" and "God cannot be known by natural theology" are not merely *contraries* in which both statements cannot be true, though both might be false; but they are *contradictions,* which means that the two premises cannot both be true *and* they cannot both be false. Hence one premise must be true and the other must be false. Herein lies the tension for the advocate of special revelation. If Paul (special revelation) teaches that natural theology is valid and Kant argues that it is not valid, then manifestly either Paul or Kant is right and the other is wrong.

We maintain that the "back of the book" method is valid only when the validity of special revelation has been established. Among advocates of special revelation, the issue of natural theology can be solved with facility by seeing what the book says on the matter, if indeed the book speaks to the issue and speaks clearly. This would not be an exercise in circular reasoning but an exercise in consistency. On the other hand, if we argue that "natural theology is valid because the Bible teaches it" and "the Bible is valid because natural theology teaches it," then we are caught in a vicious circle of *petitio principii.*

Using the back of the book method we can imagine two students agreeing that the answers in the back of the book are the correct ones to the test questions. After taking the test they disagree about the answer to a particular question and decide to settle their dispute amicably. All they have to do is turn to the answer page in the back of the book. Of course, the particular answer in the back of the book may be smudged or obscured by a printing blemish, or even stated in such ambiguous terms as to leave the question still in dispute. But if the answer is clear and undistorted, with no abiding ambiguity, then the issue is resolved according to the agreed upon method of resolution.

Before we embark on a study of the theistic proofs and evidence for special revelation we will examine the biblical texts to see if there is in fact a biblical claim to general revelation and natural theology. Different positions in apologetics often arise from differing positions on general revelation. For instance, Cornelius Van Til (whose presuppositional apologetics we will critique in Section 3) views the central issue between the Dutch theologian Abraham Kuyper and the "Old Princeton" theologian Benjamin Warfield as whether reason has the ability to interpret general revelation correctly. Kuyper's position is stated: "With the light of Scripture it is possible for man to read nature aright. Without that light we cannot, even on the Areopagas, reach further than the unknown God."[26] According to Kuyper there is a general revelation but no correct natural theology unless and until one has the light of special revelation. Here the movement clearly is a reverse flow from special revelation back to general revelation.

Warfield's position was quite different:

> Warfield accordingly attributes to "right reason" the ability to interpret natural revelation with essential correctness. This "right reason" is not the reason of the Christian. It is the reason that is confronted with Christianity and possesses some criterion apart from Christianity with which to judge the truth of Christianity.[27]

Warfield's position is that the unbeliever can and does gain a natural theology apart from and prior to special revelation. His apologetic moves from general revelation to special revelation, the opposite flow of that maintained by Kuyper. Van Til, in evaluating the Kuyper–Warfield dispute, declares, "I have chosen the position of Abraham Kuyper."[28] The authors of this book have chosen the position of Benjamin Warfield. The issue remains: Does the unbeliever have factual knowledge about God and His attributes through the creation?

CHAPTER 4

The Biblical Evidence Confirming Natural Theology

EARLIER WE MENTIONED that Western culture is not pagan, but has been secularized. Though devoid of knowledge of Christ and the Scriptures of the Old and New Testaments, paganism is established upon the basis of a thorough going rejection of the knowledge of God the Father. The pagan may be ignorant of Moses and Jesus, but he knows in his heart and understands (though reluctant to admit it) that God exists. In its variant forms, paganism represents man's attempt to flee from the God revealed in creation. With respect to the question of the existence of God, paganism's problem is not ultimately philosophical but moral. The pagan's problem is not that he does not know that God is, but that he does not like the God who is.

This, of course, is a serious charge to level against the pagan. It is a charge that applies equally to the secularized person. If it is a false charge, it is utterly slanderous as it calls into question the integrity of pagan and many secular philosophers and thinkers. It raises doubts about the intellectual honesty of many brilliant and erudite people. But this charge is not the child of our own imagination; rather it springs from the New Testament, particularly from Romans 1, the *locus classicus* of Paul's teaching on general revelation. Here the apostle charges that paganism is generated not by intellectual causes but by moral ones. The problem is not that there is insufficient evidence to convince rational beings of the existence of God, but that rational beings in their present fallen condition have a natural antipathy to the being of God.[1] In a word, the nature of God (at least the true God) is repugnant to humans—pagan and secular. Though inclined to project and create imaginary deities, humankind is antipathetic to the true God.

We also labored the point of the back of the book methodology, not so much for questions concerning general revelation or natural revelation, but to clarify the central dispute concerning an approach to natural theology. If the Bible clearly teaches natural theology, then those who affirm the normative, revelatory character of the Bible must also affirm natural theology if they are to be consistent with their view of Scripture. But even if the Bible does not clearly affirm it, we have seen that natural theology can be established from *general* revelation. To one who rejects the Bible as normative revelation, a case for natural theology may and must be made on these other grounds. Here we are addressing principally those who share our commitment to the normative, revelatory character of the Bible.

Let us examine then what the Bible does say about general revelation and natural theology.

A BIBLICAL VIEW OF GENERAL REVELATION

On numerous occasions the Scriptures make reference to God's revelation. Most significantly the "nature Psalms" call attention to the manifestations of God's glory and perfection in the created sphere. Unlike other ancient religions, in Old Testament Hebrew religion nature is never deified but is seen rather as a theater of general revelation. Other ancient religions sacralized nature by positing storm gods, flood gods, earthquake gods, and a host of other deities with each god assigned to a particular aspect of the natural realm. In Old Testament religion the power of God may be made manifest through the storm or the earthquake but the earthquake is never identified with God Himself. The fundamental principle of the Old Testament is the prohibition of idolatry, the worship of any created being or any part of the created order.

The most oft-quoted citation for general revelation in the Old Testament is Psalm 19, "The heavens declare the glory of God and the firmament shows forth His handiwork." The beauty of the skies is an indicator of the glory and majesty of the One who created them. The entire realm of creation bears witness to the master craftsmanship of its Maker.

Besides the Psalms and other allusions to God's revelation in nature, the supreme teaching of the Bible on the question of general revelation is found in Romans 1. To gain a more lucid understanding of this teaching, let us look closely at the text beginning at Romans 1:18:

> For the wrath of God is revealed from heaven against all ungodliness and wickedness of men who by their wickedness suppress the truth. (RSV)

This bold declaration of the revelation of the wrath of God from heaven is enough in itself to provoke a negative emotional reaction; the idea of the wrath of God is not popular, even in many "Christian" circles. The word the apostle uses here for wrath is the Greek word ὀργή (*orge*). The Latin version translates the Greek by the word *ira*. The wrath described here does not indicate an arbitrary, capricious, or irrational passion manifested by the deity. There is a reason for God's anger. His anger is directed against, and provoked by human evil. Paul knows nothing of a blind divine fury that rages against innocent people. According to this text, God's wrath is revealed against *ungodliness* and *unrighteousness* of men.

"Ungodliness" is a generic term capable of various forms of particular content. The term ἀσέβεια (*asebeia*) involves a general conduct of impiety and irreligiosity. It involves a posture of opposition to the majesty of God. Unrighteousness (ἀδικία, *adikia*) indicates an assault against the righteousness of God. Many commentators interpret this passage as referring to two different and subsequent types of human activity, namely, impiety and immorality. John Murray, for example, writes:

> "Ungodliness" refers to perversity that is religious in character, "unrighteousness" to what is moral; the former is illustrated by idolatry, the latter by immorality. The order is, no doubt, significant. In the Apostle's description of degeneracy, impiety is the precursor of immorality.[2]

To be sure, the broader context of chapter 1 of Romans indicates that moral degeneracy flows out of impiety and Paul structures this portion of the epistle with that order. But the immediate context of the verse indicates that Paul is describing one particular action of mankind which is, *at the same time,* both ungodly and unrighteous. We adopt the view taken by Calvin, and more recently by Kittel:

> A common view is that the reference is to sins against the first and second tables of the law, offenses against God and neighbor. If so,

it is natural to conclude, though there is no exegetical support for this, that Paul has irreligion and immorality in view, and that the former is traced back to the latter. Against this, however, is the πᾶσαν which embraces both terms and binds them closely together. Another counter argument is that the distinction between sins against God and against men is rare among the Rabbis and is certainly not a Rabbinic distinction. A final point is that in what follows ἀδικία covers both words. The δίκη against which men offend is God's righteousness. Hence ασεβέια and ἀδικία in Romans 1:18 are a hendiadys: "ungodliness and unrighteousness."[3]

Thus, by means of hendiadys, two different nouns express a single idea. God's wrath is directed against something which is considered to be both ungodly and unrighteous.

Paul does not leave us to speculate about the precise nature of the evil people commit that is at once both ungodly and unrighteous. He moves quickly from the general to the specific and isolates the particular crime which provokes God. It is the evil which *suppresses the truth*. Suppression of the truth is at the heart of Paul's indictment of paganism.

Paul uses the expression ἐν ἀδικίᾳ κατεχόντων which has been variously translated: "holding (the truth) in unrighteousness"; "hold down (the truth) in unrighteousness"; "hinder (the truth)"; "in wickedness stifling the truth"; and so on. Thus κατεχόντων is variously translated "hold," "hold down," "suppress," "stifle," and "hinder." J. H. Bavinck has suggested yet another term to get at the matter, namely, the verb "repress." He writes:

> It seems to me that in this case we should translate it by "repress." We intentionally choose a word which has a specific meaning in psychological literature. Webster's *New Collegiate Dictionary* defines the word "repression" as the process by which unacceptable desires or impulses are excluded from consciousness and thus being denied direct satisfaction are left to operate in the unconscious. This seems to agree with what Paul says here about human life. But we must mention that the word *repression* has received a wider meaning in more recent psychology. In Freudian psychology it specifically refers to unconscious desires of a more or less sexual nature. In more recent psychology it is also applied to desires and impulses of a very different nature. The impulses or desires which are repressed may be very valuable. Anything that goes contrary to the accepted patterns of life or to the predominant popular ideas may be repressed. Usually this happens and the results can be far-reaching. We are reminded of this psycho-

logical phenomenon recently discovered by Paul's usage of this word. He says that man always represses God's truth because it is contrary to his pattern of life.[4]

The primary meaning of the root verb κατέχειν in biblical Greek is "to hold fast." In its most common usage it is a positive term meaning to "hold fast" to spiritual values, for example, or to the Word of God. But the term is also used in a pejorative sense meaning to "hold illegally" or "hold in prison." In Romans 1:18, Paul obviously used the term in its negative sense. People are said to hold the truth in an evil way, in effect, to incarcerate it.

But what truth is it that is being held this way? Again Paul does not leave us to grope for the answer. Verse 19 makes it clear that it is truth or knowledge about God which is being repressed or held down. "For what can be known about God is plain to them, because God has shown it to them" (Rom. 1:19 RSV).

Here the apostle asserts that knowledge of God is not shrouded in obscurity, detectable only by an elite gnostic group or by a skilled master of esoteric mysteries. That which can be known about God is plain. The word *plain* is rendered in the Greek by φανερόν (*phaneron*) and in the Latin by *manifestum*. This knowledge (γνωστόν) is not hidden or concealed, but manifest, being clear and transparent for anyone to see. Paul goes on to say that the reason it is plain is because God shows it to them. In this case if the pupil does not learn, it is not because the teacher did not teach. There is no defect in divine pedagogy. God not only makes this knowledge of Himself available (as a professor might put specific volumes on a subject on the reserve shelf of a library for the student to peruse if he is so disposed) but God Himself shows this revelation to man. "Ever since the creation of the world his invisible nature, namely, his eternal power and deity, has been clearly perceived in the things that have been made. So they are without excuse" (Rom. 1:20 RSV). Here is the text of texts to establish the biblical basis for general revelation and natural theology.

NATURAL THEOLOGY: MEDIATE AND IMMEDIATE

Much debate has arisen in the history of the church concerning the precise meaning of this verse. The debate centers on the *mode* of God's revelation—whether *mediate* or *immediate*.[5] That is, is the revelation gleaned by reasoning from the evidence for God in the medium of creation, or is the revelation a kind of a priori knowledge immediately (i.e., without means) impressed by God upon human consciousness?

This has been a serious issue within Roman Catholic theology, as well as a point of dispute among contemporary Protestant apologists.

Immediate natural theology refers to a direct, a priori knowledge of God implanted in the mind by God. The Roman Catholic Church rejected immediate natural theology. Over against immediate natural theology, Rome endorsed mediate natural theology.[6]

Mediate natural theology refers to a knowledge of God that is not direct, but indirect; not a priori but a posteriori. That is, God is not immediately known but is known via a *medium* which points beyond itself to God. This medium is the world of nature. In this method we know God by means of nature. We are confronted by God's revelation in nature. By viewing nature, the mind is able to know the God of nature. Here Rome speaks of the ability to know God by "the natural light of reason."[7] The foundation in Roman Catholic natural theology is the conviction that we can have some knowledge of God "from the created things." The classical Roman formula for natural theology, having its roots in Thomas Aquinas, is that natural theology is "mediate, analogous, incomplete, but true."[8] Protestant theology on the other hand, did not rule out immediate natural theology. Calvin, especially developed a concept of immediate natural theology. His view of the *sensus divinitatis* and his analysis of Romans 1 and 2 give evidence of this.[9]

Mediate natural theology involves human reflection on the creation. The invisible things of God are made known by means of the visible things. In Romans 1:20, Paul is affirming that humans can in fact move from the phenomenal realm to the noumenal realm, making the dispute with Kant all the more vivid. The method of knowing here is not the immediate apprehension of the inner being of God. Nature provides no transcendental direct perception of God. The knowledge is mediate, or inferential, indicating the rational power to deduce the necessary existence of the invisible from the perception of the visible. The apostle does not indulge in metaphysical skepticism or agnosticism.

The question (whether knowledge of God is mediate or immediate) arises from a certain ambiguity in the Greek text of Romans 1:20. What does Paul mean when he says, "from the creation of the world"? Does this "from" (ἀπό) mean a temporal period? or a modal source of information? Most modern commentators favor the former and render the Greek, "since the creation of the world." H. C. G. Moule asserts:

> Man's knowledge of God began with his being as man. To see the Maker in His works is not, according to the Holy Scriptures, only the slow and difficult issue of a long evolution which led through far lower forms of thought, the fetish, the nature-power, the tribal god, the national god, to the idea of a Supreme. Scripture presents man as made in the image of the Supreme, and capable from the first of a true however faint apprehension of Him. It assures us that man's lower and distorted views of nature and of personal power behind it are degenerations, perversions, issues of a mysterious primeval dislocation of man from his harmony with God.[10]

C. K. Barrett adds the comment:

> From the creation of the world is here taken in a temporal sense, partly because the word for creation (κτίσις) refers properly to the act or process of creation and partly because instrumentality is sufficiently suggested in the words "in (or, by) *the things that he has made.*" As long as there has been a created universe, the invisible attributes of God are plainly seen.[11]

For present purposes either translation is useful for the point under consideration. Whatever the mode of revelation, the fact remains that God's invisible nature has been clearly perceived in the things that are made. Murray says:

> And this sense of the term "clearly seen" is provided by the explanatory clause "being understood by the things that are made"—it is the seeing of understanding or intelligent conception. Stress is laid upon the perspicuity afforded by the things that are made in mediating to us the perception of the invisible attributes—they are "clearly seen."[12]

The things that are clearly seen are seen in the created things, namely, nature. What are the invisible things of God which are known via natural theology? Paul identifies them as His "eternal power and deity." Natural theology includes cognition not only of the existence of God but knowledge of His nature. God is known to be eternal and powerful. He is known to have a "divine nature" (θείοτης). This points not merely to one of God's attributes but to all of His perfections. Charles Hodge commented on the invisible things:

> By the invisible things of God Theodoret says we are to understand creation, providence, and the divine judgments; The-

ophylact understands them to refer to his goodness, wisdom, power, and majesty. Between these interpretations the moderns are divided. The great majority prefer the latter, which is obviously the better suited to the context, because the works of God are expressed afterwards by ποίηματα, and because the invisible things are those which are manifested by his works, and are explained by the terms 'power and Godhead' . . . the power of God is more immediately manifested in his works; but not his power alone, but his divine excellence in general, which is expressed by θείοτης from θετος. θεότης, from θεός, on the other hand, expresses the being, rather than the excellence of God. The latter is Godhead; the former, divinity, a collective term for all the divine perfections.[13]

Later in Romans 1 another element is added to the content of general revelation. Paul adds, "they know the ordinance of God, that those who practice such things are worthy of death" (Rom. 1:32). Thus the content of natural revelation includes a knowledge of the moral character of God.

The cumulative effect of this knowledge which is clearly seen is to leave people "without excuse." This is the basis of universal human guilt. The excuse that is banished, the excuse every pagan hopes in vain to use, the excuse that is exploded by God's self-revelation in nature is the pretended, vacuous, dishonest appeal to *ignorance*. No one will be able to approach the judgment seat of God justly pleading, "If only I had known you existed, I would surely have served you." That excuse is annihilated. No one can lightly claim "insufficient evidence" for not believing in God. Though people are not always persuaded by sound and sufficient evidence, it does not follow that the evidence is therefore insufficient. The failure here is with humans, not with the evidence. The problem is not a lack of evidence, nor a lack of knowledge, nor a lack of natural cognitive equipment—it is a *moral deficiency*. We are culpable for our refusal to submit to the evidence God plainly provides.

The revelation of God in nature is mediate, but it is so manifest and so clear that it does not necessitate a complex theoretical reasoning process that could be achieved only by a group of geniuses. If God's general revelation is in fact "general," in that it is plain enough for all to see clearly without complicated cosmological argumentation, then it may even be said to be self-evident. The revelation is clear enough for an unskilled and illiterate person to perceive it. In this sense it may be said that if we but open our eyes, the revelation of God in nature is "immediate" with respect to time.

If mediate natural theology is so "immediately" recognizable, why all the labor of complex cosmological argumentation à la Aquinas? Romans 1 gives an answer to that. We read that natural theology is repressed. People refuse to acknowledge what they know to be true. Herein lies the "inexcusable" of the apostolic indictment.

The complex philosophical cosmological arguments are part of the unmasking process of those who refuse to acknowledge their natural knowledge of God. In rejecting or denying natural theology, people have used every sophisticated tool of scholarship at their disposal. If their counter arguments are sound, then we must part company with Paul. If they are not sound, it is the task of the apologist to refute them. When the church denies the validity of natural theology, she escapes the burden of refuting the Kants of this world. What the church fails to realize in her sigh of relief at not having to face the burden of intellectual defense of the faith is that in her escapist policies she is capitulating to a position that is clearly antithetical to the teaching of the New Testament.

WHAT KIND OF KNOWLEDGE OF GOD?

Many theologians make an important distinction here between the revelation God provides which is *objective* and the human apprehension of it which is *subjective*. It is a useful distinction and important, indeed, though at times it has been used to draw invalid conclusions from the text. There are those who argue that the objective general revelation is there for all to see, but that because of the fall into sin and especially because of the influence of sin on the mind (the noetic effects of sin) the objective revelation never gets through, it is not subjectively appropriated. Frequently this idea (that the revelation never yields knowledge) is buttressed by appeals to John Calvin's treatment of the problem. The famous "blindfold image" is used to support the thesis. Calvin writes:

> But as the greater part of mankind, enslaved by error, walk blind-folded in this glorious theatre, he exclaims that it is a rare and singular wisdom to mediate carefully on these works of God, which many, who seem most sharp-sighted in other respects, behold without profit. It is indeed true, that the brightest manifestation of Divine glory finds not one genuine spectator among a

hundred still neither his power nor his wisdom is shrouded in darkness.[14]

This passage from Calvin has some awkward spots in it. The blindfold image strongly suggests that the light of general revelation never gets into the mind. Blindfolded people cannot see. If this is the Geneva master's point, then we must take issue with it as this interpretation would do serious violence to the text. Even within this controversial passage, however, Calvin qualifies his blindfold image by saying that the problem is that (1) people do not meditate carefully on the revelation, (2) they behold it "without profit", (3) there is not one *genuine* spectator among a hundred, and (4), the final qualification, still neither His power nor His wisdom is shrouded in darkness. Thus the last phrase even indicates for Calvin that the light of general revelation gets through. Calvin's blindfold image probably is a reference to human *use* of general revelation and its subsequent sufficiency for salvation. Elsewhere Calvin himself makes clear that the knowledge does get through. If humanity has a blindfold on, it is on the heart, not the eyes.

Great strain is evident frequently in the treatment of this text, even by such eminent scholars as J. H. Bavinck and G. C. Berkouwer. Bavinck for example speaks of a knowledge which is not "real knowledge."[15] Against Roman Catholic natural theology Berkouwer writes, "Paul's portrait of this knowing man is quite different. It does not reveal the clear color of *true knowledge,* but is murky with vanity and foolishness."[16] Berkouwer cites Greydanus:

> Not a right knowing which leads to recognition, as the verses subsequent to this one make clear, but only a superficial notation. It touches his consciousness and is active there, but issues in no true knowledge which reveals itself in true service of God.[17]

Elsewhere Berkouwer says, "There's only reason for complaint on the part of God, for they have known Him in the irrefutability of His revelation which they have, nonetheless, refuted."[18]

The strain of exegesis here is obvious. Bavinck speaks of a knowledge which is not "real knowledge." Greydanus speaks of knowledge which is not a "right knowing" and not "true knowledge" but merely a "superficial notation." On one page Berkouwer says, "It does not reveal the clear color of true knowledge." Two pages later he speaks of people knowing God in the irrefutability of His revelation. Berkouwer first says people do not receive true knowledge. Then he says they know God. He says the knowledge is irrefutable and in the same sentence says people refute it.

Here we see an exercise in serious confusion about Romans 1; we have a knowledge that is not real knowledge; a knowledge that is not true knowledge; a knowledge that is irrefutable yet is refuted. But if the knowledge is not real knowledge, what kind of knowledge is it? If it is not true knowledge, how can people be judged guilty for rejecting it? If it is irrefutable how can it be refuted? We are surprised at these mental gymnastics. Why do such eminent scholars get involved in this obvious confusion? These writers would probably have done better to say with Jonathan Edwards that this knowledge "Don't seem real to 'em," rather than suggest that the unregenerate are devoid of real knowledge.

On numerous occasions Paul speaks of pagans as not knowing God: "Not in lustful passion, *like the Gentiles who do not know God*" (1 Thess. 4:5); "Dealing out retribution *to those who do not know God*" (2 Thess. 1:8); "However at that time, *when you did not know God,* you were slaves to those which by nature are no gods" (Gal. 4:8); "For since in the wisdom of God the world through its wisdom *did not come to know God*" (1 Cor. 1:21). Numerous other passages indicate the same negative judgment about natural knowledge of God. How do we square these statements with Paul's comments in Romans 1?

There are basically three ways we can approach the problem of the apparent conflict between Romans 1 and other Pauline passages cited above. We can conclude that (1) Paul contradicts himself, (2) that he does not mean what he says in Romans 1 or in the other passages, or (3) we can explore the nuances of the verb "to know" (γινώσκειν) in the New Testament.

The first option is eliminated *ipso facto* by those with a high view of Scripture or even by those who have the courtesy to give Paul the benefit of a second glance before convicting him of a blatant contradiction. The second option has the weakness mentioned above: It fails to do justice to the fact that Paul clearly and unambiguously asserts that people do in fact know God. The third option, in light of the multiplicity of nuances associated with the Greek verb "to know," seems to be the most reasonable and responsible way of dealing with the problem. The Bible speaks of "knowing" in many ways. It speaks of *cognitive knowledge* (intellectual awareness); *intimate knowledge* (personal intimate relationships, as, e.g., when Adam "knew his wife and she conceived"); and *saving knowledge* (knowledge unto redemption which is a correlate of special revelation). These are but a few nuances; *knowledge of intensity* could be added to the list.[19]

The most reasonable method of gaining a coherent understanding of what Paul says is to understand these nuances and apply them to the text in question. The most superficial form knowledge can take is cognitive apprehension. There can be cognitive apprehension without an intimate knowledge or a saving knowledge. But can there be an intimate knowledge or a saving knowledge without first having cognitive apprehension? To harmonize the Pauline passages all that is necessary is to point out that general revelation provides and produces a *cognitive apprehension of God*. It does not produce intimate knowledge or saving knowledge. The pagan can have one kind of knowledge of God (cognitive), while lacking another kind (intimate redemptive). This resolves the tension of the Pauline passages without resorting to statements about knowledge that is not real knowledge and knowledge that is not true knowledge; it involves no unnecessary strain and it avoids contradictory statements about refuting the irrefutable.

In fairness to Bavinck, Greydanus, and Berkouwer it must be pointed out that this is precisely the struggle that they are dealing with in their writings. It is obvious that when these men speak of true knowledge they mean something more than cognitive apprehension. By true knowledge they mean true saving knowledge, a knowledge of the redemptive truth of God. It is unfortunate that they are not clear at this point, but the context of their writings indicates that that is what they are affirming. Obviously, Berkouwer's statement that "men refute the irrefutable" is a paradoxical statement designed to call attention to the absurdity and insanity of trying to refute the irrefutable evidence of God. But the revelation is not refuted, though people make every conceivable attempt to refute it. The apostle Paul's indictment in Romans 1 is not brought against the human refusal to see or moral inability to see general revelation; it is brought against the refusal to acknowledge what all clearly do see. Romans 1 repeatedly asserts that humans do apprehend general revelation:

—That which is *known* about God is evident within them. (Rom. 1:19 NASB)
—For since the creation of the world His invisible attributes, His eternal power and divine nature, had been *clearly seen*, being *understood* through what has been made. (Rom. 1:20)
—For even though they *knew* God. . . .(Rom. 1:21)

—And just as they did not see fit *to acknowledge* God. . . . (Rom. 1:28)

—And, although they *know the ordinance of God*. . . . (Rom. 1:32)

It is the rejection of this general revelation that makes humans morally culpable. If we had no natural cognitive ability to receive general revelation, God would hardly hold us responsible for it. But no such excuse can be claimed.

To be sure, as Calvin indicates, general revelation *is* insufficient. It is insufficient to convert us. Sin creates a moral deficiency within us by which we are indisposed to truth. This factor which compounds our sin is already a result of our sin. If there is a lack or deficiency in human handling of general revelation, it is rooted not so much in our natural composition as in our moral disposition. But even fallen humanity has the cognitive equipment to know who God is. This moral problem becomes an intellectual problem when it darkens thinking and distorts judgment. But such darkness follows the rejection of natural revelation, it does not cause it. If the question of the subjective appropriation of general revelation is still in doubt, such doubt is demolished by verse 21:

> For even though they knew God, they did not honor Him as God, or give thanks; but they became futile in their speculations, and their foolish heart was darkened. (Rom. 1:21 NASB)

Here Paul unequivocally asserts that the pagan knew God. Other translators render the participle, γνόντες, "knowing God. . . ." Again, the problem is not failure to honor what was *not* known, but a *refusal to honor what was clearly known*. Thus the pagan has no appeal to ignorance. Knowledgeable people, not ignorant ones, are the objects of divine wrath and judgment.

The verb "to know" is used on different levels in the New Testament, being pregnant with various nuances. There is a vast difference between knowing God theoretically and knowing Him personally in an intimate filial relationship. There is a difference between a cognitive apprehension that God is and a redemptive knowledge that God saves. We can have the former without the latter, but not the latter without the former. There is a crucial difference between a knowledge of God and an *acknowledgement* of God, which is precisely what the apostle is dealing with here. Though the nuances contained in the word *gnosis* (knowledge) are many, there remains the decisive distinction between *gnosis* (knowledge) and *agnosis* (ignorance). Fallen humanity may not have full redemptive knowledge of God but they are not ignorant of God.

In verse 21 the apostle not only says that people fail to honor God or give thanks to Him (even while knowing Him), but also that they become futile in their thinking and their senseless hearts are darkened. Futile reasoning follows from the refusal to acknowledge God. This reasoning is futile precisely because it proceeds from a primary premise that is faulty; it produces only the final fruit already present in the initial bias. The end result is not light, but darkness that penetrates to the very heart. It ends in darkness because it abhors the light at the beginning. Had the reason first acknowledged the clear presence of the light, the fatal process of fallacious reasoning would have never begun. Brilliant and erudite reasoning may produce abhorant conclusions if it proceeds from a faulty starting point. A scientist who refuses to acknowledge facts that he knows are true can hardly be expected to arrive at sound conclusions. Any reasoning process that begins with the denial of the known and proceeds on the basis of prejudice can hardly produce light, no matter how lucid and cogent the argument may be after the initial error is made. In fact, the more consistent a dishonest thinker is the further away from basic truth his mind will carry him. By means of what is called happy inconsistency, many people begin with a faulty premise and end with a good conclusion. In this sense their good conclusions are fortuitous and not based upon a sound reasoning process.

NOT MORONS, BUT FOOLISH IDOLATERS

It is important to note that Paul does not deny the ability of natural man to reason or even to reason correctly if free of prejudice. The problem is not in the capacity for thought per se, but in the thought process that begins and is maintained by prejudice to the facts. The intellectual problem is produced by the moral problem, not the moral problem by an intellectual one.

> Professing to be wise, they became fools, and exchanged the glory of the incorruptible God for an image in the form of corruptible man and of birds and four-footed animals and crawling creatures. (Rom. 1:22–23 NASB)

This severe indictment by the apostle could easily be misconstrued as an assault upon the intelligence of natural man. A close look at this passage, however, will indicate that the passage attacks not intellectual ability but morality.

Paul's use of the term *fools* must be examined closely. In biblical categories "fool" does not necessarily indicate a person with low intelligence. The term connotes both a moral and religious judgment. To be sure, the word is capable of being used to describe persons who are dull-witted or have an extraordinarily low degree of common sense. The term *moros* is the root from which the English word *moron* derives. In classical Greek the term had a psychological flavor. Bertram points out:

> With reference to men the use is predominantly psychological. The word implies censure on man himself: his acts, thoughts, counsels, and words are not as they should be. The weakness may be due to a specific failure in judgment or decision, but a general deficiency of intellectual and spiritual capacities may also be asserted.[20]

In Old Testament terms the "fool" stands in sharp contrast to the wise man. The wise man is known not by his academic credentials but by his practical manifestation of godliness. Wisdom begins with the "fear of the Lord." Conversely, foolishness has its origin in the rejection of God. It is the "fool [who] says in his heart, 'There is no God' " (Ps. 14:1 RSV). Isaiah calls that person a fool who contemptuously breaks off fellowship with God and becomes a practical atheist. To be a fool is to fall into a negative theological category rather than an exclusively intellectual one. Likewise the fool in the New Testament is the one who fails to act prudently with respect to God, falling under moral judgment.

Paul's critique in Romans 1 is a two-edged sword. Not only is the natural man labeled a fool, he is pronounced guilty of hypocrisy as well. The one who becomes a fool is the same one who professes to be wise. There is a serious discrepancy between the profession of wisdom and the denial of God. The fool, proclaiming that he is wise, claims a state he doesn't have and thus falls under the double indictment of the apostle.

Human foolishness is manifested in the exchanging of the glory of God for idols. The word *exchange* is important to a proper understanding of the text. Many translations often render the verb to mean simply "change." But the context of Romans 1 excludes this rendition as too weak and ambiguous. The particular kind of change in view here involves a mutation or distortion by means of a substitution of the genuine with the artificial or counterfeit. The change results in idolatry which also comes under the judgment of God. Here is an example of the case where the distortion of truth results not in militant atheism but in a kind of religion. This religion, however, does not serve to exonerate man or mitigate the wrath of God, but rather compounds the felony as it adds massive insult to the glory of the immortal God. Here pagan religion is not viewed as a step of evolutionary progress on the way to a fully developed monotheism, but a flight from monotheism. Not evolution but devolution or even revolution (in the sense of revolt against God) is the pattern of pagan religion. Murray adds:

> Here the apostle sets forth the origin of that degeneration and degradation which pagan idolatry epitomizes, and we have the biblical philosophy of false religion. For hedonism, as Meyer says, is not the primeval religion, from which men might gradually have risen to the knowledge of the true God, but is, on the contrary, the result of a falling away from the known original revelation of the true God in His works.[21]

Mircea Eliade writes about the notion of a "remote God" that is found widely in primitive religions:

> Celestially structured supreme beings tend to disappear from the practice of religion, from cult; they depart from among men, withdraw to the sky, and become remote, inactive gods (*dei otiosi*). In short, it may be said of these gods that, after creating the cosmos, life, and man, they feel a sort of fatigue, as if the immense enterprise of the creation had exhausted their resources. So they withdraw to the sky, leaving a son or a demiurge on earth to finish or perfect the Creation. Gradually their place is taken by other divine figures—the mythical ancestors, the mother-goddesses, the fecundating gods, and the like.[22]

Eliade goes on to say that among African peoples, "the great celestial god, the supreme being, all-powerful creator, plays only a minor role in the religious life of most tribes. He is too far away or too good to meet a natural cult, and he is involved only in extreme cases."[23]

Thus even in primitive religion there is at least a vague recollection of God the Creator. According to Paul, religion is not the fruit of a zealous pursuit of God, but the result of a passionate flight from God. The glory of God is exchanged for an idol. The idol stands as a monument not to religious fervor but to humanity's flight from an initial encounter with the glory of God.

> Therefore God gave them over in the lusts of their hearts to impurity, that their bodies might be dishonored among them. For they exchanged the truth of God for a lie, and worshiped and served the creature rather than the Creator, who is blessed forever. Amen. (Rom. 1:24–25 NASB)

God responds to these idolaters by abandoning them to their idolatry. God lets people pursue their lusts or desires for impurity. What begins as an act of refusal to honor God culminates in the dishonoring of the human. Karl Barth comments:

> When God has been deprived of His glory, men are also deprived of theirs. Desecrated within their souls, they are desecrated also without in their bodies, for men are one.[24]

Paul's analysis indicates a progression not only from God to man but also from thought to deed. As behavior and theory are distinguishable, yet inseparably related, the moral consequences of the rejection of the knowledge of God would be inevitably manifested in moral conduct. Luther adds:

> Hence, also, the guilt is greater, for the aberration of idolatry and of an empty knowledge of God is now sealed not merely in the mind but in deed and action, thus becoming an example and a stumbling block that leads others into temptation. When, within the limits of their reverence for his holy name, they disgrace God in their thoughts by conceiving of Him in a fashion that is more than unworthy of Him, it is only right that they should fall back upon their heads and that they should think and correspondingly act in a way that is unworthy of their humanity.[25]

The "exchange" that is involved in idolatry also includes the substitution of a lie in place of the truth of God. This is the essence of idolatry, namely, the worshiping of the created realm in place of the Creator. In the practice of idolatrous religion the intrinsic antithesis between truth and falsehood is obscured. That the pagan is "religious" in no way nullifies his guilt before God. Again, the practice of idolatrous religion is not viewed as an approximate form of authentic religion but as a negation of it. It is one thing to deny the existence of God; it is another thing to add insult to the denial by worshiping as God something that is clearly of the created order. The worship and service rendered to idols may be sincere—yet is regarded as being sincerely evil. A "sincere" distortion of the truth that dishonors God evokes nothing less than the sincere wrath of God. As Paul elsewhere indicates in his reaction to the Greeks at Mars Hill in Athens (Acts 17:23), God is not particularly pleased or flattered by altars inscribed with the legend, "TO THE UNKNOWN GOD." Such worship is grounded in superstition rather than reality.

> For this reason God gave them over to degrading passions; for their women exchanged the natural function for that which is unnatural, and in the same way also the men abandoned the natural function of the woman and burned in their desire towards one another, men with men committing indecent acts and receiving in their own persons the due penalty of their error. (Rom. 1:26–27 NASB)

God removes the restraints from those who flee from Him and allows them to follow the course of their own drives. Their dishonorable degeneracy is in no way limited to homosexual practices, but is made particularly manifest by that activity. It is not strange that Paul should appeal to homosexuality as an indication of radical degeneracy in light of the Old Testament view of it. Under the Mosaic Law homosexuality was regarded as an abomination to God and was a capital crime. It was also viewed as serious enough sin to defile the land and a type of sin that was considered part of the customary practices of pagan nations with which Israel was forbidden to consort.[26] And just as they did not see fit to acknowledge God any longer, God gave them over to a depraved mind, to do those things which are not proper (Rom. 1:28 NASB).

Paul now approaches his theme in another way. The giving up to a base mind and improper conduct is not an arbitrary action of God. There is a reason for this punitive measure: "They did not see fit to acknowledge God." The judgment of man upon God was the judgment that God was not worthy of human consideration. Again the error of the human mind proceeds not from a mere logical miscalculation but from a deliberate devaluation of the worth of the knowledge of God. The error of the pagan is not fortuitous, but deliberate. The "not seeing fit" is an obstinate refusal to acknowledge that which is manifestly true.

> Being filled with all unrighteousness, wickedness, greed, malice; [they are] full of envy, murder, strife, deceit, malice; they are

gossips, slanderers, haters of God, insolent, arrogant, boastful, inventors of evil, disobedient to parents, without understanding, untrustworthy, unloving, unmerciful; and, although they know the ordinance of God, that those who practice such things are worthy of death, they not only do the same, but also give hearty approval to those who practice them. (Rom. 1:29–32 NASB)

This ghastly catalogue of crimes arising out of an initial rejection of the knowledge of God indicates that human prejudice against God is not mild. The hostility is deep and reflects not a minor disinclination but a burning rage in the human heart.

Another element is added to the content of the knowledge of God revealed in creation. Not only is God's existence known, but his attitude toward evil is likewise made manifest.[27]

The pagan knows the penalty for evil. The astonishing dimension of the pagan's madness is seen, however, not only in that he blatantly practices what he knows to be evil and knows will be punished, but in that he applauds and encourages others to participate in his madness with him. Murray remarks:

To put it bluntly, we're not only bent on damning ourselves, but we congratulate others in doing those things that we know have their issue in damnation. We hate others as we hate ourselves and render therefore to them the approval of what we know merits damnation. Iniquity is most aggravated when it meets with no inhibition from the disapproval of others and when there is collective, undissenting, approbation.[28]

This conclusion concerning the immoral character of human behavior sets in bold relief the utter folly of it. Human endeavor manifests a kind of mass insanity; insane not in the sense of behavior that is radically abnormal or atypical, but rather a kind of "normal" madness which is the inevitable result of an irrational process. Sin in the lives of rational beings begins on an irrational foundation: the refusal to acknowledge as true what one knows with clarity to be true.

The list of evils Paul ennumerates are not to be found exclusively in the confines of special isolated groups of a particularly degenerate or primitive society. Paul is not describing the savage behavior of some remote tribe of head-hunting cannibals or the moral pattern of the most calloused inmates of a maximum security prison. How many lamps would Diogenes need to find a man free from covetousness? Where could he go in his search for a man without envy? What society includes human beings free from insolence, boastfulness, and haughtiness? No, the evils elucidated in this passage are "normal" and "typical" of humans as fallen. They are manifestations of the normal *irrationalism* of the most sophisticated society.

THE PSYCHOLOGY OF ROMANS 1

To translate Paul's analysis of the human response to the knowledge of God into contemporary categories of psychology is not a difficult task, as indicated earlier by Bavinck's analysis. The basic stages of man's reaction to God can be formulated by means of the categories of *trauma, repression,* and *substitution.*

Trauma

The term "trauma" may be defined as "an injury, wound, shock, or the resulting condition."[29] This notion of injury or shock can apply to mental, emotional, and psychological shock as well as to physical. A traumatic experience generally involves something negative or threatening to the individual. (Though it is also recognized that a positive surprise can be shocking in a traumatic way.) In the case of Paul's analysis the trauma is produced by encounter with God's self-revelation. For various reasons, God's presence is severely threatening to people. God manifests a threat to human moral standards, a threat to the quest for autonomy, and a threat to the desire for concealment. God's revelation represents the invasion of light into the darkness to which people are accustomed.

On a physical plane, we are aware of the painful results produced when we emerge from prolonged darkness into the blazing brightness of sunlight. Coal miners must be careful to adjust their eyes gradually as they emerge from their subterranean labors. Even those who walk above ground in the daylight must be careful not to gaze directly into the sun lest they cause traumatic damage to their eyes. Calvin notes:

> If, at midday, we are to look down to the ground, or on surrounding objects which lie open to our view, we think ourselves endued with a very strong and piercing eyesight; but when we look up to the sun, and gaze at it unveiled, the sight which did excellently well for the earth, is instantly so dazzled and confounded by the refulgence, as to oblige us to confess that our acuteness in discern-

ing terrestial objects is mere dimness when applied to the sun. Thus, too, it happens in estimating our spiritual qualities. So long as we do not look beyond the earth, we are quite pleased with our own righteousness, wisdom, and virtue; we address ourselves in the most flattering terms, and seem only less than demigods. But should we once begin to raise our thoughts to god, and reflect what kind of Being He is, and how absolute the perfection of that righteousness, and wisdom, and virtue, to which, as a standard, we are bound to be conformed, what formerly delighted us by its false show of righteousness, will become polluted with the greatest iniquity; what's strangely imposed upon us under the name of wisdom will disgust by its extreme folly; and what presented the appearance of virtuous energy, will be condemned as the most miserable impotence. So far are those qualities in us, which seem most perfect, in corresponding to the divine purity.[30]

Encounter with the light of God's revelation is a traumatic experience. There is no trauma if the eyes are forever closed so that no light penetrates. But the eyes close in reaction to the shock of the light—after the pain has been experienced.

Repression

Repression means to check by or as by pressure, to restrain; to prevent the natural or normal expression, activity, or development of. In psychological terms, repression may be defined as the process by which unacceptable desires or impulses are excluded from consciousness and thus, being denied direct satisfaction, are left to operate in the unconscious.[31]

The memory of conscious knowledge of the trauma of encounter with God's revelation is not maintained in its lucid, threatening state but is repressed. It is "put down or held in captivity" in the unconsciousness. That which is repressed is not destroyed. The memory remains though it may be buried in the subconscious realm. Knowledge of God is unacceptable, and as a result humans attempt to blot it out or at least camouflage it in such a way that its threatening character can be concealed or dulled. That the human psyche is capable of such repression has been thoroughly demonstrated in a multitude of ways. The critical factor for our discussion, however, is that the knowledge is not obliterated or destroyed. It remains intact, though deeply submerged in the mind.

Substitution

It is because repressed knowledge is not destroyed that substitution or "exchange" (*metallaso*) takes place. Again Bavinck comments:

> This phenomenon of replacing, of substituting, is so common that we see it everywhere. It has been discovered that these repressed impulses of which we spoke, which "are left to operate in the unconscious" are not dead. They remain strong, and try to reassert themselves again and again. Surely, they play no part in man's conscious life, but they succeed in showing every now and again that they still exist. This has been illustrated by the story of the boy sent out of class at school who kept on throwing stones against the windows of the school to show that he was still there. Freud particularly has called attention to this phenomenon and inaugurated its study. He noticed that the impulses which have been exiled to the unconscious may very well reveal themselves in the errors we make, in our slips of the tongue. But they especially crop up in dreams, for then they get the chance to come to the surface.[32]

In the substitution–exchange process, the repressed knowledge manifests itself outwardly in a disguised or veiled form. The original knowledge is threatening; its disguised form is much less threatening. When dealing with deep-rooted anxieties of uncertain origin, psychologists and psychiatrists frequently explore, with meticulous care, what may be termed the symbolic activity of mankind. Dreams, Freudian slips, bodily gestures, all are carefully scrutinized by the scientist seeking to unravel the complexities of the human psyche. If in the course of a counseling interview, for example, a person exhibits an involuntary twitch or tick every time he mentions his mother, the counselor will not deem that insignificant. He will proceed to probe further in the area of the person's past relationship with his mother, even though the person may protest profusely and give every conscious assurance that there are no problems in that area of his life. In a word, what cannot be squarely and comfortably faced in the conscious mind, may be borne with a relative degree of comfort at the unconscious level. In theological terms, what results from the repression is the profession of atheism either in militant terms, or its less militant form of agnosticism, or a kind of religion that makes God less of a threat than He really is. Either option, atheism or false religion, manifests an exchange of the truth for a lie. The truth is exchanged for a lie simply because the lie seems easier to live with.

The judgment of the New Testament is that religion is, in many cases, manmade. Karl Barth pointed out that even Christianity can and often does become such a religion. This "religion" expresses not the fruit of human pursuit of God, but the product of the substitution–exchange propensity. Bavinck goes on to say of religion:

> Thus, all kinds of ideas of God are formed; the human mind as the *fabrica idolorum* (Calvin) makes its own ideas of God and its own myths. This is not intentional deceit—it happens without man's knowing it. He cannot get rid of them. So he has religion; he is busy with a god; he serves his god—but he does not see that the god he serves is not god himself. An exchange has taken place—a perilous exchange. An essential quality of god has been blurred because it does not fit in with the human pattern of life, and the image man has of God is no longer true. Divine revelation indeed lies at the root of it, but man's thoughts and aspirations cannot receive it and adapt themselves to it. In the image man has of God we can recognize the image of man himself.[33]

The idea that humans are capable of and have a proclivity for the manufacture of religion is not unique to Freud, Feuerbach, or Marx. Calvin pointed that out in the sixteenth century, appealing to sources originating centuries earlier. That religion reveals human desires is obvious. But the biblical God manifests characteristics and features that are less than desirable to most people. With numerous references to His expressions of wrath and judgment, His absolute claim over human life, is it any surprise that His appearance is traumatic?

The Christian church has had its struggle in every generation against those who would mollify or nullify the threatening dimension of God by substitution and distortion. The twentieth century is no exception. We have witnessed massive attempts to soften the demands imposed upon us by the biblical God. Consider, for example, the Bultmannian school which seeks to demythologize the Scriptures and produces a theology ripped out of the threatening character of history. An analysis of this anti-historical and anti-intellectual approach to theology inevitably raises the question as to the actual locus of mythology. Is it in the New Testament or in the reconstructed Christianity this school represents? It is equally interesting to see the end result of Paul Tillich's God-beyond-God of "ultimate concern." In spite of Tillich's literal apoplexy over the claims of his followers, he was the motivating force behind the proclamation of the death-of-God and the rise of "Christian atheism."

A strange irony attaches itself to much of contemporary theology. The "hard sayings" of Jesus are removed from the danger zone of encounter, the motifs of transcendence and "otherness" are rendered safe by demythologizing and Jesus is reduced to the realm of the "conditioned." Gollwitzer asks the obvious question, "Why should anyone attach unconditional importance to that which is conditioned?"[34] That question sounds strangely like the kind of question the prophets of Israel raised to those who fashioned idols out of wood and stone and then proceeded to bow down and worship the work of their own hands.

SUMMARY OF ASSERTIONS DRAWN FROM ROMANS 1

Let us now briefly summarize what we have learned from Romans 1:

Assertion 1   There is a general or natural revelation.

Assertion 2   There is a content to natural revelation.

Assertion 3   Natural revelation is clear, not obscure.

Assertion 4   Natural revelation has been continuous since creation.

Assertion 5   Natural theology proceeds from the visible to the invisible.

Assertion 6   Natural revelation leaves humans morally responsible for their response to it.

Assertion 7   Natural revelation "gets through," it is subjectively appropriated.

Assertion 8   People respond negatively to natural revelation, refusing to *acknowledge* the knowledge they gain.

Assertion 9   General revelation yields a knowledge of God from nature—a *natural theology.*

We conclude that the apostle Paul teaches clearly and unambiguously that humans possess a natural knowledge of God which rests upon the foundation of general revelation. The Christian, zealous to protect the biblical revelation from unwarranted intrusions from secular speculative philosophy, must be careful not to discard the baby with the bath water. In rejecting *certain forms* of natural theology, we must not discard natural theology altogether if we want to maintain a position which is consistent with the New Testament.

The final assertion we make—assertion 10—is the simplest inference of all. *If people do in fact have a knowledge of God from nature, then a natural theology is possible.* The inference is so elementary that it is precisely the type we tend to overlook when dealing with complex problems. Because certain things are possible, does not mean that people in fact do them. But if people in fact do certain things, it demonstrates conclusively that they can be done. Here we are not reasoning from the possible to the actual, but from the actual to the possible.

In the seventeenth century Spinoza ridiculed the story of people flying through the air:

> I remember once to have read in some book that a man named Orlando Furioso used to drive a kind of winged monster through the air, fly over any countries he liked, kill unaided vast numbers of men and giants, and such like fancies, which from the point of view of reason are obviously absurd.[35]

Today the exploits of a contemporary "Orlando Furioso" would not be so obviously absurd from the point of view of reason. What reason once judged to be impossible is now commonplace. The actual has vindicated the possible. If something has been done it proves that it can be done, if the conditions for doing it remain the same. But if natural revelation extended from the time of creation to the writing of Romans 1, and if the same conditions persist to the present, then we may safely assume that general revelation is still capable of yielding a natural theology. The printing of the *Critique of Pure Reason* may have done serious damage to the church's confidence in natural theology, but it did not eradicate general revelation. If the apostle Paul is correct, then Kant was in error and the Christian apologist must work to establish once again a sound natural theology.

CHAPTER 5

Toward the Reconstruction of Natural Theology: the Question of Method

THE WORD *TOWARD* IN the title of this chapter indicates the direction we wish to move: toward natural theology, not away from it. By "reconstruction" we do not mean that it is our design to *totally* reconstruct natural theology. A total reconstruction is not necessary; much of the work has already been done by others. The present chapter touches upon three parts of the task which still lie before us, namely, three elements of a proper method of moving toward the reconstruction of natural theology: (1) creativity in the reconstruction of theology, (2) the problem of disagreement among scholars, and (3) common ground among believers and unbelievers, that is, assumptions necessary to all life and thought.

RECONSTRUCTION AND CREATIVITY

Any time we are involved in the work of theology, we have to ask whether we are merely restating something that has been said before, again and again, and passing it off as something new. Reconstruction can do just that. But if the reconstruction of theology is going to be meaningful and relevant to the modern age, there must be an element of creativity in it. If, when the old structures have collapsed, we reconstruct them according to the same old blueprints, then we are asking for a repetition of the first collapse. Creativity is necessary for a viable reconstruction.

But though creativity in art and literature is exciting and constructive, some Christians view creativity in theology as mere inventiveness, an excuse for departure from the truth of God. Philip E. Hughes defines the positive role of creativity in theology:

Creativity, properly speaking, is the faculty or process of making something out of nothing. Given this definition, the cynic might be tempted to observe that the overwhelming flood of elucubrations that now pour forth from the religious publishing houses indicates that there is an astonishing number of theological technicians with a facility for fabricating intricate patterns out of nonexistent or insubstantial premises. Inventiveness, however, rather than creativity, is the category to which industry of this kind belongs. Its exponents seem intent on producing or reproducing nothing old: for them whatever is not new is dismissed as archaic and irrelevant. At the other end of the spectrum are those who seem intent on producing nothing new: for them, whatever is not old is suspect and threatening. They deal in prefabricated blocks of theological concrete. Creativity is not for them. But there is a mean between these two extremes. . . . Both the new and the old: this is the framework of theology that is truly creative.[1]

It is not enough merely to mix the old and the new. This might produce only a false and grotesque freak. If the combination is to be sound, it must incorporate what is *sound* from the old with what is *sound* from the new.

Every discipline, including theology, meets points of impasse in its development; the apparent impossibility of further progress along the same lines produces a loss of freshness and vitality. Cynicism and skepticism frequently follow. In philosophy, for example, the impasse between Parmenides (being) and Heraclitus (becoming) yielded the antimetaphysical skepticism of sophism until Socrates and Plato rescued philosophy from the impasse. The impasse between Plato and Aristotle gave rise to a shift from metaphysical concern to the more pragmatic quest for philosophical ataraxia, as exemplified in the competing schools of the Stoics and the Epicureans. So it moved down to the great impasse, with which we are still struggling, between rationalism and empiricism which carried the casket of metaphysics to the graveyard of David Hume. Kant's synthesis, Hegel's massive philosophy of history, and the advent of process thought have been attempts to resurrect metaphysics. But metaphysics and its theological counterpart, natural theology, remain in the tomb. The logical positivists cried good riddance, while the more sensitive existentialists put their hats over their hearts and quietly wept.

In other disciplines such as art and music the impasse is overcome when a creative genius emerges and changes the direction of the discipline by exploring new frontiers, stimulating a variety of new opportunities for discovery and advance. But how does this happen? By a burst of sheer intuition which comes upon him *senkrecht von oben?* (vertically from above, i.e., not on a horizontal plane of history)? Some advances do seem to occur fortuitously, as Fleming's discovery of the therapeutic value of the mold which was fouling his experiments. Normally, however, such intuitive discoveries do not take place in a vacuum. There are reasons for them. Claude Debussy, for example, stimulated by the art nouveau movement in literature and painting, achieved impressionism in music, giving to music what Monet, Gauguin, Toulouse-Lautrec, and Pissarro gave to painting. Answering a critical comment by his esteemed contemporary, Richard Strauss, Debussy replied, "Yes, I did break the rules but I got the sound I wanted."[2] He broke new ground in music by challenging the reigning musical assumptions. If there is a formula for creativity it is this: *challenge the assumptions.*

But the challenging of assumptions is easier to attain than truth. A physician can be creative without being helpful; Mengele was creative with his experiments in the Holocaust, but he was even more deadly. The department store decorator can afford to be less worried about the truth or consequences of assumptions than the cardiologist. It is not good enough to challenge assumptions arbitrarily or to dismiss previous working assumptions out of hand. Such dismissals may result in the devolution of the art or science. It is the *faulty* assumption which must be found and discarded if a breakthrough is to be achieved.

The task of isolating faulty assumptions is made difficult by the tendency of scholarship to accept certain assumptions uncritically and to enshrine them in the temple of the status quo. These uncritically accepted assumptions, elevated to the level of dogma, control the activity of a given discipline. To challenge them is to invite the wrath of those who are comfortable with the traditions. Yet the pioneering of antiseptic medicine, the work of Einstein in physics, and Bertrand Russell in philosophy would be unthinkable apart from the challenging of assumptions.

THE PROBLEM OF DISAGREEMENT

But the challenging of assumptions and the isolation of faulty ones is made more difficult and confusing by disagreement among scholars. It is useful to examine the types of error which may beset the most brilliant thinkers. One of the striking and frustrating phenomena of the history of philosophy is the myriad of brilliant minds which disagree. This recurring problem leads many to conclude that philosophy is a mission impossible, the impossible dream. When experts disagree and arrive at mutually exclusive conclusions, the tendency of the lay person is to assume that the problem is insoluble.

We have already seen the profound disagreement which attends the issue of natural theology. The question of fideism versus natural theology pits Aquinas against Scotus and Ockham, Kant versus Paul, Kuyper against Warfield. These men disagree with each other and, as we have seen, they cannot all be right, nor can they all be wrong.

Even brilliant thinkers make mistakes. Moreover, the one who comes to the correct conclusion may do so as much through good fortune as through good reason, traveling the path of the happy inconsistency. There are a multitude of errors which may short-circuit the reasoning process. For purposes of simplification we will elucidate four basic types:

1. epistemological errors
2. formal errors in reasoning
3. factual errors in empirical investigation
4. psychological prejudice that distorts conclusions

Epistemological Errors

It is not by accident that disputes in philosophy usually revert to discussions of epistemology. When one makes an assertion, the customary reply is "How do you know?" Variant epistemologies produce variant conclusions. The radical conceptualist, for example, might argue that whatever may be conceived of by the mind without contradiction must exist in reality, including Gaunilo's perfect island and Kant's gulden. The radical empiricist, on the other hand, would contend that statements about the existence of the perfect island would be meaningful only if it were perceived. These systems operate on the basis of two different and contrary tests for truth, disparate views of what constitutes verification and falsification. Of course, the two epistemologies mentioned are not exhaustive; there are several epistemologies vying for acceptance among thinkers.

Formal Errors

If a philosopher used a perfectly valid epistemology, still there would be no guarantee that his conclusions would be valid. Though the starting point may be correct, formal errors of reasoning may occur throughout the process of thought. Though not all philosophers have been rationalists, all philosophers have resorted to some kind of reasoning process in articulating their views. Even those who advocate the total inadequacy of language resort to words to state their case, and those who argue for irrationalism give reasons for their irrationality.

The question of formal truth concerns the matter of internal consistency. It incorporates questions of logic and propositions which can be verified or falsified strictly on a formal basis. Though different paradigms of logic exist and compete for universal acceptance, and though the number of inferences which are adjudged to be immediate vary from system to system,[3] all logic systems have some schema for monitoring the validity of inferences, either mediate or immediate. The examples of formal and informal fallacies, which are studied in university logic courses are taken not from the lower classes of literature, such as comic books, tabloids, or propaganda pieces, but from the finest literary products of culture. Passages from John Stuart Mill, David Hume, Cicero, Aristotle, Wittgenstein, and others are used to illustrate examples of blatant logical fallacies present in the most erudite works.

Factual Errors

Just as thinkers make formal errors, so they make errors in data collection and empirical observation. Descartes stressed the ease with which our senses can deceive us. We are aware of the limitations of our sense organs to yield total and accurate knowledge. The sensory powers we possess must be augmented by sophisticated instruments to broaden the scope of our perceptions. But even our sensitive machinery has natural limits which in turn limit the empirical process.

We are not only vulnerable to the limits of our sensibilities but we also face the problem of reaching conclusions on the basis of insufficient data. No one possesses omniscience, nor can we observe *sub specie aeternitatis*. The problem of empirical investigation is seen in the imbalance of facility between empirical verification and empirical falsification. To verify the assertion "There is gold in Alaska" is a relatively easy matter empirically. One may be fortunate enough to verify the assertion by the first turn of the shovel in the dirt. To falsify the assertion, however, is a much more difficult task. To prove empirically there is no gold in Alaska we would have to search and sift through every square inch in Alaska, wearing out a plethora of spades in the process. We must face the question of the limits of the search. How deep underground does "Alaska" extend? Even if the entire area of Alaska were searched without uncovering a grain of gold dust, we would still face the obstreperous doubter who asks if we overlooked some nook or cranny or carelessly let some particle of dust slip through our sieve. Then we would still have to search again and again *ad infinitum*.

Because of this verification–falsification differential, some theists have taken comfort in the fact that it is virtually impossible to disprove the existence of God via the empirical method. To do so would necessitate an empirical investigation of the entire universe and beyond. The theist could forever seek refuge in qualifications, adding daily to the millennium of qualifications which (in Anthony Flew's famous parable) caused the demise of God. The empirical atheist has rightly argued that because of this verification–falsification imbalance, the burden of proof is upon the affirmer rather than the denier.

Psychological Prejudice

But even a sound epistemic system, flawless deductive reasoning, and impeccable inductive procedure does not guarantee a proper conclusion. Emotional bias or antipathy might block the way to the necessary conclusion of the research. That thinkers may obstinately resist a logical verdict is humorously illustrated by John Warwick Montgomery's modern parable:

> Once upon a time (note the mystical cast) there was a man who thought he was dead. His concerned wife and friends sent him to the friendly neighborhood psychiatrist determined to cure him by convincing him of one fact that contradicted his beliefs that he was dead. The fact that the psychiatrist decided to use was the simple truth that dead men do not bleed. He put his patient to work reading medical texts, observing autopsies, etc. After weeks of effort the patient finally said, "All right, all right! You've convinced me. Dead men do not bleed." Whereupon the psychiatrist stuck him in the arm with the needle, and the blood flowed.

The man looked down with a contorted, ashen face and cried: "Good Lord! Dead men bleed after all!"[4]

Emotional prejudice is not limited to the dull-witted, the illiterate, and poorly educated. Philosophers and theologians are not exempt from the vested interests and psychological prejudice that distort logical thinking. The question of the existence of God evokes deep emotional and psychological prejudice. People understand that the question of the existence of God is not one that is of neutral consequence. We understand intuitively, if not in terms of its full rational implication, that the existence of an eternal Creator before whom we are ultimately accountable and responsible is a matter that touches the very core of life.

In light of all of the possible pitfalls of knowledge and roadblocks to achieving a sound basis for truth, the quest for a method of reconstruction of natural theology becomes all the more important. For centuries Christians have sought some epistemological common ground with the unbeliever so that dialogue can take place.

THE PROBLEM OF COMMON GROUND

The question of common ground, a place where believer and unbeliever can stand on equal terms and engage in meaningful discourse, is a controversial and complex one. If we consider common ground to mean a common perception and perspective of reality, then obviously no such common ground for discussion exists between believer and unbeliever. From the believer's vantage point every aspect of life, every bit of experience, every dimension of reality, is understood and interpreted from a theological perspective. The believer looks at a flower and knows that it is a daffodil as simply and accurately as an unbeliever identifies that flower as a daffodil. It would appear that both enjoy a univocal understanding of the daffodil. The believer's complete understanding of the daffodil, however, includes seeing it as a part of God's creation, planned and ordained by God from all eternity to grace the cosmos which God creates and rules by His providence. The believer acknowledges the *significance* of that daffodil, not as a cosmic accident, but as something that in itself bears witness to the majesty and beauty of the Creator God. This the unbeliever does not acknowledge, positing, instead, a completely opposite and antithetical understanding of the daffodil's significance.

From a different perspective, however, there is a common ground, namely the whole of creation. Believer and unbeliever live in the same universe. Each sees the same phenomena. The unbeliever and the believer can agree that two and two are four, and that certain principles of deduction are valid while others are invalid. Thus a kind of common ground is established.

Certain assumptions regarding the knowing process, for example, are virtually universal. These assumptions are shared by theists and nontheists alike, particularly when they are applied outside of the emotion-laden debate about the existence of God. We are not seeking at this point to construct or reconstruct an entire epistemology, but are seeking shared or common assumptions between theist and nontheist. We are not seeking those views which separate Kant and Paul, Descartes and Locke, Hume and Aquinas, Kierkegaard and Russel, but for those assumptions which, despite their differences, they commonly hold.

We know that different philosophers adopt different theoretical starting points and that the epistemologies present in the debate extend far beyond those employed merely by Kant and the apostle Paul. The starting point of Descartes was different from that of Locke, at least in theory. Were there, however, common assumptions operating in both Locke and Descartes, in Hume and Aquinas, in Russell and Kierkegaard? We are searching for assumptions which are neither arbitrary nor subjective, but which function by practical necessity, are objective, and are or should be nonnegotiables in any discussion of truth. In our effort to challenge assumptions, we are seeking to discover those assumptions which must remain intact if truth is to be possible. In a sense, we are proceeding in a kind of transcendental fashion asking the question, "What are the assumptions necessary for life and knowledge to be possible?" At this point we are not inquiring about ontological prerequisites to life and truth, but epistemological prerequisites.

This is not to say that other differences—formal errors, inductive errors, or emotional prejudice—are not important. They are. Some assume that only epistemological assumptions affect the partisans of the natural theology debate. If, however, some common working assumptions were present in Kant and in Paul, and other thinkers, then we would want to trace and retrace their lines of agreement in order to discern just where disagreement set in.

In our search for common assumptions, we isolate three which are held by theists and nontheists alike. There may be far more than three, but these three represent the bare minimum of working, non-negotiable assumptions. The three basic assumptions are:

1. The validity of the law of noncontradiction
2. The validity of the law of causality
3. The basic reliability of sense preception

Though we assert that these assumptions are virtually universal, they by no means enjoy universal theoretical assent. Each has been seriously challenged in the history of philosophy. People deny one or more of these assumptions with regularity, and do in fact negotiate what we are calling nonnegotiables. Our thesis, however, is that all denials of these assumptions are *forced* and *temporary*. No one denies these principles regularly and consistently. These assumptions are necessary for science in its broadest sense. They are not only prerequisites for knowledge, but are necessary assumptions for life itself. Where natural theology is attacked or denied, it is done by means of a denial of one or more of these three assumptions.

THE LAW OF NONCONTRADICTION

The law of noncontradiction is the foundation upon which all rationality is established. It is as crucial for theology as it is for all other intellectual disciplines. It creates the dimensions and prescribes the limits of all common ground for discussion. It is the necessary precondition for any and all science. The law may be defined:

A cannot be A and non-A at the same time and in the same relationship.

Aristotle defined the law by saying: "The same attribute cannot at the same time belong and not belong to the same subject in the same respect."[5]

The definition of the law is crucial. It does not say that A cannot be A and B at the same time. Because of diversity and the multifaceted character of reality many things may have more than one attribute. We can predicate more than one thing of the same object at one time. We can say that an object is both blue and square. There is no contradiction in predicating both. But a thing cannot be square and not square at the same time and in the same relationship. Something square today could be round tomorrow if it undergoes a transformation, but it cannot be square and round at the same time, and in the same relationship. An object may have many sides, one of which is square, another round. When viewed from one angle it appears square and from another angle it appears round. The qualifier "in the same relationship" applies here. The object may have a square aspect and a round aspect but not at the same time and in the same relationship (or from the same aspect).

The law of noncontradiction is a principle of rationality and as such is neutral with respect to content. By itself, it carries no brief for or against theism, as it is empty of content. If we declare that two and two are four, we are merely observing that there is a rational mathematical relationship between two sets of twos on one side of the ledger and a four on the other side. The two sides balance in a formal relationship of coherency. The primary role of the law of noncontradiction in particular and logic in general is the provision of a guide to coherency and of a formal test for truth claims. Logic monitors the formal relationships of propositions.

Logic confronts us with a critical, ontological question. Is logic limited to the realm of the formal or does it have a material, existential import? Aristotle maintained that the law of noncontradiction is more than a law of thought because it is first a law of being.[6] Must we accord ontological status to logic as Aristotle affirmed?

We were once engaged in dialogue with a group of Christian philosophers who were disturbed by our insistence on the rationality of Christianity. They obviously were agitated by the focus on reason and logic, protesting that such categories represented the unwarranted intrusion of pagan Greek thought into Christianity. We pressed the conversation by asking whether a statement can be formally valid and materially false. In other words, could a proposition meet all the tests of abstract logic, be formally valid, and at the same time correspond to nothing in existence. The philosophers agreed that this could be the case, citing the unicorn as an example. They allowed that the mind, as Locke supposed, has the ability to combine, relate, and abstract simple ideas to the point of constructing concepts of things which have no counterpart in reality. The concept of a unicorn violates no law of logic, but its rational conceivability does not guarantee its existence. The philosophers granted that statements could be formally valid but materially false.

The next question proved more difficult. Can something be materially true and formally false? The difference between the two questions is formidable: the second question asks if the real can be irrational or absurd. Does reality correspond to coherent categories of rationality or does reality itself violate the law of noncontradiction? The philosophers hesitated. Silence was followed at last by awkward and reluctant answers. After we had repeated the question several times, anomalies in science were proffered examples of how reality does in fact violate the law of noncontradiction. One man appealed to light, which under certain conditions behaves as a wave, but under other conditions behaves as a particle. Is light then a wave or a particle? Some have sought to overcome the difficulty by defining light as a "wavicle." What does this mean? Does it mean that a wavicle is a *tertium quid* or that light behaves as a wave on Mondays, Wednesdays, and Fridays, and as a particle on Tuesdays, Thursdays, and Saturdays, resting on Sunday? If a wave and a particle are mutually exclusive categories, then can light be both at the same time and in the same relationship? It is possible that waves and particles are not mutually exclusive ideas but are aspects of some deeper entity, which pushes science to new paradigms to resolve the anomaly.

Anomalies have functioned in the past as stimuli for new scientific paradigms which have unlocked previous impasses. The one paradigm that science cannot afford to follow, however, is that of irrationality. If it is determined that light is actually contradictory, rigidly and irresistibly contradictory, then science is finished as any and all knowledge becomes impossible. A single datum of irresolvable contradiction destroys both sides of the scientific method, deduction and induction. If contradiction exists in real entities, then deduction becomes functionally useless and induction functionally impossible. Induction depends on individuation for its very possibility. No individuation of anything is possible if it and its contrary can both be true. If we assume the "reality of the contrary" to any word denoting anything, then language itself becomes meaningless gibberish. Russell's attempts to avoid this problem by the rejection of ordinary language and the creation of an artificial ideal language substituting symbols for words, ended in failure.[7] So did Paul Tillich's attempt to transcend the limits of human language and get to the God "beyond God." Helmut Gollwitzer rightly observed, "There is nothing beyond theism but atheism."[8] If a universal affirmation or universal categorical proposition can be affirmed together with its contradictory, then language, whether ordinary or artificial, is impossible. When Tillich declared that God is neither personal nor impersonal but is the "ground of personality," he achieved not a transcendent breakthrough of the limits of logic and language, but nonsense. The next question a student would ask Tillich is, "Is the Ground of personality personal or impersonal?" Impersonality includes everything outside of the category of personality; there is no *tertium quid.*

After this excursion into a discussion of anomalies and variant scientific paradigms, our philosopher friends finally granted that something cannot be materially true and formally false. They were quick to add, however, that the logic which applies to the material phenomenal world does not necessarily apply to the noumenal or metaphysical realm of God.

In evaluating the contemporary religious revolt against logic, Ronald Nash discusses a common strand of thought within both neo-orthodox theology and evangelical theology, citing examples in Emil Brunner, Karl Barth, T. F. Torrance, Donald Bloesch, Herman Dooyeweerd, Cornelius Van Til, and Al Wolters: that human logic cannot be extended to a transcendent God. Human logic is restricted to this side of the ontological boundary between God and the created order.[9] Nash cites Alvin Plantinga's reaction to this kind of theological agnosticism:

> This kind of thinking about God begins in a pious and commendable concern for God's greatness and majesty and augustness; but it ends in agnosticism and in incoherence. For if none of our concepts apply to God (or if none of our inferences extend to God), then there is nothing we can know or truly believe of him—not even what is affirmed in the creeds or revealed in the Scriptures. And if there is nothing we can know or truly believe of him, then, of course, we cannot know or truly believe that none of our concepts apply to him. The view . . . is fatally ensnarled in self-referential absurdity.[10]

Our religious philosopher friends were undaunted by the specter of a self-referential absurdity and persisted in their claim that God's logic is different from human logic. They defended this claim on the basis that God is "wholly other" (*totaliter aliter*), borrowing a chapter from Karl Barth and his rigorous denial of an *analogia entis* between God and humans. We asked our friends how they knew anything at all about this wholly other God. They quickly replied that they knew of Him via His own self-revelation. But how could this God reveal anything about Himself to us if He is utterly dissimilar from us and His categories of thought are as wholly other as His being? If God is totally ontologically dissimilar, then neither He nor we have any reference point for meaningful or intelligible discourse. Communication between totally dissimilar beings is manifestly impossible. When our friends grasped this point they declared, "Perhaps we shouldn't have said that God is *totally* other."

We labor this illustration merely to note that in certain Christian circles there is a persistent allergy to rationality. It is often motivated by what Plantinga calls a "pious and commendable concern for God's greatness and majesty and augustness." The fear is that reason makes God subject to a law which is greater than Himself, making God answerable to Aristotle, rather than Aristotle to God.

But Aristotle did not invent logic or reason. Aristotle was no more responsible for the invention or creation of logic than Columbus was for inventing or creating America. Aristotle defined the logical relationships of propositions which had been functioning since the origin of human speech. Aristotle's logic was isolated from the rest of his philosophy and referred to as the *organon*. An *organon* is simply an "instrument." For Aristotle, logic was the necessary tool or instrument by which human beings can have meaningful discourse; by which science can be intelligibly carried on. When the laws of logic are violated, intelligible communication ceases.

The Christian faith affirms logic not as a law above God but as an aspect built into Creation which flows from His own character. According to Gordon Clark, "The law of contradiction is not to be taken as an axiom prior to or independent of God. The law is God thinking."[11] He goes so far as to paraphrase the prologue of the Gospel of John as follows:

> In the beginning was Logic, and Logic was with God, and Logic was God. . . . In Logic was life and the life was the light of men.[12]

Clark expects Christians to be shocked by this paraphrase, but says, "Why it is offensive to call Christ Logic, when it does not offend to call him a word, is hard to explain."[13]

There are times when the contradiction is used by thinkers to elicit a certain effect of wonderment or awe from the listeners, pointing to an alleged profundity. Think of the Zen definition of God as "one hand clapping" or Barth's purposeful use of contradiction to underscore the difficulty of penetrating the question of the origin of evil, calling sin the "impossible possibility." Talking in contradictions is nonsense, regardless of how transcendently profound it may sound.

Noncontradiction, Paradox, and Mystery. Another factor which, among Christians, provokes antipathy to the law of noncontradiction is the assumption that the content of Christianity contains contradictions. Outlaw contradiction and Christianity will be banished with it: this is the fear. Three critical doctrines of the Christian faith are thought to contain such contradictions: the Trinity, the person of Christ, and the issue of God's sovereignty and human freedom. These doctrines are understood by some devout persons as containing irreconcilable antinomies within them.

A cursory glance at these questions dispels the idea that they contain contradictions. The classical formulation of the Trinity asserts that God is one in essence and three in person. Hence God is one in A and three in B. We need not be able to comprehend the fullness of the divine mystery to see that the formula is formally sound. If we declared that God were one in essence and three in essence, or one in person and three in person at the same time and in the same relationship, we would have a bona fide contradiction. We have unity in one sense (essence) and diversity in another (persons).

The same applies in reverse to the person of Christ. The classical formula in Christology is that Christ has two natures in one person. That is, He is one in person and two in nature or essence. The perplexity arises here because we are accustomed to finding a ratio of one nature to one person. Christ represents an inductive anomaly (as He does in other ways as well, most notably in His sinlessness). Induction does not lead us to expect to find dual-natured persons; but no formal law precludes the possibility. There is nothing contradictory about Christ's being unitary in A (person) and dual in B (nature.)

The problem of divine sovereignty and human freedom is primarily linguistic and conceptual. If by "freedom" absolute autonomy is meant, then we are faced with a contradiction which no system of logic can resolve, either on this side of the Boundary or the other. Divine sovereignty and human autonomy cannot coexist. Of course Scripture nowhere teaches human autonomy in the absolute sense. From Creation onward the freedom of action which the creature enjoys is limited. It is never *ex lex* (outside of, or apart from law), but always *sub lego* (under law). Creaturely pursuit of autonomy is identified with lawlessness, the mark of the Antichrist. If God is indeed sovereign absolutely, then pure autonomy cannot exist outside of Him. Yet human language, at least ordinary language, recognizes the distinction between freedom and autonomy, which is a matter of degree. For humankind to be free and God to be sovereign requires that humans have the power of action and that God have a greater power of action. Human freedom is here limited by God's sovereignty; God's sovereignty is not limited by human freedom. By way of analogy we can think of a child living in the home of her father. The child is free and the father is free. But the father is "freer" in the sense that his power and authority stand over and sometimes against the volitional activity of the child. Sovereignty and freedom are not mutually exclusive unless we conceive of them as coexisting in creature and Creator with an equal ultimacy, which is dualism. Humans naturally have the ability to make choices, but these choices are always accountable to a sovereign God.

The desire to retain the legitimacy of contradiction within the scope of the Christian faith is sometimes provoked also by a confusion of three categories of thought—contradiction, paradox, and mystery. These three classes are sufficiently similar to create confusion, yet sufficiently dissimilar to warrant distinction.

Since we have already discussed contradiction we will proceed to paradox and mystery. The term *paradox* comes from the Greek prefix πάρα ("para") which means "alongside" or "beside," and the Greek root δοκέιν (*dokein*) which means "to think," "to appear," or "to seem."[14] A paradox is that which, when placed alongside of or beside a contradiction "seems" or "appears" to be identical with the contradiction. The similarity to contradiction has engendered confusion in English usage, which is reflected, for example, in *Webster's New Twentieth Century Dictionary's* list of definitions for "paradox":

1. a statement contrary to common belief [rare].
2. a statement that seems contradictory, unbelievable, or absurd but that may actually be true in fact.
3. a statement that is self-contradictory in fact and hence, false.[15]

Note that entry 2 preserves the classical definition while entry 3 allows the use of "paradox" as a synonym for "contradiction." We are concerned here with the classic meaning of paradox, the "seeming contradiction," which, under closer scrutiny can be resolved. We appreciate Gordon Clark's more vivid definition of the paradox as "a charleyhorse between the ears."[16]

The Bible abounds in paradox; it was a favorite pedagogical device of Jesus. Statements like "He who is least among you all is the one who is great" (Luke 9:48 RSV) frequently fall from His lips. It is one thing to say the Bible is full of paradoxes, but quite another to charge (as some have loosely used the term) that the Bible is full of contradictions.

Mystery is crucial to Christianity. Though Christianity is not a mystery religion in the ancient esoteric sense, the Bible and church tradition make use of the term. The term *mystery* derives from the Greek μυστήριον (*musterion*). Within the New Testament the term frequently refers to that which once was hidden but is now revealed.[17] It is also used in the New Testament, as well as in later church history, to refer to those elements of the things of God which remain hidden or concealed from us, to which some refer by the phrase *deus absconditus*. At certain points the Latin Vulgate translated the Greek *musterion* by the Latin *sacramentum*,[18] from which we get the English term *sacrament*.

Webster lists eight entries for "mystery" including

1. something unexplained, unknown, or kept secret.
8. In theology, any assumed truth that cannot be comprehended by the human mind but must be accepted on faith.

We would quibble a bit about entry 8. Why, for example, is theology singled out as a discipline containing mysteries while physics is spared? Who has yet unravelled the mystery of gravity or the most perplexing mystery of motion which plagued Einstein as much as it did Zeno? Or we might protest mildly about the word *cannot* in the definition, reminding the lexicographers that "has not" does not necessarily imply "cannot." But these are indeed quibbles. Christianity does have a doctrine of the incomprehensibility of God based on the maxim *finitum non capax infinitum* (the finite cannot contain, or grasp, the infinite). There are present mysteries concerning which we expect to gain future revelation, yet we do not expect ever to transcend our own finitude.

The category of mystery allows for matters which are beyond the *present* reach of reason. But there are also matters of infinity which *are* not and will never be penetrated by the finite. In this sense they are transrational. There is a critical difference, however, between the transrational and the irrational; it is the difference between the mystery and the contradiction. In terms of truth claims the distinction is important. Though the presence of mystery does not do much for verification, it does not carry the import of falsification. The contradiction, on the other hand, formally and firmly, falsifies.

It is illegitimate for the Christian thinker or any other thinker to take refuge in mystery by incorporating contradiction within it. A mystery *may* be true; a contradiction *cannot* be meaningful at all. Mystery and contradiction may be related to each other not as contradictories but as contraries in which both cannot be true but both might be false. If a contradiction masquerades as a mystery, the rules of inference must be applied to expose the hoax.

The Law of Noncontradiction as a Universal Prerequisite for Life. We have tried to show that the law of noncontradiction is nonnegotiable to Christian faith, Christian apologetics, and Christian philosophy. We said earlier that its nonnegotiability extends beyond the borders of Christianity, is universal. All people hold to it in *fact*, though some do deny it. But the denials are forced and temporary.

We are reminded of Francis Schaeffer's observation of the behavior of John Cage. An apostle of chance and indeterminacy, Cage sought to express the incoherence and irrationality of reality by composing music through the tossing of coins randomly. But he could not *live* by his own conclusions. By avocation, Cage is an exceptional amateur mycologist, whose special delight among fungi is the mushroom. But he soon learned the perils of random mushroom collecting and said, "I became aware that if I approached mushrooms in the spirit of my chance operations, I would die shortly."[19]

Cage's realization is an example (perhaps unintentional) of the application of the law of noncontradiction. He understood that certain varieties of mushrooms cannot be poisonous and nonpoisonous at the same time and in the same relationship. He knew that a repeated and enduring application of the denial of the law of noncontradiction would be fatal. We all know that. When we approach an intersection in our car and see a truck speeding toward the intersection, we assume that there cannot be a truck coming and not a truck coming at the same time and in the same relationship, and we judiciously apply our brakes.

The law of noncontradiction as a necessary presupposition or prerequisite for thought and life is neither arbitrary nor subjectivistic. It is universal and objective. What is subjective and arbitrary is the forced and temporary denial of it.

The Biblical Assumption of the Law of Noncontradiction. Though not a textbook in logic, the Bible assumes the validity of the law of noncontradiction on every page. Like any other document, it depends on the *organon* of logic for intelligible discourse. A perusal of biblical literature, especially the didactic epistles of the New Testament, reveals a high incidence of the word *therefore,* indicating a conclusion which follows logically from stated premises. As one would expect, the syllogism is rarely if ever found. On the other hand, Scripture is replete with enthymemes, a syllogism with one of the premises implicit. Gordon Clark cites Romans 4:2 as an enthymematic hypothetical destructive syllogism; Romans 5:13 as a hypothetical constructive syllogism; and 1 Corinthians 15:15–18 as a sorites.[20] The declarative sentences of the Bible are logical units with subjects and predicates, having an assumed logic embedded in them.

With the rise of neo-orthodoxy and existential patterns of theology it has become fashionable to extol the virtue of contradictions. Emil Brunner argues that

> God can speak to us His single, never contradictory Word through the priestly writings of the Old Testament as well as through the prophetic or the New Testament writings, even though these several writings are very various and in part contradictory, just as He can speak His single, never contradictory Word through the contradictory accounts of Luke and Matthew.[21]

Here the alleged contradictory contents of Scripture represent no barrier to Brunner's perception of the "single, never contradictory Word" of God. We are delighted that Brunner shrinks at attributing contradiction to God, but are perplexed by his faculty of discerning the noncontradictory Word in the midst of the contradictory words. This approach certainly frees Brunner from every form of Docetism with respect to Scripture, but throws him back into the grasp of Docetism's parent—Gnosticism.

If the Word of God is heard in contradiction, why would God ever hold anyone culpable for mistaking His commands for their contradictories? The Bible describes the fall of the human race in terms of a trial hanging on a contradiction. Adam and Eve were told by the Creator that if they ate of the forbidden fruit, they would surely die. The serpent declared that they would not die. God said, "If A (you eat), then B (death would inevitably follow as a consequence)." The serpent's counter claim was that, "If A (you eat), then non-B (no death would follow)." Here is a clear example of contradiction. If the non-contradictory truth of God can be conveyed via contradiction, why was Adam considered blameworthy for choosing one option rather than its contradictory? If contradiction is virtuous, indeed the "hall-mark of truth" as the existential theologians suppose, then Adam should not only be excused but rewarded for recognizing the Word of God in the words of the serpent, in that they carried the hallmark of truth. If such were possible, Adam's fall could not and should not be regarded as a fall but as a great leap forward.

Biblically the contradiction is the hallmark of the lie. Without this formal test of falsification, the Scriptures (and any other writings) would have no means to distinguish between truth and falsehood, righteousness and unrighteousness, obedience and disobedience, Christ and Antichrist.

The Law of Causality

The second nonnegotiable assumption for apologetics is the law of causality. We will deal in an expanded way with this principle in part 2, as it relates to the theistic proofs. In the meantime we will make some basic, preliminary observations about the types of cause, the abuse of causal analysis, and about necessary and sufficient conditions of causation.

Causal thinking is an integral part of all scientific examination. It involves a temporal element in that it concerns the quality of motion we call change. It observes the before and after of contiguous actions, events, or states. A person becomes ill; a change in the state of health takes place and the diagnostician seeks to isolate the factor which induced the change. Medicine, economics, botany, physics, and other disciplines seek to understand the reason or cause for observable changes.

Since causality functions in a practical way in the empirical world, philosophies have sought to establish the law of causality on empirical grounds as a conclusion drawn from sense perception. This method is vulnerable to the devastating critique of David Hume who rightly observed that cause itself is never directly or immediately perceived or that at least we cannot know for certain through the senses that the perceived cause is the actual cause.[22] Hume's critique does not destroy causality per se but casts a shadow on a particular method of establishing it.

Causality is established on a more firm foundation if it is seen as an axiomatic corollary of the law of noncontradiction. In a sense the law of causality is merely an extension of the law of noncontradiction; it is a formal principle which is analytically true. Its definition is tautological: every effect must have a cause. The term *effect* carries within itself the notion of cause. Because we use the principle of causality to examine and evaluate observable phenomena does not mean that causality itself is a derivative of sense perception. It is a logically prior supposition necessary for the very discrimination of phenomena. Thus we follow the procedure of asserting causality as a first or self-evident principle. Like the law of noncontradiction, it is something which all in fact believe because all *must* believe it in order to function as human beings. It is a universal presupposition necessary for life and for the ordering of knowledge. Questions may be raised about particular causes for particular effects (an inductive question), but not about the necessity of *some* cause for an event.

The aspects of change which we call effects may vary according to Aristotle's classifications of motion. Two primary types of cause must be isolated at this point—causes *in fieri* and causes *in esse*. A cause *in fieri* is a factor which brings or helps to bring an effect to pass, that which induces change. A cause *in esse* is a factor which "sustains or helps to sustain the effect in being."[23] Both types of cause are concerned with the factor of *power*—one is necessary to explain the power of being and the other power of change.

Though the principle of causality is formal, it has vital ramifications for the existent material world. It is not enough to say that things exist in contiguous or customary relationships as Hume supposed. We must deal with the question of the *power* for such customary relationships. Questions may be raised about *which* power is causing being and change, but *that* some power is involved is logically necessary. One can choose to call it by a name other than cause (Hume resorted to the term *production*) but some concept of power must be used.[24]

Of course, logical errors occur in the application of the law of causality. The fallacies of faulty causal generalization and of false cause are perils to the application of the law. False cause can be attributed either by the *non causa pro causa* fallacy which is to mistake what is not the cause of a given effect for its real cause, or by the *post hoc ergo propter hoc* fallacy which is the inference that one event is the cause of another from the bare fact that the first occurs earlier than the second.[25]

Further, we must be careful to distinguish between the category of the *necessary condition* and the category of the *sufficient condition*. A necessary condition may be defined as the circumstance or factor in whose absence the event cannot occur. It is the *sine qua non* of the effect. A sufficient condition is a circumstance in whose presence the event *must* occur. Irving Copi offers the example of the relationship of oxygen to combustion. The presence of oxygen, though *necessary* for combustion, is not a *sufficient* condition for combustion because oxygen can be present without combustion occurring.[26]

The assumption of the law of causality, like that of the law of noncontradiction, is neither arbitrary nor subjective. It too may be denied by the mouth but not by the life. Denials of this law are as forced and temporary as denials of the law of noncontradiction. We point once more to John Cage's avocation to illustrate. Aware that if he approached mushrooms in the spirit of chance operations he would shortly die, Cage was assuming not only the law of noncontradiction but the law of causality. He assumed not only that poisonous mushrooms could not be poisonous and not poisonous at the same time and in the same relationship, but he assumed some causal nexus in which the toxic mushrooms would have a deleterious effect upon his health.

The assumption of causality was also operative in Descartes's *cogito ergo sum*. The "I think therefore I am" which came out of his rigorous doubt process by which he found he could doubt everything except that he was doubting, included the assumption that doubt requires a necessary condition, namely, a doubter. Thus causality operated along with the law of noncontradiction as a necessary assumption for Descartes's self-consciousness.

Again, as with the law of noncontradiction, the law of causality is not only assumed in science and philosophy but is everywhere assumed by Scripture. The Bible offers no theory of causality but assumes its validity at numerous points. Just as the Bible uses the rationally loaded word *therefore,* so it also uses the causally loaded word *because.* Consider the reasoning process of Nicodemus in his nocturnal visit to Jesus: "Rabbi, we know that you are a teacher come from God; for [γαϱ, "because"[27]] no one can do these signs that you do, unless God is with him" (John 3:2 RSV). Nicodemus was engaged in causal thinking, seeing the imprimatur of God as a necessary condition for Jesus' ability to perform miracles. His mode of reasoning received the implicit endorsement of Jesus and the explicit endorsement of the New Testament use of the word *sign*. The signs which John records would have no significance apart from the assumption of causality. The term *sign* (σημεῖον) occurs seventy-three times in the New Testament and is frequently related to two other causally loaded terms, δυνάμεις (power) and ἔργον (work). These words concern the significance of manifestations or workings of power in the visible world. The signs demanded from Jesus by his contemporaries were demands to show that "God, in whose name He works, has unequivocally authorized Him. This authentication will take place when God does something or *causes* something to happen in relation to Jesus which will prove that any doubt concerning His divine authority is wrong."[28] Here the Pharisees were looking not only for a necessary causal condition but also for a sufficient causal condition, which the New Testament indeed attaches to the miracles of Christ. The Old Testament usage of the Hebrew counterpart to σημεῖον, אוֹת, carries the same import.[29]

The Basic Reliability of Sense Perception

The third nonnegotiable assumption for apologetics is the basic reliability of sense perception. As we move to this prerequisite for knowledge, we make a transition from the formal realm to the material realm, recognizing that the step is fraught with epistemological peril. We are convinced that an epistemology established upon a naked empiricism is doomed to travel the road to the graveyard of Hume. If the axiom *nihil est in intellectu quod non fuerit in sensu* is accepted in an absolute sense, skepticism is unavoidable. That is, if all a prioris, either of principles or abilities or categories, are excluded, we see no way to progress beyond an inchoate blob of sensations. Not a single datum can be discovered without an a priori making discrimination and individuation possible.

The Principal Limitation of Empirical Induction. The principal limitation of empirical induction is widely known—it fails to establish universals. However, a pure empiricism cannot even establish a particular. A blank mind without a priori ideas or abilities must forever remain blank of discriminate perceptions. Without a priori equipment such as Kant's pure intuitions of space and time, or Locke's abilities of combining, relating, and abstracting, or Aristotle's categories, sensations cannot give rise to perceptions. It is for this reason that post-Humean and post-Kantian empiricists are, for the most part, not pure empiricists but crypto-rationalists. The law of noncontradiction, for example, is not a conclusion drawn from sense perception but a necessary condition for sense perception.

Even if we eschew naked or pure forms of empiricism, we are still left with the question of how we acquire knowledge of the external world. Is it by recollection only, in the Platonic sense? But Plato's highest "proof" of recollection depended upon sense perception for its execution. In the *Meno* dialogue we encounter the discussion between Meno's slave boy and Socrates in which Socrates elicits from the illiterate servant, by the Socratic method, a "recollection" of the Pythagorean theorem. But Socrates does not remain strictly in the realm of abstract mathematics; he resorts to visual aids of lines and squares which are *shown* to the slave boy as Socrates feeds him the leading questions.[30]

Perhaps, then, we can leap to the Bible as our source of knowledge of the external world without depending on our senses? But the Bible itself remains inaccessible apart from sense perception. To gain any information from the Bible we must either read it visually, using our eyes, read it in a tactile way, as in Braille, using our fingers, or hear it read to us, using our ears. Without our senses the Bible remains a closed book.

The potential and actual problems attending sense perception such as the limitations of induction, the subject-object problem, and the possibility of Descartes's diabolical great deceiver all cast a shadow on the reliability of our senses. We know that our senses can be deceived and are thus not infallible and that it is possible to have hallucinations and mistake them for reality. Timothy Leary, the high priest of the drug culture of the sixties, defended the experimental use of peyote and L.S.D. at Harvard. When accused of engaging in illicit experiments with hallucinogenic drugs, he argued that L.S.D. was not an hallucinogen but was, in fact, a psychedelic, that is, not a "mind-distorting" but a "mind-expanding" drug. He elicited testimony from artists who claimed augmented ability to perceive color hues and patterns, musicians who discovered new harmonies and tonal structures, and participants in the sexual revolution claimed the ability of orgasmic elbows, all under the influence of L.S.D. Leary was claiming not a distorted view of reality but an intensified and sharper view of reality, a difficult defense to counter.

The comparative weakness of human sensibilities as compared with known sensitivities of other creatures such as the deer's superior olfactory sense (as every deer-hunter is aware of), the turkey's superior optical sense, and the dog's superior auditory sense, all point out the finite limitations of human sense perception. The telescope, microscope, radar, and other devices were built to enhance and improve our sensory powers.

Because our senses are fallible and limited we speak of *basic* or *rudimentary* reliability of sense perception rather than *total, perfect,* or *infallible* reliability. Our senses are limited but not impotent; they are problematic, but not useless. But with all these qualifiers, how can we be sure that our senses are even basically reliable and not totally distortive? We cannot. That is why we are left with the common sense necessity of assuming it. The reliability of sense perception must be a working presupposition if knowledge of the external world is to be possible. It is part of the nature or order of knowing simply because it is part of the nature or order of our being as physical, sensory-equipped creatures. Sense perception is a given of our ontological make-up. It can be augmented and enhanced, but it cannot be eliminated. The human body is the person's point of contact with the external world, the bridge from subject to object. We are creatures of sense perception; from this given there is no exit. This realization may be what most heavily contributes to recent renewed interest at the University of Notre Dame and other centers of philosophical inquiry in the Scottish realists like Thomas Reid.

The Problem of Induction and Certainty. The chief problem built into induction is the problem of classification into universals. For a universal to be absolutely established inductively requires that a comprehensive and exhaustive sampling be made. The structure of a common syllogism reveals this.

A. All men are mortal.
B. Socrates is a man.
C. Socrates is mortal.

The deductive form of the syllogism is impeccable and the conclusion flows by irresistible logic from the premises. If the premises are true then the conclusion is absolutely certain. But how do we establish the premises? The premises are established inductively, moving from the particular to the universal. Here we encounter a problem which is not quantitative but qualitative. That is, the barrier to achieving perfect universality of classification is not merely the weakness of our sensory equipment or apparatus but the limits of the *scope* of our investigation, limits that are imposed by space and time. Even if we possessed infallible sensory perception of the particulars, our finite limitations of space and time would create problems for achieving absolute universality via induction. To know with inductive absolute certainty that mortality can be predicated of all men we would have to have a universal sampling of all men. We may have astronomical incidences of the particular mortality of individual men giving us, in Humean categories, an astronomical probability quotient of universal mortality, but it falls short of absolute inductive certainty of universal mortality. Absolute inductive certainty would require the observation of the mortality of each and every human being, including those billions who are presently alive.

Assuming the basic reliability of sense perception will not solve the inductive problem in premise A. Premise B has similar difficulties. "Socrates is a man" predicates the relationship of an individual to a class, a particular to a universal. The manness of Socrates suffers from the inductive problems of Premise A. But even if we grant that there is a universal category of man we still have to identify Socrates as a member of the class. Socrates may appear to be a man but actually be a bionic replica or an hallucination of the perceiver. Our assumption of basic reliability will solve this problem of quality, but the problem of universal quantification remains.

What the assumption of basic reliability of sense perception does achieve is knowledge of the particular, without which not even relative inductive certainty of universals is possible. Without knowledge of the particular, induction cannot begin and even Hume's probability quotients crumble into ashes. There cannot be two incidences of a given phenomenon without there first being one (the particular is at least logically prior if not temporally prior to the universal).

It is because of this inherent problem of the relationship between induction and certainty that many Christian apologists have sought to avoid any dependence on empirical data for building a case for the existence of God, retreating either to fideism or sheer ontologism for their approach. To venture into the empirical realm of sense perception is assumed to necessitate a foray into the hopeless land of probability and its attending levels of uncertainty. This is why thinkers such as Descartes sought to establish the existence of God prior to facing the complexities of sense perception. (Descartes's God functioned as a safeguard against the devious ploys of the diabolical great deceiver.) This is what motivates the presuppositional apologists to begin their apologetics with the assumption of the existence of God, a move which Section 3 of this volume will endeavor to show raises more problems than it solves.

That God is ontologically prior to all human knowledge is not disputed by any theist. The problem arises, as we shall see later, when we make God a question-begging first principle of epistemology. We are seeking here not to separate ontology and epistemology but to distinguish them. Since we are concerned here with epistemology, we are restricting ourselves to matters of knowing rather than matters of being.

We dispute the skeptical notion that all matters of empiricism destroy certainty. We do not need to have universal knowledge to have certain knowledge. One empirical datum is all that is required to gain certain knowledge of God, as we shall endeavor to show in Section 2. Because induction does not yield the absolute *universal* does not mean that it cannot yield absolute *truth*. We will endeavor to show that the contingent truths of history do in fact yield eternal truth, Lessing notwithstanding. We will endeavor to show that we can move from the phenomenal to the noumenal by the application of the law of noncontradiction, the law of causality, and the basic reliability of sense perception. Like assumptions one and two, the assumption of the basic reliability of sense perception is neither arbitrary nor subjectivistic. It is an assumption all people make and all *must* make to live, the denial of which is forced and temporary, as are the denials of logic and causality.

That all must assume the basic reliability of sense perception may be illustrated by yet another visit to John Cage's mushroom patch. When he concludes that a chance approach to mushroom consumption will bring about his death, he assumes that he can at least distinguish a mushroom from a cactus with his lips if not with his eyes. Our driver at the intersection likewise trusts his senses when he applies his brakes to avoid the oncoming truck.

That Scripture likewise assumes the basic reliability of sense perception is seen in a multitude of ways. To be sure, Scripture speaks of realities which are not normally perceived, like the angels surrounding Elisha at Dothan and the invisible presence of the Holy Spirit. Yet God leads Israel through the wilderness by a visible pillar of fire and pillar of cloud. The testimony of the apostles to the person and work of Jesus is not based on mystical intuitions or upon theories or recollection. It was Philip who declared to Nathanael, "Come and see" (John 1:46). It was the apostle John who asserted:

> That which was from the beginning, which we have heard, which we have seen with our eyes, which we have looked upon and touched with our hands, concerning the word of life. (1 John 1:1 RSV)

The triad of the law of noncontradiction, the law of causality, and the basic reliability of sense perception is integral to all knowledge. Their forced and temporary denials take place in the courts of subjectivism. In instance after instance where natural theology in general and the theistic proofs in particular have been attacked, one or more of these three building blocks of knowledge has been negotiated.

CLASSICAL APOLOGETICS:

The Theistic Proofs, the Deity of Christ, and the Infallibility of Scripture

CHAPTER 6

The Incomprehensibility of God and the Ontological Argument

ANY ATTEMPT TO prove the existence of God by rational means faces two major obstacles at the outset. The first is cultural and the second is intellectual. The cultural difficulty is represented by the present anti-intellectual climate of our day. Ours is the "Age of Aquarius" in which rational argumentation is deemed not only impossible, but religiously indecent. The fact, however, that a certain apologetical malaise is evident in the culture is no justification for ignoring the task. Indeed, it merely underscores the urgent need for apologetics.

The second obstacle is the intellectual thesis of agnosticism, that it is impossible for finite beings to know anything of the infinite. If this were true and God were infinite, then manifestly a pursuit of the infinite would be a fool's errand. We agree that God is infinite but dispute the thesis that it is impossible for finite beings to know anything of the infinite.

Part of the difficulty we face is based on inferences drawn from a classical principle of theology set forth in the Latin phrase *finitum non capax infiniti*. Its origin is often attributed to Calvin but the phrase nowhere occurs in the writings of Calvin.[1] The phrase has had two primary applications in the history of theology. It was pressed into service in the Lutheran-Reformed debate over the *prasentia realis* issue of the Lord's Supper. The Lutheran view ascribes ubiquity to the *human* nature of Jesus. To the Lutheran view, Reformed thinkers objected that the finite cannot *contain* the infinite, objecting to a cryptic form of monophysitism which violated the credal limits set at Chalcedon.[2] With respect to the Lutheran concept of the Lord's Supper, *capax* is usually translated "contain." Hence the full phrase *finitum non capax infiniti* would be rendered "The finite cannot contain the infinite." The application to Luther's view of the communication of divine attributes (such as ubiquity) to the human nature would be ruled out. If the divine attribute of ubiquity were communicated to the human nature, either the human finitude would be swallowed up and annihilated by the infinite or the infinite would be swallowed up by the finite making it no longer infinite. If the finite could "contain" the infinite, it would require that the infinite be bound by finite limits of containment, and it would no longer be infinite. For the finite to contain the infinite it must first become infinite itself. If such a mutation were possible, we would be speaking of the infinite containing the infinite not the finite containing the infinite, as the latter would be a contradiction in terms.

On another theological front, the *finitum* phrase applies to the Reformed doctrine of the incomprehensibility of God. When it is applied here, there is a slight shift in the nuance of the phrase, particularly in our understanding of the word *capax*.

With respect to the doctrine of the incomprehensibility of God, the term *capax* is normally rendered "grasp." Hence the full phrase *finitum non capax infiniti* would be rendered, "The finite cannot grasp the infinite." The Latin *capax* is indeed capable of such subtle changes of nuance. It may be rendered: "able to hold much, broad, roomy, capable, receptive, contain, or able to grasp."[3]

Heinrich Heppe summarizes the Reformed doctrine of the incomprehensibility of God:

> The finite spirit cannot perfectly grasp the infinite . . . All Reformed dogmaticians present the statement which, e.g., Musculus expresses, that "what is finite cannot express the infinite," and hence despite the idea that God's nature can really be defined. . . . Similarly Cocceius "We know that God cannot be defined, not only because He is infinite, i.e., is in no wise defined, but also because every definition consists of genus and differentia. But these things are not appropriate to God; for things that consist of genus and species must needs be composite. Therefore God can only be described. . . . There is no perfect definition of God, though there are various descriptions of Him. God is incomprehensible."[4]

We observe a vacillation here in Heppe: he says God cannot be grasped but then qualifies it to "perfectly grasped," and he says that God cannot be defined but then follows this with the qualification "no perfect definition of God." This vacillation reveals the ambiquity of the use of the phrase *finitum non capax infiniti*. If it were applied full force to theology we would have to conclude that we can have no knowledge (no grasp) of God at all. If God absolutely cannot be defined, then even the "descriptions" of Him of which Cocceius wrote would be meaningless. Heppe's qualifiers, however, point to the proper function of the phrase with respect to the doctrine of the incomprehensibility of God. The doctrine does not mean that we can know *nothing* about God. Rather, it reminds us that we do not know *everything* about God. We know something, which is more than nothing, and less than everything about God. What the finite cannot grasp is the "everything," inasmuch as such total comprehension would require an infinite perspective which the finite lacks by definition.

The fact that God is infinite and we are finite does not make finite knowledge of the infinite impossible. To deny this assertion is to affirm it. When the critic declares that we cannot know the infinite, he must know something about the infinite to deny it. The critic may reply that he is talking about the *concept* of the infinite, but that he has no knowledge of infinite entities as the finite cannot know anything about infinite entities. But to attribute the *concept* of infinite to God (or any other alleged infinite entity) is to say something about the entity, namely, that He or it is infinite or nonfinite. The definition may be by way of negation (*via negationis*), but it is a definition nevertheless. Knowing that God, for example, is not finite is knowledge of His infinity.

The finite is that which has boundaries. The finite is the noninfinite. The infinite has no boundaries. The two concepts are strictly reciprocal. Knowing one is knowing the other. To know the meaning of finite demands knowledge of the nonfinite; knowing the infinite demands knowledge of the finite.

Again, what most people mean when they say that the finite cannot grasp the infinite is that the finite cannot totally, perfectly, or exhaustively comprehend the infinite. The finite can know *that* the infinite is. Not only can it know it, it cannot not know it. More than that the finite does not and cannot know except as the infinite is willing to reveal Himself further.

Another obstacle to rational apologetics is a claim alleged to follow from the incomprehensibility of God: *If God is incomprehensible though knowable, we should experience Him rather than have rational knowledge of Him.* Christianity not only teaches that we may indeed experience God, but shows how He may be experienced. Such experience is possible only because we know that He is. If we did not know rationally that He is, we would have no way of knowing that we were experiencing *Him*.

If truth is equated with or reduced to the experience of the encounter, we could not know that we were encountering God. If truth *is* encounter (*Wahrheit als Begegnung*), we can only encounter "I-know-not-whom" and erect a new altar to an unknown God.

Some may argue that we *learn* the truth or *meet* the truth in encounter, but that is far different from saying that encounter *is* the truth. "Encounter of truth" and "encounter is truth" are not identical ideas. A personal experience of God involves a knowing of God which is personal, intimate, and even subjective. It is more than gaining mere information about Him. The Bible says that to know Him in this sense is life eternal. It is life as well as knowledge. But it is eternal life through and in knowledge, not apart from knowledge. It is certainly *more* than cognitive knowledge, but it is *not less* than cognitive knowledge.

THE NECESSITY OF KNOWING GOD

For a dog to be a dog, to bark as a dog, to wag his tail as a dog, and in all ways to function as a dog, it is not necessary for a dog to know of the existence of God. Yet for a dog to be a dog the existence of God is necessary. All the dog needs is God, not the knowledge of God. The dog's master is different; he is a creature of reflection and cogitation, possessing the polar qualities spoken of by Pascal, misery and grandeur. His grandeur resides in his ability to contemplate his own existence, and his misery in his ability to contemplate a better existence than he is presently able to enjoy. He has an inner drive to probe the whence and wherefore of his own existence, questions which transcend the scope of canine inquiry.

Only an infinite being can provide satisfactory answers to these questions. So long as humans must ask questions (and as long as they exist, they must ask questions), they must know *that* this Infinite is, *who* this Infinite is, and, most important of all, *know* this Infinite who is. Augustine spoke of the human heart plagued by a restlessness which could not be quieted apart from a resting place in God. The restlessness of the heart is not a matter of cardiac irregularity or fribulations, but points to a paralyzing anxiety within the depths of the creature that is precipitated by the haunting questions of the mind. Where the mind is uncertain the heart has no peace.

We stress therefore our apology for apologetics. If there is no reasoned defense for the Christian faith there can be no sound Christianity. "There is no God and Jesus Christ is His Son." However comic this neo-orthodox statement is, it has been tragic for the church. John McQuarrie lamented that every death-of-God theologian was a disillusioned Barthian.[5]

At the same time, however, given our cultural milieu, it is not surprising that existentialism has become so attractive to religionists. For those who have a passion to believe yet despair of or despise the justifying of their faith rationally, existentialism is an appealing option. With jubilation they chisel in stone a new magna charta of faith, unfettered by reason. They declare an independence which guarantees the liberty to believe without understanding. As an added windfall they claim that after believing without understanding they find understanding because they believed.

In his *From Luther to Kierkegaard,* Jaroslav Pelikan, for example, actually finds Kant's devastating critical analysis of all knowledge, including revelation, a boon to Lutheran orthodoxy. "When the *Critique of Pure Reason* showed that basic religious and metaphysical concepts like God, freedom, and immortality cannot be reached by pure reason, it opened the way for a prophetic reassertion of the Lutheran understanding of faith."[6] Here we have another repudiation of "truth unto godliness" in favor of godliness unto "truth."

Karl Barth's successor at Basel, Heinrich Ott, maintains that if God were proven "in such a way that no reasonable objection could be made to stand, then it would mean that God is something innerworldly, something we can encompass with our human reason. . . . Understood in this way, however, God would no longer be God."[7] Ott is saying that if we prove God exists, we are actually proving that He does not exist. Ott concludes that if we prove God (the infinite, incomprehensible, unencompassable-by-our-minds-or-anything-but-Himself), then we have a mentally encompassable deity. But Ott's conclusion does not flow from his premises: Proving that an incomprehensible being exists does not require that we fully comprehend Him. Indeed (in *this* Ott is right), if we did fully comprehend Him, we would not be speaking of God. There *is* a difference, however, between knowledge and total comprehension. If there were not, we and Ott would have no knowledge of anything, for we know nothing exhaustively or comprehensively.

Where Ott cannot accept a knowable God, Jurgen Moltmann seeks to make God knowable by removing His omnipotence and making Him a suffering God. God's being is in suffering, and suffering is in God's very being. God does not measure up to Moltmann's demands: the immutable, ever-blessedness of God causes Moltmann so much pain that he must reject Him. Unless God can become miserable—infinitely miserable because infinity is an eternally present attribute of God—Moltmann will not suffer Him to live at all. He will, instead, create a God in his own image with whom he will deign to live—and die.

We sympathize with Moltmann's own suffering with a suffering world. But to make God suffer too destroys the God who alone can save the world. We agonize with the "theologian of hope," who has become the theologian of suffering, when he tells of a Jew in Auschwitz slowly dying in torment and a beholder crying out, "Where is God now?" But when the answer comes, "He is hanging there on the gallows," Moltmann's comment, "Any other answer would be blasphemy,"[8] is itself blasphemy. If Moltmann only meant what Anselm meant when he wrote *Cur Deus Homo,* we would agree. God became man—took human nature—precisely because in *that* nature He could suffer for sinful, suffering humanity. *As God,* He *cannot* suffer; that is why He became *man.* But, for Moltmann, God in Himself eternally suffers and only expresses that misery in the suffering Christ. The Savior becomes unnecessary—except as an illustration of divine pathos. Moltmann's motive for stressing divine suffering, meant to glorify the cross, destroys it. The God of theopaschitism, by suffering, suffers the loss of deity itself. A dying God is no God at all.

Karl Rahner comes close to Moltmann, but avoids implicit atheism. He also thinks that God cannot be reached by metaphysics and reason. Only by communicating Himself in suffering can He be known. This is possible because God is capable of suffering in someone other than Himself. Rahner embraces an ancient heresy by saying, "God can become something, he who is unchangeable in himself can *himself* become subject to change in *something else.*"[9] Rahner is orthodox enough to save God from suffering by having it take place in someone else. But he only verbally saves God. Indeed, he does not even verbally save Him for he continues: "God *himself* has become flesh."[10]

Rahner's effort to save God from the hands of modern theologians—Roman Catholic as well as Protestant—fails for two reasons; ironically the very same reasons Rahner gives to save Him. First, if God cannot be known, how can we know that it is He who enters history even in the sufferer? Second, if He does enter history so as to demonstrate His ability to suffer by suffering in someone else, then He at first *presents* Himself as not God (because God is eternally blessed and utterly incapable of suffering). Thus, if *He* actually does suffer in someone else, He thereby *proves* that He is not God.

Existentialism, of any variety, is futile, because one cannot even understand the meaning of the term or its presumed truth without objective standards of judgment. With existentialism, the apologetic jig is up.

But in the face of the plethora of contemporary volumes arguing the nonexistence of God and a kind of godless Christianity (compare, for example, the works of William Hamilton and Paul Van Buren), the sigh of H. P. Owen is refreshing. In the preface to his formidable work on *The Christian Knowledge of God* he remarks,

> I hope that the following pages will, in their own way, assist the restoration of a fully cognitive faith; for unless such a faith can be restored there is no ground for either Christian hope or Christian charity.[11]

THE POSSIBILITY OF KNOWING GOD

The human heart and mind may be restless without God, but that does not prove that He can be known. Air, food, and water are all necessary for human life, but they are not always available. Is it possible that God cannot be found? It is certainly possible. A dog cannot find Him because he does not seek Him. But does a human seeking God prove the finding of Him? No, but it does argue the possibility (which a dog does not have).

Have we found God without realizing it? Does realizing the possibility prove the reality? Do we know that there is a God simply because we can talk of the possibility of finding Him? If so, then we have already found Him or we could not talk about Him or about the possibility of finding Him. We may not know Him personally, but we know that He is and that there is at least a possibility of knowing Him personally.

Pure sophistry? We began talking about the possibility of knowing God. Then we argued that we already know He exists when we talk about the mere possibility of knowing of His existence. Have we arbitrarily assumed His existence? But this is precisely the point: Is it possible for us to even *suppose* or *hypothesize* God without His existence? Does the mere supposition of a possible God require an actual God? These questions anticipate the ontological argument. At this point it is sufficient to say that if there is a God, presumably it is *at least* possible to know Him, and *at most,* by asking the question, we prove that we already in fact do know Him.

Or we may ask, if it is *possible* that a necessary being (God) exists, is it therefore also *necessary* that He exists? Can we or must we move immediately from the possible to the necessary? It is certainly not impossible that a necessary being exists. The concept violates no formal rule of logic, nor is it in any way formally falsified. Thus, we must grant it is at least possible that a necessary being exists. We can formulate it simply. "A necessary being *may* exist." The formula, however, screams its own inner protest. Is it not absurd to say that a *necessary* being *may* exist? A necessary being by definition may not merely *possibly* exist but *must* exist. A necessary being, if He is truly necessary, must exist or else He would not be a necessary being. In discovering the possibility of God, we have discovered the certainty of God, unless it can be shown that the argument is done by mirrors, by linguistic legerdemain.

The "at least" of possible knowledge of God must move to the "at most" of knowledge of God. If we can think of God at all, we are compelled to think that He is. God is being. Being, in the absolute or pure sense, is God. It is undeniable that we do think of being. We cannot utter a sentence or think a thought without reference to being. Being was before Plato, even before Thales. The concept of being is pre-pre-Socratic. We can deny with our mouths that being is, but not with our minds. We cannot not think of being. Put another way, we cannot conceive of nonbeing. As Jonathan Edwards stated, the ability to dream of nothing belongs only to sleeping rocks.

Having discovered that the possibility of knowing God implies the certainty that we have already found Him, we need not discuss the probability of knowing God. We touch on it in passing merely to acknowledge a sore point of dispute between classical apologetics and the presuppositionalist approach. Presuppositionalism criticizes traditional apologetics as being merely probabilistic. We admit that much of it has been so, but not in its classical form. Many traditionalists have used probability argumentation, turning away from absolute claims. At their classical best, the theistic proofs are not merely probable but demonstrative.

Before moving on to the ontological arguments of Anselm, Descartes, Jonathan Edwards and others, let us restate what we have already set forth. Once we think of the possibility of God, everything is proven. *To think of being is to know being.* We are conscious of being. However we think, we cannot think anything but being. We are immediately aware of Him. The awareness of being is even logically prior to our awareness of ourselves. To be aware of ourselves, we must be aware of being which pervades our being and all other beings. Before we are aware of the world, we are aware of Being which pervades all other beings. Pure being must uphold and sustain "beings," finite limited, creaturely beings. Even before being aware of the laws of logic, we are aware of being because logic also has being before it has the form of its being.

ANSELM AND THE MERE IDEA OF GOD

According to Anselm of Canterbury (1033–1109), the mere idea of a being than which none greater can be conceived proves the existence of such a being.[12] If it did not, he reasoned, then it would be a being of which we could conceive a higher (namely existent) being. The principal objection offered to Anselm—that "idea" does not prove existence but only that existence is part of the idea—is effective; but only because Anselm may not have stated the argument fully. The full argument would include the implicit observation that we cannot think of the nonexistence of God. That proves God's existence, inasmuch as the inability to think of or conceive of an entity's nonexistence is the most compelling type of proof. We know we *now* exist because, while we are existing, we cannot think of our not now existing. The same is true of the chair on which we are *now* sitting. This is implicit in Anselm's argument.

But Kant argues in his *Critique of Pure Reason* that the ontological argument does not get out of the realm of idea.[13] The idea of a perfect triangle implies the *idea* of the existence of a perfect triangle and nothing more. Likewise the *idea* of a perfect being implies merely the *idea* of an *existing* perfect being.

There is a difference between these two ideas, however. We can think of the nonexistence of a perfect triangle, but we cannot think of the nonexistence of perfect being. We cannot think of the nonexistence of perfect, necessary being. Therefore, that being must exist. We simply cannot think of its not existing. We yield by necessity to the impossibility of the contrary. This is the *only* thing which we cannot think of as existing *merely* as idea. Kant could not think God out of existence, nor can anyone else.

Malcolm Diamond challenges the critics of the ontological argument at this point:

> If "something not conceivable as not existing" exists, then it exists necessarily. The contradiction glares at us in the first clause, namely, "If something not conceivable as not existing," exists. This clause involves the skeptic in simultaneously maintaining that he can and cannot conceive of the nonexistence of God.[14]

If a triangle exists, it necessarily has three angles. The very idea of a perfect triangle necessitates the existence of three perfect angles. The perfect triangle must have three perfect angles but carries no necessity of real existence. The angles of the triangle are necessary but not the being of the triangle. Nothing necessitates the existence of the perfect triangle. We can think of the nonexistence of a perfect triangle with its three necessary angles, but we cannot think of the nonexistence of a perfect being. If it is a perfect being, it is not nonexistent. If one thinks of its nonexistence, one is not thinking of a perfect being. Since everyone has an idea of perfect being, everyone has an idea of a necessarily existing perfect being. No one can think of such a being not existing. Therefore, God, the perfect being, must exist, for we cannot think of His not existing. As we said, this is the supreme proof of anything— that we cannot think of its not existing. Since we cannot think of God not existing, He must exist. Normal Malcolm asks,

> Can anything be clearer than that the conjunction "God necessarily exists but it is possible that He does not exist" is self-contradictory? Is it not just as plainly self-contradictory as the conjunction "A square necessarily has four sides but it is possible for a square not to have four sides"?[15]

The difference between this formulation and Anselm's is this: Anselm said correctly that we have an idea of a being than which none greater can be conceived. If that being did not exist, we could conceive of a being which was greater. So, the being corresponding to our idea must exist. Anselm remains in the realm of hypothetical being. It is still the being which has hypothetically the notion of existence which is greater than the hypothetically nonexistent being. All this is true enough but still hypothetical.

When one adds the simple observation that the necessary proof of anything is the inability to think of its nonexistence, this establishes the necessary existence of the perfect being. Anselm may have intended this, but did not expressly state it. He thus left himself open to the criticism that he had only proved the necessary existence of a mere idea. When one adds that Anselm's being, than which none greater can be conceived, cannot be thought to not exist, he has proven the actual necessary real existence of that being.

Anselm's idea is thought to be uniquely relevant to God. Strictly speaking, it is not. The proof of the point we are making is that we cannot think of anything which *now* exists as not *now* existing. What we cannot think of not existing must exist in our knowledge. This is the ontological proof of God and all else. God is no better *proven* than we, but He who is proven is infinitely greater than we who are proven. This may be the democratization of Anselm's proof.

DESCARTES AND THE CAUSE OF THE IDEA OF GOD

Rene Descartes's (1599–1650) form of the ontological argument (that God alone could account for the idea of God) is self-evidently true. If having the idea of God (not being able to think of God's nonexistence) proves His existence, the only ultimate cause of such an idea must be God. In the *Meditations* Descartes argues that the idea of God cannot come from nothing nor is it a matter of pure abstract thought via negation:

> What, then, shall I conclude from all this evidence? Clearly, that if the objective reality (or perfection) of some one of my ideas is such that I recognize clearly that this same reality (or perfection) does not exist in me, either formally or eminently, and consequently that I cannot myself be its cause, it necessarily follows that I am not alone in the world but that there is also some other entity that exists and is the cause of this idea.[16]

Descartes further asserted that the idea of God, though not comprehensive, was "the truest, the clearest, and the most distinct of the ideas which I have in my mind."[17] He rightly understood that the finite could not even think of the infinite or nonfinite without first having the idea of being which must come from being.

Descartes rests on Anselm. It is not as some suppose, that Descartes put the foundation under Anselm. Anselm is the foundation under Descartes. Anselm proves the hypothetical existence of God. Descartes confirms this by showing that this proof could only have come from (being proved by) God Himself.

We are simply saying that the ultimate proof of both is that that which we cannot not think is the proof of the actual existence of anything.

Let us now be more specific about the non-cogency of Descartes's form of the ontological argument.

In spite of the fact, that at this point he is cogent, Descartes does not follow through. His argument is not consistently cogent. He did actually say that "it is not in my power to think of God without existence."[18] That is correct the way it stands, but Descartes did not mean it the way it stands. He meant that, *given the idea of God,* he could not "think of God without existence." This does not get beyond Anselm, it does not get beyond the *idea* of the existence of this being. Descartes's later statement that one "cannot conceive anything but God Himself to whose essence existence necessarily pertains"[19] is still in the realm of idea. One cannot think of the *idea* of God without thinking of existence, just as one cannot think of a mountain apart from a valley.

Descartes's own syllogism shows the noncogency of his argument:

Major Premise: That which is clearly understood to belong to the nature of anything can truly be affirmed of that thing.

Minor Premise: Existence does belong to the nature of God.

Conclusion: Therefore, God exists.

This reasoning is about the idea of God and proves that existence does belong with the very idea of God. If first we knew God existed, then we could prove by this syllogism that God does, in fact, exist. Descartes seems unaware that the major premise is ambiguous. If it means that God is known to *exist,* then the conclusion is tautological. If it means that we have an *idea* of God, then the conclusion is ambiguous or gratuitous.

THE CONTEMPORARY SITUATION

The ontological argument has enjoyed a contemporary resurrection among philosophers. The most important recent proponents are Charles Hartshorne and Norman Malcolm. Since Hartshorne, cogent as he is at points, is not proving the orthodox God of Anselm (though he uses Anselm's argument) but a potential deity of his own making, we will concentrate our attention on Malcolm's reasoning to see whether he rehabilitates, reconstructs, or replaces the classical argument.

Malcolm, whose argument is the most important restatement of Anselm in the twentieth century, divides and conquers Anselm's arguments. Anselm's first ontological proof uses the principle that a thing is greater if it exists than if it does not exist. His second proof employs the different principle that a thing is greater if it necessarily exists than if it does not necessarily exist. Malcolm opts for the second proof.

Malcolm states Anselm's argument as he adopts it:

> If God, a being greater than which cannot be conceived, does not exist then He cannot come into existence. For if He did He would either have been caused to come into existence or have happened to come into existence, and in either case He would be a limited being, which by our conception of Him He is not. Since He cannot come into existence, if He does not exist His existence is impossible. If He does exist He cannot have come into existence (for the reasons given) nor can He cease to exist, for nothing could cause Him to cease to exist nor could it just happen that He ceased to exist. So if God exists His existence is necessary. Thus God's existence is either impossible or necessary. It can be the former only if the concept of such a being is self-contradictory or in some way logically absurd. Assuming that this is not so, it follows that He necessarily exists.[20]

But Malcolm is playing semantic games. Given a certain definition of God, certain attributes, for example, necessity, are involved in it. In short, what Malcolm is saying is that if God is necessary (by definition—which by our definition He is), then He is necessary. If He is necessary and this is not a contradictory notion, He exists. Though he takes some time getting to it, Alvin Plantinga is quite justified in his critique of Malcolm: "The assertion that a being so defined exists, that the definition actually applies to something, may well be, for all that Malcolm and Anselm have said, a contingent assertion."[21]

JONATHAN EDWARDS AND THE IDEA OF BEING

In our historical sampling of ontological arguments, we bypassed Jonathan Edwards (until now), for we consider his work on Anselm's argument to be superior to most others, and, indeed, to constitute the ultimate proof. According to Edwards, we have an idea of being and we cannot have even an idea of nonbeing: "That there should be nothing at all is utterly impossible."[22] This is the other side of Anselm's coin. Anselm, at least implicitly, shows that we cannot *not* think of being. Edwards shows that we *cannot* think of nonbeing. Anselm shows that being must be; Edwards that nonbeing must not—cannot—be. If nonbeing *is*, it is not nonbeing. If being is not, it is not being. Since nonbeing cannot be, it cannot be conceived; just as, since being cannot not be, its nonbeing cannot be conceived.

Therefore, we cannot think of being not being ever or anywhere:

> Where can I go from thy Spirit? Or where can I flee from Thy presence? If I ascend to heaven, Thou art there; If I make my bed in Sheol, behold, Thou art there. (Ps. 139:7–8 NASB)

Consequently, this eternal, infinite being must necessarily exist because we cannot think of it not existing; and the only ultimate proof of the existence of anything is that we cannot think of it not existing, ever.

Someone may object that the *idea* of a necessary being proves only that the idea exists (as an idea). But this particular idea *includes* necessary existence, in that we cannot think of it as mere idea, not existing. If I have an idea of a rock, for example, which I have never seen, the idea exists. That to which the idea refers, however, does not *necessarily* exist. We can conceive of the rock not existing before or after the present moment. But the idea of a necessary being does include in it eternally necessary existence. That is the only difference between the two ideas: one includes eternal necessary existence and the other does not.

W. G. T. SHEDD'S DEFENSE OF ANSELM

Our final observations on the ontological argument will be an examination of theologian W. G. T. Shedd's defense of the Anselmian ontological argument. Probably no Reformed theologian has defended Anselm more confidently. "The human mind possesses the idea of an absolutely Perfect Being. . . . But such perfection as this implies *necessary* existence; and necessary existence implies *actual* existence: because if a thing must be of course it is."[23]

Shedd seems to forget that this is all only an elaboration of the contents of the *idea*. The *idea* of perfect being does, indeed, contain the idea of the necessary existence of the being. True, the idea of an imperfect being does not contain the idea of the necessary existence of the being. It is also true that the *idea* of necessary existence implies actual existence in one instance and not in another: The *idea* of a perfect island, for example (than which no greater island could be conceived), would include the *idea* of the existence of that island. An existent island is greater than a nonexistent island because it has more being. An existent God is greater than a nonexistent God because it has more being. The necessary existence of a god is greater than the contingent existence of a god (if we can so speak) because it, too, has more being.

This leads Shedd to say that "necessity of being, therefore, belongs to perfection of being."[24] That is true, but Shedd keeps forgetting that the argument deals only with an idea. All the properties he argues for belong only to the idea.

"The idea of a tree implies the contingency that it may or may not exist; that of the absolutely perfect Being implies necessity, that he must exist."[25] But again, the *idea* of one includes contingency of being; the *idea* of the other includes necessity of being. Whether contingent trees or necessary deity we are here only dealing with idea.

Shedd does not give up easily: "If the idea of a thing implies that it must exist, it does follow from the idea that the thing does exist."[26] Why? The only thing that follows from an idea is that, if we have an idea of a contingent being and if it exists, it will exist contingently; if we have an idea of a necessary being and if it exists, it will exist necessarily.

Gaunilo, arguing against Anselm, argued that the idea of the "lost island" does not imply that there is such a thing. Anselm replied that, if Gaunilo will show that the idea of the "lost island" implies its *necessary* existence, he (Anselm) would find the island for him, and guarantee that it shall never be a "lost island" again.[27] Of course, an *idea* of a lost island does not *imply* its existence. Neither does the *idea* of a necessary being imply its existence (outside the idea).

"We are so accustomed in the case of finite beings and things to abstract necessity of existence from them, that we unthinkingly transfer this to God."[28] This is irrelevant. The idea of God indisputably includes the idea of necessity of being just as the idea of contingent things does not. But what we are debating is not the meaning of ideas but their existence in reality. Because the idea of God includes necessary existence does not prove necessary existence in reality.

"Because we can logically conceive of the non-existence of the finite, we suppose that we can of the infinite."[29] This is the cogent form of the argument, but neither Anselm nor Shedd is making it, except implicitly here (where it is wrongly thought to be synonymous with the argument stated everywhere else). It is one thing to argue that we cannot conceive of the nonexistence of infinite being; it is another to say that perfect being exists because we have an idea of it. It exists not because we have an idea of it, but because we *cannot not* have an idea of it. It is impossible to think of the nonexistence of infinite being because we cannot think of pure nonbeing or nothing. Therefore, we can only think of being, limited by nothing. *Infinite being must exist because we cannot conceive of its not existing.*

CHAPTER 7

The Cosmological and Teleological Arguments

WE ARE SURROUNDED BY things which exhibit change. We see the process of generation and decay, of growth and deterioration, of rusting and aging. We change from wakefulness to sleep and from health to sickness and back to health. The stock market snorts like a bull as the Dow Jones skyrockets, then growls like a bear when the index plummets. For all these changes we seek a cause, an explanation for the patterns of motion we call change. There is no science, no academic discipline including that of linguistic analysis which is not heavily involved with causal thinking. We know that there are causes for those changes, else we would not bother to ask *why* they change. We are concerned to locate and isolate these causes asking why the fire? Why the earthquake? Why the sickness? We may not always discover the answer but we know there is an answer. This chapter deals with this question of cause. We will look first at cause in general, before examining in detail two causal arguments for the existence of God— cosmological and teleological.

IN DEFENSE OF CAUSE

Suppose it was a match that caused the fire. We ask who or what struck the match. If we find the culprit, we ask him why, or what caused him to light the match. If it was a desire to collect insurance money, we inquire as to the cause of the desire. So it goes, *ad infinitum,* or not quite, for it cannot end in an infinite series or we would never have an answer, being left with the problem of causeless effect compounded infinitely. It is *ad infinitum,* however, in the sense of *to* the *infinite*. Our searching minds are restless until they find their rest in Him who needs no antecedent cause because He has the power of being within Himself.

The very exercise of causal thinking has been called into question, begging the question while asking the question. The first question we ask of those who attack causality is Why? What is the reason for or the cause of the attack on cause? There must be a cause for the denial of cause. The attack on cause is self-refuting, for there must be a cause for the attack. Suppose someone says there is no cause for the attack on cause. That might satisfy us because it "explains" why there need be no cause for the attack on cause. But then we must ask, what caused our satisfaction with no cause? Is the cause of the satisfaction with the causeless attack on cause that there is no such thing as cause? Here causelessness is the cause of our being satisfied with causelessness. So even causelessness is enlisted in the service of cause. Why can we not escape cause? Because.

Some have argued that there is no cause because we cannot perceive cause, only sequence or the customary relationship of contiguous events. Agnosticism of perception becomes skepticism of causality. To be sure, the perception of actual and ultimate causality has been a thorny philosophical problem for centuries. Aristotle wrestled with the complex problem of causality, distinguishing sharply among various kinds of causes—material, efficient, formal, final. The problem of perception of causes within the causal nexus reached its peak in the modern era, the debate ranging from the interactionism of Descartes to the occasionalism of Malebranche and Geulincx to the theory of preestablished harmony of the monadic philosophy of Leibniz to the substance theory of Spinoza. The issue of perception of causes informed British empiricism's concern with the primary and secondary qualities of Locke, the *esse est percipi* of Berkeley, and the radical skepticism of David Hume. Hume leaves us with no cause, only sequence.

To be sure, we cannot penetrate the causal nexus via direct or immediate perception. But there is a reason (cause) for that: the cause is not visible. It is as simple as that. Can we conclude that something has no cause because the cause is not visible? How visible is gravity? How visible is the powerful force of desire, of love, of virtue? In these invisible areas, we know cause from effects which by definition are caused.

The definition of causality is important. Some use the term as though it meant that *everything* must have an antecedent cause. Such a definition is defective for more than one reason. If everything or everyone must have an antecedent cause then God would require an antecedent cause. If God has an antecedent cause then He is no longer God, but a creature. Secondly, to argue that everything, including God, must have an antecedent cause is to argue gratuitously. The idea of an uncaused, self-existent being violates no formal law of reason. There is nothing impossible about a necessary, eternal being who has the power of existence within Himself. As long as self-existence is a formal possibility we cannot properly conclude that everything must have an antecedent cause.

It is also possible to define causality by saying that every *effect* must have an antecedent cause. Here causality is analytically true; it is true by definition. However, the truth or reality of something cannot be defined into existence. Causality as a formal principle must be presupposed or assumed. As a material force it must rely on the prior evidence of the reality of contingent beings or actions. What remains to be proven is that there are such things as effects. The tautological definition has analytical import but no necessary existential import unless or until we first establish that there are effects, actions, events, or things that are contingent, derived, subject to change or motion. Just as the term *husband* contains the notion of married man within it, so does the term *effect* contain within it the notion of antecedent cause. So we say not that everything has an antecedent cause but that every *effect* has an antecedent cause. If the sequence we observe involves effects (characteristics of contingent beings), then we may properly search for their antecedent causes. It is only in the case of necessary being, a being who is not an effect, that the search for antecedent causality may and must cease.

Another reason that cause cannot be denied in the name of sequence is that *constant sequence* is, in terms of customary usage of words, only another name for cause. Whenever A comes into contact with B, B moves. We are here saying nothing different than if we said that A causes B to move, only the language is different. We cannot take a picture of cause. One sees only the antecedent and the consequent. The effect is seen in the other object. The consequent in B, the motion of B, is what follows in sequence with A. If A is there, B moves. If A is not in contact with B, B either does not move or it does not move at that time or in that way.

This is the reason that Jonathan Edwards's definition of cause as antecedent is very precisely articulated: "Any antecedent, either natural or moral, positive or negative, on which an event, either a thing, or the manner and circumstance of a thing, so depends, that it is the ground and reason either in whole or in part, why it is, rather than not; or why it is as it is, rather than otherwise."[1]

But what about the rooster who crowed and the sun came up? Can we say that the rooster caused the sun to come up? That looks suspiciously like a coincidence rather than antecedent/consequence sequence. We do not have to wait until the rooster gets a sore throat. We can remove the rooster tomorrow morning to see whether the sun comes up notwithstanding. We then see that the antecedent of *that* consequent was not the rooster's crowing. If it had been, the morning that rooster did not crow the world would have collapsed because nothing comes to be without some cause—its own particular antecedent.

What about indeterminacy? That theory in physics would say that some things move without cause or determination. One does not have to be a physicist to recognize irrationality when he hears it. How can a physicist or nonphysicist say that any theory which says that a thing moves without being caused to move is irrational? Because the physicist or nonphysicist is immediately going to ask, "Why do these things, unlike everything else in the universe, move without being caused?" The physicists themselves seem divided on the question. Some, like Nils Bohr, argue that the explanation is ontological (in the nature of things) while others, like Max Planck, argue that the explanation is epistemological—a knowing problem. Planck seems right to lay people—this unpredictable electronic quantum movement is inexplicable *to us* at least, at this time, rather than unknowable in its nature. This could only mean that God made it with such a nature that certain of its movements are beyond finite human minds—not necessarily beyond future finite computers and certainly not beyond infinite understanding.

There must be something very different about these things or something undetectable about their causes. If the explanation is in the things themselves, then they are self-moved, which means simply that what causes them to move is something within them (rather than without them) and not a no-cause. If it is their very own nature not to require any cause at all, they would have to be God. Being things that come into being and change and go out of being, they cannot be God. Therefore, to be moved by a cause within them must be the way

God has made these things (unlike other creatures which are moved from without or at least by something other than themselves—*ab alio*).

The other explanation would be that their cause is undetectable. An undetectable cause and a no-cause are vastly different things. If this is the case, then this theory should not be called indeterminacy but indeterminableness-of-the-cause-for-the-time-being. No one would want to say that that which is undetermined now will always remain undetermined. Only omniscience could say that. The leap from un-determinableness-of-the-cause-for-the-time-being to indeterminacy is gratuitous at best and arrogant at worst. In fact, it assumes omniscience. The presumption of no-cause rests on the presumption of exhaustive knowledge of all causes, visible and invisible. The conclusion is fatal to all science for it vitiates the scientific method on two fronts. The scientific method is established on the basis of both induction and deduction. The inductive arm furnishes the scientist with the lever of empirical research including observation and experimentation. The built-in limit to all empirical induction is the limit of finitude. We never enjoy, on an inductive basis an infinite perspective. No experiment is done *sub specie aeternitatis*. Our finite research is never exhaustive because we are finite. To jump from saying we do not know the cause for the apparently random behavior of subatomic particles to saying there is *no* cause for their behavior, is to jump from the finite to the infinite. Here we see real quantum motion—in the gratuitous leap of the intellect from the finite to the infinite, doing radical violence to the limits of induction.

The second arm of the scientific method is equally violated. To argue that the event has no cause is to wipe out deduction by making a statement which is formally invalid, being unambiguously and analytically false. If the behavior is indeed an effect, then deductive logic requires that, by definition, it must have a cause. If it has no cause, it can hardly be classified as an effect. The judicious scientist makes no such absurd inferences from the data. He says instead, "We do not know why the particles behave as they do. At present they are an anomaly to our working paradigms." They may require further investigation or even modifications in our paradigm, but not the wholesale repudiation of induction and deduction which is exactly what full indeterminacy would require. That conclusion would spell the end of science.

If there were an ultimate indeterminism, it would implicitly deny causality anywhere in the universe. Thus, it would deny God's omnipotence, omniscience, providence and, by implication, all His attributes.

THE COSMOLOGICAL ARGUMENT

The world is not only being, but *orderly* being, a cosmos. If so, its Author must be an orderly mind. Order sometimes seems to happen by chance, but it would not happen all the time by chance (or really any of the time, as we will see when we discuss teleology), for then it would not be a chance happening but an ordered one. The chance would be taken out of chance. Regular order is the order of the day and the years and the ages in the universe.

All this seems self-evident, yet there are those who deny it. How do orderly human minds come to deny an orderly divine mind? By saying that order is subjective, someone's order is someone else's disorder. So, there is nothing objective about order; order is in the eye of the beholder, imposed on the external world by the perceiving subject.

The orderly mind can easily see the answer to this would-be argument. However subjective someone's order may be, it is order nonetheless, for that person is not denying order, but simply seeing order where someone else may not see it. Mrs. Jones has her own system of order. It is not her husband's, and he cannot decipher it until she explains it. Then he does see it and sees that she is a very orderly person. Do we call that order subjective? Yes, it is her subjective system, known only to her (the subject) at first. But when explained, it is seen as orderly to her husband also and to anyone else to whom it is explained. So it is quite objective order, but unperceived at first by others. It is a kind of cryptogram. When decoded it is the essence of order.

We know of a professor whose study was apparently total confusion. But when a student asked the professor for his paper, the professor went immediately to one chaotic pile and, three papers up from the bottom, extracted the student's paper. That was a very orderly chaos.

What we are saying is that subjective order is objective order. There is method in madness. The method is real; the madness is on the surface. If each person has his own system of order, that means that each person has an orderly mind and proves it by his own system, though he may be the only one who at first understands it. Such elements of order are present even within the "madness" of the clinically insane.

If one said of the recognized order in the cosmos that it is only each individual's sense of order, so far from that disproving order it would prove it. Furthermore, in the case of the cosmos just about every creature understands its code. Nature is no cryptogram but is patent and shining. Indeed, the word *cosmos* is from the Greek word meaning order.

We say that the cosmos, which almost all of us recognize, argues a Cosmic Mind, which all of us should acknowledge. If we do not, it must be for some reason other than lack of orderliness. If we refuse to see order where it exists, it must be order which is blinding us. How so? It will turn out that a priori we do not believe that there is a Cosmic Mind. Since our minds are orderly (logical) we will reason that, if there is no Cosmic Mind, there cannot be evidence of a Cosmic Mind. Consequently, because of our a priori, we will not allow ourselves to see a posteriori evidence of an orderly cosmos. None are so blind as those who will not see. If it were not for our inescapable order (which of course, did not originate with us), we would admit order. So, it takes order to deny order. In other words, we prove order when we see it and we prove order when we do not see it. (We will not argue this point here, not because it does not require it, but because it is better considered under the teleological argument for God. Teleology, or the study of purpose, involves order plus. It finds order with a purpose. Conceivably, there could be order without purpose; but purpose without order is clearly inconceivable.)

The cosmological argument has appeared in various formulations. We shall endeavor to present it in its most basic form. The simplest version argues that if something exists now, something exists necessarily; if anything is, something must have the power of being within itself. The argument does not require a universe full of contingent realities for its power. One datum is sufficient to prove its point; a single molecule, atom, or subatomic particle is enough to prove the existence of God. If we discover one molecule, we are faced with four possible explanations or sufficient reasons for the molecule. The molecule is possibly:

1. an illusion
2. self-created
3. self-existent
4. created ultimately by something which is self-existent

Illusion

The first option (illusion) poses a potential threat to the cosmological argument. If the molecule is an illusion and all other realities are equally illusory, then nothing exists. The notion that illusion exists is problematic on two counts. If all is illusion, then we must account for the illusion. What is the cause of the illusion? Who is having the illusion? As doubt requires a doubter, so the illusion requires someone or something to suffer the illusion. If someone or something suffers the illusion of the molecule, then we replace the molecule with the illusioned one as the starting point of the argument. If all we have is an illusion, then we must ask if the illusion is self-created, self-existent, or created ultimately by something which is self-existent.

The problem is similar to that faced by the Christian Scientist who, denying the reality of evil, must deal with the debater who argues for the reality of evil. Is the argument for evil a good argument or a bad argument? If it is a good argument, the case for the reality of evil is established. If it is a bad argument, then the badness of the argument proves the reality of evil. Therefore, the Christian Scientist must consign all arguments against his position into the category of illusion. He must live in a world where all arguments are sound or his case perishes.

The second problem with the conclusion that nothing but illusion exists is the utter inconceivableness of it. We have already established the impossibility of thinking of nothing, the necessity of thinking in terms of being instead of nonbeing. We *must* conclude that something, if only the illusion, exists. We then know that something exists necessarily. Unless, of course, we can demonstrate that that which exists is self-created.

Self-created

But to argue that something is self-created requires that we negotiate two primary laws of epistemology: the law of noncontradiction and the law of causality. (We have noted that virtually every "refutation" of the cosmological argument involves explicit or implicit denial of one or both of these laws.) The notion of self-creation violates the law of causality by postulating an effect without an antecedent cause. The effect is not eternal; it is contingent, dependent, and derived from nothing. In all ways it is an effect, yet it dangles there without a cause.

As already noted, the concept of a causeless effect is analytically falsified because the word *effect* by definition carries the notion of "caused by an antecedent." It suffers all the grievances of the indeterminacy problem.

The law of noncontradiction is also demolished by the concept of self-creation. For something to create itself, it must exercise causal power on itself before it exists. It must be before it is. To be before it is, it must be and not be at the same time and in the same relationship. It must be A and be -A at the same time and in the same relationship which violates the law of noncontradiction. Even Hamlet saw the absurdity of postulating a *tertium quid* in this instance.

Are we here establishing straw men or caricatures of refutations of the cosmological argument? Does anyone ever seriously argue for self-creation? Not only do some so argue, but, we maintain, most do so argue who reject the cosmological argument. French Encyclopediasts, for example, most notably Diderot and D'Holbach, advanced the "enlightened" concept of spontaneous generation for the creation of the world.[2] The concept of spontaneous generation is propositionally equivalent to the concept of self-creation. To generate something from nothing either spontaneously or gradually requires the same feat of self-creation. We have something either rapidly or slowly generating itself before it is.

What of those who argue not for spontaneous creation but for chance creation? Again, the word *chance* functions in such schemas as a propositional equivalent to self-creation. The concept of creation "by chance" is nothing more and nothing less than creation by nothing, or self-creation.

Sophisticated arguments of chance creation have been formulated which dazzle our mathematical comprehension. Formulas with exotic numeric categories overwhelm us. We are told that the probability quotient of chance creation is some astronomical ratio like a one perched precariously over a rather large bunch of zeroes. The math formula has been used invalidly by both sides of the dispute. We have read eager apologists who delight in such long odds saying the formula makes the idea of a chance creation *virtually* impossible. That is obviously not so. If there is but one chance, then it is not virtually or actually impossible. Indeed, if there is one chance in eternity for a chance creation, eternity virtually guarantees that the chance will pop up. It is not as if the opportunity for chance creation occurs but once in a cosmic lottery game—the lottery wheel is spinning through eternity. Sooner or later, presumably later, the one chance will hit the cosmic jackpot.

Both sides appeal to the formula as if it supported either a low chance creation by chance or a high chance creation by chance. The fact is, however, we have a no-chance chance creation. We must erase the "1" which appears above the line of the "1" followed by a large number of zeroes. What are the real chances of a universe created by chance? Not a chance. Chance is incapable of creating a single molecule, let alone an entire universe. Why not? Chance is *no thing*. It is not an entity. It has no being, no power, no force. It can effect nothing for it has no causal power within it, it has no *it*ness to be within. Chance is *nomina* not *res:* it is a word which describes mathematical possibilities which, by a curious slip of the fallacy of ambiguity, slips into discussion as if it were a real entity with real power, indeed, supreme power, the power of creativity. To say the universe is created by chance is to say the universe is created by nothing, another version of self-creation.

Self-existent

If we eliminate option 1 (illusion) and option 2 (self-creation), we are left with a self-existent molecule or collection of molecules or a molecule ultimately caused by something which is self-existent. By eliminating the first two options by formal reasoning, indeed, by irresistible logic, we have already established the primary assertion: if something exists now, something exists necessarily.

Some will demur at this point and say, "So what? Why can we not assign this self-existent something to the world itself or some remote part of the world? Or why must we limit the options to four? What about the possible infinite regress where we have an infinite series of finite causes such as Bertrand Russell suggested? Or a bipolar God who oscillates between being and becoming as the process philosophers advocate? Why not a 'finite God'?"

Before facing these classic objections to the cosmological argument, let us first reiterate what we have already demonstrated: Something exists necessarily. Something has the power of being within itself and is self-existent. The only significant question left for us is what or who is this self-existent eternal something? And is this self-existent eternal something transcendent?

If we discover that it is the molecule which is self-existent, eternal, and is that which exists necessarily, we can shout with Archimedes, "Eureka!" We have found it! Now we can take off our shoes in the presence of this divine molecule which has the power of being, to whom we are indebted for our own creaturely existence, and worship it without fear of idolatry. At the feet of this molecule we will be kneeling not before a finite creature but before the transcendent, infinite and eternal Creator. How so? How did we move so quickly from a self-existent molecule to a transcendent God? If it is a molecule or collection of molecules found in this world, it is therefore immanent and not transcendent. Is this not indisputably so? No, it is not indisputably so. It is indisputably *not* so. If the molecule is self-existent, it is *therefore* transcendent. How so? The confusion arises from our thinking of transcendence in spatial or geographical terms. The meaning of transcendence, however, has an *ontological* rather than a *geographical* reference. The "space" or "distance" between Creator and creature, between transcendence and immanence is one of ontic dimensions not linear dimensions. Creatureliness is defined by contingency not locality. A creature by definition is something created. It lacks the *sine qua non* of the Creator, namely the power of self-existence. If one molecule or a group of molecules possesses what all other creaturely (dependent, derived, contingent) molecules lack, then that molecule or group of molecules *transcends* the others ontologically. It is "other" by virtue of its very being. Those who seek God in some undiscovered nook or cranny "within" the universe are in fact searching for something "outside" the universe in an ontological sense.

What about Russell's infinite regress of the infinite series of finite causes (which, though Russell insisted he could conceive of it, Frederick Copleston dismissed as being "inconceivable")? Copleston:

> My point is that what we call the world is intrinsically unintelligible, apart from the existence of God. You see, I don't believe that the infinity of the series of events—I mean a horizontal series, so to speak—if such an infinity could be proved, would be in the slightest degree relevant to the situation. If you add up chocolates you get chocolates after all and not a sheep. If you add up chocolates to infinity, you presumably get an infinite number of chocolates. So if you add up contingent beings to infinity, you still get contingent beings, not a necessary being. An infinite series of contingent beings will be, to my way of thinking, as unable to cause itself as one contingent being.[3]

Copleston and other cosmologists allow for an infinite series in the abstract, such as in the case of a series of whole numbers. What is disallowed is an infinite series of finite or *contingent* beings. Russell's reply is interesting:

> I don't want to seem arrogant, but it does seem to me that I can conceive things that you say the human mind can't conceive. As for things not having a cause, the physicists assure us that individual quantum transitions in atoms have no cause. . . . Physicists' minds can conceive it.[4]

Here Russell argues that he can conceive what others cannot and appeals to indeterminacy and the ability of physicists to conceive of an uncaused effect to validate his claim. Copleston did not say, however, that no one can *say* that they conceive of the inconceivable or *say* that they conceive of a causeless effect. People say all sorts of irrational things, their very irrationality made evident by the law of contradiction they are violating when they say it. Neither Russell, nor any of his physicist allies, ever presented an intelligible proposition about his infinite series of contingent beings or his uncaused effect. He made no such intelligible propositions precisely because none can be made.

We can look at the infinite series question two ways. From one perspective, we see the *series* possessing the power of being and self-existence so that the *series* becomes our transcendent molecule. From another perspective, we see the infinite series of finite causes merely compounding the problem of self-creative infinity making us guilty of not one violation of the law of contradiction but of an infinite number of violations, as nowhere is there to be found the power of being within the causal chain. Here is the infinite absurdity. Thus, the infinite regress is not a fifth option but may be subsumed either under option 3 or option 2.

What about the bipolar God who oscillates between being and becoming, between the infinite and the finite? The same problem which is presented by the infinite regress is contained within the oscillating "God." When the mutation within God occurs by which God moves from the pole of being to the pole of becoming, does being cease to be? Can pure becoming exist by itself or must it suffer the fate of Aristotle's pure potentiality which is potentially everything and actually nothing? If some element of being remains on the becoming side of the polar continuum, then that being which remains constant and consistently self-existent would constantly and consistently continue to transcend the finite "becoming" pole and could, indeed *must,* be consistently and constantly distinguished from the finite elements on-tologically. If the entire continuum is viewed as "God," including a pole of pure becoming, we would be left with a God who at one pole is self-existent and at the other pole is self-created. But what is here "self-created" in God is nothing. The becoming pole is not a self-created something but a self-created nothing which is an analytical nonsense statement. Again, depending upon how we understand it, the bi-polar "God" is not necessarily presenting us with a new option. It might be subsumed as either a variation of option 2 (self-creation) or option 3 (self-existing "molecule"). There can be no "finite" God, for the finite dimension within God must always be ontologically distinguished from the infinite dimension upon which all that is finite depends for its existence and which ontologically transcends the finite. In the final analysis a finite God is as linguistically meaningful as a four-sided triangle or square circle.

Created by Something Self-existent

The fourth option is that our molecule is created by something that is self-existent, eternal, and transcendent, which we call God. God alone has the power of being within Himself. He alone has ultimate causal power. Without something or someone who has the power of being intrinsically, we are irrefutably left with some type of notion of self-creation which, as we have seen, is an analytically false concept. The notion of self-creation is manifestly irrational as it blatantly violates the law of noncontradiction. We have an either/or situation. Either we must postulate necessary, self-existent being, or we must flee to the absurdity of self-creation, committing intellectual and scientific suicide. The law remains intact, *ex nihilo nihil fit:* out of nothing, nothing comes.

But does not Christianity assert a doctrine of *ex nihilo* creation? Yes, in a certain sense. The great difference between the Christian concept of creation and opposing views is at the point of self-creation. Within the concept of self-creation is the idea that once there was nothing—pure nonbeing (which, to labor the point, is unthinkable), and then, "poof," there was something, like the rabbit out of the magician's hat. Only what happens is more stupendous than the feats of prestidigitation. In this magic show the rabbit comes from nothing by himself. There is no magician to bring him forth, no hat out of which to pull him, and no concealed rabbit or even partially becoming rabbit who emerges. There is nothing. Pure potentiality. Absolute nothingness. The "Genesis 1:1" of self-creation would read: "In the beginning nothing created the heavens and the earth." There is no sufficient cause for the rabbit, no efficient cause, no material cause, no instrumental cause, no formal cause, and no final cause. We have the pure effect with no cause.

The Christian view is not without its difficulties. It remains a mystery how a self-existent eternal being actually does His work of creation. The *ex nihilo* is limited in scope, however. It has primary reference to the fact that God did not use some pre-existent, external matter out of which he fashioned a world as a sculptor fashions a statue out of a mass of stone. But there is nothing analytically problematic about the notion of a self-existing eternal being. Far from falsifying the concept, logic demands it. Christianity does have a sufficient cause, an efficient cause, a formal cause and a final cause for the effect of this world of molecules.

Before we leave this subject we may note that William Rowe, in his recent analysis of the cosmological argument, comes to a conclusion that would satisfy most contemporary traditional apologists, though the authors of this book would not be among them. He concludes that the theist may claim that the cosmological argument "shows the reasonableness of belief in God, even though it does not demonstrate the existence of God."[5] More specifically, Rowe says, this argument

> makes it reasonable to believe, that a self-existent being would have some of the features the theistic God has in an infinite degree, but fails to show or make it reasonable to believe that the self-existent being has these features in an *infinite* degree.[6]

This would satisfy many of our fellow traditionalists, for they themselves no longer believe that the theistic "proofs" prove. They tend to settle for smaller mercies than Rowe offers. They see the theistic arguments as sufficiently feasible as to make theistic faith intellectually respectable. Rowe finds the cosmological argument feasible enough to make theistic faith "reasonable." At bottom, though, Rowe and some traditional apologists are saying essentially the same thing. The theistic proofs do not prove, but they are not so thoroughly refuted that they are unable to retain any feasibility or suggestiveness.

But if proofs do not prove, it is unreasonable to believe them as arguments. To do so is to say with the mind, that they do not prove and with the will, that they do prove. This is what we usually call fideism rather than rationality. If someone says that it is reasonable to believe what cannot be disproven, that may be argued; but it is *another* argument, another would-be proof, rather than the one rejected.

Having rejected Rowe's well-intentioned apologetic olive branch, we ask what makes him think the cosmological argument does not prove God to be the Creator. He grants that it proves "a self-existent being who would have some of the features the theistic God has in an infinite degree, but fails to show . . . that the self-existent being has these features in an *infinite* degree."

We maintain otherwise. The self-existent being that the cosmological argument does "show," *must* have *all* attributes in the infinite degree. If this being is self-sufficient, He exists of Himself alone and can be dependent on no other. He is unlimited or infinite in His independence. There is nothing to limit His independence. If there were anything else, it would be either dependent on Him or another independent self-sufficient being. But the cosmological argument shows that there can only be one self-existent source of the one cosmos. So if there were "another," it would not be another but the same. Any dependent beings would not be self-existent and eternal but must have been produced by this one self-existent being. So this being must be infinite and must be one. He must necessarily and eternally exist because we cannot think of His not existing. He is personal because He is the pervasive cause of all things including the purpose and the personal. So the self-existent being of the cosmological argument must be one, powerful, independent, self-existent, eternal, wise, holy being that is God.

We challenge the contention that the cosmological argument "fails to show or make it reasonable to believe that the self-existent being has these features in an infinite degree." An infinite being has all excellences in the infinite degree; otherwise He would not be infinite. So, if this is the only reason to question the sufficiency of this argument, we think that Rowe has understated his own case.

THE TELEOLOGICAL ARGUMENT

William James defines the human being as a "fighter for ends." The robin is also a fighter for ends (worms). The cat is a fighter for ends (the robin). The universe is teeming with fighters for ends. Could purposive creatures be from a being without purpose? Could there be all these fighters for ends and not be a Fighter for Ends? To put the question another way: Could the source of all beings purposelessly populate the cosmos with purpose-seekers? In this section on the teleological argument, we will examine two objections to it: (1) that it does not prove an infinite purposer, and (2) purpose cannot exist in the presence of nonpurposive or dysteleological events.

It takes no great humility to admit that we could not think of purposes of which ultimate being could not think. How then could our minds entertain goals if ultimate being cannot? Our being capable of purpose does not *prove* that ultimate being is purposive, but it is unthinkable that the creature could develop something of which the Creator is not capable.

Creatures, as we have seen, can causally argue to orderliness and structure in the Creator. The question is, Did Being unintentionally make things which revealed Himself? Being omniscient, He would have at least foreseen it. If He did not want it to happen, He could have prevented it. Therefore, He must have wanted it to happen. That is, He intended or purposed it. Since He has willed everything to come to pass that comes to pass (or it would never have come to pass), He must have purposively ordained everything to come to pass. He not only purposed the purposive but everything, whether it has a purpose in itself or not.

Kant, though ultimately critical of the teleological argument, reserved his most laudatory comments for it:

> This present world presents to us so immeasurable a stage of variety, order, fitness, and beauty, whether we follow it up in the infinity of space or in its unlimited division, that even with the little knowledge which our poor understanding has been able to gather, all language, with regard to so many and inconceivable wonders, loses its vigour, all numbers their power of measuring, and all our thoughts their necessary determination; so that our judgment of the whole is lost in a speechless, but all the more eloquent astonishment. Everywhere we see a chain of causes and effects, of means and ends, of order in birth and death, and as nothing has entered by itself into the state in which we find it, all points to another thing as its cause. As that cause necessitates the same further enquiry, the whole universe would thus be lost in the abyss of nothing, unless we admitted something which, existing by itself, original and independent, outside the chain of infinite contingencies, should support it, and, as the cause of its origin,

secure to it at the same time its permanence. . . . This proof will always deserve to be treated with respect. It is the oldest, the clearest, and most in conformity with human reason. . . . This knowledge reacts again on its cause, namely, the transcendental idea, and thus increases the belief in a supreme Author to an irresistible conviction.[7]

In spite of the "irresistible" character of the teleological argument, Kant managed to find a way to resist the irresistible, arguing that in the final analysis the teleological argument rested on the ontological argument for its cogency. If that is so, and if we have overcome Kant's objections to the ontological argument, then we would expect him to embrace joyfully the teleological argument which he found so attractive.

Kant and others talk of the dysteleological or nonpurposive in the universe. The so-called dysteleological must refer to what we do not see. We do not see the purpose of many things. Some things even *seem* to us to be antipurposive or dysteleological. But that, of course, does not prove that they are dysteleological. Since we are not omniscient beings, many things may happen which we do not even know, much less understand. But nothing happens which ultimate being does not understand and permit and therefore purpose. Consequently, that which appears to us dysteleological is teleological in fact. We do not know what the particular purpose is. But we do know that there is a purpose, for God intended whatever He permits to be, else He would not have permitted it.

We have seen that much of contemporary evangelical apologetics retains the traditional theistic proofs but in a reserved and qualified way. They are accepted as reasonable but not compelling, as persuasive but not demonstrative, as valuable but not conclusive, as evidence but not proof. Norman Geisler, for example, has so weakened the teleological argument that for all practical purposes he has virtually given it up. Though he considers himself a mild proponent of it, he ends where Kant and Jung end. He appreciates its suggestive power and even modestly claims its probability, but does not address Kant's contention that even if it were cogent it would prove merely a great architect.[8] If the argument proves only a great architect, it does not prove God who is not merely a great architect but is the infinite source of all things. Though Geisler and others appreciate the argument, they, like Kant, reject it as a proof or demonstration of the existence of a purposive, divine being.

A proof must demonstrate that something is really true. If it does not demonstrate something to be true, then it is not a proof and ought not to be referred to as such. J. Oliver Buswell is more blunt, admitting virtually that these things do not prove. Yet he thinks that they are as tenable, and more tenable, than other options. We do not think such an approach is valid, but it is, at least, a frank confrontation with the matter. It is not, in any way, urging the proofs but simply saying that teleology is no more vulnerable than other options and indeed less vulnerable. Therefore, it is acceptable, in a sense, as the lesser of various theoretical inadequacies. There is a very great difference between allowing a person a respectable, intellectual possibility of believing something that does not have compelling evidence, and presenting him with something which, if an informed and honest person, he must accept, there being no legitimate, rational alternative. These are two entirely different approaches and they ought not to be confused.

This must be said in our day, when many people are trying to preserve some semblance of maintaining the theistic argument while, as a matter of fact, they are gutting it.

It is to presuppositionalism's credit that it does not claim evidential power for the theistic proofs and insists, precisely for that reason, that we must begin on another tack. As we will endeavor to show in part 3, they are by no means consistent with that, but they at least say at times, loudly and clearly, that the theistic argument is no argument, the theistic proofs are not proofs.

Still others in the classical tradition brilliantly present the case for Christianity as "suggestive" but not "compelling." John W. Montgomery, Francis Schaeffer, and Clark Pinnock are instances of this very modern, very sophisticated, form of an essentially classical position.

Montgomery writes that even the proven Resurrection does not "force" faith because such force is against the very nature of Christianity. It is designed only to persuade persons to experiment with Christ.[9] Clark Pinnock also argues: "The intent of Christian apologetics and evidences is not to coerce people to accept the Christian faith, but to make it possible for them to do so intelligently."[10] Even Francis Schaeffer seems to think it is an apologetic sin to be demonstrative. His running criticism of Aquinas, especially in *Escape From Reason,* though his own reasoning is not altogether different, can only be explained this way.

Why the fear of coercion? Surely one need not suppose any apologist is advocating physical force to compel agreement. We are not in the age of the Inquisition. What objection is there against logical compulsion? What is logic if it is not compelling? If the case for Christianity is merely suggestive, or merely makes consideration feasible or intelligible or respectable, why should anyone convert? Someone may conceivably have good and sufficient reasons for not doing the respectable, the feasible, and the intelligible. If so, it may be feasible, respectable and intelligible not to convert. This is not what these theists want to happen. Their own arguments are too strong to let it happen reasonably. In the main, their case for Christianity is better than their own estimate of it.

Montgomery thinks that the purpose of Christian apologetics is to show unbelievers the advisability of experimenting with John 7:17 (RSV), "If any man's will is to do his will, he shall know whether the teaching is from God or whether I am speaking on my own authority."[11] But this is not the way Christ intended this statement: First, this cannot be an invitation to an unbeliever to experiment because it is morally impossible for an unbeliever to do the will of God. To do God's will one must begin by believing in Him and repenting of one's sins which, *ex hypothesi,* an unbeliever will not do. An experimenting unbeliever is a contradiction in terms. The person who says, "I believe, help thou mine unbelief," is essentially a believer, not an experimenter. Second, John 7:17 states the inner certainty given to the one who believes, that is, the one who wills to do God's will. Third, the statement is a rebuke to unbelief showing that unbelief is based not on sharp thinking but wicked living (not doing God's will.) Those who do God's will know the truth. Those who do not know truth do not do God's will. "Everyone who does evil hates the light, and does not come to the light, lest his deeds should be exposed" (John 3:20 NASB). "So they are without excuse; for although they knew God they did not honor him as God or give thanks to him, but they became futile in their thinking and their senseless minds were darkened" (Rom. 1:20–21 RSV). So far from this text being an invitation to unbelievers to experiment, it is a rebuke to them that their not doing God's will is the source of their blind unbelief.

We believe that what has happened here is what often happens with modern scholars who remain conservative in spite of their education to the contrary. They are sufficiently chastened in the process that though they are unrepentantly conservative they are not altogether unafraid. After all, to be told with great confidence by many learned men for many years that such and such notions are no longer believed (perhaps have not been believed for a hundred or two hundred years) makes it a little difficult for such Evangelicals to say, without hedging their bets just a little, that they do still believe them. But we must not take these learned cautions too seriously. At most they are the static through which the message, nevertheless, comes.

The apologetic message comes through but it is rather sophisticated and understated. Instead of strongly stressing theistic proofs these Evangelicals almost gloss over them in their eagerness to come to biblical data. But theistic proof is there. Schaeffer does not like Aquinas's five ways, but he has his own way of saying something like it. Much may be added to logic but we cannot give up logic. An important theme of Schaeffer's *Escape From Reason* is that Christianity may be more than rational but certainly it is not less.

In 1969 Montgomery delivered a lecture at DePaul University entitled "Is Man his Own God?" He presented four arguments which he believed showed the existence of a God other than ourselves. The first was a variation of Copleston's: there must be a being necessary in itself. Appealing to the concept of entropy, Montgomery argued that since the world is running down it cannot be eternal. He thinks this proves the necessity of an eternal being without gratuitously assuming a cause-and-effect universe which is supposed to violate the indeterminacy principle of modern physics. The second argument is based on God and personhood. Montgomery contends that self-transcendence is assumed by every experimenter and that this, in turn, assumes, in order to be reasonable, an ultimate transcendence. Transcendence involves freedom and freedom involves selfhood. Thus the existence of finite and infinite selves are proven. In the third argument, Montgomery sought to prove from the resurrection of Christ the efficacy of His death. Finally, Montgomery appealed to human experience of guilt that assumes one who can forgive.

One can recognize in this modern form of the classic theistic argument genuflections to the contemporary thought that is supposed to have made such classic arguments untenable. In our opinion, these arguments are suggestive rather than tight. As formulated, not one (except Copleston's which is bypassed) would endure close analysis to which we will not here subject them. We are merely noting, in passing, how modern evangelical scholars have been affected by contemporary antitheistic thought. Their heads are bloody, but *not* unbowed, though not completely bowed.

In his *Set Forth Your Case* (1967), Clark Pinnock effectively shows the futility of the attacks on theism, but his reaffirmation of the theistic arguments is subdued. In the summer of 1971, he wrote an article for *His* magazine, "Naturalism—The Losing Battle." Against naturalism, Pinnock quickly and cleverly cites eight arguments: (1) Thermodynamics (which says the world should be run down by now). (2) Rationality (if this came about from atoms we cannot rely on it and therefore we cannot rely on the notion that it came from atoms). (3) Personal freedom (if everything is determined, and therefore unbelievable, so is determinism). (4) Morality (which we feel deep down). (5) ESP (which is too far out for naturalism). (6) Hope (which is an illusion unless there is a god). (7) Meaning (craving for this cannot be satisfied here, therefore must be satisfied there). (8) Historical Christ (the historical Resurrection shows Him to be divine). But if one sorts out these arguments, he will find, differently but delightfully stated, the old arguments for God called anthropological, teleological, and possibly even the cosmological; though they are not so demonstratively stated, as in the traditional case for Christianity.

But one cannot help asking whether, if Paul had thought this way, he would ever had said (as he did in Romans 1) that they are "inexcusable" who do not worship God. Can a person be called inexcusable who does not accept noncompelling arguments as compelling? Why should they necessarily worship God when there are no arguments that demand that they should do so? On the other hand, if they are inexcusable, as Paul plainly insists that they are, then the apostle must have thought that the visible things *demonstrate* clearly that God is God. There is consequently no excuse—only willful opposition (not rational, but willful)—that accounts for people not worshiping God as God. In short, if nonworshipers of the true God are inexcusable, then they must be resisting irrefutable arguments. If they are not rejecting irrefutable arguments, they cannot really be said to be inexcusable for not accepting them.

A number of arguments have been proposed as evidence that the admission of some purpose in the universe does not require an ultimate purposer behind it.

A Merely Finite Purposer

According to one argument, even if the evidence did indicate that there is a purposer, this would only indicate that there is a *finite* purposer. This, as we have seen, is the contention of Kant[12] and others. His argument is quite plain. We see evidence of finite purpose, or purpose in finite things; therefore, if there is a purposer behind it, he need only be a finite being who is greater than all the other finite beings which presumably come from him, were designed by him, or are directed by him. Purpose and purposer must be of the same essential magnitude. A finite effect presupposes a finite purposer. Kant did not admit even that much, but simply said that *if* there is any acknowledgement of purpose in the world and any inference drawn from that, one cannot get beyond a finite purposer in any case. This would be utterly fatal to the teleological argument—the demonstration of the existence of a purposeful, infinite, eternal, divine being.

But if one said that behind finite, purposeful effects is a finite purposer, that finite purposer would himself (or itself) be another evidence of purpose. That is, if you have behind a finite, teleological event, a finite, teleological cause, then the question immediately becomes, What is the cause of that finite, purposive cause? And so *ad infinitum*. To put it another way, the finite, greater cause would be no ultimate explanation of the finite, lesser event. It would be only an approximate explanation, itself calling for an ultimate explanation. Obviously, that would apply to any other type of finite explanation one might offer. If we are going to admit, as Kant did for the sake of argument, that there are purposive events in the world, and these events require a greater purposive cause, then we cannot stop at that point (as Kant did). That greater purposive cause would itself be still a finite cause and would not explain the finite causes it is supposed to explain without being explained itself. Manifestly, the only place where one can get an ultimate resting point on which to account for finite, teleological effects would be in an infinite, teleological cause. That is what the teleological argument is meant to prove and, indeed, does prove. So, if Kant—or anybody else—will hypothetically admit that there has to be an explanation for these finite, teleological events, he is going to have to admit that that explanation must be an infinite, teleological being whose explanation is in himself and beyond whom we need not go for further explanation.

We anticipate an objection at this point: "What you have done here, is shift from the teleological argument to the cosmological argument. You are arguing from a finite effect to an infinite cause. You are not moving from teleology as such, to an infinite teleological purposer." True. But the teleological is an integral part of the effect which we are considering. Though it is perfectly true that the very existence of an effect requires an ultimate cause (as the cosmological argument maintains), there is more to this effect than just mere undifferentiated effect. Indeed, the teleological character of this effect is itself an effect which needs an adequate explanation. *Mere causality does not account for purposive effect.* There would have to be a purpose as a cause. Consequently, though the teleological is not identical with the cosmological argument, it is inseparable from it.

We must now turn our attention to the question whether the purposeful events which Kant acknowledged do exist in the world are merely hypothetical or whether they are actually compellingly logical. We maintain that the latter is the case. We do not merely gratuitously assume that there is a teleological cause of a teleological event. We say that purpose is built into the nature of the event observed. If something shows in its sheer existence that purpose is in it and is not explicable without it, then there must be some teleological explanation of it. That we find, or at least that we seek for, the cause of this admittedly teleological effect is not an option, but a requirement. Kant, in other words, is not being gratuitous in assuming this. When a person seeks the cause of a purposeful event, he is led, not hypothetically but necessarily, to the conclusion that that purposer is, indeed, an infinite, underived, eternal, purposer who has purpose in Himself and of Himself. We say "Himself" rather than "itself" because purpose, apart from intelligence, and intelligence apart from personality, is inconceivable.

Dysteleology

Let us return to the argument against teleology based on dysteleology—the presence of things in the observable universe which exhibit no purpose or prove the absence of purpose. This argument is palpably false. For even if we granted that there are some things that appear to be non- or even antipurposeful, they still do not provide a basis for concluding that the teleological does not exist. If something is purposive, the fact that something else is not purposive does not prove that the first thing is not purposive. People are normally purposeful beings. On some occasions, however, people seem to operate without any purpose or even antipurposefully. That perplexes us. We wonder why someone has behaved in such an unintelligible manner. But does that mean that all the evidence we have that such a person is, under normal conditions, purposeful does *not* constitute evidence of this person's purposefulness? Because there are some occasions when one seems not to be purposeful, is he not purposeful on other occasions? To raise that question is to answer it. Yet, many give it as a substantial argument against teleology that they see something in the universe that is not teleological. A thousand times a man tells the truth, and once he tells a lie. Is that one lie going to prove that he is not a truth-teller? Specifically, does it prove that the other thousand times he did not tell the truth? Or even if a man tells the truth once and lies a thousand times, do the thousand times prove that he *never* tells the truth?

We can hear the objectors at this point: "All right," say the objectors, "let us apply that question to God. Are you admitting that what God does a thousand times is purposive but one time out of that thousand is not? Would that not be fatal to your argument?" The answer is no and yes respectively. No, we do not believe, for a moment, that the purposive God ever did *anything* unpurposively or antipurposively. Yes, *if* we admitted that He did a single unpurposeful thing (which we do *not*) that would be fatal to our argument.

Let us explain how we are arguing here. We are simply saying that even if one could find dysteleological elements, that would not prove the absence of the teleological. We are not saying that God is dysteleological. But even if it were admitted that He did a thousand purposeful things and then one unpurposeful or antipurposeful thing, that would not prove that God could not be called purposeful. That one exception would not prove the rule; it simply would not disprove the rule. Even if a person did think that he had found some evidence of dysteleology, that would constitute no argument against teleology.

"But," it may be asked, "since you say that even if God were a thousand to one times purposeful, that one unpurposeful thing would not disprove His purposefulness, why can you not accept that criticism and still maintain the validity of your argument?" For this reason: we are talking about God as the source of purpose, and if God is the source of purpose and the only one who could be the source of purpose, then He is the source of moral purposes as well. He would also have to be omniscient to arrange everything in a purposeful way. Consequently, being God, He would be incapable of error either in planning or in intention or morality. We do not want to labor this point at the moment. We simply note it lest there be some misunderstanding. If *God* is the purposer, He cannot do *any* nonpurposeful activities.

So we have dealt with two major objections to the teleological argument. The first was that it would not provide us with an infinite purposer in any case; the second maintained that purpose could not exist in the presence of nonpurposeful or dysteleological events.

Chance

We will conclude this chapter with a fuller discussion of chance which applies to all phases of the theistic argument. In fact, chance is the only other contender for the role of creator of the universe besides God Himself.

In the context of teleology, chance is thought of as some sort of nonpurposeful entity which accounts for the existence of what is called purposeful. In other words, chance is the nonpurposeful producer of purpose. It is tacitly assumed that a purposeful event needs some sort of explanation. The obvious candidate is, of course, a purposing cause back of the event. But for advocates of chance this is what must be avoided. So they propose a *nonpurposing cause* back of the purposeful event. Without purposing to do so, the nonpurposive produces the purposive.

On the surface of it, that is an absurd statement. How can the unpurposing something produce a purposeful event? Presumably, if a purposeful event is produced, someone or something has a purpose in producing it. But it would not be traceable to this entity called chance because chance never purposes anything. If it did, it would not be chance. So, when we examine chance as a candidate for explaining purposeful events, it fails at the outset, at least in the meaning which is commonly employed in philosophical discourse in our day. How could a thing produce purposeful events unpurposively? As we say, if it has a purpose in it, it is no longer chance.

Chance does not explain a purposeful event. It could not even explain a chance event. For if we said that chance explained a chance event, then it would not be chance but it would be some deliberate (therefore, purposeful) producing of a so-called chance event. Consequently, it is an insult to the cogency of the teleological argument to treat it as merely feasible, probable, or even highly probable. For one solitary, purposeful event in the entire universe would necessitate nothing less than the eternally, self-existent, omniscient, omnipotent, designing deity we call God.

C. J. Ducasse urges as one argument against the teleological that there is imperfection in the world, proving that the world is not teleological.[13] This is something of a refinement on what we have refuted above, namely that the presence of the dysteleological disproves the teleological. Ducasse is a little more restrained than some in saying simply that there is an imperfection in the world. This is not quite as serious as charging dysteleology. Nevertheless, he intimates that the imperfection in the world would be an argument against the perfection of the purposer of the world. Ducasse seems to imply that if the purposer is God and that God would have to be perfect, then imperfection in the world would prove that the world is not His handiwork.

We certainly grant that, if there is an imperfection in the world, it would demonstrate that this feature was not a product of a perfect God. But we challenge the soundness of this argument. What is the evidence that Ducasse or anyone else would give that there is purposelessness in the universe? Is it hurricanes, tidal waves, disease, disaster, death? Does that prove that the world is purposeless? That there are tragic elements in the world does not mean that there is no purpose. Let us put the question in a still more telling manner: Is the fact that there is disaster in the world a demonstration that a moral God cannot be the purposeful creator of it? That way of putting it makes the question rhetorical. It is theoretically possible that God could be displeased with something in the world that causes Him to exhibit His wrath against the world. Still speaking theoretically, if God did treat this world in His wrath with hurricanes, diseases, and death, would that be anything other than perfection itself? Would a moral being not be obliged morally to be opposed to immorality and to show His opposition in a way that the offending being could understand as an indication of the divine wrath? If, on the other hand, there was anything immoral in this world, yet no external evidence of the Creator's displeasure, that would constitute real imperfection. Disaster is the perfect consequence of immoral behavior. Approving benevolence would mean that the Author of the universe was immoral, approving that which was immoral and not being displeased with it at all. That would be genuine, ultimate imperfection in a universe made by a moral deity, just as the evidence of displeasure is an evidence of the perfect activity of a perfect but justly angry deity.

Ducasse declares that evil lacks purpose. He fails, however, to demonstrate the truth of that arbitrary proposition. Why would evil, in the nature of the case, demonstrate purposelessness in the universe? The only reason that seems to be offered is that Ducasse cannot see any purpose in evil. What Ducasse cannot see cannot be. We presume Ducasse would be the first one to be horrified by such a statement and say, "No, I do not mean that." Yet he does say that evil has no purpose. We have already indicated above that what is usually called evil (sickness, death, and so on) could very well have a purpose if there is immorality in this world. We have given a possible reason for this that would show definite divine purpose. Ducasse offers no reason to justify the blanket statement that evil has no purpose.

It must be proven that evil in general has no purpose or that particular evils have no purpose. If it is even hypothetically possible that there is a moral God who is displeased with the behavior of persons in this world, we cannot conclude that He could not and, indeed, should not display His displeasure in symbols of wrath which we call evil. Again, if there is immoral behavior in this world, it would be the absence of evil and suffering which would be the cause for questioning purpose in the world.

Let us face the contention that purpose could come from a non-purposive source, just as computers can have powers that those who create them do not have. This argument is hardly worthy of refutation, but it is voiced so commonly in our computer age that it requires comment. The computer has nothing except the data that has been fed into it, as the familiar GIGO principle declares: Garbage in, garbage out. There is no more mathematics, no more engineering, no more accounts, no more of anything than what the computer has been told by its human designer. If by virtue of its nature, an electronic circuit can put this information together in a much more rapid fashion than the human nervous system can, this does not prove that it is doing something its designer did not teach it. Nothing new is being produced in the thing designed that was not in the human designer of it. It does not produce new ideas. It may produce new combinations of ideas but nothing is "created" in the sense of *ex nihilo* ideas. The creators had to put this information in a storage place, at memory banks, so that they can get it again much more rapidly than they could by any other present system such as books on file in libraries around the world. It is essentially no different from microfilm. One is not putting anything more on that film than is already in those books. There is nothing more in that book than is potentially in the human mind that wrote it.

Someone may insist, however, that these are new events which were not in the original cause. We simply cannot say that, because da Vinci could produce the Lord's Supper, the Creator of Leonardo da

Vinci could not produce it. If da Vinci's powers were all given to him by this ultimate source of being, what he accomplished in his artistic career was the outworking of those powers which were given to him by the source of being.

Another point needs to be kept in mind here. We are granting that *humans* may make machines that in some respects (lifing weights, combining numbers, etc.) may out-produce them. But it does not follow that creatures could ever out-produce their Creator. All things were made by Him and without Him is nothing made. Furthermore, He made all things *ex nihilo*. If He does not continually create, He must at least continually preserve what He has created. There could never be *anything* which He Himself did not either create or moment-by-moment preserve.

In conclusion, we have endeavored to update the traditional theistic arguments, trying to show that when properly formulated they are compelling certainties and not merely suggestive possibilities. It is at this point that we have attempted to answer the objections of historic opponents, such as Immanuel Kant. It is also at this point that we have tried to tighten the statements of contemporary advocates such as Montgomery, Pinnock, Schaeffer, Geisler, and others (including Frederick R. Howe, whose *Challenge and Response* was received too late for incorporation in this discussion, and C. S. Lewis, whose works are so well known as hardly to need the allusion). We are deeply indebted to these apologists and we consider ourselves essentially at one with them.

CHAPTER 8

Supernatural Revelation and Miracles

TRADITIONAL APOLOGETICS IS in two stages: the first considers natural revelation, the second, supernatural revelation. We have considered natural revelation which proves the existence of God. Now we turn to supernatural revelation. First, we will show that a presumed uninspired Bible proves inspired messengers. Second, these inspired messengers prove the Bible to be in fact inspired. The many points and sub-points of this chapter all aim to establish this linear, two-step movement.

Before we begin our argument it seems advisable to note its noncircular, linear form.

THE NONCIRCULAR CERTIFICATION OF WORD AND SPIRIT (VERSUS FIDEISM)

We often hear of the testimony of the Spirit to the Word. Prior to that, however, is the testimony of the Word to the Spirit. First, the Word testifies that there is a Spirit. Second, it testifies that this Spirit will testify to it as the Word of God. There is to be a mutual corroboration. The Word certifies the Spirit and the Spirit certifies the Word.

But this is *not* circular reasoning. The authority of the Word does *not* depend on the testimony of the Spirit which in turn depends on the authority of the Word. If that were the case, the certification of both would be the certification of neither. Each would depend on the other and both would depend on nothing. This is circular reasoning and the supposition to suppose that God reasons this way would not make it right. Two divine wrongs do not make a right. This would implicate Deity in faulty reasoning. It would suggest that in the realm of thought the Judge of all the earth could do wrong, and in fact does do wrong.

We anticipate a protest at this point. We may be charged with presuming to judge the reasoning power of the all-wise God. The creature seems to be giving the Creator lectures in logic. We seem to be telling the Logos how to be logical. We hear Paul, the protest continues, asking, "For who has known the mind of the Lord, or who became his counselor?" Now, we know. It is John Gerstner, R. C. Sproul and Art Lindsley, the ghost writers for the Holy Ghost.

But we do not claim all that. We do not intend to give the All-logical lessons in logic. We are persuaded that He made us and all our fellow creatures rational animals, incapable of *thinking* correctly any other way than logically. We are convinced that He gave us this reasoning power so that we would be capable of judging whether something was true or not. This is the principle apparatus He gave us by which to discern truth. If we have no such logical tests, we cannot distinguish between true and false claims to anything including claims to divine revelation.

If the Bible certifies the Spirit and the Spirit certifies the Bible we cannot know which certifies which. If the Bible certified the Spirit, we would first have to know that the Bible was certified. If the Bible is not a certified authority, it has no power to certify anything else. And if the Spirit is certified by something which has no power to certify it, it cannot have any authority to certify the Word, or anything else. The same applies in reverse.

Our critics have a ready answer to all this. "You have it all wrong. You should start with the Spirit who carries authority with Him. When He certifies the Word you will know by the Spirit's intrinsic authority that He can truly certify the Word. Moreover, the Word also certifies itself. It, too, has the intrinsic authority to certify anything, including its own inspiration by the Spirit. So, really, *neither depends* on the other, though both do corroborate each other. Each stands on its own foundation. The Bible is the Word of God because it says (three thousand times) that it is the Word of God and the Spirit is the Spirit of God because he says so (millions of times) in the hearts of the regenerate."

This we admit is not circular reasoning. Each carries its own evidential power. If they do that, then our critics have established their point. Neither one depends on the other at all. The Word does not need the Spirit for certification and the Spirit does not need the Word for certification. If we are going to reason this way, however, we should be very careful never to suggest an interdependence. Anybody who knows the Bible and its claims to be the Word of God knows that it is the Word of God. Anyone who has an experience with the Spirit of God knows that it is the Spirit of God. A person would not have to be a Christian or person of faith at all. All he needs is to know that the Bible claims to be the Word of God and to be able to sense any presence of the Spirit. Anyone who reads the Bible can know what it says about itself. Everyone has some kind of experience of the Spirit. If he does, then he knows that it is the Spirit of God with whom he has to do.

But alas, both of these propositions are false. The Bible is not proven to be the Word of God because it says so and the Spirit is not known to be the Spirit of God because He is said to say so. This first point—that we know the Bible is the Word of God because it says so— has a glaring weakness as an argument. The argument would seem to take two forms. First, the *Bible* is the Word of God because it, the Bible, says that it is the Word of God. Not *any* book that says it is the Word of God is the Word of God, but only this particular book. Suppose we ask, "Why is that true only of *this* book?" One cannot simply answer, "Because." There must be some reason. But whatever reason is given is fatal to the case, because then one is not believing the Bible is the Word of God because it says so; but for some *other* reason.

Suppose, second, that the argument is the general formula that *any religious* book that claims to be the Word of God must be so. Even that would be fatal for the specific case of the Bible. Even then, we would not be believing the Bible because *it* says it is the Word of God but because that is a characteristic of a certain class. That argument would be fatal for another reason. It would prove that there are many Words of God, all of them differing from, conflicting with, and contradicting one another. This would make God the author of confusion. So the notion that the Bible is the Word of God because it says so is simply not true. It would make no difference if it said so three million times—not merely three thousand—for such assertions do not prove what is asserted.

At this point we must make a crucial distinction. We are not saying that the Bible carries no evidence within itself for its being the Word of God. There is an abundance of internal evidence for its inspiration. We think of its majesty of style, the heavenliness of its content, its marvelous inner coherency and detailed consistency, its symmetrical pattern of truth and so on. These are all indicators or evidence (*indicia*) of its lofty claims for itself. What we are arguing is that the biblical claim to be the Word of God considered in itself as a naked claim is an insufficient argument for its inspiration. The claim must be vindicated, not merely presupposed to be true.

There are, nevertheless, two things to be said for this pseudo-argument. First, it would be difficult indeed to believe any book is the Word of God if it did not claim this for itself. Second, it is impressive that a book makes this claim so many times—impressive, but not conclusive.

Let us examine the notion that the Spirit certifies itself and no second witness is necessary. In fact, this is not actually claimed. No one seems to be saying that the Spirit, apart from the Word, testifies to Himself as the author of the Word.

The great principle for which Calvin, for example, is famous is the *inseparability* of the Word and the Spirit. Against the Romanists, he maintained that the Word could not really be understood apart from the Spirit,[1] and against the *Anabaptists,* that the Spirit could not be known apart from the Word.[2] Apparently, no one is advocating the notion that the Spirit is known immediately and as the Spirit, but that He is known indirectly in and through the Word.

According to the Westminster Confession of Faith, "Our full persuasion and assurance of the infallible truth, and divine authority thereof [of the Bible], is from the inward work of the Holy Spirit, *bearing witness by and with the Word* in our hearts."[3] His witness is to the Word, not to Himself.

Let us compare, for a moment, the way by which people came to know the Second Person of the Trinity, the Son of God. They did not know simply by looking at Him that he was God incarnate. As He Himself said, "Though you do not believe Me, believe the works" (John 10:38 NASB, cf. 14:11). By His words He told them who He was, but that would not have been enough, apart from His works. His words were the explanation of His works; His works the proof of His word. The disciples saw Christ and heard Him and it all added up to what He was saying, namely, that He and the Father are one (John 10:30). He, being a man, "made himself to be God," that is, claimed to be God. For this, His contemporaries were about to stone Him as a blasphemer; but the disciples worshiped Him. In both cases He was presenting evidence for His claims. The Jews did not accept it. The disciples did. In neither case was the matter resting on immediate awareness. He gave evidence (which He and the disciples recognized was compelling) of the otherwise incredible proposition that this man was indeed God. Most of the Jews could not overcome their incredulity, in spite of the evidence.

If the Son of God is any model for the Spirit of God, then, like the Son, the Spirit would not make Himself known by direct but by indirect evidence; convincing, to be sure, but indirect nonetheless. If it were impossible to know that Christ was God simply by seeing Him with the eyes, it would seem equally unlikely to be able to know that the Spirit is God simply by feeling Him in the heart. Just as going in a circle is no significant motion, so reasoning in a circle is no significant reasoning. Many Christians today are chasing their theological tails— reasoning in circles. This form of appeal clearly reduces to subjectivism, making the final court of appeal for attesting the Spirit a mere inner subjective feeling.

Getting away from these circles we resume our linear thinking. The Word first testifies to the Spirit before the Spirit testifies to the Word. There is no circle here because when the Word testifies to the Spirit it has already been established as the Word of God by apologetics. Let us first outline the steps to be developed and then elaborate them in what follows:

(1) It is virtually granted that the Bible (not assumed to be inspired) contains generally reliable history.

(2) The Bible records miracles as part of its generally reliable history.

(3) These miracles authenticate the Bible's messengers and their message.

(4) Therefore, the Bible message ought to be received as divine.

(5) The Bible message includes the doctrine of its own inspiration.

(6) Therefore, the Bible is more than a generally reliable record. It is a divinely inspired record.

THE GOSPELS AS RELIABLE HISTORICAL SOURCES

To establish this premise the standard canons of historiography must be applied as they would be to any historical document. To defend the basic reliability of the Gospels to Christians should be like carrying coals to New Castle. If the professed Christian were to assert the basic unreliability of the primary sources of information from which he knows what he knows about this Jesus whom he professes to be Lord, he reveals that his faith is, in reality, credulity. We grant that there are such persons who, while embracing a high Christology, deny not only the inspiration of Scriptures but its basic reliability as well. They thus opt for some sort of mysticism or existential variety of Gnosticism as the ground for their "faith."

To those outside the church, the case for basic reliability must be made. It is beyond the scope of this work to retrace all the steps which establish the basic historical reliability of the biblical documents. We refer the reader to such standard works on this point as Martin's *The Reliability of the Gospels*,[4] Bruce's *The New Testament Documents: Are They Reliable?*[5] and *The Defense of the Gospel in the New Testament*.[6]

The historical character of the biblical record may be granted, but a further objection is sometimes raised at this point, namely, that this history was written for a particular religious purpose and, therefore, is unreliable as history.

But even if the Bible was written for a particular religious purpose, this does not thereby make it unreliable as history. It may be even more reliable because of the religious concern. The three writers of this book, for example, admit that what they write and say is religiously motivated; but we insist that precisely because we are religiously motivated we try to be reliable. Insofar as we become careless, over-zealous, engage in special pleading, or in any other way vitiate accuracy and truth, to that degree we are *not* religiously motivated. Though the Bible is *redemptive* history it is also redemptive *history*.

Of course some scholars, seeking to make the Bible more relevant to modern people have lifted the biblical message out of history, substituting timeless, existential categories. Bultmann, for example, sought to establish a nonhistorical or transhistorical core of revelation which makes revelation punctiliar rather than occurring within the linear movement of history. Revelation occurs suddenly, *senkrecht von oben* (vertically from above), not in an objective inscripturated form.

Bultmann's own students retreated from the radical method of their master. Though far from granting total historical authenticity to the documents of the New Testament, they have increased the size of Bultmann's historical core of the New Testament. Even the radical historical critic Ernst Kasemann argues that historical context was relevant to the Gospel writers:

> This process is therefore of the greatest significance because it enables us to acquire a right understanding of the Synoptists as being composers of Gospels and not merely the gatherers of certain material which happened to be circulating at the time. Doubtless they are dominated by the interests of kerygma. But they express this in the form of Gospels, which are essentially *not* preaching, but reporting. Equally certainly, they are not historians in the modern sense. . . . At the same time they supplement the kerygma with historical touches and employ a historicizing mode of presentation.[7]

Though criticisms of biblical history still rage as evidenced in the debate between Joachim Jeremias and Kasemann, there has been a strong shift away from the existential philosophical control of the text of the New Testament. Jeremias's approach to the text proceeds from linguistic analysis of the documents rather than from philosophical controls.[8] Though some radical higher critics still deny the premise of basic reliability of the New Testament, their methods are being sharply called into question. Consider the joint statement issued by C. S. Mann and William Foxwell Albright, the dean of twentieth-century archaeologists:

> For much too long a time the course of New Testament scholarship has been dictated by theological, quasi-theological, and philosophical presuppositions. In far too many cases commentaries on New Testament books have neglected such basic requirements as up-to-date historical and philological analysis of the test itself. In many ways this preoccupation with theological and metaphysical interpretation is the unacknowledged child of Hegelianism. To this should be added the continuing and baleful influence of Schleiermacher and his successors on the whole treatment of historical material. The result has often been steadfast refusal to take seriously the findings of archaeological and linguistic research. We believe that there is less and less excuse for the resulting confusion in this latter half of the twentieth century.
>
> Closely allied with these presuppositions is the ever present fog of existentialism, casting ghostly shadows over an already confused landscape. Existentialism as a method of interpreting the New Testament is based upon a whole series of undemonstrable postulates of Platonic, Neo-Platonic, left-wing scholastic, and rela-

tivistic origins. So anti-historical is this approach that it fascinates speculative minds which prefer cliches to factual data, and shifting ideology to empirical research and logical demonstration.[9]

MIRACLES AS BIBLICAL, RELIABLE HISTORY

It is important that God should reveal His inmost intentions concerning our justified damnation or merciful salvation. If it is important that He should do so by human messengers, it is equally important that He should accredit these as His messengers. Many may claim to have the Word of God and not be messengers from Him. There must be some way that He can infallibly certify authentic messengers, distinguishing them from those making fraudulent claims. Otherwise, it would be worse than there being no messengers from God at all. Without clear certification we would probably follow the false messengers who pander to our wishes and lusts. If, by chance, we fixed on the true messengers it would only be by chance, not rationally, which would hardly please the All-wise One who sent them. If God is willing to reveal His will by prophets, surely He will certify them beyond any reasonable doubting.

Now if God would certify His messengers to us—as we have shown He would if He intends to send them at all—He would give them credentials that only He could give. Thus, we would know indubitably that they are to be received as the messengers of God.

What would God give His messengers that all could see could come only from God? Since the power of miracle belongs to God alone, miracles are a suitable and fitting vehicle of attestation.

Is this circular reasoning? Are we using the Bible to prove miracles and miracles to prove the Bible? No, we are not engaged in circular reasoning, because we are not using the Bible to prove miracles and using miracles to prove the Bible *in the same sense*. From an *uninspired* Bible we are arguing for miracles, and from miracles we are arguing for an *inspired* Bible.

The definition of "miracle" must be understood in its technical and theological sense rather than in its popular sense if we are to avoid confusion. A miracle is a visible deed done by God in a manner other than, and contrary to, His usual way of acting, commonly called natural law. A miracle proper is visible and is explicable only by supernatural agency. (God does other supernatural works that are both supernatural and extraordinary but which are invisible, such as His work in the hearts and souls of people. These are not miracles.)

Luther referred to conversion as a "miracle," using the term in the broadest sense of including all God's supernatural works both visible and invisible. Technically, however, miracles are visible and external and perceivable by both converted and unconverted alike, carrying with them the power to convince, if not to convert. Certainly, as far as apologetics is concerned, the visible miracle is indispensable to the case for Christianity which case would thereby be demonstrated sound whether anyone believed it or not, whether anyone was converted or not, whether anyone experienced an internal "miracle" or not. The proof would be demonstrative even if all people willfully refused to acquiesce in it.

A miracle is a deed done by God in a way other than or contrary to His usual acting. All activity is (ultimately) the doing of God; miracles are the special workings of God. All works call attention to the presence of God; miracles *especially* call attention to Him. All workings call attention to God creating and preserving. Miracles call attention to God revealing and re-creating. God's regular working calls attention to creation, His special working in miracles to re-creation.

We say that miracles are "other than" or "contrary to" God's usual manner of working called "natural law" (*contra naturam*). It matters little, if any, whether miracles are merely other than or contrary to nature. In either case, they call attention to God's special presence which is their specific purpose. They do not need to be *contrary* in order to show the action of special divine presence, as the *difference* alone will suffice. Perhaps being contrary to nature would make God's special presence the more conspicuous, but the argument over the terms is not necessary. We do not need to know whether the miraculous working is ultimately contrary to natural law. What appears contrary may be based on a law of which we are not presently aware. We know that God is present by the mere deviation from His established pattern of visible behavior which deviation He alone can effect.

The definition also notes that God's usual way of working is what is meant by natural law. We have already seen that God is eternal causality. He is the only one who exists of Himself, has all power, and brings all to pass. The omnipotent is also the *only* potent. What we call "second causes" are still God's actions indirectly. His acting according to a regular habit is the only law. Natural law is not an independent order or law which nature possesses, but is God's law of acting in nature. The regularity of the normal pattern evidences divine wisdom and benevolence in itself, and also sets the stage for special revelation.

THE NECESSITY OF NATURAL THEOLOGY AS A GROUND FOR MIRACLES

We have noted that natural theology is necessary even for the definition of a miracle. There are at least two other ways in which natural theology is necessary as context for miracles: to prove that there is a God who could perform miracles, and to test the messengers themselves.

Necessity of Natural Theology to Prove That There Is a God Who Could Perform Miracles

Natural theology shows that there is a God. If there is a God, miracles are possible. If a God exists who created the world and operates it, there can be no doubting that He can modify His *modus operandi*. On the other hand, if we did not know that there is a God, we would have to step into an irrational view of the operation of nature by chance. Miracles, if they could be defined, would have no significance in such a framework. They would be chance occurrences, as everything else would be, and could prove nothing but a chance occurrence among chance occurrences.

John W. Montgomery does not seem to understand this, for he writes, "we may properly infer his [Christ's] deity from his resurrection." What Montgomery is saying here is that, since Christ conquered death by His resurrection and gives us the gift of eternal life, "no more worthy candidate for deity is in principle imaginable than the One who conquers death on mankind's behalf."[10] Montgomery says that Christ's own explanation of His own resurrection was, "He rose because he was God."[11] According to Montgomery, miracles prove, first, the existence of God and, second, the existence of Jesus Christ as God. We have already shown, however, that miracles cannot prove God. God, as a matter of fact, alone can prove miracles. That is, only on the prior evidence that God exists is a miracle even possible. Manifestly, if miracles cannot prove God, they cannot prove that a particular man is God. Montgomery says that Christ claimed that miracles prove Him to be divine. Needless to say, no texts are cited. We are afraid that there are no such passages because Christ did not claim miracles as proof that He was God. He did cite miracles as evidence that He was authenticated by God and was a messenger to be believed (John 10:38).

Since this trustworthy messenger from God said that "he who has seen me has seen the Father" (John 14:9) and "I and the Father are one" (John 10:30), we know that this trustworthy messenger of God is, indeed, God. In this indirect way the miracles prove that Christ is God, but by itself the fact that Christ does miracles is not immediate proof that he is God. All we would know immediately by Christ or anyone else doing miracles would not be that that person is God but that that person has the power of God. Receiving this power of God, he has received credentials from God which authenticate him as a messenger of God and, therefore, to be believed in whatever he says. The only person who had that power and who actually claimed deity was, of course, Christ. He was thereby proven to be what He *claimed* to be—that is, God.

Because this argument has been used promiscuously, many thinkers have been driven to presuppositionalism. If it is true that arguments such as Montgomery gives are not sound, this tends to create the impression that another approach is absolutely necessary. But another approach is not necessary because miracles, properly understood and properly used for what they properly prove, do indeed demonstrate the special relevation of God, the special Word of God, the special incarnation of God.

Montgomery cites M. A. Boden: "The fact that theological underpinnings are necessary to the very identification of a miracle in the first place, is one reason why miracles could never be regarded as a proof of the existence of some God, or God, to an unbeliever."[12] Of course, Montgomery does not agree with Boden and assumes that this type of remark is based on Lessing's famous statement that the accidental truths of history can never prove the necessary truths of reason. Montgomery seems to agree with Lessing's statement and thinks that Lessing and perhaps Boden are confusing God with a merely analytical statement. Only in analytical statements (mathematical, for example) are propositions possible that are certain. Since God is not an analytical statement or condition, we cannot have absolutely certain evidence; and since the affirmation of God is one based on the observation of data, it falls short of the absolutely certain. Consequently, in such a matter, probability would be quite adequate evidence of the existence of God. Thus Montgomery argues against Boden and Lessing.

Montgomery then makes an unfortunate comment: "Granted the proof will never reach 100% (faith will have to jump the gap, from plausability to certainty), but such proof is the basis for all our factual decisions, so we cannot summarily dismiss is just because a vital religious question is at issue."[13] In other words, Montgomery, an orthodox theist, does not think we have absolute certainty even of God's existence. Montgomery defends his own belief in God on grounds that evidence for a divine being cannot possibly be certain but only probable. Therefore, it is appropriate to bridge the gap psychologically by the assertion of belief.

If probability does not *require* belief but only makes it possible, then, presumably, an individual who did not want to believe would not be required to have faith in God. A belief in God would be an open option for persons to accept if they felt a need for it and reject it if they did not. The psychological factor would be determinative. A person would be as justified in disbelieving as in believing. One person would be utterly justified in not believing and another person would be utterly justified in believing. The difference would be in the individual, but not in any objectively compelling evidence. It would *not* be a sin for a person (who did not have the psychological need) to disbelieve in God. It would be a sin for the other type of person not to believe in God. Montgomery would not want to allow the proposition that it is a sin for some persons to disbelieve in God and not a sin for others, yet we do not see how he can avoid this conclusion if a belief in God is psychologically determined. Montgomery might conceivably try to convince a person who felt no desire for God, that he ought to feel such a desire. But he does not say that.

There is a more serious concern than this psychological issue. We defend Boden's proposition that miracles cannot prove God because they necessarily presuppose God. *It is the nonmiraculous natural order that proves the necessity of God.* Boden is right, therefore, in making his assertion. Montgomery is unfortunate in denying Boden's assertion and unfortunate in using miracles to prove God. What is a miracle if there is no God? Normal events and unusual ones could, of course, occur as they do regularly occur. But the unusual is certainly not necessarily the miraculous. The miraculous would be an event that could not be explained by the order of nature. If there is no order, how can there be anything which would require an explanation by deity?

What Lessing meant and what Lessing said may be two different things. We will concentrate only on what he said. He said that "the accidental truths of history can never be the proof of the eternal truths of reason."[14] This is utterly true. Accidental events cannot be the proof of anything. But if Lessing intended this as evidence against the rational significance of miracles, his conclusion does not follow. Miracles are not accidental events. By definition, miracles are events in the external world that could only be wrought by God. Obviously, anything wrought by God would be no accident. Lessing is trying to win an argument by definition and manipulation. He is subtly defining miracles as accidental events and then, with a great flourish of victory, trying to demonstrate that miracles as such cannot possibly prove necessary laws of reason. He is clever but not sound. Let us restate Lessing's remark using the word "miraculous": "The miraculous events of history can never be the proof of necessary truths of reason." The *accidental* truths of history can never become the proof of necessary truths of reason, but miraculous events in history most certainly do become the proof of the necessary truths of reason. They prove that God is revealing Himself and what God reveals must be rational, pure and simple.

This all shows that sound apologetics cannot begin with the inspired Bible or even with a divine Christ. If we did not know that there is a *God*, no one could prove that Christ is the *Son of God*. If we did not know that there is a *God*, we could not prove that the Bible is the *Word of God*. If we did not know that God manifests Himself at all times in the things He has made, we could never know that He manifested Himself in a special way at the time of special revelation.

Necessity of Natural Theology to Test the Messengers Themselves

A professed messenger of God would bring things out of his treasure new and old. He undoubtedly speaks in the name of God who is already known by nature but gives a message not known from nature. One prerequisite of a prophet is that he confirm what is already known as well as reveal the unknown. Therefore, if he came in the name of God but proclaimed the lies of the devil, we would know him for a false prophet that he must be, no matter what he does. He may be a very clever deceiver working lying wonders, but we would know (even if we could not see through his counterfeit miracles) that he was no prophet of the true God. This is precisely why theologians have defined true miracles as *contra peccatum* as well as *contra naturam*.

We have already shown that the Bible records that miracles occur throughout its history and also how it uses them. It is sufficient here simply to remind ourselves that miracles are a part of biblical history which cannot be removed without violating the whole fabric. Some scholars have indeed tried to separate the miraculous from the life of Christ. But, as Karl Adam once said: Christ's life is a blaze of miracles from his virgin birth to his bodily resurrection. Albert Schweitzer has shown that the quest for a merely naturalistic life of Christ is futile.[15] Wrede found that Mark, theologically, was as "bad" as John.[16] More recently, McCasland has noted that demons simply cannot be exorcised from the biography of Christ.[17] The Bible paints history with its warts (miracles) and all. Scholars are not about to accept the view of Robert Pfeiffer who said that, when he encountered a miracle in the Old Testament, he skipped over to the historical section.[18] The question is whether this is a scholarly, rational (not to mention devout) way to behave. It is indeed, *if* it can be proven *a priori* that miracles are not possible, or that the record of them is unreliable. But Dr. Pfeiffer did not endeavor to do so and, if he had endeavored to justify his attitude rationally, he should first of all have had to prove the nonexistence of God. Some people think that it is difficult to prove the existence of God. Our sympathy is reserved for those who undertake to prove the nonexistence of God. Unless one establishes the nonexistence of God, he cannot rationally insist that miracles are impossible.

Since we have proved that God does exist, we cannot deny the historicity of miracles on the ground that miracles are impossible. Very few have ever attempted to prove that God does not exist.

But David Hume (while he did not attempt to prove that miracles were impossible) succeeds in proving to many persons' satisfaction that they were highly improbable. His clever argument amounts to this: that there is vastly more evidence for the undeviating uniformity of nature than there is for any deviation (miracle). "No testimony is sufficient to establish a miracle unless this testimony be of such a kind, that a falsehood would be more miraculous than the fact which it endeavours to establish."[19] Thus, he argued that these deviations are highly improbable. This is clever, but also spurious reasoning. The argument makes it seem that since we have some billions upon billions of instances of uniformity of natural law over against relatively few seriously claimed instances of nonconformity, the probability ratio eliminates the miracle. But this is a false antithesis. Trillions upon trillions of instances of natural law are not against miracles, or even against one occurrence of miracle. If God is the author and preserver of natural law, that simply means that it is His pleasure usually to act in that regular fashion. We can see the benefits for His creatures. But it in no way militates against His acting differently, on rare occasions, for the benefit of these same creatures. All that He has shown of the regularity of His usual behavior makes His exceptional behavior the more conspicuous and significant, so that these two patterns of behavior complement each other rather than exclude each other. Consequently Hume's statement that it is "contrary to experience that a miracle should be true," is simple question-begging.

Hume's argument proves more than he desires. By this schema of argument not only would miracle be made *a priori* incredible, but so would all unusual and extraordinary events. We would be consigned to a world of the utterly commonplace, as any slight deviation from the normal (not to mention a miracle) would be unbelievable, for it would lack sufficient evidence to overcome the probability quotient of the normal.

Uniformity itself rests upon repetition, a series or sequence of same or similar events. But the series can never be established because before there can be two such similar events there must first be one. The first, however, would be unique and therefore incredible. Its repetition cannot resurrect it because repetition becomes impossible by definition.

It is especially ironic to have Hume appealing to an inviolable natural law. ("A miracle is a violation of the *laws of nature,* and as a firm and *unalterable* experience has established these *laws,* the proof against a miracle, from the nature of the case, is as entire as any argument can possibly be imagined."[20]) Hume is the greatest opponent that causality and its fixity has ever had. Cause, according to him, is merely a habitual way or "custom" of thinking about relationships. There is no "efficient" causation in the nature of things. For the great skeptic to be talking about "laws" and "laws of nature," at that, not to mention "unalterable experience" is mind-boggling. He should be the first one to argue that things like miracles could well happen. He may be somewhat aware of his inconsistency when he falls back on "experience" but then, with gross inconsistency, calls that "unalterable" which, in the nature of the case, cannot possess causal fixity. The only thing more surprising than Hume's grossly contradictory argument is that two hundred years later empiricists, of all people, are still holding his supposedly shattering argument.

Of course, the canny Scot has another thing working for his sophistical argument and that is the counterfeit miracle. For every biblical miracle there are thousands of manifest counterfeits. As with all good counterfeits, they expose the genuine to suspicion. But we cannot say because some are counterfeit that all are. The opposite is probable: where counterfeits abound, there usually is something genuine they seek to imitate.

The biblical miracles need to be considered on their own merits. Their impossibility, or even improbability, has never been demonstrated. We have positive evidence for their occurrence. The reasonable person will believe that they occurred as recorded.

These miracles authenticate the Bible message. We have already shown above how miracles accomplish this, prosecuting the argument without circularity. That is, these miracles are seen generally as a reliable part of the reliable Bible account, without assuming that the Bible is anything more than that—a reliable account. Treating the Bible as any other historical record, we find compelling reasons to believe that the miracles it records occurred and proved the divinity of its message by certifying the divine authority of its messengers.

THESE MIRACLES AUTHENTICATE THE BIBLE'S MESSAGE

Further, these miracles, being done only by the power of God, certify His endorsement of the miracle-worker's message.

Since God alone controls the natural He alone can act above it. If any human being has that power, it could have come only from the one source—God. God, therefore, is the certifier of the messengers who carry His exclusive credentials.

"Rabbi, we know that You have come from God as a teacher; for no one can do these signs that You do unless God is with him" (John 3:2 NASB). Nicodemus made the point. Christ claimed the same argument Himself. On the occasion of healing the paralytic, He asked, "Which is easier, to say to the paralytic, 'Your sins are forgiven [which only God can say]'; or to say, 'Arise, and take up your pallet and walk'? But in order that you may know that the Son of Man has authority on earth to forgive sins," He said to the paralytic, "I say to you, rise, take up your pallet and go home [which only God can effect]" (Mark 2:9–11 NASB). Even more explicitly, He says at the time of raising Lazarus from the dead, "Father, I thank Thee that Thou heardest Me. And I know that Thou hearest Me always; but because of the people standing around I said it, that they may believe that Thou didst send Me" (John 11:41–42 NASB). Indeed, even God Himself used miracles to authenticate Jesus Christ when He spoke from heaven saying, "Thou art My beloved Son, in Thee I am well-pleased" (Luke 3:22 NASB).

Therefore, the Bible's message ought to be received as divine. This point is self-evident. If something is seen to be from a divine source it is immediately received. There can be no further debate, unless one chooses to assail the credibility of the divine.

Although thousands of volumes have been written on this subject and controversy has raged, there is virtually no question that the Bible claims its own inspiration. The questions concern different degrees of inspiration; what books are included in the Bible; the method of inspiration (whether inspiration is mechanical or dynamic); and a variety of essentially intramural questions. That is not to say that all who are agreed that the Bible teaches its own inspiration believe what the Bible teaches about itself. But if our argument is sound, then rational and honest people must not only believe *that* the Bible so teaches but they must also believe *what* the Bible teaches.

That the Bible claims its own inspiration would not, in itself, guarantee the truth of the claim. If the claimants, however, are certified by God, attested by miracles, then the claim is validated. This is true not only for the apostolic writers but for Jesus as well.

At the core of the controversy regarding biblical inspiration and authority is the issue of the authority of Christ Himself. The authority of Scripture is inseparably linked to the authority of Jesus. If we know anything of the *ipsissima verba* of Jesus, we know that He taught a very high view of Scripture. There is little doubt among contemporary scholars that Jesus Himself taught the inspiration of the Bible. Jesus' view, however, is frequently dismissed as irrelevant to the debate on the grounds that touching His human nature Jesus was not omniscient and therefore is excusable for presenting misinformation about Scripture because He was bound by the knowledge available to Him in His day. To ascribe greater knowledge or omniscience to Christ is to commit the heresy of docetism. C. H. Dodd comments:

> We need not doubt that Jesus, as He is represented, shared the views of His contemporaries regarding the authorship of books in the Old Testament, or the phenomena of "demon-possession"—

views which we could not accept without violence to our sense of truth.[21]

Emil Brunner agreed that Jesus shared the high view of Scripture of his Jewish contemporaries: "The Scriptures are to Him the revelation of God."[22] Yet Brunner had no problem criticizing Jesus' understanding and use of the Old Testament, saying that "the Bible is full of errors, contradictions, erroneous opinions concerning all kinds of human, natural, historical situations."[23]

The facility with which Protestant theologians have rejected Jesus' view of Scripture is based on the Protestant rejection of docetism which charge may accurately be leveled against the Roman Catholic tradition. But an important point is overlooked in the debate. There is a vast difference between the omniscience of Jesus and the infallibility of Jesus. The two concepts must be distinguished carefully. Omniscience refers to comprehensive knowledge, a knowledge which presumably only God could have. If God is omniscient He is also infallible, unless we conceive of God in a blasphemous way as to have Him "fail" or "err" on purpose. The only way an omniscient being could err would be by intentionally telling a falsehood. In reality, since God is both omniscient and altogether righteous, His infallibility is established by His omniscience.

Omniscience, then, carries with it the notion of infallibility, but the reverse is not the case. One can be infallible without being omniscient. It is theoretically possible for a person with limited knowledge to speak infallibly if certified by divine power. An apostle could write infallibly if inspired by God to do so, without resulting in the deification of the apostle. The apostle can be rendered infallible without being rendered omniscient.

The same can and must be said of Jesus. Jesus, in His human nature, was not omniscient; but He was, indeed He had to be infallible. He was certified by miracle as a truth-teller. A deeper theological and Christological issue emerges which men like Dodd and Brunner overlooked. Connected to Jesus' teaching office is the matter of Jesus' sinlessness. It would have been no sin for Jesus to be less than omniscient in His human nature. It would have been sin for Him to make claims about Himself which were not true. He claimed to be the Truth, to be sent from the Father and to speak nothing on His own authority, but rather on the authority of His Father. None of these claims demand omniscience for their consistent application, but all of them demand infallibility. Can one who is Truth speak falsely? Can Jesus, on the authority of His Father (which the Father certifies by miracle), teach erroneous doctrines? To ask such questions is to answer them.

What is at stake here is not the omniscience of Jesus but His sinlessness. For Jesus to teach falsehood either consciously or unconsciously in light of the magnitude of His claims to authority would be to violate biblical canons of truth and to face the severe judgment Scripture reserves for teachers (James 3:1). As a teacher of falsehood Jesus would be culpable. If He so sinned, even if it were a minor peccadillo, He would not qualify to mediate redemption for Himself, let alone for us.

The modern theologian who, in cavalier fashion, dismisses Jesus' view of Scripture not only negates Jesus' sinlessness but violates Jesus' own pedagogy. Jesus rebuked His contemporaries, "If I told you earthly things and you do not believe, how shall you believe if I tell you heavenly things?" (John 3:12 NASB). We have an entire generation of scholars who do precisely that. They refuse to accept Jesus' teaching regarding earthly matters such as biblical authorship yet extol Jesus' celestial teaching. They strain out the gnat and swallow the camel. Therefore, the Bible is more than a generally reliable record. It is a divinely inspired record.

We have travelled not in a circular path back to where we began but up Jacob's ladder anchored on earth in a merely human and historical Bible into the heavenlies of a divinely inspired Word of God.

What is the relation of the Holy Spirit to this reasoning? The argument is found apart from the Holy Spirit's illumination; but probably will not be acknowledged apart from Him. As the Westminster Confession of Faith says, persuasion comes only from the Holy Spirit witnessing by the Word in our hearts. Acquiescence, as we have seen, is the key word in Calvin's brilliant discussion in the *Institutes,* 1.7.

A greater than Calvin, Paul, has said that only God can give the repentance which leads to the acknowledging of the truth. "And the Lord's bond-servant must not be quarrelsome, but be kind to all, able to preach, patient when wronged, with gentleness correcting those who are in opposition; if perhaps God may grant them repentance leading to the knowledge [*epignosis*] of the truth" (2 Tim. 2:24–25 NASB). *Epignosis* is usually translated "acknowledging," as the Greek word indicates more than mere knowledge. Berkeley translates it "acknowledgement of." The point is clear. The apologist provides the knowledge; the Holy Spirit the acknowledgment.

IMPOSSIBILITY OF TRUE MIRACLES BEING PERFORMED BY FALSE MESSENGERS

We have just proved the evidential power of miracles; the essential case for Christianity. We have shown that miracles can be performed only by the power of God and therefore that messengers who are enabled to do miracles carry the imprimatur of heaven on their utterances in the divine name. John Locke was correct—miracles establish the "credit of the proposer" of doctrine. Nicodemus was correct when he said, "Rabbi, we know that You have come from God as a teacher, for no one can do these signs that You do unless God is with him" (John 3:2 NASB).

Now comes the company of well-meaning Christians who say that emissaries of the devil in his name (or, worse yet, in the name of God) do miracles as well. These may be lying wonders; but some lying wonders are *true* lying wonders, they say. That is, they are true miracles called "lying wonders" not because they are not truly wonders or miracles but because they are done by the chief of liars; that is, they are supposed to be true wonders in the service of lies. After all, they say, the devil could speak through a serpent and that is a miracle. The devil could speak through a possessed person, and that is a miracle. He was allowed to afflict Job with boils, and that is a miracle. And what about the witch of Endor? they ask, and the wonder-working magicians of Egypt?

The first thing we would do by way of answer is to make an empirical observation. By listing these instances of apparently true miracles by false messengers, we have almost exhausted the biblical list. Reference to lying wonders of the devil relatively are few and far between. While the miracles of the Bible are concentrated in a few periods of time they were quite numerous during those periods. Someone has counted, for example, eight miracles done by Elijah and sixteen by the prophet Elisha, who prayed for a double portion of his spirit. Of Christ's miracles, John writes: "Many other signs therefore Jesus also performed in the presence of the disciples, which are not written in this book" (John 20:30 NASB). Paul's, too, are numerous. The devil's works (whatever they were) seem a dark shadow against the light of God's presence. We are merely making an observation which may be suggestive; but we are not calling it an argument.

Furthermore, Satan being able to overpower and use even human agents is not a miraculous phenomenon, though it would qualify for a wonder. He is a spirit who is represented as able to devour us, deceive us, and overpower us. He is subject to God's sovereign power, of course; but unless God does restrain him, it is no wonder at all that he deceives and overpowers humans. It is, therefore, no more a miracle that Satan could possess Legion and use his vocal cords than a heavy-weight champion could beat up the average person.

To continue with our discussion of satanic activities that are not necessarily miracles, let us consider Job. Satan was permitted to afflict Job by taking away his wealth, his family, and his own health (though 2:3 has the Lord saying to Satan, "You incited Me against him, to ruin him without cause"). None of this was done miraculously but apparently naturally.

None of those satanic activities qualify for the title, miraculous. And if they were not necessarily so interpreted, they could not serve the function which true miracles alone can serve.

After all this, along comes the skeptic who has been listening to the Bible believers disputing with each other, and he raises an objection of his own: But we know all this from the Bible itself which we have not yet fully established. True, but notice that we may know this apparent objection from the Bible also. The problem seems to emerge from the phenomena of Scripture and is answered by the phenomena and teaching of Scripture. But if someone insists that the problem exists outside the Bible also (demonic activity certainly has existed outside the Bible), we reply, heathen reason shows that such phenomena are not necessarily miraculous, unlike the miraculous phenomena of the Bible. Why? Because from this world alone, we do not know that there are not invisible spirits in our world which may come even from another world. As far as we know, they may quite conceivably have the power attributed to devils. Such activities (unless indisputably miraculous) would not require special divine power.

If infinite natural power is the ultimate argument for the existence of God, infinite supernatural power (miracle) is the ultimate argument for the revelation of God. If Satan could do miracles, we could prove neither God nor His revelation. If true miracles could be done by God or Satan, we would learn precisely nothing from them. They would establish the credit for either "proposer" because they would establish credit for both. Nicodemus would have to say, "We know that you are a teacher sent by God (or the devil) for no one does these works you do unless God (or the devil) is with him." Christ would have to pray: "Father, I thank Thee that Thou heardest me. I know that Thou hearest me always, but I have said this on account of those standing by, that they may believe that Thou (or the devil) didst send me." The disciples, after seeing Christ still the waves, would have cried out: "What manner of man is this (a man of God, God Himself, or the devil incarnate) that He commands the waves and they obey Him." As for the elect being deceived, we would read: "For false Christs and false prophets will arise and will show great signs and wonders, so as to mislead, if possible, even the elect" (Matt. 24:24).

Some may object that others besides apostles have the power of miracles in the New Testament, as the apostle Paul clearly taught in 1 Corinthians 12–14. This is true, but apparently, their power came from the laying on of hands by the apostles and faded out with those from whom they had received power.

Do we not exclude all other miracles by definition? No, we have defined a miracle as a visible deed done by God in a way other than and/or contrary to His usual way of acting which is commonly called natural law.

Do we not rule out the miracles of the Egyptian magicians by simply saying that they are not acts of God? No. First, we say that the records show that their deeds were done by their secret arts. Second, those persons were called magicians. Third, they themselves acknowledged, by contrast, that Moses' works were done by the finger of God. Fourth, they were unable to continue, giving up after apparently simulating Moses' works for one and a half miracles—through the "production" of frogs but stopping with the removal of them. If they had miraculous powers, why would one work be more difficult than another? removing the frogs more difficult than creating them?

Turning the Nile into blood would by our definition be a miracle. If the magicians did that we would claim that they wrought miracles as certainly as Moses did. It is not by definition that we rule this out as a miracle. We rule it out by the account of their activity. The narrative tells us that they were not doing miracles but tricks. It does not take God to do tricks. Clever men can do that. Tricks are not miracles, they are not supernatural, nor do they require any special activity of God above or contrary to natural law.

Since the magicians were opponents of God and on the side of Satan, is it not possible that they did their works by the power of the devil and thereby proved that the devil has power over nature? But their tricks are not represented as the work of the devil. Someone's advancing the cause of Satan does not necessarily prove that he does so by a supernatural power of Satan. Furthermore, there is no evidence of power over nature in the activities of the magicians.

We conclude, therefore, that no miracles were done by the evil magicians of Egypt or the devil behind them. They did not prove that false messengers may perform true miracles.

Does the witch of Endor not prove the miraculous power of false messengers? Certainly the narrative (1 Sam. 28) represents the dead Samuel as being present on this occasion, seen by the witch, and speaking to Saul. We are inclined to think that this is all phenomenological. It presents the incident as it appears to King Saul who had solicited it. The Bible nowhere else actually represents the witches as having power to conjure up the spirits of the dead and it is the Bible that is rendering the incident. We admit, however, that we cannot *prove* this narrative to be merely phenomenological and that, if it is a literal happening, we must conclude that necromancy, though strictly forbidden by God as an abominable art, is a possible natural art not necessitating miraculous power.

Miracle without truth is spurious. That is, we accept miracles in harmony with known truth as the proof of Scripture as a revelation of God. Now we have thus proved that the Bible is the Word of God on this formula: Natural revelation plus miracle plus claimed revelation proves revelation. The Bible is established and its teaching is therefore to be accepted. This would include its teaching about miracles. That is, if the Bible says that the miracles themselves prove that the miracle-worker is a messenger of God, then (quite apart from the natural theology of the worker) we may accept the fact on authority that miracles per se authenticate an authority. The doer is a messenger of *God* and not of anyone else. This the Bible does in fact teach. As we have seen, this was given as proof of Moses' mission and Christ's. Even if we were unable to prove *a priori* that miracles must in themselves alone demonstrate the doer to be a messenger of God we can, without circularity, prove it from the Bible. That is, the Bible which we may prove by natural theology and miracle teaches that miracle alone is sufficient.

Christian sects claim miracles in support of their errors. For example, the Roman Catholic Church is a professing Christian body that teaches many orthodox Christian doctrines. She also teaches some doctrines which she claims are taught by, or at least consistent with, the Bible which Protestants contend are either implicitly or explicitly contrary to the Bible. Roman Catholic miracle-workers may claim and have claimed that a given miracle confirms a Roman teaching which is erroneous according to the Protestant interpretation. For example, the immaculate conception of Mary is said to be supported by a miracle performed for Bernadette who claimed that Mary appeared to her and said, "I am the immaculate conception." The Roman Catholic church accepts that dogma and the miracle that confirmed it.

This alleged miracle is easy to disprove. First, and most fundamentally, it is claimed in support of a palpable falsehood—the immaculate conception. If we can prove our charge that the immaculate conception is demonstrably false doctrine, even the Roman Catholic Church would admit her error in endorsing Lourdes. She is not about to grant that God contradicts Himself—least of all, by miraculous proofs. Rome will agree with us that, if the immaculate conception doctrine can be proven false, then the miracle of Lourdes is proven counterfeit (and all the miracles that are supposed to have followed from the counterfeit are spurious as miracles).

There are two arguments against the immaculate conception which Rome cannot deny. One is exegetical and the other is logico-doctrinal.

First, the Bible plainly teaches that all humans are sinful. Paul establishes this beyond any doubt. "All alike have sinned." "There is none who does good, there is not even one" (Rom. 3:12 NASB). Monsignor Knox's translation of Romans 3:12 is to the same effect: "All alike are on the wrong course . . . not one of them acts honourably, no, not one. No human creature can become acceptable in his sight by observing the law" (Rom. 3:12, 20). "Therefore, just as through one man sin entered into the world, and death through sin, and so death spread to all men, because all sinned" (Rom. 5:12). It is no surprise that Bonaventura and Thomas Aquinas[24] strenuously opposed the sinlessness of Mary, which doctrine, in turn, led to the doctrine of her sinlessness at birth or the immaculate conception. The Bible which Rome claims to be infallible opposes Rome's dogma of the sinlessness of Mary.

Second, Rome's doctrinal logic also opposes the immaculate conception. The regress of doctrine led, of course, from sinlessness to sinless conception. If Mary was thought to be sinless it was logically concluded that she had to be so from birth and at birth. Therefore, she must have been supernaturally conceived so as to avoid contamination by her sinful parents.

But here Rome is caught in her own logic. If Mary had to be pure in order not to contaminate her Son, would her parents not have had to be pure in order not to contaminate her? No, comes the answer, because she was miraculously prevented from her parents' contamination by miracle. But if they argue that way, the objection against the immaculate conception immediately arises that it would not be necessary because Mary was, by the miracle of the Virgin Birth, prevented from passing on her contamination to her Son. If a miracle could prevent the passing on of contamination in one case, it could in the other and if it could not in one case, neither could it in the other.

In all arguments such as this, when Rome is demonstrated to be in error she is tempted to "pull rank." She has the infallible magisterium. Therefore, she cannot err and all who prove that she can and does must themselves be in error. Her argument rests ultimately on this arbitrary appeal to infallible magisterium, demanding a *fides implicitum* from her adherents.

We need not go into a deep discussion of this fundamental error of Rome—her claim to errorlessness in dogma. It is sufficient simply to remark that we are dealing with miracles as proof of divine revelation. Rome uses them just as we do as part of her apologetic for Christianity. It is only after there is proof that revelation has occurred that the recipients can settle further hermeneutical questions concerning the church and her authority. But the authority rests on the miracles—not the miracles on the authority.

In summary, we stress again the indispensability of genuine miracles. They and they alone ultimately prove that Christ is the Son of God and that the Bible is the Word of God. All other "evidence" is corrobative. This is the reason we have pursued the theme of miracles to our own time arguing that all claimed since the apostolic age are "counterfeit miracles." We are aware that this contention is not only greatly controverted even by contemporary *traditional* Christian apologists but that our viewpoint has become a minority report. We have submitted our report nonetheless because we believe that the cessation of miracles is almost as essential to the case for genuine miracles as miracles are for Christianity.

If contemporary works of God are called miracles in the technical theological sense of the word, then all miracles self-destruct. They are claimed today by heretical and orthodox variations within Christianity and by unbelief outside it, making God the author of confusion.

CHAPTER 9

The Spirit, the Word, and the Church

BEFORE WE SHOW HOW the Spirit persuades of the Word of God let us first take note of how the inspired Word persuades of the Spirit of God.

When Christ was present on earth in the flesh, the Holy Spirit was, to a degree, in the background. Christ bore witness to Himself and to the Spirit before the Holy Spirit bore more full witness to Him. At first the disciples themselves hardly recognized who Christ was; they were even less cognizant of the Spirit. But there were allusions to and anticipations of the work of the Spirit during the earthly ministry of Christ Himself. In this chapter we will follow this historical and biblical pattern, treating first the witness of the Word to the Spirit, then the witness of the Spirit to the Word.

THE WITNESS OF THE WORD TO THE SPIRIT

One epochal allusion to the Spirit occurred at Caesarea Philippi where Christ first asked who people said the Son of Man was, and then asked who they (His disciples) said He was. Peter said, "You are the Christ, the Son of the living God" (Matt. 16:16 RSV). Whereupon Christ declared, "Blessed are you, Simon Bar-Jona! For flesh and blood has not revealed this to you, but my Father who is in heaven" (Matt. 16:17 RSV), thus explaining the source of Peter's understanding. On an earlier occasion, commenting on the diverse responses to His ministry, Christ had said, "I thank thee, Father, Lord of heaven and earth, that thou hast hidden these things from the wise and understanding and revealed them to babes; yea, Father, for such was thy gracious will" (Matt. 11:25–26 RSV). In both instances Christ speaks not of the Spirit but of the Father as the one responsible for giving understanding of the Son. Yet we know from later New Testament revelation that it is not the first person of the Godhead but the third person, the Spirit, who is the agent of revelation and illumination.

What, then, is the significance of Christ's referring to the Father rather than to the Spirit when illumination is the subject? Apparently two factors are at work here. First, by this Christ emphasizes the divine sovereignty in illumination. The Father is the executive head of the Godhead and He, supremely, expresses the absolute sovereignty of the divine decisions. By this manner of speaking Christ calls attention to the ultimate source of divine illumination—the sovereignty of God—which was fundamental to the fact and fundamental to the disciples' understanding of the fact. A second reason is that the Holy Spirit's supreme redemptive activity is in the application of the Son's work. Hence, the Spirit's activity is not stressed at this time but later when the work of Christ is finished.

The appropriate stressing of the Father's role and the subordinating of the Spirit's probably accounts for the way in which the Son Himself explains the illumination of His own ministry: At the very outset of Christ's ministry, John the Baptist had defined his Lord's ministry in relation to his own. He had baptized in water in anticipation of the coming of the Christ who would baptize in the Spirit. "And I did not recognize Him, but He who sent me to baptize in water said to me, 'He upon whom you see the Spirit descending and remaining upon Him, this is the one who baptizes in the Holy Spirit.' And I have seen, and have borne witness that this is the Son of God" (John 1:33). So Christ Himself was baptized with the Spirit and "baptizes in the Holy Spirit." It was Christ's baptism with the Spirit and the fact that He was going to baptize in the Spirit that convinced John that "this is the Son of God."

During the ministry of Christ, the Holy Spirit was eclipsed by the Father and by the Son. His time had not yet come, as it were, though He was by no means unknown. But throughout His ministry, Christ did prepare for the special coming of the Holy Spirit. In his discourse with Nicodemus, for example, Christ not only insisted that a person must be born again in order to see the kingdom of God, but that the new birth was by the Holy Spirit. "Unless one is born of water and the Spirit, he cannot enter the kingdom of God" (John 3:5 NASB). Long before the pouring out of the Holy Spirit, Christ made it very clear that the Spirit is absolutely essential to Christ's own ministry and to the saving responses to it.

The divinity and sovereignty of the Holy Spirit are also strongly accented in this discourse. "Do not marvel that I said to you, 'You must be born anew.' The wind blows where it wills, and you hear the sound of it, but do not know whence it comes or whither it goes; so it is with every one who is born of the Spirit" (John 3:7 RSV). Just as the Father who is the Lord of heaven and earth does what is well-pleasing to Him, so the Holy Spirit, like the wind, blows where He pleases. As the psalmist had said long before: "Our God is in the heavens; he does whatever he pleases" (Ps. 115:3 RSV). Though the Holy Spirit is sent at the command of the Father (according to the Caesarea Philippi discourse) and at the command of the Son (as we shall see in a moment), in a later disclosure it is clear that, being equally sovereign, He comes as He Himself pleases. There is a divine triumvirate here.

It is also interesting to notice how Christ's references to Himself come to a climax in reference to the Holy Spirit. In one passage Christ moves from a discussion of *bread* to Himself to the Holy Spirit; while in another He moves from a discussion of water to Himself to the Holy Spirit. Speaking of the bread which came down from heaven in the days of Moses, Christ indicated clearly that He was that bread and that He must be eaten if His people would be alive spiritually. His language, often taken to be eucharistic, is very strong:

> Truly, truly, I say to you, unless you eat the flesh of the Son of man and drink his blood, you have no life in you; he who eats my flesh and drinks my blood has eternal life, and I will raise him up at the last day. For my flesh is food indeed, and my blood is drink indeed. He who eats my flesh and drinks my blood abides in me, and I in him. (John 6:53–56 RSV)

If this were to be taken literally, one could understand Martin Luther's simple, intransigent insistence at the Colloquy of Marburg upon the phrase "This is my body." But before Christ's discourse is finished we hear Him saying, "It is the Spirit that gives life, the flesh is of no avail; the words that I have spoken to you are spirit and life" (6:63 RSV). Once again, in the midst of the strongest, most literal-sounding speech about eating flesh and drinking blood, Christ refers not to His own body (though His sacrifice is the basis of it) but to His own divine Spirit, the Holy Spirit, the Spirit of God.

In the same manner, Christ makes the transition from the water of life to the Spirit of God:

On the last day of the feast, the great day, Jesus stood up and proclaimed, "If any one thirst, let him come to me and drink. He who believes in me, as the Scripture has said, 'Out of his heart shall flow rivers of living water.'" Now this he said about the Spirit, which those who believed in him were to receive; for as yet the Spirit had not been given, because Jesus was not yet glorified." (John 7:37–39 NASB)

The word given is not in the Greek text but is supplied by the translator to convey the meaning. Probably *poured out* would have been a better term than *given* because the Spirit was already present and active as we have seen (and will see even more clearly when we consider John 14:17 where the Spirit is said to be "with" the disciples at the time but to be "in" them later at Pentecost). The main point, with which we are here concerned, is that the water of life is nothing other than the Spirit of God. Again Christ is calling attention first to Himself, but then to the Holy Spirit as the One who brings people to Him, the Word of God.

The principal introduction to the ministry of the Holy Spirit comes, however, at the very end of Christ's ministry. John 14–17 is replete with references to the special coming of the Holy Spirit. John 14:1–15 is a summary of the evidence that Christ Himself is the Son of God. "He who has seen Me has seen the Father" (14:9 NASB). Then He begins to talk in earnest about the Holy Spirit. "And I will ask the Father, and He will give you another Helper, that He may be with you forever; *that is* the Spirit of truth, whom the world cannot receive, because it does not behold Him or know Him, *but* you know Him because He abides with you, and will be in you" (14:16–17 NASB). Here is the classic transitional statement about the Holy Spirit who had been "with" them but would soon be poured out upon them. They already knew this one for whom Christ is going to ask and whom the Father "will" give. Obviously there is something old and something new—a greater degree of outpouring and indwelling which awaited the disciples who are about to be bereft of the presence of the Son of God in the flesh. They had already been baptized with the Spirit, they had already drunk of that water and eaten of that bread which is the Spirit, but a magnificent new dimension of spiritual experience is about to come when the Son leaves. "But I tell you the truth, it is to your advantage that I go away; for if I do not go away, the Helper shall not come to you; but if I go, I will send Him to you" (John 16:7 NASB).

In foretelling the special coming of the Spirit, Christ tells something about Him who is to come that is of major importance for the second part of this section, namely, the witness of the Spirit to the Word: "But the Helper, the Holy Spirit, whom the Father will send in My name, He will teach you all things, and bring to your remembrance all that I said to you" (John 14:26 NASB). Here the two concepts are conjoined: the witness of the Son to the Spirit and the witness of the Spirit to the Son. The Son is saying that the Spirit will come and the Spirit will say that the Son has come. But notice, as we observed before, that the order is this: *first* the Son speaks with authority and *then* we know (when we hear the Spirit speaking as Christ said He would) that the Spirit too speaks with authority.

Much more is said by the Son of God about the coming of the Holy Spirit in these closing chapters, but we take time for just one more. John 16:8–10 (NASB) especially reveals the coming work of the Holy Spirit. "And He, when He comes, will convict the world concerning sin, and righteousness, and judgment; concerning sin, because they do not believe in Me; and concerning righteousness, because I go to the Father, and you no longer behold Me; and concerning judgment, because the ruler of this world has been judged." We have what amounts to a parallel to this in the Great Commission (Matt. 28:20), where Christ promises to be with His witnesses to the end of the age. The Holy Spirit who would thus be Christ's agent by whom they would make disciples of all nations, just as in John it is said that by the Holy Spirit people will be convicted of sin, righteousness, and judgment.

The climax of the unveiling of the Holy Spirit comes at Pentecost. Here we have the actual outpouring of the Spirit in whose power the apostles preached and by whose power many were converted. The Old Testament is fulfilled as people from all over the world learn by experience that it is " 'not by might nor by power, but by My Spirit,' says the Lord" (Zech. 4:6). What the Son of God has said about the Spirit of God is beginning to be fulfilled. The process is still going on and will go on until the end of the age as the Son of God is "with" His witnesses by the Spirit of God.

On the solid foundation of the established Word of God, we have overwhelming evidence of the Spirit of God, His presence, His imminent outpouring, and His work. Thus, the Word of God testifies to the Spirit of God. We now consider how the Spirit of God testifies to the Word of God.

HOW THE SPIRIT OF GOD CONFIRMS THE WORD OF GOD

If apologetics rests on divine causality in natural revelation and in special revelation, it comes to final rest on divine causality in the soul. A miracle in nature must prove the gospel to the sinner and a miracle in the soul must persuade the sinner of the gospel. In apologetics, as in life in general, God will have mercy on whom He will have mercy. He will make those blinder who will not see, while opening the eyes of others that they may see things that eyes have not seen, nor ears heard, nor have entered into the heart of man (1 Cor. 2:9).

Predestination is taught throughout the Bible; it is a daily fact of life for the apologist. We know persuasion is not by apologetic might, nor rational power, but by the Spirit of the Lord. We see the wise turning away mocking and the children perceiving the truth of God (Luke 10:21).

Is truth caught or taught, after all? Both. It is taught and caught. It must be taught by us; but it will not be caught unless God changes the minds and hearts of those we teach. It may be taught and not caught (God is sovereign), but it will not be caught without being taught (God is gracious.)

Without God, we cannot persuade—we are utterly futile. Apart from God, we even harm human hearts and make them fitter for destruction. Who is not humbled by the realization that all he does, insofar as he alone does it, only alienates those whom he would win? At this point we would be prone to despair. Then we realize that without us God will not change hearts. So we think as hard as we can, and we reason as well as we can, and we batter down the intellectual strongholds of Satan, and seek, as Calvin put it "to stop the mouths of the obstreperous."[1] After listening to us argue, a visitor from outer space would no doubt report to his peers that Christian apologists on earth think they can reason people into the kingdom of God. But we know that in apologetics, as in all else, at the end of our journey as at the beginning, we depend completely on the grace of God.

We have seen that God and logic go together, though some, as we noted, have thought that these were an odd couple, in fact, mutually exclusive. "Ignorance," they say, "not knowledge, is bliss." Not truth which can be understood, but paradox which calls for crucifixion of the intellect must be the way to God. Not a carefully constructed bridge from reason to belief but a leap of faith is called for.

We are alluding, of course, to Kierkegaard; but the man in the street often thinks the same way. Indeed, the Christian scholar some-times thinks that way. On Monday morning he expects to use his head; but on Sunday he leaves his brains with his hat in the vestibule and goes into the sanctuary to feel with his heart. He considers himself irreverent if he uses his head in the pew. Thus the caricature is born that the scientist thinks without feeling and the theologian feels with-out thinking.

Since we have the authority of the Word of God for the belief that the Spirit of God will indeed come and be a river of life, the bread of life, the indwelling of Christ, and the one who confirms Christ's Word, that very experience in the Christian heart is a divine confirmation of "the infallible truth and divine authority" of the Word of God. This is genuine confirmation that the Bible is the Word of God. How so? The proven Word of God said that the Spirit of God would come into human hearts and bring these very experiences. When we have these experiences, therefore, we know experientially or internally what we knew before merely rationally or externally. This is a new dimension or aspect of evidence. It is not really new *evidence,* nor is it fuller or better. The Bible's declaration is the perfect evidence. Experience can-not offer higher evidence than the testimony of the written Word of God.

We have already seen some anticipatory statements about the witness of the Holy Spirit to the Word especially in the promise of Christ that the Spirit would "teach you all things, and bring to your remembrance all that I said to you" (John 14:26 NASB). In bringing to men the remembrance of Christ, the Holy Spirit is doing more than the mere written record could do. That which is written does remind us of Christ, being the basic source of our knowledge of Him. The work of the Holy Spirit is other than that, since it obviously is not identical with that.

But this witness of the Spirit is not *apart* from the Word of God either, for He communicates no information. The Westminster Con-fession of Faith, therefore, puts it well in speaking of the work of the Spirit as bearing witness "by and with" the Word in our hearts. This witness would have to be by the Word, as we have said, because the Holy Spirit does not communicate the information on which we are dependent. So His witness is *by* the Word but also, more than that *alongside* it or *with* it (in addition to it).

Romans 8:16 also has a powerful, though concealed, reference to the Spirit's witness to the Word. "The Spirit Himself bears witness with our spirit that we are children of God." The "Spirit" is here distinguished from our "spirit." We witness that *we* are the children of God and so does He. The Holy Spirit and our spirits are inseparably united but not indistinguishably. There is a union here, not of equals, but an intimate, personal union nonetheless. Thus we are conscious of being the children of God as the Word of God says we in fact are and of having the right to call him by the familiar "Abba," Father, as the Word of God says we have the right to do. But in addition to that, the Spirit Himself gives us the right to call Him Father. His Spirit bears witness with our spirits. By confirming the Word's promises in our experience, the Holy Spirit indirectly testifies that the Scripture is indeed the Word of God.

But what does this have to do with the Word of God? It is clearly a witness of the Spirit of God to the church of God, but how is it a witness to the Word of God? As we say, the text is a concealed or implied allusion. How do we know that we are the children of God except that the Word of God says that we are? The Spirit of God does not "tell" us this. So it is in connection with our faith in and re-membrance of the Word of God that our spirits know that we are the children of God. It is the 'Spirit *in that connection* who Himself bears witness with our spirits that we are the children of God. This must imply that our confidence is truly in the Word of God. Our confidence is justified or the Spirit would not Himself bear witness with—but against—our spirits. So He makes us aware that we are the children of God by assuring us that the testimony of the Word is true as is that of our own spirit. Indirectly, this is a very powerful witness of the Holy Spirit to the Scripture as the very Word of God.

Romans 10:17 is another concealed reference to the witness of the Spirit of God to the Word of God. "So faith comes from hearing, and hearing by the word of Christ." The context makes it very clear that the initial hearing in this text ("faith comes by hearing") refers to the outward hearing of the call of the gospel. This is probably the strongest chapter in the entire Bible stressing the absolute necessity of hearing outwardly the Word of God if faith is to arise. But Paul is noting that not everyone who hears believes. He cites Isaiah to that same effect.

That leads Paul to make the remark that more than a hearing of the outward Word of God is necessary, although that is indispensable. That other hearing is called "hearing by the word of Christ," that is, hearing "of or concerning Christ."[2] One is helped much more by the context than by the language of the text. The language about the "word of Christ" is puzzling except that it is here being contrasted with the outward hearing of the word of Christ and therefore seems to refer to another, an inward hearing of Christ. Since Christ Himself has sent the Spirit of God to make the things of Christ real, calling them to remembrance in the hearts of His people, what else but that can be in mind here? What else than the hearing by the Spirit of Christ? So once again the Word of God is certified experientially by the Spirit. Why have they not "believed our report"? Because they have not heard it inwardly through the witness of the Holy Spirit, and thus they do not know it savingly.

In Hebrews 4:12 we have a strong but not obvious reference to the work of the Holy Spirit in convincing the soul of the Word of God:

> For the word of God is living and active and sharper than any two-edged sword, and piercing as far as the division of soul and spirit, of both joints and marrow, and able to judge the thoughts and intentions of the heart. And there is no creature hidden from His sight, but all things are open and laid bare to the eyes of Him with whom we have to do. (NASB)

In this case, the Spirit is not even mentioned and one might not notice that He is assumed, though if we recall Paul's reference to the Word as the sword of the Spirit in Ephesians 6:17 we could not fail to make the connection. The Spirit is not explicitly mentioned, but everything but His name is used. Notice the movement of the passage. The description is of the Word of God as *living, piercing, judging,* leaving no creature "hidden from *His* sight, but all things are open and laid bare to the eyes of *Him* with whom we have to do." The writer himself knows that he is describing no mere word but God Himself. He very naturally moves in verse 13 from a description of a living-piercing-judging *word* to a *person,* who alone could have such qualities. Who would this person be but the third person of the Trinity? The Spirit is so merged with His word that the Word becomes Person and no mere Word. There could be no stronger witness of the Spirit of God to the Word of God.

There are many other passages in the Bible to the witness of the Spirit of God to the Word of God. We will consider only one more which may be the most explicit:

> As it is written, "THINGS WHICH EYE HAS NOT SEEN AND EAR HAS NOT HEARD, AND *which* HAVE NOT ENTERED THE HEART OF MAN,

ALL THAT GOD HAS PREPARED FOR THOSE WHO LOVE HIM." For to us God revealed them through the Spirit; for the Spirit searches all things, even the depths of God. For who among men knows the thoughts of a man except the spirit of the man, which is in him? Even so the thoughts of God no one knows except the Spirit of God. Now we have received, not the Spirit of the world, but the Spirit who is from God, that we might know the things freely given to us by God, which things we also speak, not in words taught by human wisdom, but in those taught by the Spirit, combining spiritual thoughts with spiritual words. (1 Cor. 2:9–13 NASB)

This passage may well be the best in all of Scripture for putting together the revelation of God, the inspiration of God, and the illumination of God. The revelation is described as that which proceeds from the very thoughts of God which could only be known by the Spirit of God. The inspiration is referred to as the "words taught not by human wisdom, but in those taught by the Spirit," and the illumination, which especially concerns us here, by the expression "that we might know the things freely given to us by God." The revelation which comes from the mind of God is communicated to us by the words of God and we are illumined by the Spirit of God so as to "know" the things freely given to us by God.

Once again it is the Spirit who enables us to know the Word of God, the Scripture and, of course, to know that it is the Word of God. The Word comes from the mind of God, through the words of God, by the enlightenment of God: from revelation to inspiration to illumination. Without revelation there would be no Word of God; without inspiration there would be no inscripturating of the Word of God, and without illumination there would be no true understanding of the Word of God.

So the testimony of the Spirit is no *utterance* that what we are reading is the only Word of God, but *enlightenment* in the spiritual meaning of what we read whereby we understand not only what it says but that it is God who says it.

Our study of God and the Word of God has reached its penultimate stage. We have seen how the Son of God certifies the Word of God. We have seen how the Word of God in turn certifies the Spirit of God. Now we have seen how the Spirit of God persuades and assures us of the infallible truth and divine authority of the Word of God. It remains only to study the church of God to see how the Word of God brings the church of God into being and then how the church of God, in all ages, testifies to the Word of God.

HOW THE CHURCH TESTIFIES TO THE WORD OF GOD INCARNATE AND WRITTEN

We have seen how the Spirit of God gives His testimony to the Word in the church. Now we will see how the church has given her testimony to the Spirit in the Word.

Of the writing of histories of the doctrine of inspiration it seems that there will be no end. Recently Jack Rogers wrote one for *Biblical Authority*,[3] and it was answered by an essay in *Foundations of Biblical Authority*.[4] Now Rogers and Donald McKim have written a longer one[5] to which John Woodbridge has written a lengthy response that amounts to another survey.[6] The reason for the vast divergence among scholars on what would appear to be a simple historical subject—what the church through the ages has thought about the Bible—is not so much divergence in the data as the function of *non sequiturs* in the researchers' minds.

There are at least five common *non sequiturs:*

1. Phenomenal *non sequitur:* Supposing that when the Bible speaks of things as they *appear*, it is speaking of things as they *are*.

2. Accommodation *non sequitur:* Supposing that because the Bible accommodates or adapts itself to human ways of speaking, it therefore accommodates itself to human errors.

3. Emphasis *non sequitur:* Supposing that because the Bible *emphasizes* one thing, it is therefore unconcerned with the accuracy of incidental matters.

4. Docetic *non sequitur:* Supposing that because the Bible was written by humans, it could not also have been written by God without reducing humans to a mere appearance.

5. Critical *non sequitur:* Supposing that when a scholar tries to determine critically whether a text belongs in the Bible, he is assuming that the Bible may contain errors. We cannot point to a single recognized teacher of the Christian church, past or present, who actually says that God errs or even that the Word of God errs.

In those historical surveys in which inerrancy is attacked, the writer usually points to views of various historical teachers of the church who taught things that, in the opinion of the author, are inconsistent with inerrancy. But these authors never quote any church father as explicitly stating that there are errors in the autographic Bible. In other words, the historical surveyor is drawing conclusions from the historical teachings. But these conclusions are *non sequiturs,* conclusions that follow in the mind of the reviewer but not necessarily in the mind of the teacher of the church. We have to face the fact that some very learned scholars (who should be respected for their learning) draw some very dubious conclusions from their own vast data.

Assuming that the view of the inspiration of Scripture presented earlier in this chapter (the testimony of the Word to the Spirit and of the Spirit to the Word) is the historic position of the church, we now ask, what is the significance of it? To this question there are essentially three utterly disparate answers. The first is that of thinkers like Kirsop Lake,[7] namely, that the church has been wrong for all these centuries. This is *reason against the church.* The second is the official Roman Catholic answer; namely, that regardless of the verdict of rational evidence, the church has been right for all these centuries. This is the *church against reason.* The third is our own Protestant and Reformed answer; namely, that the verdict of rational evidence favors the position of the church for all these centuries. This is *reason for the church.*

Reason Against the Church

Lake and others, who admit that the church has indeed taught the inspiration of the Bible through the ages, think that the church has been wrong. Usually they think that, though there has been more excuse for it in the past than in the present, nevertheless, the doctrine of divine inspiration is and always has been untrue. In their view, the weight of historical support for our position turns out to be a ball and chain from which the church still finds it difficult to sever herself. An idealistic young friend of ours made this observation about inerrancy: "As I have grown older, I have discovered that the torch which I used to hold proudly aloft has turned out to be a hot potato!"

Why do the liberals think that the inerrancy of Scripture is nothing but an academic hot potato and that no one who values his scholarly reputation will hold onto it another moment? They have differences among themselves, of course. Nevertheless, their reason for repudiating biblical inspiration is essentially the same: Even if they believe in God and even if they believe in the natural revelation of God, they all reject supernatural revelation. However much they may differ from one another in other things, they stand back to back as antisupernaturalists. God does not walk on water; God does not raise the dead; God does not beget children without male sperm; God does not separate seas; God does not dispatch chariots of fire for departing prophets; God does not enable people to know things that are going to happen centuries hence; God does not reveal Himself supernaturally and then supernaturally inspire humans to record what He has revealed. These things do not happen. Every liberal knows this. Every radical knows this. Every reasonable person knows this. Every Christian ought to know this.

What do we say to these things? Shall we triumphantly declare that we will be fools for Christ's sake? Christ does not want us to be real fools; only to look like fools to a world which only thinks it is wise. But if all these things that liberals say about the Bible are true, then we would indeed be fools to believe the Bible.

We do not need to prove the antisupernaturalists wrong. They have to prove themselves right. This is clear from the following hypothetical dialogue:

Orthodox: Do I understand you to deny the inspiration of the Bible?

Liberal: If you mean the miraculous, supernatural inspiration of the Bible, I most certainly do deny it. Any intelligent person denies miraculous inspiration. Aren't you an intelligent person?

Orthodox: I think so, and I know many others who seem to be intelligent who believe that the Bible is supernaturally inspired. Can't God do miracles?

Liberal: Oh, I guess He *can* do them.

Orthodox: Let us take the guesswork out of this. Do you admit that God can do a miracle?

Liberal: O.K., God *can* do a miracle.

Orthodox: Then you grant that He *can* inspire a Bible?

Liberal: Oh, I guess he can even inspire a Bible.

Orthodox: Again let us take the guesswork out of this. Do you grant that he can inspire a Bible?

Liberal: O.K., I have to admit that God *can* inspire a Bible if He wants to, though I don't know why He would ever want to.

Orthodox: I will let that go for the moment. The point is: you do admit that God can inspire a Bible.

Liberal: Yes, I admit that God can inspire a Bible.

Orthodox: Then why do you deny that He did inspire the Bible? You admit at least that you cannot deny it a priori; that is, you do not say that there cannot be such a thing as an inspired Bible.

Liberal: Yes, I must admit that I cannot rule it out beforehand.

Orthodox: If you or anyone else did do so, you will admit that would not be very intelligent, will you not?

Liberal: Touché. I admit—though this is going to be hard on some of my friends—that it would not be intelligent to rule out inspiration a priori.

Orthodox: Well, then, since you do not rule out inspiration a priori, why do you deny it at all?

Liberal: I guess when it comes down to it that I don't believe miracles do happen, though I admit they could.

Orthodox: This is not being intelligent, is it—saying that miracles do not happen, when you admit that they can, without showing why they in fact do not happen?

Liberal: Touché again. I admit it's not being smart to say, without proof, that miracles do not happen when you yourself think that they may.

Orthodox: Fine; but why then do you think that they do not happen?

Liberal: I guess it is because I have never seen one or met anyone who has seen one. But I know what you are going to say about that. I'll admit in advance that not to believe miracles happen because one has never seen one is not very sound either.

Orthodox: Thanks, then why not join with us in believing in the inspiration of the Bible?

Liberal: Now wait a moment. Enough is enough. I have gone fairly far in even admitting that the Bible could be inspired. That is not the same as saying that it is. In fact, why should I believe the Bible is inspired?

Orthodox: I grant that you are not obliged to believe that something is miraculous just because you admit that it may be. In fact, it would not be very intelligent to do so. The burden of proof is on me now that you have removed the initial obstacle to all proof, the notion that something could not possibly be. Let me begin at this point. . . .

We need not continue this dialogue any further here. The main thing with most liberals is to get over that a priori hurdle. If they open themselves (as they must if they would be as liberal and reasonable as they claim to be) to the possibility that miracles did happen and that one of the greatest of them was the inspiration of the Holy Scriptures, their major objection has been removed.

Most liberals are very lame in their reasons for not believing in the inspiration of the Bible. They often admit that the church through the ages has believed this, but do not believe it themselves. They think that we are wrong in believing it but they seldom say why. Most of them belong to a "no miracles" fraternity. A condition of membership is that you admit "no miracles"—not that you are able to give a reason for the nonfaith which is in you.

All that we will say here and now is that liberalism has not yet come up with a sound argument against the miracles of the Bible, much less against the miracle which is the Bible. Therefore, whatever they have against the church's historic position, it is not reason. It is not reason but unreason parading as reason that is against the church's testimony to the Word of God.

The Church Against Reason

A priest once wrote that he believed the Bible is the Word of God because the Roman Catholic Church says that it is the Word of God. That was the only reason. If the Church had said that Matthew was not the Word of God, he continued, he would have believed that Matthew was not the Word of God. If the Church had said that *Aesop's Fables* were the Word of God, this priest would have believed that *Aesop's Fables* were the Word of God. For this priest there was only one reason for believing this or any other dogma or not believing this or any other dogma—whether his Church affirmed the dogma or denied it. His stance was determined by the *fides implicitum* concept of submission to whatever the Church teaches.

The Roman Catholic Church is not usually considered antirational or even nonrational. There is a profound sense in which this priest and the whole tradition which would agree with him, without expressing itself quite so flamboyantly, is rational. If the Church's magisterium is able to know what the individual cannot know, then, however absurd it may appear, the intelligent thing would be to believe whatever the Church does teach.

Protestants would never say this about the church, but we would say it about God. What God says is true, is true no matter how it appears to us. If God told us that Matthew was not inspired and that *Aesop's Fables* were, we would believe confidently that Matthew was not inspired and *Aesop's Fables* were. Ignatius Loyola believed that his Church had this God-like role when he said that if what he saw as black the Church said was white, he would believe that what he saw as black was white.

We admit an admirable rationality in Rome at this point: that whatever divine authority says, must be true no matter what we as individuals might think. We agree. We differ with Rome in that we do not believe God has given infallibility to the Roman Catholic magisterium. If God had indeed given the infallibility which Rome claims, she would be eminently rational in exercising it as she does and her members in accepting it as they do. If, however, Rome does not have the infallible magisterium which she claims (after Vatican II as well as before), then to proceed as she does is to pit the Church against reason. (This is precisely what Hans Kung and others in the Roman Catholic communion are saying today.[8])

We will not attempt here to prove that Rome does not have an infallible magisterium. The fundamental argument is that Rome is circular in her reasoning:

1. The infallible Church certifies the inspired Bible;
2. The inspired Bible certifies the infallible Church.

Reason for the Church

Reason is not against the church's doctrine and the church need not be against reason's verdict. The church and reason join together in the verdict that the Bible is the Word of God. We have seen that the church indeed does confess the Bible to be the Word of God; but how can we say that reason does the same? Even if reason's attempts to discredit the testimony of the church were futile, as we have shown, how does it follow that reason's testimony actually *supports* the church's testimony? It is one thing not to be against and still another thing to be in favor of.

First, we have shown that the Son of God affirms the Bible as the Word of God. If the Son of God says the Bible is the Word of God, no better reason could be advanced. If reason thought that it had evidence that the Bible were not the Word of God, as soon as it learned that the Son of God said that it is the Word of God, reason would know that its judgment was not reasonable. The only reasonable thing to do is to agree with the infallible God incarnate. Reason would be pure folly if it thought that it knew the infallible One to be wrong. The Son of God, who is the Logos, could not be illogical. Once the Son of God rendered His verdict, reason forever after would only say that it is reasonable to believe that the Scripture is nothing other than the very Word of God.

Second, the Spirit of God testifies to the Word of God. The Spirit of God is also God, fully God, and therefore omniscient. It is no more possible for Him to be in error than it is for the Father or for the Son. Any person in the Godhead would establish the reasonableness of believing in the inerrancy of the Bible, and here we have no less than two distinct persons in the all-wise Godhead saying the same thing.

Third, the Word of God itself says that it is the Word of God— three thousand times. We have proven, independently of the *inspired* Bible, that the Bible is the Word of God and the Word of God itself confirms that it is indeed the Word of God. If we say the Bible is the Word of God, we cannot add to our statement that it has or contains errors. The formula "The Word of God which errs" is at once irrational and impious.

No, reason is not against the church's testimony nor need the church's testimony be against the verdict of reason. Rather the testimony of the Christian church and the rational mind join in antiphonal response to the inerrant Word of God.[9]

So the Son of God certifies that the Bible is the Word of God; the Spirit of God illumines us concerning the Word of God; and the church is created by the Word of God and is that by which the world comes to know that the Bible is the Word of God.

As we said at the outset, the church through the ages has taught that the Bible is the Word of God, and the historians of the church have recorded it almost as many times as the Church has said it. So why say it yet again?

For one thing, it needs to be told to the generations which come after. They always begin in ignorance and if someone does not tell them, they will remain in ignorance.

An even more important reason is that our generation is not only normally ignorant but abnormally so. That is, we not only have scholars who do not know the history of the church's testimony, but we have those who tell it like it was *not*. One of these, on an occasion when he heard us mention that the historic position of the church has been inerrancy, said that he had never heard that before. And he had been around a long time. Nor did he mean, "Thank you for informing me" but, "How can a historian of Christianity be so ignorant as to think such an absurd thing?"—so absurd that this scholar had never even heard it before. We have heard that another instructor told his class that no scholar has believed in inerrancy for two hundred years.

We must keep telling the old story. We must labor the point until this error of errors—that the Bible has error—perishes from the face of the earth. The Word incarnate says of the Word written that "not the smallest letter or stroke shall pass away from the Law, until all is accomplished" (Matt. 5:18 NASB).

SECTION III

A CLASSICAL CRITIQUE OF PRESUPPOSITIONAL APOLOGETICS

CHAPTER 10

An Outline of Presuppositional Apologetics

PRESUPPOSITIONALISM HAS BECOME the majority report today among Reformed theologians, although it cannot even be called a minority report of church history. If Charles Hodge is right, that what is new is not true and what is true is not new, presuppositionalism, being new, falls of its own weight. Nevertheless, an intellectual movement of such force and extent merits and demands close attention—especially by evidentialist apologists and Reformed theologians, which the authors consider themselves to be. To our knowledge, this volume is the first extensive study of classical traditionalism (evidentialism) and presuppositionalism.

Many other traditional apologists and theologians have spoken and written about presuppositionalism. Perhaps, the best collection of such writings is found in the festschrift for Cornelius Van Til entitled *Jerusalem and Athens.*[1] Clark Pinnock, John W. Montgomery, Gordon R. Lewis among others oppose Van Til's presuppositionalism. Their critiques are necessarily brief, though useful. This collection displays some in-fighting among presuppositionalists, such as Herman Dooyeweerd, Robert Knudsen, and others, who differ with presuppositionalist Van Til. A large-scale critique has not been made, however, by any of the above writers.

Cornelius Van Til is, without doubt, the leading exponent of presuppositionalism. Van Tillianism is almost a synonym for presuppositionalism, though the school is much broader than any one thinker. The dedication is our tribute to Dr. Van Til. John Gerstner had the privilege of studying under him more than forty years ago and finds him still one of the two best teachers at whose feet he ever sat.

Van Til is also as gracious and generous in his speech as he is scorching, profound, and polemic in his mind. Though this book is intended as a refutation of Van Tillian apologetics, our tribute to Van Til is utterly genuine. We have no doubt, whatever, that he loves Jesus Christ and is thoroughly convinced that he learned presuppositionalism at His feet. The stalwart Reformed testimony of Van Til's disciples is impressive evidence that they, too, believe their Van Tillianism to be true biblical apologetic.

The readers may well wonder why the authors of this book so much fear an apologetic whose authors they so much love and admire. The answer is simple: the implications of presuppositionalism, in our opinion, undermine the Christian religion implicitly. The advocates love and promote Christianity, we gladly admit. However, their principles work against their intentions. If and when presuppositional principles are carried out consistently, they destroy what their advocates love.

We are already seeing this deadly work. The Institute of Advanced Christian Studies (Toronto) has departed, unconsciously perhaps, from the Reformed theology with which it began. Throughout this volume we will be citing instances of this in Herman Dooyeweerd, H. Evan Runner, Bernard Zylstra, James Olthuis, John Vander Stelt, and others. In fact, we will show that presuppositional principles, carried out consistently, undermine the Christian religion itself. These grave assertions will be spelled out and defended in the pages that follow.

BETWEEN TWO FIDEISMS

Even thinkers who oppose Van Til sharply are often essentially presuppositional or, at least, fideistic in their own principles. This is true for James Daane, for example. Fideism is the real culprit. We are aware that Van Til and others deny that they are fideistic, but while we honor their sincerity, we will try to prove their self-estimate wrong. Mark Hanna is another who is very critical of fideism, but his "veridicalism" does not really escape it.[2]

In fact, contemporary apologetics is between a rock and a hard place. The rock is ever more fideistic traditionalism. Contemporary Evangelicalism, that is, is basically experience oriented (the Charismatic movement being merely an extreme manifestation of a general trend).

If traditionalism is in danger of the rock, presuppositionalism must beware of the hard place. This school of thought has not suffered from a lack of nerve but has boldly rejected the traditional theistic proofs and Christian evidences. It has become the ultimate form of fideism riding under the banner of a super-rationality. Gordon H. Clark, the major rational opponent of Van Til, nevertheless outstrips Van Til's fideism with his own absolute fideism, while calling himself, in his latest book, a "spiritual rationalist."[3]

May God enable us, therefore, to help bring essentially sound traditional apologetics to its rational moorings where it can join with one of its greatest exponents, Jonathan Edwards, in saying:

> We first ascend, and *prove a posteriori,* or from effects, that *there must* be an eternal cause; and then secondly, *prove* by *argumentation,* not intuition, that this Being *must be* necessarily existent; and then thirdly, from the *proved* necessity of his existence, we may descend, and *prove* many of his perfections *a priori.*[4]

In one sentence affirming natural theology, the word *prove* occurs four times. Edwards, heralded as America's "greatest philosopher-theologian,"[5] displays himself as an equally great evidentialist in his rational case for the inspiration of the Bible.

Presuppositionalists insist that all traditional apologetics, such as that of Edwards, is futile, and worse than futile—false, and worse than false—blasphemous. Traditionalists may mean well, say presuppositionalists, but they do not think well. They may intend to do God service, but in fact they obscure His glory. Thinking themselves able to do for God what only God can do for Himself (and for them), they make mockery of reason and substitute arrogance for piety.

This serious indictment is based on several allegations. First, the traditional procedure, according to presuppositionalism, starts off on the wrong foot—*autonomy.* Traditionalists think that they can begin their thinking without God, being a law to themselves. They think themselves to be the measure of all things including the God who made them.

Second, even if this false apologetic ever could get started—as it cannot—it could never reach its goal. For if it begins with man, it is going to end with man, it will never end with God. The only way to end with God is to begin with God.

Third, the presuppositionalist insists that if the traditionalist did reach his goal, it would be an unworthy goal. The evidentialist cannot begin where he begins, cannot reach his goal if he does begin there, and if he thinks that he has reached his goal, that very conviction is his ultimate folly. Manifestly, beginning with a finite start and going through finite steps, he must finish at a finite end.

All the above criticism is negative. But the presuppositionalist claims to do far more than prove that the traditionalist is wrong. He would also prove that his own approach is right: If we start where we ought to start—with God—we not only end at the right place but grasp all else as well, including ourselves. This is what apologetics is supposed to do—give a reasoned defense for the Christian religion.

Let us now flesh out this skeleton of the presuppositionalist argument.

THE PRESUPPOSITIONALIST ARGUMENT

Presupposing God, we can prove everything and incidentally confirm God Himself. The fundamental fallacy of the traditional approach is in not recognizing that without knowing everything one cannot know anything. Thinking one can know anything without knowing everything is the initial error of traditionalism that plagues all its subsequent steps and wipes them out as fast as they are laid down. Everything is in relation to something else and that something else, of course, affects other things. If those other things are not known, then something about the thing in question remains unknown, and if something about it is unknown, then it in itself is not known.

It is like the problem of the flower in the cranny wall. As the poet lyricized, one cannot know the flower in the cranny wall unless he knows the world and all. On the other hand, if one can somehow know the world and all, then he can also know the flower in the cranny wall.

The presuppositionalist knows how he may know the world and all. This is the glory of presuppositionalism. It has found the secret of knowledge; the open sesame to all truth. A brute fact is a mute fact; but presuppositionalism opens the mouth of mute facts by changing them into part of the world which the presuppositionalist will tell us how to know.

His secret, of course, is God. God does know all—the world and everything in it. All theists have been aware of this for some time, but how does this help *us* to know the world? To be sure, God knows it as we have known all along that He does; the difficulty arises at the point of *our* knowing anything if *we* have to know everything.

Presuppositionalism's answer is that God reveals Himself and His knowledge to us in Scripture. If He did not do this, we would be back in futile traditional apologetics, trying to reach Him by our brute-mute facts.

At this point another question arises: Granted that God reveals Himself to us in Scripture, how does this help *us*? Our problem, presuppositionalists say, is that our brute facts are mute facts. How does it help us to know that God knows all facts and that they are not brute-mute facts for Him? That solves the problem for God who never had a problem, but how does it help *us* who still have the problem?

According to presuppositionalism, God enables us to think His thoughts after Him. That is the whole point of His revelation—not only to tell us that He knows, but to show us that we, too, presupposing Him who knows, can know also. How does God show us that because He knows we too can know? By analogical thinking. We cannot know as He knows, to be sure. But in his light He permits us to see light. That is, He permits us to posit knowledge of the facts because He knows the facts and vouchsafes knowledge to us by analogically thinking His thoughts after Him.

Still another problem arises for the presuppositionalist. The Bible teaches that humans are sinners and are therefore not willing to come to God at all, much less think all His thoughts after Him and be dependent on Him for everything. The solution is pure and unmixed Calvinism: God must open our eyes and change our hearts, we must be born again.

And if I am not born again? Then I will never see or understand what the apologist is telling me. The basic error in traditional thought, being principally Arminian, is that it overlooks the noetic influence of sin. That is, it does not notice that sin blinds the mind. Only God can remove sin and let the light in.

Thus, for the presuppositionalist, theology and apologetics are inseparable. A sound theology is essential for a sound apologetic. All traditional apologetics is considered Arminian even when developed by Calvinists, such as Hodge and Warfield, who simply forgot their Calvinism when doing apologetics. Calvinism teaches that people are blind and can only grope in the dark until they are born again. True apologetics must begin with rebirth. One may be born again without being presuppositional; but no one can be presuppositional without being born again. For prior to rebirth, presuppositional thought will appear foolish and obscurantist.

Presuppositionalism teaches heteronomy instead of autonomy, regeneration instead of the noetic influence of sin; analogical rather than univocal thinking; presupposing instead of proving. It departs from evidentialism at every apologetic point, just as it shows evidentialism to be in error at every apologetic point.

But evidentialism dies hard. Once again it asks: If we presuppose rather than prove, have we not abandoned apologetics rather than performed it? Feasible as all the presuppositionalist answers sound, do they not beg all the questions? If they displace evidentialism, do they not do so by abandoning apologetics in the process?

This is something of a sore spot for the presuppositionalist, the point where he comes closest to admitting that he has a problem. What we hear him saying is this: We may not *prove* in the ordinary sense of that word, but we do *confirm*. That is, to assume God at the outset is the foundation for all knowledge. Is that not proof? Real proof? Confirmation? Is that not losing one's intellectual life in order to gain it? Does not the traditionalist try to save his apologetic life only to lose it?

That is a pious answer, but it is also circular and paradoxical. The charge of circularity would demolish all other forms of thought; but for the presuppositionalist, it is the call to arms. Yes, indeed, he declares, but what a glorious circle! What a divine circle. All thinkers, evidentialists included, think in circles; but they are human circles. Ours is divine and given by God Himself. Presuppositionalists travel only in the very best circles.

Having presented an outline of the presuppositionalist position, we turn now, in the remainder of this volume, to the critique of presuppositionalism. First, we will glance at the history of apologetics to hear its testimony. We will show that this new apologetic was virtually unheard of for eighteen centuries, only coming into its own in this one. Those claimed points of contact with great apologists gone by we will see are more apparent than real. The real historical point of contact comes not with Christian apologetics of the past but with that which brought its modern eclipse—the Enlightenment. The third part of this book will present and refute current arguments for presuppositionalism and end in a reassertion of the traditionalism of the ages.

CHAPTER 11

General Apologetic Tradition on Reason and Faith: Augustine, Luther, and Calvin

COMPETING CLAIMS AND assertions of various apologetic positions make necessary the attempt to establish the historic position of the church on the relation of reason and faith. We will consult three towering figures in church history—Augustine, Luther, and Calvin—taking them as representative of the church's historic position.

AUGUSTINE ON FAITH AND REASON

Augustine is often considered a fideist. Contemporary commentators note little if any priority of reason to faith in Augustine's thought.[1] Perhaps the reason for this widespread belief that Augustine is a fideist is that in a number of places he emphatically stresses the acceptance of authority as a prerequisite for reason.

It has not generally been noticed that in Augustine's thought there is a place for reason both before and after accepting authority. Reason provides grounds for accepting an authority. Once that authority is established, then reason has a subordinate role helping to explain and confirm various doctrines found in that authority. In the latter case, the acceptance of the doctrine is not dependent on the ability to defend it rationally. Reason, in this case, can help but must ultimately submit to authority.

Many of the quotes brought forward to show Augustine's "fideism" only show reason in this latter role. In Augustine's thought reason also has the role of showing why a claim to revelation ought to be accepted. We see reason used in this sense in Augustine's conversion and in his subsequent writings.

Augustine's conversion experience had a definite influence on his later emphases. In order to understand his position on reason, authority, and faith it is important to see how he came to faith. It is especially important to see why Augustine rejected the Manichean position on reason. Prior to his conversion to Christianity, Augustine had been a Manichean. The central argument that had drawn Augustine and his friend Honoratus into that sect was their condemnation of the superstitious faith of Christians. The Manicheans promised reasons for all their teachings. Augustine recalls:

> You know, Honoratus, that I fell among these people for no other reason than that they would put aside all overawing authority, and by pure and simple reason would bring to God those who were willing to listen to them and so deliver them from all error. What else compelled me for nearly nine years to spurn the religion implanted in me as a boy by my parents, to follow these men and listen diligently to them, than that they said we were overawed by superstition and were bidden to believe rather than to reason, while they pressed no one to believe until the truth had been discussed and elucidated.[2]

During his time as a Manichean, Augustine came to see that, although this sect had promised reasons for their teachings, in actuality he was being asked to accept some rather fantastic accounts of reality without any reasons being offered. Irrational and unverifiable tales were offered for belief solely on the authority of Mani and the Manichean teachers. Augustine saw that they asked for acceptance on authority, even while they spoke of the necessity of reason.

Augustine also came to see that belief in authority was necessary in everyday life. In his *Confessions* he says that the Lord

> little by little, with a gentle and most merciful hand, drawing and calming my heart, didst persuade me taking into consideration what a multiplicity of things which I had never seen, nor was present when they were enacted, like so many of friends, so many of physicians, so many now of these men, now of those, which unless we should believe, we should do nothing at all in this life.[3]

Augustine thus began to see *reasons* why he must accept some kind of authority. After a meeting with the celebrated Manichean teacher Faustus, Augustine was disillusioned. He was sorry that he had become involved with that sect. He began to search in earnest for the truth. He began to consider the possibility that if truth was to be known, perhaps it would be known through divine authority. Augustine saw that:

> Possibly the manner of seeking truth might be concealed and would have to be accepted from some divine authority. It remained to inquire what that authority might be, since among so many dissonant voices each one professed to be able to hand it on to me. An inextricable thicket confronted me, most tiresome to be involved in; and here without any rest my mind was agitated by the desire to find the truth.[4]

First, Augustine came to see that some authority was necessary to life. Second, he came to consider the possibility of there being a divine authority. The question that remained was where to find that authority. There were so many claims to such authority. Augustine had chosen the wrong way before and did not wish to do so again.[5]

It was particularly through the preaching of Ambrose that Augustine began to believe that which he once thought to be absurd:

> For now those things which heretofore, appeared incongruous to me in the Scripture, and used to offend me, having heard divers of them expounded reasonably, I referred to the depth of the mysteries, and its authority seemed to me all the most venerable and worthy of religious belief.[6]

Later Augustine advised Honoratus to do what he had done. If it appeared that ridiculous things were taught in the church, then "seek for someone both pious and learned"[7] to help in the search for truth. Throughout his life, Augustine was opposed to credulity. Although he stressed the importance of accepting authority, he did not accept that authority or ask others to accept it without any reasons. We see this priority of reason to faith in a number of Augustine's writings.

Reason Prior To Faith

In one of Augustine's earlier treatises, *Of True Religion* (A.D. 390), he speaks of two functions of reason—one following after authority, the other in relation to authority itself:

> Authority demands belief and prepares man for reason. Reason leads to understanding and knowledge. But reason is not entirely absent from authority, for we have got to consider whom we have to believe.[8]

Reason first decides whom to believe then reason leads to a deeper knowledge and understanding of the authority that is believed.

Later in the same work, Augustine again indicates the importance of evaluating an authority before believing:

> It is our duty to consider what men or books we are to believe in order that we may rightly worship God, wherein lies our sole salvation. Here the first decision must be this: Are we to believe those who summon us to the worship of many gods or those who summon us to worship one God?[9]

He argues that belief in one God is "more worthy to be believed."[10] Again Augustine does not ask for the acceptance of authority without reason. It is our duty to consider which men or books we are to believe.

In one of his letters, Epistle 120 (A.D. 410), Augustine clearly spells out the role of reason prior to and following faith. He says that faith ought to precede reason because this is in itself reasonable. This letter is a response to Consentius, a monk who had written to Augustine concerning christological and trinitarian questions. At the beginning of his letter (Epistle 119),[11] Consentius had laid down the principle for himself that "divine truth is to be grasped by faith more than by reason."[12] Augustine responded to Consentius by warning him not to underestimate the value of reason.[13] On points of salvation, which we cannot grasp by reason, let faith precede reason, in a provisional sense. It is important to understand, however, that to allow faith to precede reason is itself a reasonable principle:

> It is, then, a reasonable requirement that faith precede reason, for, if this requirement is not reasonable, then it is contrary to reason, which God forbid. But, if it is reasonable that faith precede a certain great reason, which cannot yet be grasped, there is no doubt that, however slight the reason which proves this, it does precede faith.[14]

Thus we see that for Augustine the principle that faith precedes reason is itself proved by reason. It is certainly not "contrary to reason, which God forbid." In this citation as in the rest of his writing, Augustine downplays the role of unaided human reason after it has found authority. He calls reason prior to faith "slight" and reason after faith "great." This is consistent with his rejection of the Manichean emphasis that all truths must be accepted on the basis of reason. Nevertheless, Augustine does give a place to reason prior to faith.[15]

One of the "reasons" that helped to establish authority was miracles. Miracles establish authority and authority demands faith. According to Augustine, Christ

> by his miracles gained authority, by his authority deserved faith, by faith drew together a multitude, thereby secured permanence of the tradition, which in time corroborated religion. That religion neither the foolish novelty of heretics working deceitfully, nor the ancient error of the nations in violent opposition, will avail to pluck up and destroy in any part.[16]

In the *City of God* Augustine placed the Resurrection and Ascension at the center of the miracles. The apostles' miracles testified to this one great miracle:

> For they who had not seen Christ risen in the flesh, nor ascending into heaven with His risen body, believed those who related how they had seen those things, and who testified not only with words but wonderful signs. . . . That the one incredibility of the resurrection and ascension of Jesus Christ may be believed, we accumulate the testimonies of countless incredible miracles.[17]

The resurrection and ascension of Christ are confirmed by the apostles' miracles. These miracles in turn confirm the creed. The purpose of miracles is to confirm the creed and ultimately to lead to faith.

> But we cannot deny that many miracles were wrought to confirm that one grand and health-giving miracle of Christ's ascension to heaven with the flesh in which He rose. For these most trustworthy books of ours contain in one narrative both the miracles that were wrought and the creed which they were wrought to confirm. The miracles were published that they might produce faith and the faith which they produced brought them into greater prominence.[18]

Prophecy as well as miracles help to establish that Christ is God. Along with a "multitude of very striking miracles which proved that Christ is God, there were also divine prophecies heralding Him, prophecies worthy of belief, which being already accomplished we have not, like the fathers, to wait for their verification."[19]

Although Augustine argues that there is sufficient evidence to confirm faith in authority, he does not believe that this evidence will persuade sinful people. We may "accumulate the testimonies of countless miracles, but even so we do not bend the frightful obstinacy of these skeptics."[20] The "world's belief in Christ is the result of divine power, not of human persuasion."[21] Evidence is the ground of faith, but it is not the cause of it. Augustine presents evidence as sufficient to establish authority, fully aware that only "divine power" will persuade to accept the authority. Reason does not produce faith, except as God leads the heart to accept it.[22]

Faith Prior to Reason

The priority of reason to faith described above has not been given sufficient notice, because there are so many strong statements in Augustine's writings to the effect that faith and authority precede reason. Augustine says, for instance, that "there is no sounder principle in the Catholic Church than that authority should precede reason."[23] The method of all heretics is to "counter the supremely strong foundations of the authority of the Church by the specious title and appeal to reason."[24] This was certainly the case in Augustine's experience with the Manicheans. His later emphasis is easily understood in light of his own discovery of divine authority. Once authority was determined, then reason could exercise its highest role—that of understanding authority.[25]

Augustine's position was not taken for granted among his contemporaries. Few in the church had the philosophical training Augustine had. Few desired to understand authority by reason as Augustine did. In his first work, *Against the Academics* (A.D. 386), he says:

> No one doubts but that we are helped in learning by a twofold force, that of authority and that of reason. I, therefore, am resolved in nothing whatever to depart from the authority of Christ—for I do not find a stronger.[26]

When Augustine dealt with what had been rationally established as divine revelation, he bowed to authority, but even then was quick to desire a deeper understanding by means of reason. When reason probed matters of revelation, its role was definitely subordinate. No teaching or doctrine of revelation was accepted because it was rationally defensible. Authority, not reason, was then the basis for accepting the individual teachings of revelation which reason can elucidate.[27]

Reason can help clear up obscurity in understanding a doctrine. Yet the danger is always present that mysteries might be believed only when they are understood. It is important to begin with "at least authority." In order to obtain understanding, we are

> necessarily led in a twofold manner, authority and reason. Authority has a temporal priority, but reason an actual one. One takes precedence in the order of action; the other is judged to be of higher value as an object of desire. . . . For all who desire to learn great and hidden goods, only authority opens the door. . . . When he has become teachable through these precepts then at long last will he learn how much reason was embodied in those precepts which he had observed before rational understanding. . . . I do not know how I could call those happy who, while they live among men, [are] content with authority alone and either despising or unable to be instructed in the liberal arts.[28]

Once recognized, authority is the door to understanding. It comes first in the "order of action." It has a temporal priority. Reason has an actual priority because it has a "higher value as an object of desire." It can lead us to a deeper understanding of God. Augustine does not see how anyone could be content with authority alone. The liberal arts help us to arrive at a deeper understanding of revelation.

Notice that in the above quotations reason is subordinate to authority in dealing with divine matters. Reason may establish authority as a whole. Once that authority source is discovered, however, its individual teachings are accepted on the basis of its authority and only clarified by reason. Individual doctrines like the Trinity do not need to have inherent rational proofs in order to be accepted. It may be possible, as Augustine attempts to do in *The Trinity,* to provide a rational justification for revealed teaching. But divine matters are not always capable of being understood by reason:

> For in human things, reason, although lacking the certitude of truth is thought secure. But when it approaches divine things, it turns away unable to behold; it trembles, pants and burns with love, and, driven back from the light of truth, returns, not from choice but from exhaustion, to its familiar darkness.[29]

Reason, on its own, is not always able to penetrate divine revelation. Nevertheless, it can be a great help toward understanding revelation.

Each time "reason" is used in Augustine's writings it is necessary to determine in what respect it is being used. Those passages in which faith or authority are said to precede reason point to the inability of reason to determine divine things. Augustine does not deny that reason is prior to authority when the question is which authority to believe. Reason tells us whom to believe. Once that is known, it is reasonable for faith to precede reason.[30]

LUTHER AND REASON

Martin Luther is notorious for his opposition to reason. In various of his writings he calls reason "carnal," "stupid," a "beast," an "enemy of God," and a "source of mischief."[31] He refers to it as a "whore," "Frau Hulda" who seduces the innocent. His verbal assaults on Aristotle who is synonymous with scholastic philosophy are well known. In Luther's eyes Aristotle was the "destroyer of pious doctrine," a "mere Sophist and quibbler," an "inventor of fables," "ungodly public enemy of the truth," "the stinking philosopher," "the Clown of the High Schools," "trickster," "rascal," "liar and knave," "the pagan beast," and "billy goat."[32]

While many strong statements like those given above, can be brought forward to show Luther's hostility toward reason, a fuller study of his writings shows that it is necessary to distinguish between Luther's various uses of the word *reason*. There are passages where Luther attacks reason, and other passages where he praises reason. In *Grace and Reason*, B. A. Gerrish holds that it is necessary to maintain a threefold distinction when considering Luther's view of reason. Luther uses reason as (1) natural reason ruling within its proper domain; (2) arrogant reason trespassing on the domain of faith; and (3) regenerate reason dealing with spiritual matters, but always subject to the Word.[33] Luther's attack on reason focuses on the second of these uses; he praises the other two. Gerrish says

> that the real problem is not that Luther's statements exhibit a uniform hostility towards reason, but that they present a strangely ambivalent attitude, alternatively heaping upon reason extravagant praise and unqualified opprobrium.[34]

Despite Luther's harsh words for Aristotle, a number of considerations qualify Luther's opinion about philosophy in general and Aristotle in particular. First, Luther saw value in some of the teachings of Aristotle and other philosophers. He maintained that Aristotle's teaching could help in the conduct of life. For instance, Luther liked the discussion of *epieikeia* in the *Nicomachean Ethics*,[35] and found Aristotle's *Logic, Rhetoric,* and *Poetics* helpful as textbooks. Second, not all philosophers were judged as harshly as Aristotle; Luther preferred Cicero's practical emphasis to Aristotle's emphasis on logic. Aristotle believed that God exists, but Cicero also maintained that God cares. "If you want real philosophy," said Luther, "read Cicero."[36] And in another place:

> Aristotle is an utter Epicurean. He does not believe that God cares for human affairs—or, if he does so believe, then he considers that God governs the world as a drowsy nursemaid rocks a child. Cicero, on the other hand, went much further.[37]

Luther did not dispute the value of natural reason in philosophy in general or in Aristotle in particular. His primary objection to Aristotle was his association with the scholastic system of salvation which Luther opposed. He states this clearly in his *Address to the German Nobility,* "Almost the whole of Aristotle's *Ethics* is the worst enemy of grace."[38] This Lutheran antipathy toward Aristotle reaches a peak in the classical Protestant reaction to Aquinas. Such dread of infection from Thomistic–Aristotelian soteriology cast a shadow over the whole of Aristotle and Aquinas.

Luther had studied under nominalist philosophers at Erfurt and Wittenberg. He was greatly influenced by William of Occam, Gabriel Biel, and other nominalists who were critical of Aristotle. And when Luther reacted violently against the scholastic system of salvation, it was the nominalist separation of reason and faith that enabled him to break out of the scholastic soteriology.

Sometime before 1513, Luther had a spiritual awakening. One of the catalysts to this new insight was his biblical study. Texts such as Isaiah 28:21, Ezekiel 33:11, and Romans 1:17 were particularly important. On Christmas of 1514, Luther preached his last speculative scholastic sermon. His sermons on the Decalogue, beginning in 1516 and continuing to February 24, 1517, were directed against scholasticism.

This religious experience together with the nominalistic separation of reason and faith made the rejection of the scholastic synthesis possible. Although Luther tended to separate reason and faith, it needs to be determined in what sense this separation was made. Gerrish maintains that for Luther the problem of relating reason and faith is not so much an epistemological problem as a soteriological one. There is a

> certain speciousness to the case of critics who place him in the succession of Christian irrationalists which goes back at least to Tertullian. But your argument so far has been correct, what is wrong with the critics' case is simply that for Luther the problem of faith and reason is not so much an epistemological question (as they clearly suppose): it is a soteriological question. His critique of reason is theological through and through. "Faith" and "reason" stand, so we have maintained, for two different ways of salvation; and "rationality" (if we dare use so vague a term) is not more characteristic of the one type than the other.[39]

This is perhaps why Luther did not object when Melanchthon, Luther's chief lieutenant, included theistic proofs in his *Loci Communes* (1511). It is unlikely that Melanchthon could or would have done this without Luther's approval. At the very least, Luther allowed the proofs to remain.

Although Luther made strong statements against reason, he did appreciate the value of natural reason and philosophy. He objected to the use of reason where it had distorted a theological doctrine such as justification by faith alone.

CALVIN AND REASON

There has been considerable debate about the nature of Calvin's position on the knowledge of God. Various answers have been given about whether Calvin had a "natural theology." Some (Karl Barth, Peter Barth, Wilhelm Niesel, and T. H. L. Parker) maintain that there is no natural theology in Calvin. Others (Emil Brunner and Edward Dowey) give a limited role to natural theology, seeing it as possible for the Christian. Still others (e.g., B. B. Warfield) see in Calvin a natural (though not saving) knowledge of God present in all people.

There is one point at which all the above positions agree, namely, that for Calvin knowledge of God is at least available to all people through the creation. Calvin stated emphatically that God has shown Himself clearly in nature. When we look at the creation we see that God has there "engraved unmistakable marks of His glory."[40] God "daily discloses himself in the whole workmanship of the universe. As a consequence men cannot open their eyes without being compelled to see him" (1.5.1). The heavens and the earth contain "innumerable evidences" of God's wisdom (1.5.2). When we look at God's works, whether individually or as a whole,

> God's powers are actually represented as in a painting. Thereby the whole of mankind is invited and attracted to recognition of him, and from this to true and complete happiness. Now those powers appear most clearly in his works. (1.5.10)

There is not even a need to go outside ourselves. The "signs of divinity" are within as well as without (1.5.4).

Calvin maintained that there is a *sensus divinitatis* or *deitatis* present in all people: "There is within the human mind, and indeed by natural instinct, an awareness of divinity" (1.3.1). God has sown a "seed of religion in all men" (1.4.1). This sense of divinity does not seem to be a faculty of the soul,[41] but it does include a rational understanding of some basic truths: that "there is a God and that he is their Maker" as well as an "understanding of his divine majesty" (1.3.1). Along with this sense of the divine majesty is a sense that God ought to be worshiped and that He will show His vengeance towards sin (1.3.1-2). According to Calvin, even the "unity of God has been engraved upon the hearts of all" (1.10.3).

Another point at which all the varying positions agree is that for Calvin this knowledge of God available in nature does not lead to salvation. This natural knowledge does not lead to "real piety" (1.4.1). Because of their "carnal stupidity" (1.4.1), all distort the true knowledge of God. Nature would have led us to a "primal and simple knowledge" of God "if Adam had remained upright" (1.2.1). Although the knowledge of God in nature is clear, it only serves to leave all people without excuse:

> While the heavens bear witness concerning God their testimony does not lead men so far as that thereby they learn truly to fear him, and acquire a well-grounded knowledge of him; it serves only to render them inexcusable.[42]

The point of issue is whether this natural knowledge of God gets through to the unbeliever. For instance, Niesel says that "the knowledge of God which we may acquire from His works and deeds is subjective and unreal."[43] Because of sin the capacity to recognize the signs of divinity in nature has been lost. The evidence for God's existence and majesty are available in nature but unbelievers are totally blind to it. The evidence is objectively adequate but not subjectively appropriated. Parker says in his work on *Calvin's Doctrine of The Knowledge of God:* "Is God then known by means of a consideration of the universe and history? Ideally—or rather originally—yes. In fact, no."[44] Brunner and Dowey hold a similar view (although they differ with Niesel and Parker on the place of a Christian natural theology).

There are passages in Calvin which appear to justify this position. Calvin, commenting on the psalmist, says,

> But because most people, immersed in their own error, are struck blind in such a dazzling theater, he exclaims that to weigh these works of God wisely is a matter of rare and singular wisdom, in viewing which they who otherwise seem to be extremely acute profit nothing. And certainly however much the glory of God shines forth, scarcely one man in a hundred is a true spectator of it! (1.5.8)

In another passage the "minds of men" are said to be "more than stupid or blind" when they "pursue heavenly mysteries" (1.5.12). In yet another place, Calvin wrote that though the "invisible divinity is made manifest" in the universe, "we have not the eyes to see this" unless illuminated by God's "inner revelation" (1.5.14).

But despite these images of unbelievers as "struck blind," more than "blind," and having "not the eyes to see," other passages indicate that they are blind not to natural knowledge of God's majesty, but to the things of salvation. Commenting on Romans 1:20, Calvin wrote that

> the manifestation of God by which He makes His glory known among His creatures is sufficiently clear as far as its own light is concerned. It is, however, inadequate on account of our blindness. But we are not so blind that we can plead ignorance without being convicted of perversity. . . . We are prevented by our blindness from reaching our goal. And yet we see just enough to keep us from making excuse.[45]

The argument of this passage illuminates what Calvin said in other passages on "blindness": God has shown Himself to His creatures in the creation. This evidence is "sufficiently clear." But it is "inadequate" because of our "blindness." How is this knowledge inadequate? Is it inadequate because it is never really known? Or is it inadequate, because of our blindness, to lead us to salvation? Calvin clearly maintained that it is not the former. We are "not so blind" that we can plead ignorance. We "see just enough" to keep us from making excuses. Our blindness, however, prevents us from "reaching our goal." What is this goal? Since our blindness does not prevent us from seeing "enough," our inadequacy to "reach the goal" must be with respect to a fuller, more complete knowledge of God, a *saving* knowledge of God. Our blindness is not to a natural knowledge of God, but to the "goal" of saving knowledge.

Other passages indicate that this knowledge of God's majesty continually breaks through our "blindness." The sense of the divine majesty is "ever renewing its memory" (1.3.1). God "repeatedly sheds fresh drops" (1.3.10). Some conception of God is "ever alive in all men's minds" (1.3.2). This "sense of divinity . . . can never be effaced" (1.3.2). Even though unbelievers wish to extinguish this knowledge it "thrives" (1.3.1). Unbelievers wish they were totally blind to God, but the knowledge of the divine majesty

> strikes their consciences all the more violently the more they try to flee from it. Indeed, they seek out every subterfuge to hide themselves from the Lord's presence, and to efface it again from their minds. But in spite of themselves they are always entrapped. Although it may sometimes seem to vanish for a moment, it returns at once and rushes in with new force. (1.3.2)

Thus we see that unbelievers are not blind to the divine majesty, in fact, they are never totally blind to it.

Another consideration which implies that this natural knowledge of God gets through is Calvin's use of pagan philosophers. Calvin uses Cicero, for example, to support the idea of a universal sense of divinity: "Yet there is, as the eminent pagan says, no nation so barbarous, no people so savage, that they have not a deep-seated conviction that there is a God" (1.3.1). And he uses Plato to support his argument for the importance of knowing God: "Plato meant nothing but this when he often taught that the highest good of the soul is likeness to God, where when the soul has grasped the knowledge of God, it is wholly transformed into his likeness" (1.3.3). He even quotes Plato on the subject of prayer, commenting that the "heathen man is wise in that he judges how dangerous it is to seek from the Lord what our greed dictates" (3.20.34). These philosophers were not so blind that they could not see some fundamental truths about God. Although Calvin did not believe that natural knowledge of God would lead to salvation apart from God's work, nevertheless he emphasized that enough knowledge does get through to leave unbelievers without excuse, the point Brunner was so jealous to make in his famous debate with Barth.

There is some controversy also about Calvin's attitude to the theistic proofs. According to B. B. Warfield, Calvin had a "special interest in the theistic argument" and "he asserts their validity most strenuously."[46] T. H. L. Parker responds that this contention of Warfield "comes from reading back into Calvin another motive and other thoughts, culled from the course of scholastic Calvinism, which is not to be found in Calvin, but do violence to the motive of his theology."[47] Parker does not see where "all this activity is to be found."[48]

When we look particularly at *Institutes* 1.5.1-13, we see a variety of arguments being used. Edward Dowey maintains that in this section of the *Institutes* every single Scripture verse could be dropped out without in any way affecting the argument.[49] Phrases such as "Therefore as the prophet aptly exclaims" (1.5.1) or "For the same reason David exclaims" (1.5.3) are given in confirmation of a rational argument rather than vice versa. Dowey continues:

> In the description of how it should function Calvin uses in simplified form some arguments from nature that would do credit to Herbert of Cherbury. . . . The rational quality of the arguments we are about to analyze and the active contribution to them of the human mind on the level of ordinary logic are unmistakable. . . . The arguments from design and from sufficient cause are held up as norms for the mind, and the immortality of the soul is maintained in opposition to Aristotle on purely rational grounds.[50]

Calvin's arguments are usually quite compressed. They are not elaborated in a philosophical manner and defended against objections. Nevertheless, Calvin used theistic argument. Calvin constructed an argument from design:

> In regard to the structure of the human body one must have the greatest keenness in order to weigh, with Galen's skill, its articulation, symmetry, beauty and use. But yet, as all acknowledge, the human body shows itself to be a composition so ingenious that its Artificer is rightly judged a wonder-worker. (1.5.2)

He sketched a cosmological argument:

> This very might leads us to ponder his eternity; for he from whom all things draw their origin must be eternal and have a beginning from himself. Furthermore, if the cause is sought by which he was

led once to create all these things and is now moved to preserve them, we shall find that it is goodness alone. (1.5.6)

Calvin argued for the immortality of the soul against Aristotle (1.5.5), and against the Epicurean's idea of chance (1.5.4). He argued against Virgil's pantheism, pointing out that this philosophy necessitates the idea that the universe is self-creating: "As if the universe, which was founded as a spectacle of God's glory, were its own creator" (1.5.5). Calvin regarded the few arguments that he gives "sampled at random" as so "very manifest and obvious" that "no long or toilsome proof is needed" (1.5.9) to show the divine majesty. The proofs can be "observed with the eyes and pointed out with the finger" (1.5.9). Many philosophers today would disagree with Calvin's optimism about the transparency of the proofs. It appears, however, that Calvin regarded them as compelling. In fact, he regarded them as so obvious that they do not need "long or toilsome arguments to demonstrate their validity."

Yet another area of controversy in Calvin scholarship is over the role of the internal testimony of the Holy Spirit in relation to Scripture. The central question is whether the Holy Spirit works apart from or along with evidence for biblical inspiration in producing certainty in the heart of a believer.

There are those who believe that Calvin opposed a rational apologetic for Scripture. Bernard Ramm, for instance, in *The Witness of the Spirit* writes that Calvin

> opposed rationalistic Christian apologetics for several reasons. To begin with, the Scriptures themselves do not agree with this method, for the prophets and apostles do not appeal to rational arguments, but to the sacred name of God (1.7.4). A rational apologetics gives human assurance where only divine assurance is suitable (1.7.4). Such proofs are matters of probable supposition, the product of disputation, and the human mind is always left in suspense with such proofs. Calvin says that even if he debated with a man and convinced him of the truthfulness of the faith, the man would not have any substantial assurance (1.8.1).[51]

It is true, according to Calvin, that the prophets and the apostles do not "dwell upon rational proofs" but call upon the name of God. We must "seek conviction in a higher place than human reasons, judgments, or conjectures, that is, in the secret testimony of the Spirit" (1.7.4). He frequently pointed to the difference between human assurance and divine assurance. No doubt Calvin did believe that rational evidences would not produce "substantial assurance." The inadequacy of evidence to produce divine certainty does not mean, however, that evidences are to be rejected. The question is not whether the Holy Spirit's assurance is the ultimate basis for certainty. That is granted by all. The question is, how does the Holy Spirit relate to evidence in producing that assurance?

There is no doubt that Calvin regarded the testimony of the Holy Spirit as the ultimate basis for the believer's certainty:

> But I reply: the testimony of the Spirit is more excellent than all reason. For as God alone is a fit witness of himself in his Word so also the Word will not find acceptance in men's hearts before it is sealed by the inward testimony of the Spirit. (1.7.4)

It would be a false inference, however, to conclude that, because the testimony of the Spirit is "more excellent" than reason, Calvin necessarily maintained an irrational basis for belief in biblical authority. Clearly, Calvin did not disregard arguments for biblical authority. He devoted a whole chapter of the *Institutes* (1.8) to evidences for the Scripture's authority. The credibility of Scripture is established by proofs such as its superiority to human wisdom, its antiquity, its majestic style, its miracles, and its witness by the blood of the martyrs. Calvin believed that this evidence is compelling:

> There are other reasons, neither few or weak, for which the dignity and majesty of Scripture are not only affirmed in godly hearts, but brilliantly vindicated against the wiles of its disparagers. (1.8.13)

Calvin asserted that the evidence is so overwhelming that he could silence many unbelievers by using it.

> Although I do not excell either in great dexterity or eloquence, if I were struggling against the most crafty sort of despisers of God, who seek to appear shrewd and witty in disparaging Scripture, I am confident it would not be difficult for me to silence their clamorous voices. (1.7.4)

Yet, despite the overwhelming amount of evidence available to establish biblical authority, the highest testimony is the inward testimony of the Spirit.

> Scripture will ultimately suffice for a saving knowledge of God only when its certainty is founded upon the inward persuasion of the Holy Spirit. Indeed, these human testimonies which exist to

confirm it will not be vain if, as secondary aids to our feebleness, they follow that chief and highest testimony. (1.8.13)

Notice that no amount of evidence can produce "saving knowledge." The inward persuasion of the Holy Spirit is the "ultimate" testimony. Evidence alone will never produce a "firm faith in Scripture" (1.7.4). Only the testimony of the Spirit can give Scripture the "certainty it deserves with us" (1.7.5).

Still it may be asked whether the Holy Spirit's testimony moves against reason or beyond it. There is reason to believe that Calvin maintained the latter. Evidence cannot produce a firm faith until the Spirit works:

> Of themselves they [evidences] are not strong enough to produce a firm faith, until the Heavenly Father, revealing his majesty there, lifts reverence for Scripture beyond the realm of contro-versy. (1.8.13)

Although the evidences are strong, and can stand up in controversy, they are not "strong enough" to produce firm faith. What the Holy Spirit does is to take the debate "beyond the realm of controversy."

The question that remains is whether the evidences are only for the confirmation of faith or whether they can be a preparation for it. Some passages suggest that the primary role of evidence is to confirm faith (1.8.13). Other passages clearly teach that evidences can be both. Calvin wrote in his commentary on Daniel 3:28 that

> faith cannot be acquired by any miracle or any perception of the Divine power; it requires instruction also. The miracles avail only to prepare for piety or for its confirmation.[52]

Notice that miracles are not only for confirmation of piety but for its preparation as well. Calvin's comments on Exodus 4:5 provide a similar perspective. The miracle in this case is Moses' rod changing into a serpent.

> It would be tedious here to dilate expressly on the use of miracles, suffice it briefly to lay down, that they sometimes serve as pre-paratives to faith, sometimes for its confirmation. We see an example of both in the metamorphosis of the rod by which Moses was the more animated and encouraged to gather strength, al-though he already believed in God's promise; but the Israelites, who were both incredulous and unteachable, were prepared and compelled to believe. Besides the miracle opened the door of faith

> with the Israelites, that being persuaded of his prophetical office, they might submit to be taught. . . . For although the Almighty begins further back and refers to the adoption of the patriarchs, and this was calculated to lay the foundation of the hope of redemption, it still does not follow that they were prepared to receive Moses until the authority of his ministry had been established. Wherefore, I have said that their faith was commenced by the miracle.[53]

Again we see that the evidence of miracles can be both a preparation for and confirmation of faith. Through the miracle of the rod Israelites were "prepared and compelled to believe." This evidence "opened the door of faith." Their faith was "commenced by a miracle." This kind of language supports the view that Calvin regarded evidence as a foundation for faith. Evidences "open the door" to or "commence" a process which is continued by instruction in the truth and by the internal testimony of the Holy Spirit. In light of these passages, it is difficult to say that for Calvin testimony of the Holy Spirit was apart from or opposed to evidence.

Still another complex issue in Calvin scholarship is Calvin's use of religious language. The principle of "accommodation" has received some recent discussion, as has Calvin's use of analogical language. The question is, did Calvin believe that it is possible to have knowledge of God as He is in Himself? In other words, did Calvin follow the traditional philosophy of analogy of being?

Roy Clouser maintains that Calvin rejected the analogy theory.[54] A number of well-known passages of Calvin are brought forward to justify this point. It can be shown, however, that in each case the passages actually support the opposite opinion. For instance, it is argued from *Institutes* 1.5.9 that Calvin did not believe it was possible to know God in Himself:

> Consequently, we know the most perfect way of seeking God, and the most suitable order is not for us to attempt with bold curiosity to penetrate to the investigation of his essence, which we ought more to adore than meticulously to search out, but for us to contemplate Him in his works whereby he renders himself near and familiar to us, and in some manner communicates himself. (1.5.9)

But note that this passage does not say that God is without an essence or that that essence is unknowable. Calvin was arguing here simply that God does have an essence but that we are not to pry into it. God *can* be known in Himself, but ought more to be adored than "minutely discussed." Calvin disapproved of a false emphasis on knowledge of God's essence, he did not deny the possibility of that knowledge itself.

> [God's] powers are mentioned, by which he is shown to us not as he is in himself, but as he is toward us, so that this recognition of him consists more in living experience than in vain and high flown speculation. (1.10.2)

If we note the context of this passage, we see that Calvin was arguing against an emphasis on speculation, but not against a knowledge of God in Himself. The passage being expounded is Exodus 34:6–7 (NASB): "The LORD, the LORD God, compassionate and gracious, slow to anger, and abounding in lovingkindness and truth, who keeps lovingkindness for thousands, who forgives iniquity, transgression and sin." In this context Calvin says, "Here let us observe that his eternity and self-existence are announced by that wonderful name twice repeated," then he proceeds to discuss God's "powers." Calvin's point is that the emphasis of this passage is not on God's incommunicable attributes (God as He is considered in Himself), but on His communicable attributes (God in relation to us). But by this Calvin did not deny that God's eternity and self-existence are known. In fact, he explicitly argued that they are known in this passage. Yet the emphasis of this passage and of Calvin is on His "powers"—God in relation to us, not God in Himself.

When dealing with biblical passages where God is said to repent, Calvin wrote that

> because our weakness does not attain to his exalted state, the description of him that is given to us must be accommodated to our capacity so that we may understand it. Now the mode of accommodation is for him to represent himself to us not as he is in himself, but as he seems to us. (1.17.13)

Calvin's point is that God changes His *actions* toward us, not that He changes what He is in Himself. Calvin is quick to emphasize, however, that

> neither God's plan nor his will is reversed, nor his volition altered, but what he had from eternity foreseen, approved and decreed, he pursues in uninterrupted tenor, however sudden the variation may appear in men's eyes. (1.17.13)

God does not change in Himself, even though when His actions toward us change He portrays Himself as repenting, and thus *seems to us* to change. The use of the word *repent* is in some ways like the way God is (changing His actions toward us), and in other ways not as God is (in His unchangeable essence.) This "accommodation" is very close to the traditional analogy of being. In fact, a study of Calvin's use of the principle of "accommodation" would show that Calvin covered the functions of analogy of being by use of this term.

We provide this historical reconnaissance of Augustine, Luther, and Calvin because of the widespread assumption that presuppositionalism represents orthodox Reformed apologetics. Because of presuppositionalism's pervasive influence among contemporary Reformed theologians, and the general pervasive influence of fideism, it is thought by many that presuppositionalism *is* the classical view, indeed the very touchstone of orthodoxy. It claims to be Augustinian, Calvinistic, and Reformed. In historical perspective, however, it would be more accurate to speak of it as Neo-Augustinian, Neo-Calvinist, and Neo-Reformed with the accent on the "Neo."

THE AGE OF ORTHODOXY

The seventeenth-century development of Protestant orthodoxy, Lutheran and Reformed, was not, as falsely charged, a change of course from the Reformers but a development and a systematization. This is quite evident in natural theology, concerning which seventeenth-century Reformed theologians spelled out the Reformers' views more fully, systematically, and scholastically.

Lutheran Orthodoxy

Following Melanchthon's *Loci Communes*, Orthodox Lutheran systematic works began with natural theology. E. D. Hirsch illustrates the Lutheran view by citing J. Musaeus, who, in *Introductio in Theologiam* (1679), writes typically: "God, through the guidance of the light of nature, is known by two different ways; first, through innate knowledge, and then through acquired."[55] The objection is then considered that no one now comes to God by natural revelation, and the answer given that that is true. Natural revelation in the Garden of Eden, however, *was* sufficient to bring Adam to God; but because of the Fall and sin, that is not possible now. Nevertheless, Musaeus concludes, natural theology is still necessary and is not essentially different from special revelation: "all difference between them concerns only degree."

What was true of Lutheran orthodoxy was true of orthodoxy in general: Roman and Eastern as well as Protestant. That Reformed orthodoxy, for example, took essentially the same position can be seen in Heppe's *Reformed Dogmatics*.[56] Puritan orthodoxy, although more active than its counterpart on the continent, followed the same pattern. Among the heirs of the Reformation, the reason–faith synthesis continued into later eras also.

Reformed Orthodoxy

One institution which continued this synthesis was Princeton Theological Seminary. It was probably the mightiest champion of Reformed orthodoxy in the nineteenth century. That it was an advocate of traditional theism and of theistic proofs has been shown by two recent doctoral theses. One studies the rise of the Princeton theology at the beginning of the nineteenth century.[57] The other studies the school's demise as such a bastion in the beginning of this century with the passing of B. B. Warfield, who died there, and J. G. Machen, who left in protest of Princeton's new stance.[58] Archibald Alexander was Princeton Seminary's founding father, his evidences represent a traditional approach. Charles Hodge, Princeton's most famous theologian, devotes many pages of his three-volume *Systematic Theology* to the proofs.

B. B. Warfield, whom some consider the last and greatest of the great apologists at Princeton, wrote much on this subject. Of general and special revelation, he wrote typically:

> Each is incomplete without the other. . . . Without general revelation, special revelation would lack that basis in the fundamental knowledge of God as the mighty and wise, righteous and good, maker and ruler of all things, apart from which further revelation of this great God's intervention in the world for the salvation of sinners could not be either intelligible, credible or operative.[59]

Before we leave this survey, we may observe that not only were the Princeton Calvinists in what we call the classic tradition, but so were most of their non-Calvinist contemporaries. A striking illustration is C. G. Finney, who was not merely un-Calvinistic but anti-

Princeton, yet outstripped his opponents in the area of theistic proofs. Finney not only advanced the traditional arguments for God but taught that they were effectively persuasive, and that people could no more resist these demonstrations than a seed could resist life.

Eastern and Roman Orthodoxy

We should remember also that Eastern orthodoxy, as expressed, for example, in her classic theologian John of Damascus, and Roman orthodoxy, everywhere, maintain the same essential theistic position. Not only has Pope Leo XIII declared Thomas Aquinas the teacher of his church, but Pius IX in his encyclical *Qui Pluribus* (1845) expressed the classic Christian view of the relation of reason and faith as well as it has ever, to our knowledge, been put:

> Even if faith is above reason, nevertheless, no true dissension or disagreement can ever be found between them, since both have their origin from one and the same font of immutable, eternal truth, the excellent and great God, and they mutually help one another so much that right reason demonstrates the truth of faith, protects it, defends it, but faith frees reason from all errors and, by a knowledge of divine things, wonderfully elucidates it, confirms, and perfects it.[60]

We have attempted to show by historic sampling that the classic Christian view accepts and advocates the theistic proofs—we say *proofs,* not suggestions, not psychological confirmations, not partial proofs but full, theistic proofs. From the Apologists to the dawn of our own era, this has been the central tradition of the church, Eastern, Roman, Protestant, the teaching of the creeds and of the theologians. Even some who were thought to have been opposed, we have shown were supporters.

We do not say that this view has been universally held by all Christians at all times, past and present. We specifically mentioned that the late medieval scholasticism which influenced Luther argued that there could be no arguments for God. And, of course, Henry Dodwell, Jr., is not the only Protestant who could have written a book entitled *Christianity not Founded on Argument,* nor is Karl Barth alone in thinking that what is philosophical is not Christian and what is Christian is not philosophical. Tertullian could separate Athens and Jerusalem in a sense and, more radically, Pascal could insist that the

God of the philosophers is not the God of Abraham, Isaac, and Jacob. We wish these views had not been held but we cannot deny that they were and are—especially in this age of Kierkegaard. But we hope, on the other hand, that presuppositionalists and other fideists think wishfully that the traditional position supports them will grant that it does not.

To be sure, the fact that presuppositionalism is a post-Kantian departure from classical Reformed apologetics does not, in itself, vitiate its claim to truth. What is vitiated is its claim to an expression of classical Reformed theology. Clearly, it is a departure, a modern innovation and must be recognized as such, standing or falling on its present merits. Protestantism claims no infallible tradition to assure orthodoxy, but rather embraces the principle *semper reformanda*. Yet because the Reformed tradition is held in high esteem among its advocates, temptation is great to claim its support for current expressions of theology. Presuppositionalism claims to be a "more consistent Calvinism," which claim we dispute.

We will now endeavor to show that presuppositionalism is not only a departure from classical Reformed Christianity, but that the departure, so far from being an improvement on the classical position, is a fatal blow to apologetics in particular and classical Christianity in general.

CHAPTER 12

The Starting Point: Primacy of the Intellect and Autonomy

THE STARTING POINT

APOLOGETICS IS A JOURNEY—an intellectual journey. And like any other journey, it must start somewhere. In the case of apologetics, we consider it self-evident that it must start with the person who is making the intellectual journey. One simply cannot start outside himself. To begin outside oneself, one would first have to depart from himself. As the farmer told the tourist who asked for directions, "You shouldn't start here."

The issue of starting point is crucial to the debate. The presuppositionalist maintains that you cannot get to God by starting with the self (cf. chap. 10), and the traditionalist argues that the self is the only possible starting place (cf. chap. 11). Just as the tourist *had* to start where he was, the protests of the farmer to the contrary, so must both traditionalist and presuppositionalist start where they are.

From time immemorial all people have assumed that they must begin their thinking with themselves for there is no other place where *they* can begin. Christian and non-Christian thinkers alike, being human, have found no starting point but in the human subject. Just as we cannot get out of our physical skin, neither can we escape our intellectual skin. Rationalism and empiricism have debated whether the starting point of the self is first person (subjective) or third person (objective), but in *both* the self is the point of departure. Certainly, Cornelius Van Til will be wearied by this criticism. He has heard it all before—from Charles Hodge,[1] from J. Oliver Buswell, Clark Pinnock, Stuart Hackett, John Warwick Montgomery, and Gordon Lewis, not to mention James Daane[2] and especially from Gordon Clark.[3] He has responded to it patiently each time.

But he has never really answered this criticism, even when he thinks he has. Let us look, for example, at what Van Til undoubtedly considers a thorough and adequate reply obviating all our criticism long before we wrote it here:

> I do *not* maintain that Christians operate according to new laws of thought any more than they have new eyes or noses. The non-Christian uses the gifts of logical reason in order to keep down the truth in unrighteousness. The question is not that of the law of contradiction as a formal principle.[4]

This is no answer to our objection. Non-Christians cannot use reason and logic to "keep down the truth." They have to *violate* them to "keep down the truth." Reason would not be functioning but malfunctioning if by it the truth were kept down. That is the whole point which (we fear) Dr. Van Til does not get and which he does not answer.

Dr. Van Til adds, "The more consistent his [the sinner's] logical reasoning is, the more certainly will he end up with a finite god which is no God."[5] Human reason, which is a God-given instrument for truth, has become an instrument leading to error. In that case, human mental faculties (not only holiness) have been eradicated by the Fall. Humans must be given a new mind in regeneration—despite all that Van Til says about the mind, the eyes, the nose, being the same for the Christian and the non-Christian. The body has somehow survived the Fall, the mind has not. This is a theological error, as well as an apologetic fatality. Van Til has not answered his critics because, believing as he does, he cannot.

The reason these Christians do not see what they could not help seeing if they would look at it, is that something else is diverting their attention. That something else is the conviction that God cannot be proven. He is beyond the reach of reason. No syllogism can attain to Him. He must be accepted on faith. That translates into the working conviction that to find God we must begin with Him and not with ourselves. They do not seem to realize that even if *they* did find God by beginning with God it is *their* conclusion nonetheless. They begin with themselves even while they argue that they cannot begin with themselves. It is *they*—the finite—who are thinking that the finite is not capable of the infinite. Consciously or unconsciously, presuppositionalists are beginning with themselves as much as we are, and there is no point to contesting the necessity of so doing. Even if they argue this point with us, it will be *they* who are arguing with us: one man with another.

Nevertheless, for Van Til, theoretically, the proper starting point is not man at all, but God. If man were the starting point, we all would have this in common and thus an initial point of contact. But this is not so, there is no point of contact—nothing in common. Therefore, "the Calvinist cannot give reasons because he has no *point of contact* with the non-Christian."[6]

It is interesting to find Charles M. Horne commenting on Van Til vis-a-vis E. J. Carnell and Hackett, noticing (with approval, unfortunately) the same thing. "Ultimately these three positions are reducible to two alternatives: either we assume that God is the origin of all predication or we assume that man is."[7] If Horne meant the ontological point of origin, this would not have been a point of difference among these three apologists. He must mean epistemological and this is a fatal difference. This shows that he and Van Til are supposing that God is the epistemological starting point. We do not start within ourselves, they say, but outside ourselves. But this is patently absurd, though starting within ourselves will lead us to see that we *were started* outside ourselves by our God in whom (we then know) we live, and move, and have our being.

Again Van Til says that "if God did not exist we could know nothing."[8] This would be true if he had said, "If God did not exist *we would have* known nothing and *been* nothing." But God made us so that we know facts whose ultimate validation can come only from Him. It is by really knowing these things that we ultimately realize that they—and we—must have come from God. If we did not know some things, we could never have arrived at the knowledge of God. Knowing these things, our minds are restless until they find their resting place in God. If we did not start with ourselves, we could not have come to Him.

The inevitability of beginning with the human self is admitted occasionally even by presuppositionalists. For example, Van Til acknowledges that

> all agree that the immediate starting point must be that of our everyday experience and the "facts" that are most close at hand. But the exact charge we are making against so many Idealists as well as Pragmatists is that they are taking for granted certain

temporal "facts" not only as a temporary but as an ultimate starting point.[9]

This is a very significant point not often made by Van Til. As a matter of fact, it is never made consistently as a part of his system. If it were, much of his criticism would collapse. Van Til repeatedly insists that we must always begin our thinking with God. According to the Vantillian presupposition, even the man at the tip of a diving board (in a well-known Van Til illustration) who has only the board and the water in his purview must actually know the world and all even to understand the diving board and the water.

Otherwise, there would be no real difference between Van Til and the traditional starting point. As Van Til, in this very quotation, goes on to say, some pragmatists and idealists make that temporary provisional starting point into the permanent one; but that is his charge against anybody, including theists and even orthodox Calvinistic theists, who start at that point. We contend that the "'facts' . . . most close at hand" are merely a starting point just because they are the only place at which anyone *can* start. If we do start at that point, we learn from the evidence that surrounds us that there is a God who alone can explain the ultimate meaning of everything.

If Van Til were willing to begin with us at that starting point and then argue from the observation of the world around that God alone explains everything, we could not agree more. C. S. Lewis makes a good deal of the fact that one could not confidently think without ultimately assuming a rational being at the head of the universe; but he does not begin with this rational being. By contrast, Van Til insists that a person must begin at that point. We find it difficult, therefore, to understand his casually saying that, of course, everybody begins at the common-sense, proximate starting point. We wish Van Til would acknowledge this all the time, instead of almost always supposing that anybody who starts there makes a fatal error because he necessarily ends there. No, the traditional theist does not end there. And yes, the presuppositionalist too must always begin there. Van Til's exception in the above case shows him to be inconsistent. This is apparent when any line of Vantillian thinking is pursued. He vacillates from one position to another—without being aware of it, for he certainly does not defend vacillation, though he does defend circularity of reasoning. He glories in circles. But we do not find even Van Til glorying in vacillation. Van Til consistently confuses God as the ontological starting point with God as the epistemological starting point; from this confusion arises his vacillation.

On another level, Van Til confuses the sinner's *rejecting* sound knowledge with *not having* sound knowledge. Therefore he represents the unregenerate as having and not having knowledge. In his *Psychology of Religion*,[10] for example, he observes that a person may reason soundly but not submit, may *see* where to go but not *want* to go. Precisely. Such a person *does* see and *does* know and is not ignorant and is not presupposing God. Here the orthodox Van Til is advancing a genuine Calvinistic conception of the "noetic influence of sin," asserting that sinners have knowledge which they suppress.[11] He says in *The Defense of the Faith,* "The intellect of the fallen man may, as such, be keen enough. It can therefore formally understand the Christian position . . . [but] the result is that however much they may formally understand the truth of Christianity, men still worship the dream and figment of their own heart."[12] Precisely. But they *know* what they are doing and the apologist has that point of contact. How, therefore, can Van Til write: "The Calvinist cannot give reasons because he has no point of *contact* with the non-Christian"?[13] Furthermore, Van Til is always *proving* to the non-Christian that predication is impossible without presupposing God, obviously assuming that the non-Christian can understand his argument.

Thom Notaro's way of stating Van Til's view makes our point quite clear. "Autonomous man will not accept God's revelation in Scripture—that is agreed."[14] It is indeed "agreed" that unregenerate, autonomous persons will not "accept" (i.e., "welcome" or "acquiesce in") God's revelation in Scripture—or nature, for that matter. But they may "accept" it in the sense of receiving it as a fact (which they do not welcome). The devils do this all the time and there is evidence that unregenerate people also "know" God. So they can and do, if they reflect at all, grant the facts and then spend their lives trying to refute what they can neither deny, on the one hand, nor welcome on the other.

Van Til reaches his own nadir in this realm when he says that, if we grant someone "an autonomous reference point for interpreting the facts, we cannot deny his right to twist the facts of Christianity at any point."[15] We grant no right to "twist" any facts, anywhere. Nor can Van Til grant any such "right" to do wrong. Since Van Til admits, as we have seen, that the unregenerate can and do have sound ideas of God and revelation which they attempt to suppress (or twist), he can and does call that inconsistency with themselves to their attention. To deny that is to deny that they have any of the natural (not merely moral) image of God left after the Fall. To say that is to leave Calvinism for hyper-Calvinism which we believe is, indeed, the implicit theological error which parallels Van Til's apologetic error. The former is more serious than the latter. It is not, that Hodge and Warfield were implicitly Arminian in their theology as presuppositionalists suppose, but that presuppositionalists are implicitly hyper-Calvinist in theirs.

Though Van Til does, on rare occasions, acknowledge the inevitability of our starting with ourselves when thinking even about God, the real Van Til insists that we must not start there but with God. We do not begin from below but from above. Absurd as it may be for us who are here below to begin where we are not—above—Van Til insists that it must be done. We must begin *von oben*, (from above). Strange as that statement may be coming from a human, Van Til actually attributes it to *God* Himself: God says we must begin not where we are but where He is.

Van Til writes that we know we must begin *von oben* not because we are wiser than other men but because we have been saved by grace:

> By the regenerating power of the Spirit we have been able to see that the foolishness of God is wiser than men. But having been saved by grace we now also see that there is no place for the fruitful exercise of the human intellect except within the totality view granted us in Scripture. There is no logic or reality neither is there any relation between the two which we as creatures may consistently hold to unless both logic and reality have their very being in the Creator-God of Scriptures. If men do not accept this totality view by faith in the absolute authority of Christ, then there's nothing left to them but the fearful looking forward to the crucifixion of the intellect by which they are seeking to defend themselves against the approaching judgment of the self-attesting Christ, who shall judge all men by words which He has spoken.[16]

This is a very important statement for understanding the Vantillian approach. Let us therefore consider it line by line:

By the regenerating power of the Spirit we have been able to see that the foolishness of God is wiser than men. First, we must suppose that the phrase "foolishness of God" in Paul (from whom it comes) is satire, it being nonsense to speak literally of the "foolishness" of an all-wise Being. For anyone to think of the wisdom of God as foolishness only proves that person to be foolish, as the unbelievers, of whom Paul is speaking, undoubtedly are. Regeneration is not necessary however, to see that the "foolishness of God" is "wiser than men." Any rational person can see that. If the unregenerate do not "see" it, it is only because they *will not,* not because they *cannot.* Their wills and not their minds need to be changed because their problem is not in knowing this but in acknowledging it. Indeed, they *do* know it. That is the reason they know they do not like it and therefore contend that they do not even know it.

One might suppose that this is what Van Til means too, but the evidence is against it. In his whole system, Van Til argues that the unregenerate cannot reason rationally without presupposing God which they do not do. So they, without regeneration, cannot understand anything including the obvious fact that an all-wise Being cannot be foolish.

Van Til would be tempted to demur here, because as we state his position it does sound absurd. How could anyone, unregenerate or not, fail to see that an all-wise Being cannot be foolish? But that is what Van Til almost everywhere contends. If the unregenerate could see this and other obvious verities, such as that a thing cannot begin to be without a cause, they would be capable (as traditionalists argue that they are and Van Til argues that they are not) of seeing the cogency of theistic evidence even though, while unregenerate, they are unwilling to acknowledge it.

We must fault Van Til here for representing unregenerate persons as incapable of understanding the self-evident. Instead of saying that by the regenerating power of the Holy Spirit people are enabled to "see" that the foolishness of God is wiser than men, Van Til should have said that by regeneration people are enabled gladly to acknowledge this verity.

But having been saved by grace we now also see that there is no place for the fruitful exercise of the human intellect except within the totality view granted us in the Scripture. Our objection here is essentially the same as the critique just offered. The God who is revealed in Scripture is indeed the only one who can afford a rational, "totality view." But one does not have to be a Christian to see that. He needs to be regenerate to *admit* it, but not to *understand* it.

An unregenerate person can well understand that if there is such a deity as Scripture describes, He (and *only* He) can indeed perfectly account for everything which is. The unregenerate simply cannot admit that such a Being does in fact exist because the sinner loves the darkness and this Being must be the light which the unregenerate hates. Once again, the problem is not with the head ultimately but with the heart. The unregenerate "know God" as Paul says, but they do not honor (that is, acknowledge) Him as God (Rom. 1:20).

On occasion, Van Til strongly insists that the unregenerate know God. Man "knows God as Paul says so specifically in his letter to the Romans."[17] But even here Van Til implies that that person does not really know God who does not know Him ethically. So he takes back with one hand what he gives with the other. Let the reader not be confused here. All Calvinists admit that the unregenerate are devoid of *saving* knowledge of God, but they do not say that the unregenerate lack any knowledge of God whatsoever. Van Til seems to be saying the same thing, but he is not. This becomes quite clear when he writes that "what is meant by knowing God in Scripture is *knowing and loving* God; this is *true* knowledge of God; the other is false."[18] That puts it beyond dispute that, in spite of statements which affirm it, Van Til does not believe the unregenerate have knowledge of God. Their "knowledge" is not "true" knowledge; it is "false" knowledge. If it is totally false, then it is no knowledge at all. This is consistent with his fundamental principle that one must *presuppose* God in order to have "true" knowledge of Him or of anything. On most occasions, as here, Van Til cannot admit that the unregenerate know God (without destroying his own system), for then they would not need to presuppose Him.

This is a gross inconsistency on the most fundamental point in the presuppositional position: Unregenerate persons can and cannot "know" God. Whether Van Til acknowledges this inconsistency or not, he appears to feel it as a logical thorn in his side. He seeks relief by explaining knowledge of the unregenerate as a divine sense (*sensus divinitatus*). But that does not remove the problem. A sense or awareness of something is not necessarily knowledge of it. One may have a sense or awareness of something moving in a dark room without knowing what it is or even being certain that it is anything. We believe that Paul, in Romans 1:21, refers to cognitive knowledge and not to a mere awareness or sense. Van Til is caught on the horns of a dilemma. When he says that the unregenerate have no knowledge, his statement is patently false and unscriptural. When he says that the unregenerate do have knowledge, he contradicts his contention that one must presuppose God, as well as his assertion that their "knowledge" is "false."[19]

There is no logic or reality neither is there any relation between the two which we as creatures may consistently hold to unless both logic and reality have their very being in the Creator-God of Scriptures. With what this statement says we agree; but we disagree with what Van Til intends by it. True, the *ultimate* justification of logic (in the sense that logic deals with reality) can come only from God. But from this valid insight Van Til infers that we cannot begin our thought with logic but must presuppose God. That, too, is true if we would be *certain* when we first use logic that it does indeed deal with reality. But whether we know that logic deals with reality or not, we must begin all our thinking with logic, for that is the only way that we can think. We cannot even presuppose God except logically. In other words, even to think of the God who alone can validate logic, we must first think logically or rationally. Through the exercise of this logic and reason we come to realize the existence of the God who validates the logical process by which we have arrived at the knowledge of Him. So we begin with logic because we *must*, and in the end we come to the God who proves that we *may*.

Not only in his *Metaphysics of Apologetics*, but throughout his writings, Van Til stresses his divine starting point. For example, in his *A Survey of Christian Epistemology*, he writes:

> The question we must ask constantly is how anyone has conceived of the relation of the human mind to the divine mind. It is on this point that the greatest difference obtains between the theistic and the non-theistic position. The former cannot think of the human mind as functional at all except when it is in contact with God; the latter presupposes it to be possible that the human mind functions normally whether or not God exists.[20]

This commonly echoed sentiment of Van Til's is false both to himself and to those whom he criticizes. When he says that the Christian cannot think of a human mind as functional at all except when it is in contact with God, he is denying his fundamental proposition that the Christian thinker can show the non-Christian thinker that his non-Christian thought is not intelligible. He is presumably—that is the Christian is presumably—*ad hominem,* not in contact with God but only in contact with the data of the non-theist when he makes this observation. Van Til is assuming, in other words, that the human mind is quite functional without being in "contact" with God. He, of course, believes himself to be in spiritual contact with God but he is not presupposing God when he makes this observation. He is not, in other words, in intellectual contact with God which is a presupposition necessary to proving to the non-theistic philosopher that his philosophy is not intelligible.

This is parallel to our earlier assertion that Van Til proceeds inductively in the ordinary sense of the word, not presuppositionally, when he shows the insufficiency of non-theistic thought. Van Til is misrepresenting the non-theist and the non-presuppositionalist Christian when he asserts that they both have their own presupposition, viz., that the human mind functions normally whether or not God exists. All that the non-theist actually does in a case like this is observe himself in the world around him. He is not presupposing anything with regard to the invisible. He is simply going on with what he does see and can reflect upon. He is theoretically open to the possibility that there is a God. But he does not know. It is not proper to say that he presupposes the nonexistence of God. It *could* be said that he is not presupposing the existence of God. But that is not the same as saying that he is presupposing the nonexistence of God. Van Til does not keep this distinction clearly in mind; in fact, we do not remember that he ever makes it. Without this distinction, Van Til observes constantly and falsely that anyone who begins with himself and the world without presupposing God is presupposing non-God. This is his grievance against Bishop Butler as well as non-theists. It is incorrect to say that non-theists and theists like Bishop Butler presuppose the nonexistence of God simply because they do not presuppose the existence of God. It is unfair to Van Til himself because he argues *ad hominem* that non-theist philosophers are capable of seeing that they must presuppose God or they must acknowledge God if they are going to be intelligible. He must admit that he is not the only one who has seen that or called that to their attention.

We are not denying that Van Til *thinks* he has a point of contact in his system. "If God is absolute," he contends, "man must always remain accessible to him. . . . God may therefore use our reasoning or our preaching as a way by which he presents himself to those who have assumed his non-existence."[21] But Van Til cannot have it both ways. He cannot say that the unregenerate Person assumes no God and at the same time assumes God. To say that God by His omnipotence can become accessible to a person who necessarily assumes He does not exist is untenable. Nothing in the neo-orthodox theologians is more paradoxical.

What makes matters even worse for Van Til is that the knowledge which the unregenerate have of God (when God makes Himself "accessible") is certainly no "presuppositional" knowledge of God, and, therefore, to presuppose God is not the necessary and sole way of knowing God. If this simple statement stands, Vantillianism falls and traditionalism is vindicated. If Van Til stands, this statement and all like it must fall.

Suppose that Van Til counterattacks by objecting that we are beginning *hypothetically* with logic and, when we discover God, we conclude *certainly* that logic is valid. This, he may charge, is inconsistent, for a *certain* conclusion is reached from a *hypothetical* premise. If the premise is hypothetical, the conclusion must be the same. How can one be certain about a God who is reached from an uncertain rational foundation? Our answer to this is: we cannot think any other way. We must think logically if we would think at all. We must conclude that there is a God if we think logically. If the whole process is hypothetical then we must think hypothetically. We have to assume that our thinking is valid. We cannot assume anything else. It is certain that, if we are going to think at all, we must think in such a manner, as must all other persons.

Suppose Van Til persists and argues: Then you must admit that reason, and God whom it reaches, may be an illusion, unreal, hypothetical, and that you can be certain about nothing. No, we reply, that does not follow. We must begin with our reason even before we know that there is a God who validates it. But that beginning is not hypothetical, it is a *certain* beginning. We *must* begin by relying on our reason. When we say that such a beginning leads us ultimately to God (who as the Creator validates His creation, reason), that does not mean that the reason was uncertain before the divine validation. We could not think of it as uncertain or we could not have thought. It was certain from the beginning that reason was reliable, but we did not know then that it was a creation of God. When it leads us to God because it *is* reliable, it leads us to One who does not *then* make it reliable but shows that He is the One who made it reliable when He made it, which was before we came to know Him by means of it.

But suppose someone suggests that God may be playing tricks with us. Would we not have to admit that possibility? No. We not only would not have to admit that possibility, we *should* not. We cannot rationally deny the reliability of reason, and when our reason leads us to God we cannot rationally deny God. It is a simple rational impossibility. We cannot think that God is not and we cannot think that God is playing tricks on us. If (to suppose the unthinkable) God *were* playing tricks on us, we could not conceive of it. To imagine that God was playing tricks, we would have to rely on our minds. But if God were playing tricks, we could not rely on our minds. Since we do and must rely on our minds, we cannot imagine that they are unreliable, that is, that God is playing tricks.

But a last-gasp objection may be: "You are saying that God *may* be playing tricks on us though we simply cannot conceive of it." That is a contradiction, of course. We are not saying and cannot say that God may be playing tricks, because the expression has no meaning for us, we cannot conceive of it. The objector may use the meaningless expression and we may, for argument's sake, use the same expression only to show that it has no meaning, being inconceivable. We may use the expression "square circle" also, though it is meaningless, for the purpose of showing that it is meaningless.

If men do not accept this totality view by faith in the absolute authority of Christ, then there is nothing left to them but the fearful looking forward to the crucifixion of the intellect by which they are seeking to defend themselves against the approaching judgment of the self-attesting Christ who shall judge all men by words which he has spoken. This statement shows Van Til at his best and at his worst. At his best, for this is a truly prophetic statement reminding all that they must believe in Jesus Christ if they would be saved from the wrath of God. We honor Van Til, a true prophet and witness of Christ Jesus, for he never permits anyone to think that apologetics is a game but is a matter of eternal life and death. That makes it all the sadder that Van Til has associated an unsound apologetic with eternal destiny.

To briefly recapitulate our discussion of the starting point: we have given three arguments why we must start with ourselves rather than God:

1. It is psychologically impossible for *us* to start with *God* (as it is impossible for *God* to start with *us*).
2. It is logically impossible for us to start with God for we cannot affirm God without assuming logic and our ability to predicate.

According to the law of noncontradiction, one cannot assert anything without assuming that its opposite is excluded. If we say, "That is a dog," the statement must imply that the dog cannot be a not-dog. "A" must exclude "not-A" or "A" itself is meaningless. "God" must exclude "not-God" or "God" is not a meaningful expression. So we could not meaningfully refer to God if it were not for the law of noncontradiction. Manifestly, if we cannot conceive of God without logical laws we cannot presuppose Him in order to arrive at logical laws. Therefore, to say that we must presuppose God in order to validate logic is, without logic, not even a valid statement. It is true that we do not know that logical laws are ultimately valid until we learn that there is a God who made these laws and the creatures who think according to them. But that we must use them and assume their validity before we come to know God is indisputable, because we cannot even define Him without them. First we use logical laws; then we learn of the God who made them. We cannot begin with God, as God began with God, and then move to logic as God then moved to logic. We must begin with logic and then learn that He is the One who made these laws and validates them ultimately. The well-known principle is that the order of knowing is the reverse of the order of being. The order of being: first God, then logic. The order of human knowing: first logic, then God.

3. It is logically impossible to show the rational necessity of presupposing God except by rational argument.

This is implicit in what is said above but again let us spell it out more fully. The presuppositionalist cannot use the word *God* without assuming the law of noncontradiction. Obviously, it is impossible to show the necessity of presupposing God before using logic, when it is essential to presuppose logic in order to meaningfully use the word *God*. So, the presuppositionalist (like the man who said: "I am an atheist, God knows."), if he would show the necessity of presupposing God before we can use the laws of reason, must use the laws of reason to do it and this is a contradiction. Van Til would be saying, "Reason dictates that we must presuppose God in order to use reason."

Dooyeweerd, the presuppositionalist, calls the starting point the Archimedean Point. It must satisfy three requirements. First, it must be related to the origin and meaning of God. Second, it must transcend the diversity of meaning. Third, it must not be separated from our own objective self. The "heart" is related to origin because it is the religious root of human experience—the supratheoretical, religious root of human nature. It determines a person's relation to God, accepting, as it may, or rejecting Him.

We need not enter into a study of Dooyeweerd's views on the soul and self, that having been done by David Freeman, William Young, Ronald Nash, and others.[22] We can see that this starting point is different from Van Til's but just as arbitrary. Van Til would regard it as another autonomous beginning[23]—not the autonomous mind of the traditionalists, but autonomous nonetheless; it begins with humanity rather than with God. Dooyeweerd's starting point is just as arbitrary as Van Til's though more down to earth. Beginning with the heart, he at least begins with man (where we must always begin). So we have sympathy with Dooyeweerd here. He is returning to home base and is offering something which is at least thinkable.

Why not begin with the heart rather than the mind? It is admitted that the heart is more basic than the mind. This is, as Dooyeweerd and the Bible indicate, where the issues of life are determined. While all that is true, the heart is still not the *starting* point. It may affect the starting point but it cannot be the starting point. It cannot be the starting point because it cannot even be recognized as the heart apart from the mind. The mind must interpret the experience of the heart in logical terms. The experience must be simultaneous with logical apprehension, to be sure. But it cannot even be *known* as the experience of the heart except by logical apprehension. A and not-A apply to the human heart just as they do to the being of God. We cannot presuppose a heart any more than its Maker without the instrumentality of the mind.

Rousas Rushdoony is another eminent presuppositionalist who thoroughly rejects any point of contact. He wrote that "Jesse Deboer and Orbebeke, for example, profoundly disturbed Van Til. They begin with a self-contained God-Scripture instead of a man's reason and the self-contained facts of this physical universe. From these facts they would prove God. But any God that is added to a universe of self-contained facts is irrelevant to it."[24] Rushdoony is making the same criticism which Van Til makes of that type of approach. The way he makes his mistake, however, is not the way Van Til makes his. Rushdoony says that the view he is criticizing (Deboer's and Orbebeke's) is guilty of adding to the universe the God to be proved. He does not seem to recognize that this approach does not add God to the universe. Deboer and Orbebeke try to prove that this God is the author of the universe. That they begin with a "self-contained God-Scripture" does not satisfy Rushdoony. In Rushdoony's opinion, proving God is adding God because he assumes that, when one proves God, he is altogether without God when he begins his argument. But Deboer and

Orbebeke begin without God only in the sense of not assuming God. They do not assume His nonexistence. Rushdoony cannot see any difference between beginning without assuming God and beginning by excluding God. For him, as for Van Til, they are one and the same.

It is interesting that a few pages later, we find Rushdoony himself saying, "An objective revelation of God is given to man, both through the world about him and through his own created nature, upon which God's impress is unmistakable."[25] This is precisely what a number of theists have said. They observe the world about them and recognize its created nature. They find God's impress upon it unmistakable. They are observing exactly what Rushdoony here observes. But when they do so, Rushdoony accuses them of thereby adding God to the universe. When Rushdoony does it, he does not see himself as guilty of that same fault. He would probably say that he had already presupposed God. But in the quote above, he is saying that there is an objective revelation of God in and to humans. Presumably, God's impress is on the world. If so, the impress is not the same thing as the presupposition or the so-called "objective revelation."

The neo-Reformed Karl Barth, is more thoroughgoing than Van Til in his denial of point of contact. The fall of man has not defaced but effaced the image of God and all possible points of contact with the Creator. Van Til is too Reformed to say this but he does infer and teach it implicitly and constantly. Barth seems to have the courage of his unfortunate convictions:

> Man's capacity for God, however it may be with his humanity and personality, has *really been lost*. We cannot, therefore, see that at this point there comes into view a *common basis of discussion* for philosophical and theological anthropology, the opportunity for a common exhibition at least of the possibility of raising the question about God.[26]

This is what Van Til, if he would be consistent with his own principles, should say. But he has too much rationality left in him to be consistent with his antirational apologetic. He would prove to the unregenerate what they cannot understand (because they do not presuppose God) and what they cannot admit (because they are unregenerate). Barth will have none of this prevaricating. He is more consistently irrational. Using a Word humans cannot understand, God creates a faith in what they cannot understand either. This is quite preposterous, of course, but it merits praise for consistency in madness. If humans can be regenerated by what they cannot understand, why can he not believe it as well?

In Van Til the method triumphs over the madness. That is, he too represents humans as not understanding but nevertheless believing when regenerated. But, as if realizing the error, he covertly slips into rationality at the cost of consistency—by importing the notion that people can *falsely* understand without regeneration and when regenerate can *truly* understand.

PRIMACY OF THE INTELLECT

Closely related to the question of starting point is the issue of "the primacy of the intellect." Van Til will have no truck with any primacy of the intellect in the ordinary sense. In this ordinary sense, primacy of the intellect refers not to a *priority of excellence* but to a *priority of order*. Primacy of intellect means that we must think about God before we can actually know Him. Primacy of intellect does not mean that the intellect is of a higher order or excellence than the God whom we discover by means of it. That would be a blasphemous notion. "Primacy" means strictly priority of order. As far as primacy of *importance* is concerned, that which is known—the divine being—is comparably and infinitely more important than that by which He is known.

In a debate with Gordon Clark, Van Til traced Clark's errors to his doctrine of the primacy of the intellect:

> Failing to make the distinction between a primacy of the intellect that is based upon the Creator-creature distinction and a primacy of the intellect that is not based upon the Creator-creature distinction as is the case with the Greeks, Clark argues that it is the primacy of the intellect that saves from skepticism. But the primacy of the intellect as the Greeks held it has historically and logically led to the skepticism of modern irrationalists.[27]

Note the paradox in "a primacy of the intellect that is based upon the Creator-creature distinction." If any primacy is based on something else, it does not have primacy. Since Van Til maintains that he can teach a primacy of the intellect based on the Creator-creature relationship, he necessarily teaches a secondary primacy or a subsequent primacy. One is reminded of Jonathan Edwards's Arminian animal from Tierra del Fuego who always took one step before the first.

"The primacy of the intellect . . . based upon the Creator–creature distinction" means, for Van Til, that if we first acknowledge the Creator and that we ourselves are the creatures, then, and only then, may we accept the primacy of the intellect. But if we recognize the Creator–creature relationship prior to recognizing the primacy of the intellect, we have recognized that the Creator–creature relationship is known apart from and prior to the use of the intellect. However that knowledge comes, it does not first come through the gateway of the mind. Whether that is a sound view is not the question at the moment. What is the question of the moment is how, if that be the case, there can be any meaning to the expression the "primacy of the intellect." Usually, "the primacy of the intellect" refers to the assertion that prior to anything being encountered, experienced, or in any way coming into the human psyche, it must pass the gate of the intellect. Manifestly, there cannot be anything but a secondary role for the intellect if the knowledge of the Creator–creature relationship precedes the functioning of the intellect.

That that relationship does precede the functioning of the intellect in Van Til's theory goes without question. It ought also to go without question, no matter what Van Til says, that he rejects the concept of the primacy of the intellect. To suggest that he accepts it with that qualification is a kind of serious joke. In Van Til's system, standard terms are used time and again, but scarcely ever with their standard connotations. Van Til is an honest man, not trying to deceive anybody; but he seems to confuse his readers without trying. He believes in many traditional concepts but gives them an extraordinary definition. (In chapter 16, for example, we will discuss his unusual concept of common grace.)

According to Van Til, the intellect is not functioning in its traditional role until the knowledge of the Creator is assumed. But if so, then it is a mystery how we can know the Creator–creature relationship except through the intellect. How do we come to know the Creator–creature relationship if it is not first comprehended by the intellect? According to the traditional position, one cannot believe anything without first knowing it by the intellect. Van Til has cut off that bridge to knowledge. How then does he get any knowledge to accept or believe? There is no denying that this matter of a Creator–creature relationship is a knowledge item. It must have been comprehended somehow. But how can it be when the apprehending instrument, the mind, is not yet functioning? According to Van Til, it cannot function until this relationship is first of all ascertained and acted upon. Yet this relationship cannot be known without the mind. We find no answer to this very elementary and elemental question. No answer *can* be found because to give an answer means that the reason is already functioning, which Van Til denies to be the case.

The question is how Van Til ever came to such a notion. Apparently it was because of his ever-present desire to glorify God. We must always give Van Til credit for a passionate desire to praise God. We have no doubt that this is his intention. But neither do we have any doubt that this is not his accomplishment. Since, prior to the presupposition of God, there is no instrument which can give us knowledge of the Creator–creature relationship, there can be no knowledge of this relationship. Therefore, however much Van Til wishes to glorify God and give Him the primacy, he succeeds only in taking away the possibility of any knowledge of God. He seeks to glorify God and succeeds only in nullifying Him. Desiring to give a sounder view of the priority of God, he gives no view at all.

Earnestly desiring to glorify God and give Him the lordship over all things including the intellectual process, Van Til has taken this position, not noticing—once again—the difference between priority in the *order of being* and priority in the *order of knowing*. Of course, Van Til, an accomplished philosopher, is familiar with this time-honored expression and, on occasion, uses it. He seems not to consider it here. Any meaningful statement by Van Til about intellectual priority pertains to the order of being and not to the order of knowing. God is indeed first and is indeed the Creator of the human intellect. If that is what Van Til wants to say, we heartily agree. But given the proposition that God is first in order of being and the human intellect is second, does it follow that in our thinking we are able to move in the same order? It does not at all follow. The exact opposite follows. If we are endowed with intellect, then our intellect has *first* to function in apprehending the nature of God who created the intellect for that purpose. Once it has comprehended God, it immediately recognizes that its own primacy is strictly in the area of knowledge and not in the area of being. Using the intellect first (the *primacy* of the intellect), we then discover that the order of being was indeed prior to the order of knowing. That is, first God exists and creates the intellect and then the intellect by the primacy of knowledge reasons to the prior existence of God.

How do we explain Van Til's apparent blindness to such an

obvious matter? It is his overall thinking which controls him here and pulls him out of the rational order. That is, he believes we cannot know anything, including the primacy of the intellect, without this prior commitment to the revelation of God as the Creator and ourselves as dependent creatures. But one simply cannot know before he knows.

Gordon Clark defends the usual meaning of primacy of the intellect. He argues that apart from this primacy of the intellect there is nothing but skepticism.[28] Skepticism entertains some knowledge about which it is dubious or noncommittal—skeptical. But if the primacy of the intellect is denied in its true and proper meaning, there can be no knowledge at all, no knowledge about which to be skeptical. Van Til should notice that Clark is being very easy on him, easier than he should have been. If there is no primacy of the intellect there is simply no knowledge at all. There can be knowledge apart from its apprehension by the only instrument of apprehension with which we are endowed.

We conclude that Van Til himself is forced to operate on the basis of primacy of the intellect even with respect to the Creator–creature relationship. First, he does claim to know the Creator–creature relationship. Second, he does not have any means of knowing that he himself has ever introduced or claimed, other than the intellect. Therefore, third, though he will apparently not admit it, Van Til himself has arrived at the notion of the Creator–creature relationship by virtue of the primacy of the intellect. In Van Til's thought, as in Clark's and every other rational being's thought, the intellect has to precede even his thought of God. This does not detract from God, since it is He who made us this way. By starting faithfully where we are, we will indeed arrive where He is, that is, at the knowledge of Him. It certainly does not glorify God to try to reach him by some other route than He Himself was provided.

Dr. Van Til insists that the law of noncontradiction also has no meaning apart from its locus in the Creator–creature relationship. But we have already shown that there is no understanding of the word *Creator* or *creature* or anything else without a prior understanding and use of the law of contradiction. Therefore, we cannot bring in the law of noncontradiction after the knowledge of God is achieved. The same is true of the law of excluded middle and every other logical law which Van Til wants to bring in after God. God Himself made it impossible to bring them in after Him.

AUTONOMY

There is no charge more commonly made against the traditional starting-point than that it implies autonomy. That is, the person who begins with himself necessarily assumes that he is a law to himself. "Man is the measure of all things." The creature exalts himself above the Creator.

To avoid autonomy, it is argued, one must begin at the very outset with God, the divine lawgiver. Instead of autonomy one should practice heteronomy. One should start all his thinking with the Creator, not with the creature. To fail to do this is to worship the creature rather than the Creator.

Needless to say these are serious charges. No Christian will knowingly be guilty of worshiping himself rather than his God. If the traditional apologetic does this, it is a form of idolatry.

Presuppositionalists bring this indictment against all other approaches to thought. Van Til, for example, constantly makes this charge not only against non-Christian thought but against traditional Christian thought as well. He cites Aquinas and Butler, especially, and even the Old Princeton School. Kuyper, Dooyeweerd, Runner, Vander Stelt, and probably a majority of contemporary Christian apologists agree with Van Til. In fairness to presuppositionalists, it must be said that they do not charge traditionalists with being non-Christian idolators. They grant that we may be Christians unaware of our own implications. As Christian brothers we sincerely appreciate that and entertain the same charity toward our presuppositionalist brethren.

What do traditionalists say to these serious charges? We admit the charge of autonomy, but not its guiltiness. That is, we admit that we begin autonomously, but where is the sin, not to mention idolatry? If this were idolatry, we would abandon it instantly. So far from abandoning it, we defend its legitimacy, as well as its intellectual necessity. We will even try to prove that our critics practice it also, though unconsciously.

Autonomy is bad only after heteronomy is known, not before. We *must* begin with ourselves, that is, autonomously. At that point, autonomy is no sin but a necessity and a virtue. The situation is like Cain's seeking a wife. If the race began with a single pair, Cain, their son, had to marry a blood relative if he were to marry at all, and he had to marry if the race were to continue. His violation of the subsequent law of consanguinity was no sin as ours would be. So, at the beginning of our quest for knowledge, autonomy is as much a necessity and a virtue as its exercise, after it leads us to God, is unnecessary and vicious.

Van Til writes:

> If to any extent we allow the legitimacy of the natural man's assumption of himself as an autonomous reference point for interpreting the facts, we cannot deny his right to twist the facts of Christianity to any point. Autonomous man will not accept God's revelation in Scripture [and it is] no easier for sinners to accept God's revelation in nature.[29]

Van Til thus rejects any element of neutrality in the non-Christian mind.

This statement makes clear how Van Til is using the word *autonomy*. Apparently, he uses the two ingredients of the word (*autos* and *nomos*) to signify that the individual is a law to himself in the sense that he may arbitrarily make the laws which control him. So he is a self-legislator, according to Van Til's understanding of the word *autonomy*. From *that* definition all of these appalling deductions do follow rather logically. Nevertheless, it is a strange thing to say that an autonomous man, even in that sense of the word, has the "right" to "twist" the facts. We know what Van Til means by that. He is assuming that God is the lawgiver and that a person who is a law to himself may by his own self-legislation twist the legislation of God. But if each person is a legislator, then what he legislates is not a twisted law but actually the correct and authentic law. For Van Til to accuse him of twisting the laws is assuming his heteronomy when as a matter of fact, according to Van Til's view, he is autonomous.

But surely when we begin by using the laws with which we are endowed, this is not the same thing as self-legislation. This autonomy is part of our composition. Whoever made us intended that we operate according to these laws which we find within us. These laws are not our own product, they do not originate with us. They are given to us, not created by us. This distinction is never recognized, as far as we have seen, in any of the writings of Van Til. He always assumes that the person who begins to examine the universe without presupposing the existence of the divine Lawgiver necessarily presupposes his own status as a lawgiver. That is by no means a necessary assumption of the person who begins by examining the data which he has at hand. The concept of *moral* autonomy is not analytically contained in the notion of self-consciousness. Some people do come to the conclusion that they can legislate for themselves, but this is not a necessary conclusion. Though the vast majority of humankind does begin autonomously, they do not assume that, because they have to operate according to the laws by which they have to operate, they are therefore the creators of those laws. Nor do they commonly feel they have any right to twist data so as to meet their preferences. On the contrary, they draw conclusions about the laws of thought with which they have been endowed. Van Til sees all of this as a twisting because he assumes that one who operates according to these laws is in opposition to God. But people do not necessarily consider themselves in opposition to God, whose existence they do not even know at the outset. They do not necessarily deny the divine being as Van Til insists they do. People do not assert their autonomy against an initially known God as Van Til insists they do. They simply operate according to human nature. Traditionalist Christians would say that if a person followed the data in accordance with the laws which are instilled in his very being, and did not try to suppress conclusions because they threaten him, he would arrive at heteronomy. He fails to do this not because he is human, but because he is a sinner. If he follows the laws of his own nature, autonomously if you please, he will come to the conclusion that there is a God. That, of course, will be the end of his autonomy.

We may observe at this point that Van Til has an "autonomy" of his own. He argues that if we presuppose God, we have an intelligible view of the facts of the universe. Therefore, we ought to presuppose God. But why does Van Til draw those conclusions? In practice, he is as autonomous as anyone else. Van Til concludes that, without presupposing God, we cannot predicate and it is therefore wrong not to presuppose God. If we can predicate by presupposing God, it is right to presuppose God. That is Van Til's *autonomous* conclusion. God does not tell him that. If God does tell him that, he, Van Til, is the one who decides that he ought to believe it.

Van Til does not really begin with God. God functions in the Vantillian system as a postsupposition. There is something prior to God, though it is often concealed. Van Til begins with the supposition that we should be able to predicate; an inability to predicate is fatal. We agree. We observe, however, that this is his autonomous conclusion (as well as ours). If autonomy is wrong for us, it is wrong for him also.

Van Til goes on to say that autonomous humanity will not accept

God's revelation in Scripture, and with that we agree. Given Van Til's notion of autonomy, it is agreed that autonomous humanity cannot accept any higher authority. As we have shown repeatedly, however, that is not a proper usage of autonomy. Starting from what Van Til calls autonomy, many have come to the conclusion of heteronomy. As a matter of fact, Van Til himself admits that autonomous (i.e., unregenerate) humanity knows God, which demonstrates that autonomous humanity does grasp God's revelation. Besides, in this context, Van Til is saying that these persons will not only reject the revelation of God in Scripture but the revelation of God in nature. As a matter of fact, they accept both if they know God. If they accept Him, it makes sense that they know there is a God even from their own allegedly autonomous principles. That is what is agreed rather than the opposite.

If Van Til is playing on the word *accept,* then, of course, he should say so. It is agreed by all Christians that, in their unconverted condition, people do not *acquiesce in* the knowledge which they have of God. All we claim is that though they do not acquiesce in it, do not act according to it (Rom. 1:18f.), they do accept it as a fact. This knowledge is suppressed. They do not worship God as God. They will not keep Him in their thinking. They try to suppress Him, to eradicate Him. This implies, however, that they "accept" or grasp the fact that He exists.

Van Til does not keep these two usages in mind. He tends to vascillate between them, without indicating the divergence. This brings repeated confusion into the discussion. Van Til and all the rest of us agree that natural, unregenerate people who do not presuppose God at the outset, nevertheless know God. Since Van Til does not make the distinction between accepting and acquiescing in Him, his statement that they do not accept this knowledge is simply not true. They do "accept" the fact. They "accept," they "grasp" the fact, they "admit" the fact, they even, reluctantly, "confess" the fact that there is a God. They do not "accept" it in the sense of acquiescing in it. This distinction is vital. The difference is profoundly significant.

To make this whole debate about autonomy more apparent, we submit an imaginary dialogue between Dr. Van Til and the traditionalist:

VT: If you begin your thinking relying on your own logical principles and observations, you are guilty of autonomy.

T: You mean that in that case we make ourselves a law to

ou selves instead of acknowledging God as the only rightful lawgiver?

VT: Precisely.

T: When we begin our thought we do not deny that God is the
only rightful lawgiver. We simply do not know, when we
begin to think, that there is a God. If we did, we would
certainly admit that He is the only rightful lawgiver.
Would you suggest that we recognize God as the only
rightful lawgiver when we do not know that there is a
God?

VT: I admit, of course, that you cannot recognize God as the
only rightful lawgiver if you do not know that there is a
God. But, if you are ever going to know that there is a God,
you are going to have to presuppose Him. If you do presuppose Him you will recognize Him as the only rightful
lawgiver and deny your own autonomy.

T: We grant that if we presuppose God we will in so doing
presuppose that He is the only rightful lawgiver. From that
moment on, we will cease believing ourselves to be autonomous. But, if *we* did presuppose God, would it not be *we*
who presuppose Him? That is, would it not be the old
autonomous selves that would now be presupposing God
and only then giving up our autonomy? When *you* presuppose God, is it not *you*, Dr. Van Til, who presupposes Him?
Are not you then as we in that case, exercising your own
autonomy?

VT: Perish that thought. You may proceed autonomously if
you insist, but I—never!

T: We realize, Dr. Van Til, that you do not now consider
yourself autonomous (nor do we, for that matter, since we
too believe in God); but, when you decide to presuppose
God, do you not do so of yourself—autonomously, that is.
If not, please explain how you avoid so doing.

VT: I presuppose God because that is the only way that I or
anyone else can think.

T: Do you think so? Is the very fact that you do think so not
an autonomous intellectual act? It is you who do that presuppositional thinking, is it not? It is not God who presupposes God is it? It is Cornelius Van Til is it not? Autonomous Cornelius Van Til?

VT: No, it is not God who presupposes God, but Cornelius Van Til who presupposes Him, to be sure. However, I am not autonomous in so doing because He reveals Himself to me and enables me to presuppose Him.

T: Do you think so? You see the point of our rhetorical question. It is always Cornelius Van Til who does the thinking, even the presuppositional thinking. Do you not autonomously judge that God has revealed Himself to you in the Scriptures? And in your heart by the Holy Spirit? Can "private judgment" be avoided by anyone, including you?

VT: Maybe you have a point there. But, after that initial revelation in Scripture and illumination in my heart by the Holy Spirit which I myself do accept, I yield any conceivable autonomy. Therefore, I do not try, as you traditionalists do, to prove God autonomously.

T: Please note, Dr. Van Til, that we too (once we are convinced that the Scripture is the Word of God and that the Holy Spirit has illumined our soul) yield our autonomy as you do. The difference between us, at this point, seems to be that you claim to accept Scripture and the internal testimony of the Holy Spirit on faith while we require evidence. We both admit that we accept these acts as autonomous acts, but your autonomous acts require no evidence whereas ours do. You, therefore, consider yourself now free of the charge of autonomy while we still labor under it. Is that the way you see it?

VT: Essentially, now, do you plead guilty to the charge of autonomy?

T: Yes, we do but we remind you that you have already pled guilty to it also at an earlier point. The question is whether we are holding on to autonomy too long or whether you gave it up too soon. May we ask you a question?

VT: Yes.

T: Why do you believe that the Scriptures are the Word of God?

VT: That is an easy question. I believe that the Bible is the Word of God because the Bible says that it is the Word of God.

T: Then *you* have *that reason* for accepting the Bible and your autonomy is alive longer than you thought, is it not? Previously, it had seemed that you merely accepted the Bible as the Word of God. Now, we see that you have a reason for your faith; namely, that the Bible claims to be the Word of God. Presumably, you would not accept the Bible as the Word of God if it had not so claimed.

VT: I had not thought of it quite that way. I guess you can say that, believing the Bible is the Word of God because it says it is, is a kind of reason for faith in the Bible. Nevertheless, I do not need any other evidence as you traditionalists do.

T: We wonder about that. There are other religious books which claim to be the Word of God that you do not believe are the Word of God. Why is that?

VT: Because. . . .

T: Let me interrupt long enough to say that the very word "because" means that you do not accept the Bible as the Word of God merely because it says that it is. Whatever you put after your "because" is some additional reason beside the mere affirmation. Perhaps you will say: "Because the Holy Spirit convinces me that the Bible is the Word of God"?

VT: That is true: The Holy Spirit does convince me that the Bible, and no other book, is the Word of God.

T: The Bible you can see and read; but, how do you recognize the Holy Spirit?

VT: I am immediately conscious of His presence.

T: How do you know that the presence of which you are immediately conscious is the Holy Spirit? Does He say that He is the Holy Spirit?

VT: Of course not; not in so many words or in any words, in fact. I am a Reformed theologian, you know.

T: Indeed we know that you are an eminent Reformed theologian and we honor you as such. But we still would like to ask you how you know that it is the Holy Spirit in your heart?

T: I know the answer you are fishing for and what you will do with it when you get it. But here goes: I know that it is the Holy Spirit in my heart because the Bible tells me so. Go ahead now and accuse me of circular thinking—you seem to delight in that.

T: We will not disappoint you. We accuse you of circular

reasoning. You believe the Bible is the Word of God because the Holy Spirit tells you so and you know the Holy Spirit tells you so because the Bible is the Word of God. We can well anticipate what you will say to that, but please tell us whether you admit that you are reasoning in a circle.

VT: I do not admit it; I glory in it! What a glorious circle! From God the Word to God the Spirit and back again. Why don't you travel in such a divine circle?

T: Seriously, Dr. Van Til, you certainly see that you are proving neither the Word of God nor the Spirit of God by such a tactic. You are a reasonable person and you know as well as anyone that making the Bible's inspiration rest on the Spirit and the Spirit's testimony rest on the Bible's inspiration gets you nowhere at all.

VT: I am sorry that you think so. That circle gets you everywhere, so to speak. That is, the Word of God gives the answer to all our questions. Apart from that revelation we cannot even predicate and on the basis of it we can (thinking God's thoughts after Him) understand everything.

T: Ah, now we are getting somewhere. Now we hear something that sounds like an argument—an autonomous argument at that.

VT: What do you mean?

T: We find you contending for the Bible as the Word of God because it explains the world of reality and that it only does. Are you not saying this?

VT: Indeed I am. Is it not true?

T: We agree most heartily. It is true that the Bible is the Word of God and that it explains everything and that without it we cannot understand everything or anything ultimately.

VT: You sound like a VanTillian. Are you being converted at long last?

T: It is Van Til who has become the traditionalist. You are giving a reason now for believing the Bible—and not a circular reason either. You are saying that you believe the Bible is the Word of God because it answers questions only God could answer and makes predication possible. You are giving a reason for believing the Bible that we, or any autonomous individuals, can understand and weigh. Van Til is no longer the VanTillian and his autonomy is still alive. Furthermore, we suspect that he does not see himself as thereby making the creature greater than the Creator simply because he has a reason for believing that the Creator has revealed Himself in the Bible.

Certainly there are differences between presuppositionalism and traditionalism concerning the type of arguments offered for believing that the Bible is the revelation of God. The crucial point, however, is that there is no real difference on the matter of autonomy. Do we not together admit the necessity of exercising personal judgment until we know that God exists and that He has spoken? At that point, we both give up our autonomy. From there on, we both are instantly obedient to the recognized authority of God.

"Whether the unbeliever claims to know all things or not, he in effect asserts that he knows all things if he sets up his own judgment as the standard."[30] This statement is from Robert Knudsen, a Dooyeweerdean who disagrees with Van Til at some crucial points. Nevertheless, it states what virtually all in the presuppositionalist camp reiterate. They assume that if a person proceeds to make his own judgment the standard at the outset, he therefore thinks he "knows all things."

Presuppositionalists persistently attribute an implied omniscience to those who begin where they actually are. But they cannot carry this charge through consistently. Every now and then they admit that there is a valid, finite starting point in human reason which does not imply human omniscience. Similar statements may be found in the writings of Gary North, John Frame, Greg Bahnson, Rousas Rushdoony, and others.

This is a most unfortunate misunderstanding because it is a root matter. We are dealing with the beginning of the whole process both for the secular and the presuppositional mind. To have a misapprehension of the situation at a point so fundamental must have far-reaching effects.

CONCLUSION

All's well that ends well? Hardly. Certainly in the realm of thought nothing can end well that does not begin well. We have shown that presuppositionalism does not begin well even though it begins with God because it begins with God when God requires us to begin with ourselves. To start from above when we are below is simple absurdity and this fundamental absurdity will plague presuppositionalism to the very end. And the whole of Reformed theology, which presuppositionalists proclaim, will be denatured with the best of intentions. As we shall see in the following chapters, no Reformed doctrines escape this underlying derationalization.

CHAPTER 13

The Noetic Influence of Sin

IN A SENSE, what we have just been considering—the presuppositionalist view of starting point and autonomy—is supposed to show *how* the nonpresuppositionalist errs. The subject we now consider—the presuppositionalist view of the noetic influence of sin—is supposed to show *why* the nonpresuppositionalist errs. As background for this subject, we will first note briefly how classic Calvinists have viewed the influence of sin on the mind, taking Calvin, Voetius, Heppe, and Edwards as representative of this tradition.

CLASSIC CALVINISTS ON THE NOETIC INFLUENCE OF SIN

The basic Calvinist position is implied in the eighth chapter of the first book of Calvin's *Institutes:* "So Far as Human Reason Goes, Sufficiently Firm Proofs Are at Hand to Establish the Credibility of Scripture."[1] Calvin begins this chapter by reminding the reader that unless certainty "higher and stronger than any human judgment be present, it will be vain to fortify the authority of Scripture by arguments." He insists that arguments do not produce persuasion which is the work of the Spirit discussed in the preceding chapter. But he does not deny that arguments do prove, and can be seen to prove, that the Bible is the Word of God. Referring to the miracles of Moses, for example, Calvin asks, "Was not God, from heaven, commending Moses as his undoubted prophet?"[2] Later, Calvin refers to "a proof too clear to be open to any subtle objections."[3] The "truth" of the New Testament "cries out openly that its writers must have been instructed by the Spirit."[4] "There are other reasons . . . brilliantly vindicated against the wiles of the Bible's disparagers."[5] Yet they all "are not strong enough to provide a firm faith, until our heavenly Father, revealing his majesty there, lifts reverence for Scripture beyond the realm of controversy."[6] What can Calvin mean by this lifting "reverence for Scripture beyond the realm of controversy"? If the Bible is established by "sufficiently firm proofs so far as human reason goes," what can this "revealing his majesty" be except the internal, nonrational, super-rational, testimony of the Spirit? And if the testimony of the Spirit is necessary, what does that imply about Calvin's view of the noetic influence of sin? It means that the mind is not destroyed by the Fall for it sees the "confirming proofs." Something is wrong with the heart—not the mind—which needs the nonrational, super-rational revelation of divine majesty.

Heinrich Heppe quotes Voetius as evidence that the next century's Calvinists did not depart from Calvin:

> We presuppose that the supernatural truths of divine faith surpass the reason of man as such. He does not perceive them unless he is raised up and informed by a higher light. But they are not repugnant to him *per se* as such, only through the *accident of corruption and the wicked disposition which inheres in our mind*.[7]

Voetius traced the effect of sin to the disposition, not the cognitive power of mind.

Heppe continues:

> Generally then *religio naturalis* and *religio revelata* are so related to one another, that the latter is the confirmation of the former (since it absorbs it into itself); and the latter mediates revelation's point of contact in man. Yet it must by no means be concluded from this that reason, i.e., "the faculty of the rational soul in man by which he apprehends and adjudicates upon things intelligible" (Voetius I, I) may *in any way* be the principle of knowledge by faith. Not for a moment can this be said of the reason unillumined by revelation. On the contrary, the sole principle of religious knowledge must be the light from which even the Christian's reason has its illumination, namely, revelation; or (since as a matter of order God only reveals Himself by the Word) the word of Scriptures.[8]

Jonathan Edwards taught total depravity totally. He was also very sensitive to the way that depravity of the heart always tries to make the mind its flunky. In spite of this indirect noetic influence of sin, the mind as an instrument survives and is utterly indispensable at least eight ways:

1. Reason must prove the existence of God the Revealer.
2. Reason anticipates revelation.
3. Reason must grasp the message of revelation.
4. Reason must demonstrate the rationality of revelation.
5. Reason must verify the supernaturalness of revelation.
6. Reason argues the dependability of revelation.
7. Reason defends the mysteries in revelation.
8. Reason must interpret the inspired contents of revelation.[9]

It was inevitable that the general editor of the Yale University Press edition of *The Works of Jonathan Edwards* would conclude that "Edwards accepted totally the tradition established by the Reformers with respect to the absolute primacy and authority of the Bible, and he could approach the biblical writings with that conviction of their inerrancy and literal truth."[10]

Edwards also recognized the limitations of reason:

1. Reason cannot make the knowledge of God "real" to the unregenerate.
2. Reason cannot yield a supernatural salvific revelation.
3. Reason cannot determine all that revelation may reveal.
4. Reason cannot apprehend revelation as revelation.[11]

We suggest that classic Reformed orthodoxy saw the noetic influence of sin not as direct through a totally depraved mind, but as *indirect* through the totally depraved heart.

PRESUPPOSITIONALISTS ON THE NOETIC INFLUENCE OF SIN

We turn now to a sampling of presuppositionalists' handling of the noetic influence of sin: first, Van Til; second, Greg Bahnsen; third, Rousas Rushdoony; fourth, Herman Dooyeweerd; and fifth, H. Evan Runner.

According to Van Til, the traditional approach is unable to account for the scriptural view of human nature. The traditional position suggests, he maintains, "that the Scripture is not correct when it talks of 'darkened minds,' 'willful ignorance,' and 'bad men' and 'blind people'!"[12]

Traditionalists, of course, do *not* say that the Scripture is incorrect. They do not believe that. They would repudiate their own apologetic if they thought it really implied that the Word of God erred. The question is, then, how traditionalists do account for the blindness that is attributed to people in Scripture. The interesting thing is that they account for it the same way that Van Til does. Traditionalists agree that men do think and they do "see" that God exists. However blind their minds may be, they are not so blind that they cannot see that. They see it very plainly. It is transparent to them, according to Romans 1:21. Traditionalists say, with Van Til, that fallen humans proceed to suppress this knowledge. The very fact that they are suppressing knowledge of God indicates that the knowledge is always present. According to evidentialists, men are quite unsuccessful in suppressing it. The knowledge is not only present but it remains present. Apparently that is Van Til's thinking, too, on occasion.

What, then, is the darkening of the mind? Traditionalists and presuppositionalists agree that it is not that the mind cannot think clearly any more. As a matter of fact, it cannot help thinking God. However, because sinners are at enmity with God, the knowledge which the mind discovers is repugnant to them. They try to eradicate it. That is the way the mind becomes darkened. None is so blind, according to our Lord, as one who will not see. Throughout Romans 1, Paul insists that people *will not* have God in their thinking. The mind itself is not reprobate but sinners will not let the truth penetrate their inmost being. Because they "became vain in their thinking," God (then) gave them over to a "reprobate mind." God punishes sinners by letting them have their own way. In other words, the noetic influence of sin is the influence of a sinful heart on the use of the mind, leading the mind to suppress information which the mind (as a reliable instrument of knowledge) cannot help apprehending.

It is not traditionalism which has a problem here. It is presuppositionalism. Traditionalists of Reformed persuasion certainly account for the blindness of the mind as a willful suppression of the information which the sinner's perceiving mind does apprehend. How does Van Til account for it, since he repudiates the traditional approach? He will not allow the noetic influence to be an indirect influence through the wicked heart acting upon an instrumental reason. What option has he left except to suppose that the mind itself has been destroyed? But he will not say that. He realizes how problematic that is. But if he contrasts his position with the traditional, what option does he have but to say that the effect of the Fall is the obliteration of the functioning mind? That is hyper-Calvinism. Van Til does not want to be guilty of it. As a result, he vascillates between the position which he repudiates as autonomous (namely the classical Calvinist position of the serious noetic effect of sin) and the position which he infers as a part of his presuppositionalism, as we have shown in the preceding chapter dealing with the primacy of the intellect (the radical noetic effect of sin). A further indication that Van Til sees the noetic influence as virtually destroying the logical functioning of the mind is his conception of the absurd. "We do not say *Credo quia absurdum*. We say rather that all wisdom that has not its source in Christ is folly. We cannot fathom logically how the eyes and minds of self-deceived and satan-deluded men may be opened. But that they can be and are being opened that we know."[13]

The Latin quotation above originates with Tertullian and in essence is repeated by Kierkegaard, Brunner, Barth, Reinhold Niebuhr, and Tillich. Most twentieth-century dialecticians have the same pattern of thought, though each prefers or objects to one word or another: "absurd," "inconceivable," "paradoxical," "mythical." Van Til rejects the term, "absurd," but defends the concept. "We *cannot fathom logically* how the eyes and minds of self-deceived and satan-deluded men may be opened." But some are opened to the understanding of truth and it should be easy for Van Til to "fathom logically" how God can open their eyes and minds by regeneration to welcome the truth.

Is Van Til a dialectical theologian? He says that he rejects their absurdity doctrine even while he illustrates it in his own thought. What is the difference? Perhaps Van Til is inconsistent while the neo-orthodox theologians are not. They see all revelation doctrines as incapable of logical explanation. For Van Til the God of revelation is somehow coherent and the basis of all creaturely comprehension. The inevitable question is how a God whose revelation is not capable of logical comprehension can Himself be the principle of comprehension? Is Van Til's not an absurd denial of the absurd or the most absurd of all absurdities?

Greg Bahnsen insists that Tertullian's *Credo quia absurdum est* ("I believe *because it is absurd*") should have been "in spite of its apparent absurdity."[14] This Vantillian is not with his mentor at this point. It must be admitted, however, that Van Til does try (unsuccessfully) to represent Christianity as not absurd. Let us see whether Bahnsen can succeed.

According to Bahnsen, when Paul "came to Corinth, he did not rely upon the intellectual tools of the Athenian philosophers; instead, he came with the powerful demonstration of the Spirit in order that faith might not be in *the wisdom of men* but in the power of God."[15] Bahnsen explains: "Paul did not oppose the use of persuasion and philosophy that were patterned after man's alleged self-sufficient intellectual abilities."[16] This presuppositionalist is allowing Paul the use of some form of persuasion and philosophy (as long as it is not of the autonomous variety). As if to imply that not all of unregenerate, human reasoning is that way, he maintains:

> One of the key reasons why Paul did not exalt and trust the intellect or reason of man is found in his doctrine of *total depravity*. That depravity, held Paul, extends to the intellect of man. "The carnal mind is at enmity against God; for it is not subject to the law of God, neither indeed can it be."[17]

Defending Van Til, Bahnsen claims that "standing firmly within the circle of Christianity's presupposed truth, we reason *from the impossibility of the contrary*."[18]

Bahnsen is a study in arbitrariness. First, he says that Paul did not "rely upon the intellectual tools of the Athenian philosophers," though Paul did not say that, and even cited one of their poets. Furthermore, reliance on the "demonstration of the Spirit" is *more* than, not other than, intellectual argument. Third, while admitting that Paul was not against persuasion and philosophy, Bahnsen tells us that Paul rejected them though he gives no evidence of this in his Mars' Hill sermon. Fourth, the appeal to "total depravity," though not arbitrary generally, is arbitrary when applied to the Areopagus sermon because Paul makes no mention of it. Fifth, the appeal to Paul's teaching that "the carnal mind is enmity against God" is arbitrary in two ways. It is certainly not cited or alluded to in Acts 17 and, more importantly, the very phrase *carnal mind* shows that Bahnsen is not thinking clearly enough. The carnal mind would not welcome what is opposed to the fleshly interest. In so doing it would have to go counter to pure intellectuality which seeks truth and not the justification of other interests. If someone insists, "But that is the way the mind of fallen humanity functions," we grant it. But the mind *knows* what it is doing, can be shown what it is doing, and if it continues, will be aware of the rape of the mind by the flesh. In other words, we can appeal to the mind (as Paul obviously did appeal to the carnal minds at Athens) knowing all the while that, unless regenerated, this mind will try to justify rationally the heart's unbelief.

Bahnsen does not avoid the hyper-Calvinist notion of the noetic influence of sin, but we sense his movement back toward a Reformed center. Statements against *Credo quia absurdum est*, the acknowledgement that Paul did not oppose the use of "persuasion and philosophy," and especially the declaration that "standing firmly within the circle of Christianity's presupposed truth, we reason *from the impossibility of the contrary*," are inconsistencies in Van Til's thought and the minor themes at that. They may be the same in Bahnsen, but their emphatic utterance by a young scholar at the beginning of his intellectual ministry gives us hope. If Bahnsen will truly *reason from the impossibility of the contrary*, he will realize that he is assuming a legitimate autonomy, the primacy of the intellect, and a genuine point of contact in the meaningful, traditional, Calvinistic, understanding of those terms. If he does that, he will therein cease to be a presuppositionalist.

Rousas Rushdoony's view of the noetic influence of sin is indicated by his remark that William Hallack Johnson, C. H. Dodd, and other scholars "have their own bias, each in his turn predetermining the facts on the basis of certain philosophical presuppositions. . . . Man neither is nor can be 'objective' and 'impartial.' "[19] This very general statement about scholars being necessarily subjective or biased presumably applies to humanity in general as well.

Rushdoony is himself both a scholar and a man, and if his statement is true, he too is biased and partial. And, presumably, his presuppositionalism would be biased and partial also. If bias and partiality vitiate the thinking of Johnson, Dodd, and other scholars, would they not vitiate the thinking of Van Til, Rushdoony, and other such scholars also?

No doubt, Rushdoony would reply that the grace of God by regeneration makes him unbiased. We do not doubt that, but how would he prove it, especially to scholars like Johnson and Dodd? If he tries to prove it, he tacitly admits that these men are not necessarily biased intellectually or they could not hear (understand) what he is saying. If he does not try to prove it, the counter-charge of his own bias is unrefuted. Then his charge against others' bias cannot stand.

Coming to Dooyeweerd, we wish to point out the similarity between Dooyeweerd and Van Til as presuppositionalists, and, at the same time, the vast dissimilarity between them due apparently to the *total* lack of rational orientation in Dooyeweerd. Unlike Augustine, Dooyeweerd would develop a Christian philosophy in which philosophical questions are not handled within the framework of an elaborately developed systematic theology. He would instead subordinate philosophy to revelation (not to theology, in a scientific sense, since theology, for Dooyeweerd, is in itself subordinate to revelation). This is not because philosophy arbitrarily is thought to be the servant of theology, but because "*a theoretical analysis of the nature of philosophical thought is able to disclose an essential unity between faith and reason.*"[20] Dooyeweerd agrees with Augustine's withdrawal from the external world seeking truth in the inner consciousness.

David H. Freeman claims that the Reformation viewpoint was overtaken by Scholasticism. But he asserts that Dooyeweerd, with Calvin, rejects any conception of philosophy which affirms a self-sufficiency of reason. Dooyeweerd would found philosophy upon the basic articles of the Christian faith: Creation, fall into sin, and redemption in Jesus Christ. Freeman insists that Creation, Fall, and redemption in Dooyeweerd are not to be understood in their theoretical, theological sense, but rather as motifs of the Word of God.[21]

Dooyeweerd cites this as the thesis that he would defend, throughout his entire writings: Philosophical thought is dependent on non-philosophical thought—on religious motives. A religiously neutral objectivity is impossible.

In other words, the Fall has so affected the mind that it cannot function as a mind. It must yield to revelation before it can function. Otherwise, if it asked any questions, used any rational criteria, this would be affirming the "self-sufficiency of reason." Dooyeweerd and his expounders, like Freeman, never state the matter so bluntly. They would argue that this is not what Dooyeweerd is saying. True, Dooyeweerd does not say this in so many words, but it must be what he means. For what else can he mean? If he means that he does not want reason to be *totally* self-sufficient, we ask, why does he not say so? In traditional thought that is what is said. Reason finds the evidence for revelation, but it is no substitute for revelation (as is the case in rationalism). When it finds evidence of divine revelation, it knows that it can no longer doubt the truth of what that revelation contains. To do so would be to claim rational self-sufficiency and this is not reasonable. Augustine, Aquinas, Calvin, Hodge, Edwards—all have said as much. But Dooyeweerd says far more. If he gave a reason for revelation, he would not be *beginning* with revelation. When he begins with revelation, he does not give a *reason* for so doing.

This, we say again, implies that the Fall has essentially destroyed the reason. To be sure, reason can be used, after being remade or regenerated, to interpret and apply the arbitrarily accepted revelation. But Dooyeweerd gives no reason for accepting revelation in the first place. At bottom, Dooyeweerd would seem to say, the human is an unthinking animal, below even the dumb animals because their minds, at least, can judge about the external world. The proper human mind, according to Dooyeweerdian thought, has no more power or right to question the data on the basis of which it operates than a computer has. It carries out all its theological and other computations as mechanically as a machine. If we give a rational ground for the mind operating as it does, we have not kept revelation at the beginning.

In his festschrift, Van Til makes an interesting comment on Dooyeweerd's contribution. With respect to traditional apologetics, Van Til had "agreed with Kuyper as over against Warfield on this point. Still, further, when I saw that Kuyper, though opposing Warfield, yet retained elements of a scholastic methodology in his thinking, I proposed that we must *go beyond.*"[22]

In the same article, Van Til finds Dooyeweerd deficient in the same way, bringing to light (as Dooyeweerd himself remarked) "important differences between your [Van Til's] view of a Christian philosophy and that of the Philosophy of the Cosmonomic Idea."[23]

> You see then, Dr. Dooyeweerd, that I hold two points about Christian apologetics which apparently you do not hold. In the first place I believe that Christian apologetics, and in particular Reformed apologetics, is not really *transcendental* in its method unless it says *at* the outset of its dialogue with non-believers that the Christian position must be accepted on the authority of the self-identifying Christ of Scripture as the presupposition of human predication in any field. Then, secondly, I believe that a Christian apologist must place himself for argument's sake upon the position of the non-believer and point out to him that he has to pre-suppose the truth of the Christian position even to oppose it.[24]

Before proceeding further with the Van Til critique of Dooyeweerd, let us critique Van Til. These two points which he rightly charges Dooyeweerd with denying, he himself cannot maintain consistently. His first point is that we must tell unbelievers that they must presuppose the truth of Christianity or the truth of Christ. Such a statement is utterly arbitrary and dogmatic. Unbelievers in possession of their rational faculties will not accept it or enter dialogue with one who does.

But suppose we listen to point two. What do we hear? A flat contradiction of point one. He will now show the unbeliever an irrefutable *argument* for the presuppositionalist position. If this had been point one, the unbeliever might have been interested in having someone prove it. But as Van Til's argument stands, point two is a flat contradiction of point one which says that there is no argument for being a Christian except being a Christian—there is no reason to believe Christ except to believe Christ. If Van Til protests that point one refers to believing the self-identifying Christ of Scripture, we see no difference. This is believing Christ because Christ said He is to be believed. If Van Til still insists that he added the qualification, "as the presupposition of human predication in any field," this makes no difference. It sounds like an argument—in fact, it sounds like point two—but it is not point two and it is not an argument. If it were an argument, then Christ would not be arbitrarily accepted because of His own assertion. He would be accepted because it can be proved that predication is only possible by presupposing Christ. We would have an argument *before* the presupposition is accepted, making the presupposition actually a conclusion or *post*supposition.

Van Til replies to Dooyeweerd, "You seem to me not to have given them [Creation, Fall and redemption; that is, the Word of God] their proper place at the outset of the argument, and you have *not presented them as the presupposition of the possibility of analyzing the structure of theoretical thought and experience.*"[25] In other words, Dooyeweerd has momentarily lapsed into a rational pattern of thought. He has analyzed the nature of theoretical thought before presupposing the Bible as the Word in order thereby to analyze the nature of theoretical thought.

It would be easy to view this as the pot calling the kettle black. But this Dooyeweerdian kettle is even blacker (more irrational) than the Vantillian pot, because Dooyeweerd thinks with his heart, whereas Van Til thinks irrationally but with his mind. Van Til is implicitly rational and explicitly irrational; Dooyeweerd is explicitly rational but implicitly irrational.

H. Evan Runner takes the view that man suppresses the Word of

God, does not hear it. "He suppresses it, because he pushes it down from the place it *has* in virtue of God's creation-ordinance."[26]

One cannot but notice how studiously Runner avoids saying "knowledge." In Romans 1, Paul says that the sinner will not have God in his *thinking*. He suppresses that knowledge or attempts to suppress it. That implies the primacy of reason. Reason is the means by which a person first has knowledge and encounter with God. The Dooyeweerdians, wanting to avoid that intellectual content and locate the beginning in the heart, logically have to avoid this initial knowledge. Hence we find Runner referring to the suppression not of knowledge but of God's "creation-ordinance." Even in that case, however, there would be an *implicit* knowledge of this creation-ordinance if there is any suppression of it. Runner seems determined to make that suppression by the heart alone. He tries to avoid the involvement of the mind in the first instance. He makes it a secondary, reflex action, in order to avoid the principle of the primacy of reason. Later he writes about the sinner's "substituting something else for the Word of God." Here again, however, the Word of God would have to be something rationally grasped before one could attempt to substitute something else for it. In the next sentence the truth wins out: "This at once brings a distortion of the Truth at the very center of the unbeliever's life."[27] Notice that the word *Truth* is capitalized. One suspects that Runner wants to talk in terms of the Person (God) and try to separate Him, if possible, from knowledge about Him.

We also notice, in this connection, that the reference throughout is to power, ordinance, and direct encounter with God. There is careful avoidance of a knowledge referrant. The values the human is always attempting to suppress in the "imagination" (which again seems to be something other than thought) would presumably imply knowledge. Runner does not explicitly deny the knowledge content, though he does not expressly acknowledge it either.

Runner frequently refers to the "re-publication"[28] of the Gospel. The Gospel is a "re-publication" of the truth of creation-light. This brings to mind the deistic use of that expression. Here is Runner's concept of re-publication: "God's Word in Christ is a reiteration of what God said when in his deed-revelation he created the world."[29] The resemblance to the famous deist Matthew Tindal (1653–1733) cannot be coincidental. The title of Tindal's "Deist Bible" was *Christianity as Old as the Creation: or, The Gospel, a Republication of the Religion of Nature*.[30]

251

Surely Runner does not want to say that nature contains the gospel. "God was in *Christ* reconciling the world" (2 Cor. 5:19) surely is not the "reiteration of what God said when in his deed-revelation he created the world."

If we are rightly sensing Runner's thinking, we must say that the presuppositional opposition to the traditional doctrine of the noetic influence of sin is reaching a nihilistic terminus. The Vantillians implicitly deny that the mind functions before it is enlightened by a presupposed revelation Word of God; the neo-Dooyeweerdians, in their intellectual leader, deny that the mind functions before a presupposed creation-Word of God.[31]

CHAPTER 14

The Attack on the Theistic Proofs

PRESUPPOSITIONALIST CHRISTIANS stand back-to-back with the world against the traditional theistic proofs. The oddest of couples appear in perfect harmony. Kant is no more insistent than Van Til that God's existence cannot be proved. Clark and Hume make common cause against miracle as evidence for truth. Lessing and Dooyeweerd are together on this side of the "Great Ditch." Carl Henry and Karl Barth agree that you must arbitrarily believe if you are ever going to understand supernatural Christianity.

PRESUPPOSITIONALISM'S AGREEMENT WITH NEO-ORTHODOXY

Van Til disagrees profoundly with Immanuel Kant, but not with his rejection of the theistic proofs. In a lecture on "Immanuel Kant and Protestantism," Van Til writes:

> In his *Critique of Pure Reason* Kant sought, it would seem, first of all to save science rather than to lay a foundation for faith. But in his *Critique of Practical Reason* and in his *Critique of Judgment* it appears that his ultimate purpose, even in the *Critique of Pure Reason,* was "to make room for faith." More than that, in the last analysis, Kant saw no way of even *saving science* except by making room for faith. Though all the "proofs" for the existence of God, including the moral proof, do not *prove* the existence of an unconditional being, yet nature, without such a being, is unintelligible.[1]

Van Til takes up J. W. N. Sullivan's work on *The Limitations of Science*[2] which, like Kant's, was written to make room for faith by destroying knowledge. Perhaps, Sullivan says, we will have to endow the atom with a rudimentary form of consciousness. In Sullivan, science has become humble, recognizing its partiality. It now allows us to make traditional allegations about aesthetics, etc.; moreover, it admits that it is highly probable that all scientific theories are wrong.[3]

Making room for religion, this dualistic religion is in turn followed by a monistic one. The principle of continuity has enabled scientists to see that freedom is no longer something that must be held to in spite of science but is something which may be believed in terms of a higher concept of science. Whitehead admitted that there is no alternative to recognizing in "God" the origin of all evil as well as all good.

Likewise, Van Til quotes Kroner who, with Kant, asserts "that the principle of free-will, which is the final term in reference to which nature, morality and religion must be referred, cannot be known by man himself to be a fact of the intelligible world, a thing-in-itself."[4] Kroner thinks that Kant has neglected imagination which he himself is going to develop. This leads him to say that Jesus is the Son of God because He knew Himself to be so; being and knowledge are here inseparable, because both are imaginative.[5] While "appreciating" Kroner, Van Til notes that, "in Greek thought, too, it is man that makes himself the final reference point in predication. True, this fact is not so obvious in Greek thought as in the case of Kant."[6]

Again,

> It was not possible, said Kant, to find unity between the manifold contradictions of human thought by means of logical analysis. Appeal had to be made to ethical experience and therewith to intuition. But, in so doing, Kant did not do what Luther or Calvin did, really make room for faith in the Christian sense of the term. Rather he made Christian faith more impossible than ever. He made room for faith, to be sure, but for faith that must forever be faith in the indefinite.[7]

The standard critique of Kant, apart from Scottish Realism, is his starting point and his ending point. For Kant, a thing-in-itself, God, and the soul are unknowable; nevertheless, he speaks about them. He assumes that they may be the cause lying behind the world of perceptions. While agreeing with Kant's rejection of theistic proofs, Van Til repudiates his rejection of Christian revelation.

Van Til is at one with twentieth-century neo-orthodoxy in his stance on the theistic proofs. Neither neo-orthodoxy nor Van Til's orthodoxy grant the cogency of the proofs or the possibility of a natural theology not based on biblical revelation.

We have already seen Barth's opposition to natural theology. Emil Brunner's famous debate with Barth concerned natural revelation not natural theology. Brunner was almost as convinced as Barth was that there could be no vital natural theology. He was not as certain as was Barth that the "proofs" had no cogency; but, being abstract, they were devoid of life.

> The God of rational Theism . . . is He of whom love can only be predicated *per accidens* and without certainty, who does not enter into history, and who therefore stands nearer to the God of Deism—who is remote from the world, and cares nothing about human beings—than he does to the Living God of Faith.[8]

Since mid-century, there has been some revisiting of the theistic proofs in nontraditional circles as we have seen, with—of all things— rehabilitation of the ontological argument which neither St. Thomas nor the traditional Protestants such as Charles Hodge defended. Norman Malcolm and Charles Hartshorne are examples of the rehabilitation of the ontological argument. Hartshorne, after showing that the idea of a necessary being is possible, argues that the idea of a necessary being, being possible, proves its necessary existence. Nevertheless, the God at the end of his syllogism is only potentially infinite and therefore not the infinitely real God. Malcolm's God is even more abstract. With friends such as these, theistic proofs have no need of enemies. Hartshorne and Malcolm may as well join Kierkegaard, Barth, Brunner, and Van Til pose as defenders of theistic faith. (We have attempted to refute them along with their opponents in the first part of this volume.)

Insofar as Van Til dispenses with traditional proofs, he is in the mainstream of contemporary thought. As a defender of orthodoxy, his up-to-dateness gains many a contemporary hearer who would be annoyed immediately by the mere mention of a cosmological or teleological argument. Usually, skeptical rejection of proofs of deity is a litmus test of the *avant garde* thinker, free from the tradition of the past. Imagine the surprise when an unabashed and unreconstructed

Calvinist steps forth to agree with the antitheists on this vital matter. It is no wonder that L. Harold DeWolf remarked that Van Til proves that intellectual orthodoxy is not dead yet,[9] an orthodoxy that has survived and even embraced the modern onslaughts and emerged a triumphant champion.

Van Til finds in Calvin a sixteenth-century presuppositionalist.[10] According to Van Til, Calvin recognized clearly the main principle that the finite consciousness must, from the outset, be conscious of God. Accordingly, Van Til argues, Calvin used the "theistic arguments" more *theistically* than they had been used before. He did not separate the "what" from the "that." He took into his purview the absolute God, the absolute Christ, the absolute Scripture, and absolute regeneration and maintained that all of these must be taken or nothing can be taken. He cleared from Christian theistic thought much of the Platonism that had clung to it until then.

We have already shown that Calvin argued, in fact, that people know God independently of "the absolute Christ, the absolute Scripture and absolute regeneration." These must be present for a *saving* knowledge, he maintained, but not for *any* knowledge of God at all. As B. B. Warfield has well written:

> It will repay us to gather out from their matrix in the flowing discourse the elements of Calvin's doctrine of God, that we may form a fair estimate of the precise nature and amount of actual instruction he gives regarding it. We shall attempt this by considering in turn Calvin's doctrine of the existence, knowableness, nature, and attributes of God.
>
> We do not read far into the *Institutes* before we find Calvin presenting proofs of the existence of God. It is quite true that this book, being written by a Christian for Christians, rather assumes the divine existence than undertakes to prove it, and concerns itself with the so-called proofs of the divine existence as means through which we rather obtain knowledge of what is, than merely attain to knowledge that God is. But this only renders it the more significant of Calvin's attitude towards these so-called proofs that he repeatedly lapses in his discussion from their use for the former into their use for the latter and logically prior purpose. *That he thus actually presents these proofs as evidences specifically of the existence of God can admit of no doubt.*[11]

So we give Kant and others to Cornelius Van Til (and to other modern Calvinists as well), but John Calvin and the Calvinistic tradition in general is against him. Unlike Barth, presuppositionalists do argue for general revelation. "All men know not merely that a God exists, but they know that God, the *true* God, the *only* God exists. They cannot be conscious of themselves without being conscious of God."[12] We question whether they can be conscious of God without first being conscious of themselves. Calvin, at least, assumed that unregenerate people know the God of whom they are conscious.

Unregenerate people have knowledge of the true God. Does not Van Til say that the unregenerate have this, only they keep it deeply suppressed? He does not say, as we do, that they *try* to suppress it. He says that they suppress it and do not have it in their thinking which is always autonomic. Does the unregenerate know the true God or not? Van Til stresses knowledge of God (γνοντες τον θεον). But there is a dilemma here. If the unregenerate know God, then how can they be autonomous thinkers living on borrowed capital? If they are autonomous and cannot predicate from contingency, how can they have this knowledge (true knowledge) of God?

According to Van Til, "They constantly conclude that God does not exist."[13] But according to the Bible, humans conclude that God does exist but they pretend He does not in a desperate effort to "think" Him out of existence. This seems occasionally to be Van Til's position, but he misunderstands the traditional position: "You [the traditional theist] say that by virtue of man's creation in the image of God, he knows God, and at the same time you say that these image-bearers interpret all things amiss since they do not know God."[14] Not so. What we say is that these image-bearers interpret all things amiss because of their willfulness and in spite of the fact that they know God.

Let us examine Van Til's approach as seen through the eyes of Rousas Rushdoony. He writes that the theistic arguments assume the neutrality of the mind, whereas Calvin was convinced of the enmity of the human mind against God. Moreover, the "proofs" of God to be arrived at first assume the independence of the human mind and of natural facts from God. Thereby they "concede to the opposition rather than advance the theistic cause."[15] We think it is correct to say that theistic argumentation assumes the neutrality of the mind in the sense that the mind is an instrument which does not feel but cogitates. When Rushdoony refers to the neutrality of the mind, he has in view the neutrality of the *person,* the heart as well as the mind. Surreptitiously, he gathers up the heart and will into the concept of the cognitive faculty or mind. Because his concepts are not clear, confusion follows.

Aquinas, Edwards, Butler, Reid, Warfield, Beattie, Orr, and others who used theistic reasoning with non-Christians were not assuming that there was no Fall, no sin, no hostility to God in the human heart. They were assuming, rightly we believe, that the mind as a faculty or power remained and functioned as it was intended to do. Therefore, it can and does survey the evidence and it can and does draw the proper conclusions, with detachment and neutrality. But as soon as it reflects on the visible things and concludes that there is an invisible Being behind them, the hostile heart immediately tries to suppress that evidence, not being willing to worship the God whom the mind discovers in its perusal of visible things. In a word, we are saying that Rushdoony's "mind" is not neutral because he is thinking of it as the heart. Apologetic ships are passing in the night without meeting each other at this particular point. Rushdoony implicitly affirms that the mind is neutral because he acknowledges that with the mind fallen, autonomous humanity *knows God*. If the cognitive faculty, the mind itself, were hostile, that enmity (as Rushdoony is here suggesting) would never even admit the knowledge of God. So the mind, as such, would be at enmity with God and would deny that it even knows God. Because of this lack of clarity, Rushdoony is attributing something to the traditional position which does not belong to it.

Van Til writes, "If there were an absolute God it is *ipso facto* out of the question to apply the categories of thought to him in the same way that they are applied to man."[16] We say, on the contrary, that if there is a God who made man in His own image, in His own rational image, then the categories of thought would apply to both God and man essentially (not modally). The difference would be a difference in degree and not of kind. God would understand in the infinite mode immediately, intuitively, infallibly, unchangeably. The finite creature would be liable to error, change, and all those things to which finitude is heir. But if people can think God's thoughts after Him, as Van Til insists regenerate people can, then they must be following the same pattern of thought as God's. The presuppositionalists do not escape this implication by their reference to analogical thinking. They believe that is a solution to their problem, but actually it is not. According to their view, they think God's thoughts after Him analogically. That is, regenerate humans in their own finite way understand what God has given them to know. If there were an absolute difference and no applicability of the laws of human thought to the divine being or the divine being to the human thought, then there would be no such thing as analogical thinking. If God were *totaliter aliter* in an absolute sense, knowledge of Him would be utterly impossible by any means. A dog cannot think God's thoughts after Him even analogically. He does not have the equipment because he was not made in the image of God. His owner, having been made in the image of God, is able to think as God thinks though without the infinite, perfect, and infallible qualities that belong to divine thought. God can reveal knowledge to the dog's owner as He could never reveal to dogs or other parts of the creation not made in the divine image.[17]

PRESUPPOSITIONALISM'S DISAGREEMENT WITH TRADITIONAL ORTHODOXY

Having observed presuppositionalism's agreement on the theistic proofs (Van Til's in particular) with contemporary neo-orthodoxy and secularism, we will now observe its disagreement with traditional orthodoxy. We will consider its debate with such thinkers as the Scholastics, Aquinas, Bishop Butler, Scottish Realists, and some contemporaries such as John Montgomery, Clark Pinnock, and Stuart Hackett.

No Knowledge Except by Special Revelation

On Scholasticism in general, Van Til states the issue as follows:

> The point in dispute is not whether there is some knowledge that must be acquired by revelation, but whether there is any knowledge that can be acquired without redemptive revelation. We hold it to be definitely anti-Christian to say that any man can have any *true knowledge of anything* except through the wisdom of Christ.[18]

In other words, Van Til does not disagree with the Scholastics' claim to special revelational knowledge, but with their claim that there is any other. In the above repudiation he refers plainly to "any knowledge" without qualification, though in a following sentence he specifies "any *true* knowledge." That knowledge which Augustine, Anselm, and the early and late Scholastics (the Protestant scholastics included) confidently affirmed, Van Til as confidently rejects. Indeed, he labels such a claim "definitely anti-Christian."

The Scholastics' erroneous conclusion is traced by Van Til to a mistaken epistemological method. "The Scholastics made the same mistake as the Greeks. Both took for granted that words must be used either simply univocally or simply equivocally."[19] Van Til implies that words may also be used analogically.

This supposed mistake of the Scholastics led to an even more unfortunate one, Van Til contends: "Accordingly the main question in epistemology, i.e., that of the relation of the infinite to the divine mind, was subordinated to the less important question of the relation of the finite mind to finite laws and 'facts.'"[20] So the Scholastics became apt in the horizontal, human, epistemological questions and neglected the vertical divine-human relation. We do not see that this is so since univocal and equivocal relate to finite/infinite. If words are univocal, then what is said of God by them is true, *mutatis mutandi*, of humans also. If words are equivocal, then what is said of God by them is not true, or not necessarily true, of humans.

What Van Til really infers is that there is no proper univocal or equivocal use of words pertaining to God and man but only an analogical use. He simply differs with the Scholastics' contention, but is not justified in saying that they were subordinating the "main questions" to lesser ones. They viewed the "main question" differently. It remains to be seen whose viewpoint is correct.

Thus far we have been speaking about Van Til and the realistic Scholastics. He comments on the nominalistic Scholastics as well. Of the greatest of them he remarks:

> Duns Scotus, the father of Nominalism (in his commentary on the *Sententiae of Lombardus*) carries this idea through until for him chance really ruled above God. If God's will is a will of indifference not led by his intelligence, chance is higher than God. And chance amounts to necessity once more.[21]

It is true that the Nominalism of Duns Scotus (unlike the Realism of Aquinas) led logically to the deification of chance, as Van Til comments. This is the Calvinistic determinist critiquing the voluntarist. But Van Til's conclusion that "chance amounts to necessity once more" is surprising. The usual determinist conclusion is that indifference leads to chance and chance to chaos, not to necessity. Though this is a minor matter for our inquiry, it reveals once again Van Til's persistent tendency to depart from his own tradition.

Van Til's Critique of Aquinas and Butler

Van Til's main critique of Scholasticism is reserved for Thomas Aquinas. "Then as now," he writes,

> I was convinced that the old Aquinas–Butler type of apologetics had always been unbiblical and therefore inadequate. What needed to be done was to point out that man himself, the subject of knowledge, must interpret himself as the creature of God, as a sinner in the sight of God, and as forgiven through the work of Christ and his spirit. All men know God, but all men as sinners seek to suppress their knowledge of God. They do this particularly by means of their various philosophical systems. This fact must be pointed out. Hath not God made foolish the wisdom of this world? It was not till later years that I received much help in my understanding of philosophy from D. H. Th. Vollenhoven and Herman Dooyeweerd.[22]

This is Van Til's original criticism of the traditional apologetic. As we have noticed, he agrees with the traditionalists that "all men know God," but, he continues, "all men as sinners seek to suppress their knowledge of God." Traditional apologetics, as we have shown, has always recognized this fact also. And it has pointed it out. When he says that all men know God, he is referring to all people before they recognize themselves as sinners and before they attempt to suppress this knowledge which they have. The point is that he admits that people have this knowledge even in their fallen, sinful, unconverted state. So, they do not have to presuppose God to know God. All human philosophical endeavors are attempts to think out of existence the God whom they already know to be in existence. Van Til seems strangely blind to two things: that his own system admits that sinners can think about God, and that the traditional position admits that these sinners, while thinking about God, try to think God out of existence. Thus, on this occasion, he overestimates the unique efficacy of his own system and underestimates the reach of the traditional.

Van Til will probably charge us with gross unfairness here, reminding us that he constantly insists that unregenerate people know the true God while always suppressing this knowledge. But what he admits in one breath, he takes back with the next.

Admittedly this is a tricky point but let us try to follow it (once more) through the intellectual thicket. First, Van Til grants that unregenerate, fallen, autonomous humans know the only true God. Second, this is not a mere sensory knowledge, but actual, cognitive knowledge. Third, such knowledge, according to Van Til the apologist, is only possible on the basis of the revelation of God in Scripture. Fourth, since autonomous humans never reason other than autonomously, they must, by autonomous reasoning, err about God. Fifth, the whole history of fallen humanity's autonomous thought, according to Van Til, shows that they never, on these principles, arrive at the knowledge of the true God. Therefore, sixth, history is supposed to show that autonomous humanity cannot possibly arrive at knowledge of God and that, nevertheless, they most certainly do. The seventh point, the *piece de resistance,* is that Van Til constantly tries to prove the impossibility of this knowledge, or indeed any true knowledge, ever being attained by autonomous humanity, thus reneging on the first point.

To confound confusion further, unregenerate humanity's knowledge is supposed to be merely knowledge-after-a-fashion, which they need not and do not suppress. But Van Til simply cannot have it both ways. If natural man has only knowledge-after-a-fashion or "false knowledge," he need not suppress that, and if he has to suppress knowledge, it must be true knowledge, which Van Til is always showing that he cannot, but does, have. A final touch, is that according to Romans 1:18–19 this true knowledge which Van Til inconsistently admits that the unregenerate have come from natural, not special, revelation.

If our analysis is sound, the traditional Aquinas-Butler apologetic is immune to Van Til's criticisms, while his alternative is inconsistent. Thomas and Butler are faulted for assuming that unregenerate humanity can reason soundly about God and the world. This is thought to be inconsistent with fallen, sinful human nature. A sound view of the Fall, however, does not entail that the very essence of human nature—rationality—was lost. Moreover, Van Til himself admits that fallen sinners do know God. So it turns out here that Van Til does *not* think that human rationality is lost in the Fall.

Such behavior on the part of sinners does not imply that they are ignorant of God because of their autonomy. Just the opposite, it is precisely because they do know God, that they must suppress such knowledge because, as Paul says, it leaves them without excuse for not worshiping God. Traditional apologetics is quite correct to proceed by showing sinners that they do know but do not act accordingly. Seeking to justify themselves, sinners say they do not know (suppression of the knowledge). The sound apologist will not let them escape, but will remind them of arguments which they cannot deny, though they will keep on trying for they have a vested personal interest in succeeding. This dialogue will go on until the sinner dies or is reborn.

Now let us examine Van Til's inconsistent alternative. He takes the sinner's lying allegations of ignorance seriously. Instead of pointing out, as the sound apologist does, that unconverted persons are not at all ignorant, Van Til agrees with them but tells them they must presuppose God in order to know God. He thus gives them an excuse for sin. On their own principles, sinners know God and Van Til should never let them forget it. But Van Til not only lets them forget, he justifies this avowed ignorance by arguing that on autonomous principles sinners cannot know God or anything. This is comforting those who wish to be excused from knowledge of God. Another of Van Til's comforts for the unregenerate is the notion that they cannot know God without presupposing Him and, as unregenerate sinners, cannot presuppose Him. Thus, this false apologetic preaches that sinners cannot know God where they can and that they can know God where they cannot.

It is a sad historical irony that Van Til took the wrong fork at the very outset of his intellectual odyssey. He was then, as now, "convinced that the old Aquinas–Butler type of apologetics had always been unbiblical and therefore inadequate." That was the initial mistake which he has devoted his entire strenuous, brilliant, academic career to defending, developing, propagating. It was not Butler who erred but Van Til and not Butler's essential soundness which needs to be repudiated but Van Til's tragic aberration which is shaking the very foundations of the Christian religion. However orthodox Van Til's affirmations and convictions may be, the foundations on which he bases them are not a bit less paradoxical than those of Karl Barth.

Furthermore, Van Til charges that when Aquinas "says that reason (by an Aristotelian method) can prove that God exists, this is pointless inasmuch as he adds that it *cannot say what God is*."[23] We add that this is a caricature of Aquinas who says a great many things that natural revelation shows God to be. He simply maintains that we cannot know His very essence. But to this Van Til responds:

> If he [Aquinas] tones his contrast down sometimes by saying that man by reason can know something of the *general characteristics of God, this is merely inconsistency*. Every man must and does

say something about the nature of God. He is clearly consistent
with his starting point in Aristotelian logic only when he asserts
that man can say nothing of the nature of God.[24]

He continues that it is as impossible to know God by the logic of
Aristotle as by the logic of Kant. Says Van Til, Wilbur Smith's mistake
in his *Therefore Stand*[25] was that he did not notice this. It was overlooked also by traditional apologetics generally and even by Gordon
Clark in his article "The Primacy of the Intellect."[26]

The Presuppositionalist Critique of Evidentialist Apologetics

Another aspect of the presuppositional departure from traditional
orthodoxy is its critique of theistic evidence. Here we will examine
only the formal relationship of the presuppositionalist and the evidentialist approaches to theistic evidence. In chapter 15 we will discuss in
detail their substantive differences. Van Til gives his attention to many
evidentialists, including Clark Pinnock, John W. Montgomery, J.
Oliver Buswell, and Stuart Hackett. We will consider only Hackett.
Hackett is Arminian. Not all evidentialists today (nor in the past) are,
by any means, Arminians, though Van Til supposes that Arminian
theology is implied even by avowed Calvinists.

Van Til cites Hackett as saying we must "have 'a rational justification for the metaphysical ultimate.' "[27] In Hackett's opinion, apparently, Calvinism denies this, making puppets of human beings. Since
humans are actually responsible, the irrationality of Calvinism has to
be rejected.

Van Til then shows the fundamental differences between Hackett's
and his own understanding of the message of Christianity.[28] His critique of Hackett is first of all, that he accepts the mind of the flesh.
Second, Hackett's basic charge that Calvinism is determinist and irrational is simply not true. Calvinistic divine sovereignty has nothing to
do with the physical, causal determinism of the philosopher. This is
indeed true, but Van Til gives no proof (as Edwards did in *The Freedom
of the Will*). It is true, however, that, according to Calvinism, God does
ordain all things, including physical causes which affect humans. How
then does Calvinism avoid Hackett's charge? A mere denial is not a
refutation.

Van Til next defends Calvinism against the charge that it has no
point of contact. It is Hackett, he says, who has no point of contact
because the principles on which he and others proceed are not sound.

On Hackett's view of "fact," unbelievers cannot know anything. So there cannot be any real point of contact. The Calvinist point of contact, by contrast, is rooted in the *"actual state of affairs."*[29] The particular point of contact claimed by Van Til is that he can show that the non-Christian explanation is no explanation at all; the non-Christian is living on borrowed capital, and so on. Notice that here again Van Til assumes that the unregenerate is able to understand in spite of his autonomous thinking.

Van Til refutes Hackett's charge against "Calvinistic" irrationality by saying that it only seems irrational to the *supposed* reasons and proofs of the unregenerate. By contrast, "the Christian offers the self-attesting Christ to the world as the only foundation upon which a man must stand in order to give any 'reasons' for anything at all."[30]

The objections to this contention are several. First, Christianity is true because it makes rationality possible. This is the traditional position which Van Til rejects. It gives a reason for faith which presuppositionalists say cannot be done. Second, the unregenerate presumably *can* see this point, which they are supposed to be unable to see because of the *noetic* influence of sin. Third, the self-attesting Christ is a "foundation" on which "reasons" rest. Mere self-attestation is not evidence, though Van Til says that it is; and reasons validate it, but Van Til says it needs no validation.

Vantillians reply that the unregenerate, *left to themselves,* will proceed autonomously; but a presuppositionalist can, *ad hominem,* show them that they cannot predicate on their autonomous principles. But if people could see *that,* they could understand that presupposing the God of Scripture is necessary to predication and they would not require regeneration. Van Til would probably respond, "Precisely, the problem is merely *ethical.*" Our reply is: "That is true on the *traditional* Reformed position, not on yours, because you maintain that people must be regenerated even to have *true* knowledge (let alone *saving* knowledge)." If we could persuade our presuppositionalist friends on this simple point, presuppositionalism would be a thing of the past, and we could close apologetic ranks and stand united before an unbelieving world.

Clark's Presuppositionalist Critique of Traditional Theism

Gordon H. Clark, perhaps the most thoroughgoing presuppositionalist of them all, is not less critical of the theistic proofs than Van

Til is, but his attack is different. There are great differences between Van Til and Clark but these do not include their common antipathy to traditional theistic argumentation. We will follow Clark here as he criticizes the cosmological argument as developed by Aquinas.

Clark charges that Aquinas's argument for a first-mover is circular. It includes a theory of motion which asserts that nothing can move itself. This theory in turn rests on the concepts of potentiality and actuality. Aquinas defines motion as the reduction of potentiality to actuality: The cause of a motion must be actually what the thing moved is potentially. And since nothing can be both actual and potential in the same respect, it follows that nothing can move itself. Unfortunately, the concepts of potentiality and actuality remain undefined. (Aristotle tried to explain them by an analogy.) In the context, motion is used in the definition and then the concepts of potentiality and actuality are used to define motion. The argument therefore is circular.[31]

Clark detects another phase of circular reasoning in Aquinas. According to Clark, Thomas argues against infinite regress because "it would rule out a first-mover."[32] If Thomas argued this way, it would indeed be circular because it would be proving the necessity of a first-mover because of the infinite regress argument and the infinite regress argument would be proved by the necessity of a first-mover. Thomas may have been infelicitous in some of his expressions, but there can be no doubt that he was using the argument independently. Regardless of Thomas's cogency of expression, the argument from infinite regress stands. If there were an infinite regress of causes, no cause could account for the existence of anything after itself. That is, everything which begins to be must have a cause and if every cause ultimately needs a cause, there is no such thing as an independent cause to account for anything.

The third reason which Gordon Clark offers against the validity of Aquinas's argument concerns the identity of the unmoved mover. Clark does not think that Thomas's "first mover" and "God" are the same being. "The argument taken at its full face-value would prove the existence merely of some cause of some physical motion; one might say that it could prove the existence of some physical cause."[33] But Clark obscures Aquinas's point. If the infinite regress is an unsound concept, then the physical cause is the originator of the reason of the unsound concept. The physical cause would require another physical cause which in turn requires another *ad infinitum*. Positing another physical cause does not end the infinite regress, but requires its continuance. The first-mover would have to be of the nature of that which is being moved. It could not be a mover which must be moved and yet be unmoved. Therefore, it cannot be in this physical sequence. It must be a being which is able of its own power to originate this sequence. We have already shown that it could not be physical; it is equally evident that it must be nonphysical or spiritual. At least, it could not have a physical cause, which it could not need.

Clark, retreating a little from his earlier assertion, states, "At any rate, it is quite clear that the Unmoved Mover of the proof has no qualities of a transcendent personality. . . . There is nothing super-natural about this cause."[34] On the contrary, Thomas is quite right when he says that everyone understands this Unmoved Mover to be God. This Unmoved Mover is not in this series which apart from Him would be in infinite regress. He is the Being who is able to be the First Mover, Himself being unmoved. If this Being does indeed start this process, He must have chosen to do so, which is a highly personal act of will. (Quite apart from the cosmological and teleological argu-ments, it is plain that order cannot be the product of anything other than deliberation, the activity of a person. And it must be super-natural, because if it were natural, it would be a part of the infinite regress which we have already observed could not explain any causality whatever.)

Clark concludes this paragraph with a remark taken from Pascal: "If the argument is valid, and this Mover explains the processes of nature, the God of Abraham, the God of Isaac and the God of Jacob is superfluous, indeed impossible."[35] It is precisely the God of Abraham, Isaac, and Jacob whom the Bible declares to be not only the Redeemer, but also the Creator. Being the originator of the universe in no way militates against the idea that He is also the Redeemer of humankind. True, introducing Him as the only one who could explain a natural, cosmological sequence would in itself not require that He be the Re-deemer. When we are talking about the cosmological argument in that restricted sense, however, we surely are not telling the whole story. Everything that exists needs an explanation: the God who explains the world also explains humanity and answers the predicament of human fallenness. The Creator who also redeems is anything but superfluous.

In this same work, Clark attacks the cosmological argument, appealing to Karl Barth's argument. Barth argues that God can only be known by God because we are talking about the Christian God, the triune God, whereas the cosmological argument of, e.g., Vatican

Council I leads to a partitioning of God and therefore to another God.[36] Clark also appeals to the fact that the God of revelation is the Redeemer-God and that, therefore, the Cosmic Beginner cannot be separated from the triune God. Surely, the knowledge of God as the beginning and end can coexist with the knowledge of God as Redeemer. And how can we know God as the Redeemer without knowing Him as the beginning and end of all things?

The criticism we have made of Clark and his allusion to Pascal, applies even more to Barth. Barth simply acknowledges no natural revelation or natural theology apart from special revelation. In chapters 3, 4, and 5, we have shown that there cannot be recognizable special revelation apart from natural theology. Barth has put the theological cart before the theological horse. Special revelation is based on general revelation, not the other way around. It is true that people do not acquiesce in the God of natural revelation until they are illumined by the God of special revelation. But saying that there is no *acquiescence* in natural revelation apart from special revelation does not deny natural revelation. Barth never seems to have recognized this. Gordon Clark echoes the same sentiment.

Clark raises a fourth argument against Thomas's cosmological contention. He says that Aquinas is using his chief terms in two different ways. Clark is referring to Thomas's insistence that no term, when applied to God, has precisely the same meaning it has when applied to humans or things. For example, the word *exist* has a different meaning in the proposition "God exists," than it has in the proposition "Man exists." But Clark maintains that if the term is not used univocally, the syllogism is violated.[37]

This is not quite fair to Thomas either. Aquinas denies the univocality of the knowledge of God and man, but he does not maintain the equivocality. Instead, he maintains the *analogous* character of such knowledge. Human knowledge of existence is analogous to God's. It is not univocal, not equivocal, but analogical. That means that it bears some resemblance to God's knowledge which is infinite and free of any blemishes, whereas human knowledge may possess limitations and faults. Consequently, if Aquinas's reasoning is sound, we must always remember that while the knowledge of God's existence must be placed in a class by itself, *sui generis,* it is not without a certain analogical relationship to knowledge of human existence.

Thomas has proven, by cosmological argument, that God does exist. He simply reminds us that God's existence has a certain difference from ours, without thereby invalidating the fundamental argument.

Assuming that he has demolished Thomas's argument, Clark notices that some Protestants think that the logical argument is valid even while disagreeing with Thomas's formulation. Clark now takes up Hume's objections, the first one of which is that even if the cosmological argument were valid it would not prove that God is any more than sufficiently powerful to be the cause of what we observe.[38] This is essentially the same Pascalian argument, about the first mover not being the God of Abraham, Isaac, and Jacob, or even adequate for the role of Creator. We have already shown a valid objection to this contention whether made by Pascal, Gordon Clark, or David Hume.

The point is that the argument is not otherwise sound. William Paley's famous analogy *assumes* that the universe which needs a maker is like a watch which needs a maker. Hence the universe needs a divine maker. Hume questions the analogy: Is the universe a machine? It seems much more like an organism, says Hume. Granted, there are many events which may require a cause, but does the universe as a whole have to be an effect?

Clark thinks Hume's question is a good one. He next examines Hodge's effort to answer Hume. Hodge argues that "since all the parts of the cosmos are dependent and movable, the whole must be dependent because the whole cannot be essentially different from its constituents."[39] This is untrue, says Clark. The whole is essentially different from its parts, just as Rembrandt's "Night Watch" is more than pigments and canvas.[40] Here Clark equivocates, committing the fallacy of ambiguity, as the meaning of the term *essential* changes in the course of his argument.

The canvas, no matter how composed of pigments, is still a caused entity requiring adequate causes to produce. Applying pigment to canvas does not change the basic character of the pigment and canvas. To be sure, Rembrandt's genius has entered into the picture. But Rembrandt the man can produce only finite, temporal effects; the "Night Watch" reproduces the same kind of characters as the one who produced it. Hodge is simply saying that a temporal creature produces temporal products. These do not take on a character other than the temporal. Surely, it is quite inconceivable that a universe made up of things that have come into being by specific causes—trillions and trillions of such causes—itself can be an uncaused entity. Admittedly, a cosmos or universe has a character which the individual ingredients do not possess. But it is inconceivable that every single entity in the universe requires a causal explanation while the sum total of them all requires none. The universe cannot be an uncaused entity.

Hodge continues: "An infinite number of effects cannot be self-existent. If a chain of three links cannot support itself, much less can a chain of a million links. Nothing multiplied by infinity is nothing still." And Clark responds: "Analogies are never valid arguments, and this analogy is particularly bad. In the first place, the picture of a chain whose first link is held by a hook is a far from adequate picture of the connections of the parts of nature."[41] This may well be an inadequate picture of a living organism—the universe—but this does not invalidate Hodge's analogy. We cannot think of *three* links hanging together in mid-air. They must, in the nature of the case, depend on something. Can the myriad links which constitute the universe be suspended on nothing? If we cannot think of three such links suspended in air, then neither can we think of the universe so suspended. Clark has not refuted Hodge's analogy. Nor does he refute the cogency of the analogy by saying that analogies are never valid arguments. Here is an argument from analogy which is quite valid: as three dependent links cannot be independently suspended, *a fortiori,* three trillion dependent links in nature cannot be independent. That is self-evident.

Clark is not finished. He says, second, whether it is three million links, or just one link, the fact that it cannot float by itself in the air provides no rational basis for concluding that the universe is not self-existent.[42] Eternal self-existence is quite a different concept from that of a link hanging on a hook. Clark is right, but he is also missing the point. It looks as if Clark is overwhelmed by the vastness of the universe. He is so traumatized as not to see the basic cogency of the argument which Hodge is using. An eternally self-existent entity, every part of which is not self-existent and which requires a cause, is exactly the same concept (on an incredibly vaster scale) as the idea of a link hanging in the air by itself or a link suspended without a hook. If a link needs a hook, vast multitudes of "links" need a hook too.

Finally, Clark writes:

> Hodge's first sentence bears the form of the main argument, clearly attached to the preceeding. He had just said that what is true of three links must be true of a million; but now he adds that nothing multiplied by infinity is nothing still. Aside from its doubtful connection with the preceding, he has not mentioned that zero

multiplied by infinity is zero, as one can easily see by realizing the fraction $2/0$ and the fraction $3/0$ are both infinity.[43]

Here Clark faults Hodge's mathematical terminology. Perhaps Hodge should have avoided mathematical terminology, but surely there can be no question of the cogency of what Hodge is saying. An infinite "amount" of nothing is still nothing. Let us see if we can phrase it without any mathematical terminology. If A, B, and C links are events which come into being and therefore require a cause, then X, Y, and Z links would therefore likewise be things that come into being and must require a cause because the word "link" means the same thing in both cases. That which characterizes a link is that it needs a cause and is not self-explanatory. As long as something is an entity coming into being then the human mind cannot think of its coming into being without a cause. Manifestly, if one link would require a cause, a million links would require a million causes. We can safely say that much, without involving any mystery of infinite numbers.

Clark is at his best as a critic of pure forms of empiricism. And he thinks that Hodge, like empiricism, is guilty of circular reasoning: assuming something in order to prove it. Empiricism, for example, assumes space: "But if space is learned by comparing houses and tables, we must first be able to perceive the table before we can compare it with a house in space."[44] That is to say, space is an idea of comparison, but if we do not already have an idea of space, we cannot produce tables and houses by selecting simple ideas through the use of space. Empiricism, therefore, has blundered fatally. It has surreptitiously inserted at the beginning of the learning process an idea of space which does not exist until after the process has been well-nigh completed.[45] Thus it needs Kant to bail it out.

But Hodge's argument is not a case of circular reasoning. On the contrary, it is a movement from the implicit to the explicit. According to empiricism, we know tables and we know houses. That is a datum, a given. Later reflection shows that it is impossible to compare these except by assuming that space separates them. All that is necessary is that empiricism, when it first observes tables and houses, recognize space as an implication. Later reflection makes this implication evident to the empirical mind and it explicitly articulates it. Only after observation and reflection does it become conscious that at the very beginning it was making its comparisons by using the concept of space. This is not a case of proving space by comparison when space was assumed for comparison in the first place. This is a case, rather, of being unconscious of space at first and becoming conscious of it by means of reflection.

It is interesting that Clark *at this point* does not give the usual objection against empiricism as a way of reasoning. He brings it in later in his discussion of Kant. This objection is that empiricism, because it is inductive, can never come to a conclusion about the infinite. No amount of finite observation can justify conclusions concerning the infinite.

This fundamental, virtually axiomatic criticism against empiricism is usually referred to as the cumulative fallacy. The empiricist who argues for the existence of God is supposed to have committed this fallacy: having concluded by cosmological argumentation, that the many, many finite data require an infinite cause. The empirical apologist is accused of making a vast logical leap.

Some empiricists do fall afoul of the cumulative fallacy. Properly stated, however, the empirical apologist is not guilty of this error. It does not argue that so many finite effects require an infinite cause. If it makes a blunder at all, it is far more elementary than that. Empiricism holds that *no* finite effect can be caused ultimately by anything short of an infinite cause. It is not merely that such a vast number of finite effects can only be explained by an infinite cause. A vast number of finite effects, if they can be explained in terms of finite causes, would not require a greater than finite cause. That is granted. But that is not the true empirical argument. The empirical argument is that *no* finite event can be explained by anything less than an infinite cause. Why is that? Because anything beginning to be can never be explained by a finite cause since that finite cause itself must have begun to be and needs a cause, and so on *ad infinitum*. Therefore, only something that never begins to be can be the explanation of anything that ever begins to be. A finite cannot account for itself. Even though it does exist, it cannot account for the effect it produces. Why so? Because it does not exist of itself and consequently cannot continue to exist of itself. Therefore, it needs the not-finite, the infinite, to account for its continuing to exist. If it effects something else, it must be the infinite which effects that something else through it. Apart from the infinite, the finite cannot account for itself or anything else.

Accurately stated, the cosmological argument maintains that any beginning-to-be ultimately requires an infinite cause. Any true cause is an infinite cause, a cause which exists in and of itself, an Unmoved

Mover. In other words, the only way there could be even a single, finite cause would be if "in the beginning, God created the heavens and the earth," every blade of grass, every pebble on the seashore, every star in the heavens, everything which begins to be. Every solitary thing which begins to be can be explained only in terms of a Being which never begins to be, the "I am that I am." That is what the Bible says and that is the only thing which the human mind can conceive. Failure to see this leads to the notion that empiricism is guilty of the cumulative fallacy.

This means, incidentally, that the term *second cause* must be used with very great care. Strictly speaking, there is no such thing as a "second" cause. There can only be a first (and only) cause. God is the only possible cause. He is the Alpha and Omega, the first and last cause. In Him we live and move and have our being. What we mean by "second cause" refers to the fact that God acts in a certain way in producing certain effects. Instead of exerting His power immediately and obviously, He exerts His power subtly in a sequence of steps which he puts into the production of the totality of things. In other words, then, "second" causes have efficacy because, and only because, of the first cause.

Let us illustrate. It is certainly within the infinite power of God to have made the universe, everything that is in it, everything that has happened in it, and everything that ever will be in it or ever will happen in it, yesterday or a moment ago. This would be easy for infinite power. Now God did make the universe, everything that is in it, everything that has happened in it, and everything that ever will be in it or ever will happen in it but not yesterday or a moment ago; in fact, in less time; indeed, in no time. What He does He does in the eternal mode of His being. We finite creatures apprehend His timeless works only in time or sequence as antecedents and consequents. The antecedents we call "second causes" since God who causes all, causes them in the antecedent-consequent sequence. Antecedents are called, or miscalled, causes or second causes in distinction from the first and only ultimate cause.

If one says that we are perilously close to pantheism at this point, he is right. This is perilously close, but it is not pantheism. God is indeed in everything and everything is in God, but God is not everything. He could not be in everything if He were everything or everything were He. Because He is in everything, everything exists. It is because He is in everything that everything has the power to exist. If

He were not in things, things would cease to exist. Everything lives, moves, and has its being in Him. He is not thereby identified with everything. The very fact that we can talk about everything as something other than God Himself is an indication that there is something which He has created which is other than Himself. All things depend, moment by moment, on Him for their continuance in being and power, causal power.

Robert Knudsen's "Indirect Proof"

As we have seen, Clark and Van Til have their differences but not about the validity of theistic proofs. Another interesting debate is that between Dooyeweerdean presuppositionalist Robert Knudsen and Van Til. While both reject the traditional position, Knudsen says:

> Van Til has asserted again and again . . . that one cannot prove Christianity directly. That is an impossible undertaking, because it is impossible to assume a stance outside of Christianity in a meaningful way from which such a proof could proceed. Thus, as we have said, Van Til must entrench himself within the walls of the Christian faith and he must argue from the impossibility of the contrary. This method seeks to establish an indirect proof of the faith.[46]

Knudsen is right, but he does not seem to recognize the nature of this apologetic game either. We have noted already Van Til's vascillation in saying, on the one hand, that we cannot prove Christianity while proceeding nevertheless to do so. Knudsen simply recognizes Van Til's denial of the ability to prove but calls what he does do an "indirect proof." We maintain that this "indirect proof" is no proof at all, there is either proof at both levels or no proof at either. Let us explain. Assuming Christianity, Van Til does indeed claim to prove that it is true because it makes predication possible while the opposing position makes predication impossible. In this argument, Van Til assumes that the unregenerate mind is able to see that, on its own principles, it cannot predicate and that, on Van Til's principles, it can predicate. If this argument is valid, Van Til has shown the unregenerate mind (1) the futility of secular thought and (2) the validity of presuppositional thought. The only alternative is that there is no knowledge or no proof in either case. For if by accepting secular viewpoints we cannot prove the truth of Christianity, then certainly we cannot do so by presupposing either. Secular mentality is represented as being autonomous and contingent and categorically rejecting any kind of revelational knowledge. Therefore, Van Til cannot prove anything indirectly, any more than he can directly, to the unregenerate mind which is carnal and unwilling to accept either the futility of its own viewpoint or the validity of the presuppositional viewpoint. It is a case of all or nothing. One must either prove everything or prove nothing. Van Til is not willing to admit that, and so vascillates. Knudsen does not admit it either, but resorts to the use of the terms *direct* and *indirect* proof—terms which suggest a distinction but are in fact without a difference.

We conclude simply that while presuppositionalism argues that theistic proofs are not cogent, its own argument rests on an unsound *pre*-presupposition.

CHAPTER 15

The Attack on Christian Evidences

BATTERED BY antisupernaturalists and presuppositionalist super-naturalists (as we have shown), as well as some others, traditionalists have retreated to Christian evidences alone for their apologetics. We call this Halfway House Apologetics, for it is a fatal compromise. It is a halfway house enroute to presuppositionalism rather than to traditionalism. Traditional apologetics *begins* with theistic evidences, arguing that there can be no evidence for the Son of God if there is no evidence for God. But it does not rely on Christian evidences *alone*. The pure evidentialists are very much besieged—they are being attacked by us, their friends, for their incompleteness, and by their enemies for the alleged unsoundness of the evidence itself.

But what is the evidence and what the attack? As we have seen, the traditional Christian evidences are essentially three: the witness *to* the Bible as the Word of God, the witness *of* the Bible as the Word of God, and the effects of the Bible as the Word of God. Both presuppositionalists and evidentialists affirm the Bible as the Word of God. The dispute between them centers on the method of argumentation for the Bible as the Word of God. Presuppositionalists reject prophecy and miracles as arguments for the Bible; evidentialists reject self-attestation as a sound argument.

The arguments from prophecy and miracle reduce to one, argument from miracle, because prophecy is a species of the generic category of miracle. It is the miraculousness of prophecy which makes it an argument, while what makes miracle an argument is that it requires God to account for it. Thus for evidentialists, prophecy and miracle are evidences for the revelation of God. For the presuppositionalist, the self-attesting God validates prophecy and miracle.

One would suppose that since the traditionalists and presuppositionalists both make use of the Bible's self-attestation, they would agree on this argument and join apologetic ranks. But they do not, because, for the presuppositionalist, appealing to self-attestation as *evidence* means that humans are thinking autonomously and sitting in judgment on the Word of God. The Bible's self-attestation, according to the presuppositionalist, must simply be accepted; it must not be seen as evidence that what the Bible says is true. Evidential arguments for the Bible are especially objectionable to the presuppositionalist when applied to the Word of God itself because they presume to substantiate its divine truth.

Van Til puts the whole matter summarily: "The Bible must be true because it alone speaks of an absolute God. And equally true is it that we believe in an absolute God because the Bible tells us of one."[1] Van Til cannot reverse the order of these two sentences. If we put the second sentence first, we must ask why we need to believe in an absolute God simply because the Bible speaks of one. A reason would have to be given or the assertion would be uncompellingly arbitrary and obscurantist. The reason is the first sentence: "The Bible must be true because it alone speaks of an absolute God." When we ask why that is so, the answer is all of Van Til's apologetic—that ultimately we cannot know anything at all unless we presuppose the God the Bible reveals. If Van Til's apologetic is sound, then he *proves rationally at the outset* with his mind *as it is* to the other minds *as they are* the *necessary assumption* (not *arbitrary presupposition*) that the Bible, which alone reveals this God, *must be true* (indeed, the Word of God).[2] "We must begin with the actuality of the book. We must not pretend that we have established the possibility of the book and the necessity of it in terms of the philosophy that we did not get from the book."[3]

Supposedly, the Bible is the foundation of Van Til's thought. Actually, it is the foundation of the foundation. For what is crucial is not merely the Bible, but the way by which Van Til comes to the Bible. He claims a sound approach to the Bible; we think he has an unsound approach to the Bible. But we agree on one important point: the Bible and the approach to the Bible are absolutely essential to his view of the Christian religion.

Note by way of historical orientation that here again Van Til is departing from the traditional approach Roman Catholic, Eastern Orthodox, and classicial Protestant theologians as well begin their theologies with prolegomena. In that prolegomena, they typically argue for the very thing that Van Til is rejecting here, namely, the possibility, and even more importantly the necessity of a divine revelation in a book. All Reformed theologians recognize that unless God opens His mouth and speaks to us we will not know what He intends to do with us sinners. Furthermore, this approach is made traditionally precisely "in terms of the philosophy that we did not get from the book." That is, before we approach the book we already have a philosophy about data in general, about truth and the way it is apprehended, and the laws under which it is systematized. All of this is out of bounds according to Van Til.

We will now examine the three items to which Van Til takes exception (first, that humans establish the possibility of the book; second, that we establish the necessity of the book; and third, that we do have—and must have—a philosophy with which we do both before we approach the book) and show why he should not take exception to any of them.

THE POSSIBILITY OF THE BOOK

Traditionalists have reasons for arguing the possibility of the Book. According to traditional apologetics, natural theology proves the existence of God, His rationality, and His ability to communicate. Even though God is infinite, eternal, and unchangeable, thus possessing many incommunicable attributes which distinguish Him from His creation, natural theology also shows that the Creator of rational creatures certainly is able to communicate with them. Though he cannot communicate eternality, infinity, and immutability, He can communicate knowledge that can be apprehended by mutable, finite, temporal creatures. By such arguments, traditionalists establish the possibility of such a book as the Bible, the Word of God. God could write in the sky if He wanted to. He could speak perpetually from the heavens if He pleased. He could also write on tablets of stone or pieces of papyrus if He wished. It is also obvious that, if He chose to use human instruments to communicate His message, He certainly would find that easy enough to do, if He had reason to do it. This is the type of thing one finds in standard theological textbooks of all branches of orthodoxy, in all ages.

It is quite different with the unorthodox Immanuel Kant. Kant tried to prove that God cannot be known. Since human creatures are incapable of knowing the divine being, Kant concluded, logically, that God cannot communicate Himself to them. So, *ex hypothesi,* according to Kant there cannot be any possibility of a book by God. At most the Bible could be a book *about* God, but certainly not *by* God. And even if it were a book about God, it would be wishful thinking because God cannot be known.

So, no book exists which is truly the Word of God. It is not even a possibility in the thinking of men like Kant. But that is not the thinking of traditional theologians. They argue that God exists and, though transcendent and beyond our knowledge (if He chooses to remain beyond our knowledge), is quite capable of condescending to our capacities and making Himself known to us. That is all that is necessary to establish the possibility, the mere possibility, of a book such as the Bible, God's Word.

The question is, why does Van Til deny that we can establish the possibility of this book and assert that virtually the whole orthodox tradition has been in error on this matter? According to Van Til, we cannot know anything unless we begin with the Bible. It is impossible, he argues, to begin somewhere else and know the Bible or even the possibility of the Bible. There is no denying that Van Til is consistent with his philosophy at this point. It is indisputably true that, if we cannot know anything without beginning with the Word of God, we cannot know about the possibility of the Word of God. The reasoning is impeccable; the premises, however, are unreasonable.

According to Van Til, unless we presuppose the knowledge which this Book gives us, we cannot know anything. Very well. How do we presuppose the knowledge that this Book give us? We would have to know what this Book is telling us before we could presuppose what it is telling us. But, if we know what it is telling us, then we already have some canons of judgment at the very outset before we start to presuppose what the Bible tells us. In other words, we cannot recognize the Bible unless we first of all have recognized its possibility and the possibility of understanding it. Or, to put it another way, unless we have principles of interpretation *before* we approach the Bible, we cannot interpret the Bible so as to make it the foundation of our principles of interpretation. Again, if we do not know the possibility of the book at the outset, we could never recognize it in actuality.

THE NECESSITY OF THE BOOK

Let us now consider the second point, according to which the traditionalists are supposed to have erred when they have argued the necessity of the book. Van Til is quite correct in saying that the traditionalists not only argue the possibility of special revelation but the absolute necessity of it. (It is necessary, that is, if God is inclined to tell us, more specifically than nature does, what He intends to do with us.) We noted above (chap. 5) that the necessity of divine revelation is based on the fact that, if people are to know what God would do with them, He has to tell them specifically what He has not revealed by nature. Paul makes a natural theological observation when he says (1 Cor. 2:11) that if only the spirit of a person can reveal his thoughts, only the Spirit of God can reveal what is in the mind of God. Therefore, if we are dependent for knowledge of one another's inmost thoughts upon revelation from one another, manifestly we are dependent upon the divine revelation of God's inmost thoughts for knowledge of Him. This is taught in Scripture, to be sure; but it is taught in Scripture as a perfectly natural observation which anybody, with or without knowledge of Scripture, could see immediately.

Why then does Van Til seem to stumble on such an obvious matter? As before, the answer lies in his conviction that there is no such thing as knowledge of anything, necessary or otherwise, without presupposing the revelation itself. The necessity of revelation cannot be known because nothing can be known without the revelation itself. But we have already shown that we cannot recognize the revelation as revelation unless we have principles by means of which we conceive that it is a revelation. If we do have these principles, it follows that, on those principles, we may very well deduce the necessity of the revelation before we ever encounter it. We say "if" because God has no obligation to reveal Himself savingly. But if He were going to save us, He would have an obligation to tell us and that would spell the necessity of the Bible.

WE APPROACH THE BOOK WITH A PHILOSOPHY

Van Til's third stipulation underlies the first two. He argues that we must not approach the book in terms of a philosophy that we did not get from it. But that is the only way we can approach it. It is obvious that we must have developed a philosophy before we could even learn to read and understand. We can only apprehend the book when we are able to read and understand. If we cannot read when we are forming in childhood a basic philosophy of understanding, manifestly we cannot begin with a book which must be read to be understood. This would imply that we cannot think until we get to the philosophy of the book. Vast numbers of people, then, never learn to think and those who do are well advanced in years before they begin. It will not do any good to hand an infant emerging from the womb the best version in baby-talk of Holy Scripture. He simply cannot do anything with it. But he has already started to observe the world in his own infantile way, and soon he will be drawing conclusions about it: he determines the fastest way to his mother's breast and how he can compete for toys with his siblings as he grows older. Where he came from and how he is related to the Creator will come later on his agenda.

That "philosophy" to which Van Til refers includes the basic laws of logic and the laws of thought, as well as any metaphysical conclusions which a person draws as he observes himself and the surrounding universe. It does not refer to a specific form of philosophy such as materialism or monism or dualism and the like. Many people think metaphysically only implicitly. All of them, however, are more or less conscious of the laws of identity, noncontradiction, and excluded middle, even before they know how to express them. John Cotton once argued that even dogs have an understanding of the law of noncontradiction. At a fork in the road, if you show a dog a bone, cover his eyes, and throw the bone down one of the roads, when the dog is sent to search for it and goes down the wrong road, he immediately concludes that it must be on the other road where he next goes and finds the bone.

Human beings bring similar basic logical equipment with them to the Bible. Earlier, they had used that same equipment to observe the universe. We cannot even observe without the law of noncontradiction. Babies cannot even conceive of their mothers' breasts unless that excludes something which is not mother's breast. In other words, long before children can say "Mamma" or "Daddy" they operate according to the law of noncontradiction. They cannot operate any other way. To say that long afterwards when these people approach the Bible, they must do so without a philosophy derived from something other than the Bible, is requiring the impossible.

MIRACLES AS EVIDENCE

In traditional apologetics, miracles (as we have seen in chapter 8) play an absolutely crucial role. They are the evidence that certifies messengers sent by God. Nicodemus, who had far greater standing in Israel than Jesus did, came to learn from Jesus because he recognized, from the miracles that Christ did, that He was a messenger specially sent from God. Although Nicodemus had difficulty with some of Christ's teaching, he was prepared to accept Him as divinely authenticated because of the miraculous attestation of Christ's ministry.

Miracles have no such role in the presuppositionalist apologetic. Of themselves, they are just "brute facts" which are "mute facts." They prove absolutely nothing about either God or revelation. They must themselves be proven by His revelation. The tables are totally reversed. Instead of miracles being the proof that it is God speaking, God's speaking is the proof of miracles.

We cannot but notice that the great liberal, Friedrich Schleiermacher, was the one who first made Christ the prover of miracles rather than miracles the prover of Christ. Now the orthodox Van Til is doing the same thing. We do not deny that the Christ of Van Til and the Christ of Schleiermacher are not, by any means, identically the same. Nevertheless, neither in the theology of Schleiermacher nor of Van Til does Jesus of Nazareth, in the role of miracle worker, prove anything special about the identity and authority of Jesus of Nazareth. Both of these theologians vindicate miracles by Christ Himself. The miracles need to be apologized *for* rather than being apologized *with*. Everything is in the one presuppositionalist basket. If that goes, everything goes. If that stands, everything stands. Once again, Rushdoony is very blunt: "To accept miracles or Scripture on any other ground [except presuppositionalism] is in effect to deny their essential meaning and to give them a pagan import."[4] The miracles do not prove the revelation. The revelation proves not only miracles but the very definition of miracles. Rushdoony continues: "No God, no knowledge." No God presupposed at the outset, no knowledge of any kind, including miracles.

At this point, Christian lay people must become uneasy about presuppositionalism. Historically, miracles have played a major role in the proof of Christianity. They still do in the thinking of most people. To be told that they depend for their very meaning, not to mention their validation, on a presupposition, must shake people. They realize now, if they did not realize it earlier, that this is a root-and-branch critique of the usual approach to Christianity.

For many people, the bodily resurrection especially is a central miraculous attestation of the truth of Christ and all that He said about Himself and the Word of God. For Van Til, the resurrection of Jesus Christ (which he believes fervently and preaches vigorously) proves absolutely nothing. If it is once accepted in the context of the presuppositionalist approach, then and only then, it *corroborates* the teachings of Jesus. One can see immediately that this corroboration depends entirely on the validity of the system itself. It has no independent testimony to offer. It is absolutely dependent upon this theoretical approach. This "corroboration," therefore, is empty. It is empty because it adds nothing to the presupposition. Presuppositionalism is all there is. It needs no corroboration and "corroboration" does not corroborate.

Van Til writes, "We must allow that it is quite possible that at some future date all the miracles recorded in the Bible, not excluding the resurrection of Christ, may be explained by natural laws."[5] According to Van Til, this would be the result of adopting the so-called natural, scientific method and he notices that this is the traditional position of apologetics as represented by no less than Warfield.[6]

We presume that what Van Til means is that at some future date a scientist may learn how to revivify dead bodies. We agree that is not inconceivable. But that is not the same thing as saying that science may in the future work miracles. The definition of miracles which Van Til is addressing is "an event in the external world that could have been wrought only by the immediate power of God." Suppose by the year 2000 scientists are able to revive dead bodies. That is not the same thing as saying that in A.D. 29 it was a natural phenomenon to revivify a dead body. If the scientist has achieved that ability by A.D. 2000, does that prove that it was not a supernatural event two thousand years earlier? Because one could resurrect a body in A.D. 2000 by natural means does not imply that that was the case two millennia earlier. Manifestly, raising a body from the dead, as Christ's body was raised, was something which could have been done—at that time in any case—only by the immediate exercise of divine power. Whatever scientists may be able to do in the future could hardly disprove a past miracle. Something may be a miracle in A.D. 29 that is not a miracle in A.D. 2029. Of course we must allow for the "possibility" of Jesus' possessing an esoteric knowledge of a natural law of resurrection two millennia before anyone else discovered it. If so, that would be the miraculous source of the miracles.

Consider the miracle of the crossing of the Red Sea. The biblical record indicates that a strong wind caused water to stand up and cause an appearance of dry land between the two banks of water. Even in the biblical narrative there is the indication of the use of natural forces (winds). Why was that considered a miracle? Not because winds blowing very mightily could cause water to pile up and separate. That is not miraculous in itself, though it would be, without doubt, extraordinary. The miracle was in the fact that those winds blew at the very time that Moses raised his hand and prayed, as the fleeing Israelites had the advancing Egyptian army behind them and the threatening sea before them. Scientists in our time can very well get winds to blow with such might that they can hold waters back. Are they any closer to being able to raise their hands in prayer and produce an effect like that? The fact that modern scientific advances can "duplicate" an ancient miracle is no evidence that all of the circumstances under which the original event occurred are being duplicated. In other words, the miracle in the case of the separation of the Red Sea is not that winds blew the waters apart but the occasion on which they so blew. We are not any closer four thousand years later to being able by the raising of hands to make the wind blow and hold back the sea.

Again, consider the coin in the fish's mouth (Matt. 17:27). There is nothing miraculous in a fish swallowing a coin or in the fish being caught and the coin being discovered when the fish is cut open. Yet, the finding of that particular fish with the very coin which Christ used to pay the temple tax did meet the definition of a miracle—not in the fact that a fish swallowed the coin and later on yielded it, but in the fact that Christ told his apostles to go to a particular place where a particular fish was brought out of the water with precisely the right amount of money to pay the tax. Are we any closer to duplicating that kind of phenomenon now? Is there any indication whatever that modern science will get to the point where it can actually tell not by means of some electronic devices but by natural understanding where a certain fish is which has a certain specified amount of money in its body? Our point here is that it is easy to say that the time may well come when science can produce "miracles." But if one considers the characteristics of the original miracles, it is not at all easy to say that such a possibility does actually exist. What is true, of course, is that we understand more and more about the operation of natural law, and we are also able to manipulate it more and more. Thus, we are able to come more and more into the sphere of what looks externally like a miracle. But the more we examine the nature of a miracle the more we realize that advances in science do not bring us any closer to the actual supernatural, miraculous character of the original events to which we refer. To put the matter in a sentence: If every body which died after A.D. 2000 were resurrected, that would not take away an iota from the miraculous significance of what Jesus did in A.D. 29.

Van Til has taken away the significance of miracle and given us really nothing in its place. Miracles are used by God throughout the Bible as evidence—certification of the spokesmen whom He sent to address His people. If miracles lose their significance of certification, then we have left no way by which a messenger of God was actually accredited by God.

How do presuppositionalists interpret the Bible? James Olthuis writes, "Even as it is totally God's word, fully reliable and fully trustworthy, it is fully creaturely."[7] Before we read any further in this essay, we want to make a tentative comment. We wonder if the author realizes that the Bible is not fully creaturely in the proper sense of that word. For something to be fully creaturely it has to be liable to error because a creature—as merely a creature—is liable to error. This is proven by the fact that man, even as created in original righteousness before the Fall, was able to sin or not to sin. The only man who was not able to sin was in hypostatic union with the second person of the Godhead. All others who are unable to sin are in heaven and they are unable to sin only because God has promised to preserve them from it. It is not their creatureliness which removes them from this possible liability but their union with, and preservation by God. So Olthuis is already opening the door to error in the Bible by the use of the word *creaturely*. He may close the door, or by that term he may leave it open a crack. We will see. As he continues, he labors the necessity of a pre-understanding of the Bible and opposes any notion of a *tabula rasa*.

It is only a slight jump from "creaturely" to the various existential theories of hermeneutics. The "dynamic equivalence" of Eugene Nida, for example, is hardly other than the "creaturely" viewed as the immediate, cultural context. The "new hermeneutics" becomes hermeneutical subjectivity.

Barth would argue that the inerrantists must allow for the "creaturely" in the form of cultural background.[8] But Barth has a problem. If the background shapes and distorts everything so that we cannot know anything as it is, then Barth himself cannot distinguish between background and foreground. But if he can—even long enough to make this criticism—then he contradicts himself by assuming that he has— at least for the moment—escaped his own distorting background.

We gladly acknowledge that almost all presuppositionalists such as Van Til himself, John Frame, Greg Bahnsen, Rushdoony, the late J. Barton Payne, and a host of others are staunch inerrantists. For this we are profoundly grateful. At the same time, our criticism of presuppositionalism, even at this point, continues unabated. The presuppositional *basis* for inerrancy is utterly arbitrary. It is no stronger than the presuppositional argument in general. If and when that goes—as it must as soon as its inherent weakness is seen—everything including the Bible goes logically with it. The presuppositionalist has nothing to fall back on. He cannot argue from miracles, from prophecy, from consistency, from effects, from anything. It is an entirely *abitrary* assumption, a *mere* presupposition that the Bible is the Word of God, which has no ultimate escape hatch from pure subjectivism. We realize that the presuppositionalist does not admit or realize this because of his core inconsistency, his vacillation between reasons and no reasons for his faith.

The *Institute for Christian Studies* in Toronto, as seen in Runner and Olthuis (and could be shown in others) is the handwriting on the wall. Their very consistency in the arbitrary, antirational feature of presuppositionalism is already spelling doom for inerrancy, for Calvinism, and for the Christian religion. Westminster Theological Seminary, and other presuppositional institutions, are being spared for the present only by their inconsistency.

Presuppositionalism burns its evidential bridges behind it and cannot, while remaining presuppositional, rebuild them. It burns its bridges by refusing evidences on the ground that evidences must be presupposed. "Presupposed evidences" is a contradiction in terms because evidences are supposed to prove the conclusion rather than be proven by it. But if the evidences were vindicated by the presupposition then the presupposition would be the evidence. But that cannot be, because if there is evidence for or in the presupposition, then we have reasons for presupposing, and we are, therefore, no longer presupposing.

CHAPTER 16

The Self-Attesting God

THE HEART OF THE presuppositional apologetic is a God whose proof is solely in Himself. All other systems argue *to* God—this one, *from* God. All other systems are supposed to fail because God cannot be reached at the end of a syllogism, this one claims to succeed because here the syllogism is derived from God. Furthermore, there is only one God—one true God—and He reveals Himself exclusively in Holy Scripture. His trinity solves the problem of the one and many; His sovereignty solves the problem of freedom; His self-attesting character solves all problems at the beginning and His paradoxicalness solves all problems at the end. In presuppositionalist thought, it is not God's nature that is paradoxical, but his revelation.

It may well be that its most significant theological principle, inseparably connected with the self-attesting God, is paradox. This indeed is the way in which God attests and reveals Himself. At bottom, presuppositionalism is a form of paradox theology. But, as we shall see, it is more paradoxical than Paradox Theology, because it is paradoxical in handling its paradoxes.[1] That is, it denies paradox even while falling back on it constantly. Just as it fideistically repudiates fideism and irrationally repudiates irrationality, so it paradoxically repudiates paradox. It makes Karl Barth look like the champion of "system" and Emil Brunner the most consistent of theologians. This feature of presuppositional thinking is plainly visible in its treatment of several traditional doctrines.

PARADOX: ELECTION AND REPROBATION

Perhaps the best doctrine by which to examine the presuppositional paradox is supra- and infra-lapsarianism. Supra-lapsarianism teaches that God's decrees of election and reprobation are determined with man-as-man (*homo creabilis*) before the divine mind. Infra-lapsarianism teaches that God's decrees of election and reprobation are determined with man-as-sinner (*homo lapsus*) before the divine mind.

What follows is Van Til's paradoxical interpretation of the decrees:

> Supra- or infra-lapsarianism, taken as some advocates of the views have taken them, were faulty in their imposing of the reach of human logic upon the data of revelation. Is it not thus with us who love the Reformed Faith today? Do we not need to come to an agonizing re-appraisal; with respect to the whole matter? Our witness must come clearly before the world. We all love to honor God for the work of the Reformers. That work found its climax in the idea of the sovereign grace of God freely proclaimed unto men.[2]

This shows that the rational explanation which both infra- and supralapsarians give is not acceptable to Van Til precisely because it is rational. He wants to end with mere sovereign grace of God which is mere *arbitrary* grace of God. That is perhaps the heart of this tract as far as any theological understanding is concerned. Its very simple language addressed to the general public lays bare an irrationality so bizarre that any layman who runs may see. Dr. Van Til is a very learned man and he has many learned disciples, and they write learned books in which learned scholars get lost, but the glory of plain speech is that it puts plain error in plain view for plain people to see.

Dealing with those who say that reprobation is not to be equally ultimate with election,[3] Van Til writes:

> But surely, it is apparent that such a point of view leads us off the highway of the Reformed faith and tones down our witness to the world. The world needs the sovereign God of Scripture. Hence we must say that reprobation is not ultimately an act of justice with respect to the sin of man. It is rather an act of the sovereign will of God.[4]

Of course, reprobation *is* a decree of God, as truly and therefore as ultimately as election. We would indeed be off the Reformed "highway" if we denied this. But at the same time, it is unfortunate and misleading to suggest that reprobation is not "ultimately an act of justice." That is true in the sense that God *first* reprobates (decided not to give grace to the reprobate, but to give them over to continuing in chosen sin). But it is misleading in the sense that the reprobate are not damned *on the ground of reprobation* but on the *ground of their sin* (which is the ultimate and only *just* ground of damnation). We concur with Van Til's concern that God be shown to be as sovereign in withholding grace as in bestowing it; but we wish that he had made it clear that reprobation is grounded in justice.

Van Til continues: "Hence, too, we dare not say that Adam could, in the last analysis, have chosen to be obedient as well as disobedient."[5] This statement can hardly be interpreted other than as denial of the universally held Reformed-Augustinian principle that Adam was created *posse peccare and posse non peccare*. By rejecting the latter possibility—that it was possible for Adam *not* to sin—Van Til has reversed the traditional Reformed position. Adam, he holds, was created only *posse peccare*—only able to sin. Adam, as created, was not able not to sin.

Van Til does not want to make God the author of sin, but he has succeeded without trying, for God has created a sinner—a man only able to sin. Van Til observes, of course, that the Bible also teaches that God made all things good and made man upright. Once again, he presents hard-core paradox (God makes man evil; God does not make man evil). Van Til insists with Herman Bavinck, that the Fall is only an approximate cause of reprobation; there is an ultimate decree:

> Quite properly Bavinck refers in this connection to the reply that Calvin gave to Pighius when the latter objected to the counsel of God as a final source of the determination of the destinies of all men. In dealing with the ninth chapter of Romans and, therefore, with the difference between Esau and Jacob, Calvin says: "Now if this being '*afore prepared* unto glory' is peculiar and special to the elect, it evidently follows that the rest, the non-elect, are equally '*fitted* to destruction' because, being left to their own nature, they were devoted already to certain destruction so that they were 'fitted to destruction' by *their own wickedness*. It is an idea so silly that it needs no notice. It is indeed true that the wicked procure to themselves the wrath of God, and that they daily hasten on a falling of its own weight upon their heads. But it must be confessed by all, that the apostle is here treating of the difference made between the elect and the reprobate, which proceeds from the alone secret will and counsel of God."[6]

Here Van Til is apparently thinking of people like Berkouwer (as Calvin thought of Pighius), who deny a real decree of reprobation. He is not thinking of infra-lapsarians who do believe in a permissive decree. Calvin's statement here about the falling of judgment upon reprobates who are left to their own nature certainly is compatible with an infra-lapsarian, permissive decree.

We cannot help but think, in this connection, about another difference between Van Til and typical Reformed orthodoxy, especially such as Edwards's and Shedd's. In the traditional approach, the rational evidence is given alongside the biblical evidence. With Van Til, the rational evidence turns out to be a paradox, and the explicit biblical evidence has to override it. But a sovereign God, even one who is not paradoxical and irrational, is not inimical to evidence and rational proof.

In a very profound sense, Van Til is paradoxical at the core. We have just examined a typical example of it in the way he handles reprobation: "The first and basic answer is that Scripture teaches it."[7] Now comes his "rational" explanation: "But then we can see that in order to be disobedient and, therefore, to be punished for their own sin, they must be confronted with God in all that they do."[8] Of course, they would have to be confronted with God; but to be confronted with God does not require necessarily the possibility of being disobedient. Saints will be confronted with God eternally without that possibility.

Van Til concludes that "we can also see that, therefore, the restraint of God by which men are kept from greater sin and from greater punishment is something that is an unmerited favor unto them."[9] This is meant to show that there really is common grace. But Van Til has shown no real basis for disobedience in the first place nor, in the second place, that God restrains further disobedience. So that while this sounds like a rational statement, it rests on no foundation. It is questionable whether God's restraint on reprobates can be called "unmerited favor." Favor suggests that God is pleased with the wicked, when in fact he is angry with them everyday (Ps. 7:11) and His wrath abides on unbelievers (John 3:36). That less anger and wrath than is possible rests on them is their good fortune, to be sure, but can God's "forbearance" be equated with "favor" and called common "grace"?

Van Til cites Bavinck, and ends with a comment of his own:

> Moreover, when I add with Bavinck that though sin and its eternal punishment for some men is a part of the plan of God and, therefore, in a sense willed by God, yet they are not willed in the same sense and in the same manner as are the grace and salvation

of the elect—I have not thereby met the objection of him who charges the Christian religion with contradiction. We shall need simply to hold both to the genuine meaning of historical causes and to the all-inclusiveness of God's will as the ultimate cause.[10]

Here Van Til simply asserts God's will as an ultimate cause without any rational address to the problem, leaving us with pure paradox. There is candor later:

Let us, rather than try to meet the objector's desires for supposed consistency and logic, not deny the fact of God's revelation of His general favor to mankind or the fact of God's wrath resting upon the non-elect. To meet the objector and satisfy him we should have to deny the meaning of all history and of all secondary causes. We should need to wipe out the difference between God and man. To the objector it is contradictory to say that God controls whatever comes to pass and also to say that human choices have significance.[11]

Our point is that this is contradictory to Van Til also; but God makes it necessary for him to believe it. It is an error to say that a rational God makes us believe absurdity. Divine "control" and significant human choices hardly constitute a rational difficulty or apparent contradiction, not to mention paradox.

PARADOX: COMMON GRACE

If anything clearly shows Van Til's paradoxical thought, it is his doctrine of common grace. On God's attitude, Van Til writes: "And loving mankind, He offered them eternal life. It was seriously meant that they accept it, apparently; but, he meant that they not accept it. It was no farce."[12] But once again, there is no satisfactory explanation of this. It is left as a mere, arbitrary assertion of an obvious contradiction, inescapably implying divine insincerity. The obvious paradoxical (contradictory) character of the statements is utterly unalleviated and is unobscured by any sophisticated scholarship. He adds, "Sinners are said to have their understanding darkened and to be enemies of God at the same time that they are told that they do know God and have knowledge of right and wrong."[13] There is a perfectly rational explanation of that sort of thing; but the way Van Til articulates it requires a crucifixion of the intellect and conscience in order to accept it. Here, for example, is Van Til's comment on the Synod of the Christian Reformed Church in 1924:

> So even after the fall God gives his good gifts to men everywhere, thereby calling them to repentance and to performance of their task. The Christian view of God in relation to man must always begin, as Berkouwer has emphasized, from this idea that God at the beginning of history was favorably disposed to mankind. And then in amazement we note that even after the fall, when mankind as a whole has become the object of His wrath, God still continues to give good gifts unto men and by these gifts he calls them to repentance. . . .
>
> Now how can this universal call to repentance be harmonized logically with the doctrine of election? God did not intend that all men should repent. Indeed he intended from all eternity that some should not repent. How could they repent unless they heard the Gospel of salvation through Christ. . . . How can God have any attitude of favor unto those men whom he so obviously has not included in the number that could possibly be saved through the Gospel of the blood of Jesus Christ?
>
> Well, the answer is that we cannot comprehend how it is possible but that the scriptures reveal it to be true.[14]

Suppose we see something as black, we cannot see it as anything but black. God says that it is white. What do we say? We say that we see it as black but it must be white for God. We cannot, without lying, say that we see it as white. We can only see it as black. If it really is white for us, then our eyes deceive us and they can no longer be relied upon for color vision. If we then see something else as yellow and someone asks us the color, we must answer that we cannot know what color it is until God tells us.

Van Til is saying something like this about the "eyes" of our (regenerate) minds. We see something as a contradiction. We cannot see it as anything but a contradiction. God says it is not a contradiction. We say that in God's mind it is not a contradiction; in our mind it is. If God says that to our minds it is not a contradiction because He says that to our minds it is not a contradiction, then we can only truthfully say that our minds are no longer to be relied upon and that we can know nothing unless God tells us what we know. Even then we do not know it by contemplating the rational object with our minds; only by knowing the revealed mind of God can we say that we know that. He knows it and we *would* know it if we had reliable minds which we do not have even by regeneration. Van Til will not say that, however, but encourages us to believe something to be intelligible which is an unalleviated contradiction. This is not mystery but contradiction.

PARADOX: VAN TIL'S DEFENSE AGAINST PANTHEISM

Another illustration of ultimate paradox or contradiction is seen in Van Til's defense of Calvin before the criticisms of A. M. Fairbairn. Fairbairn charges Calvin with the pantheism of Spinoza because according to Calvin God's will is the only efficient will in the universe.[15] Van Til dismisses Fairbairn's criticism because Calvin, unlike Spinoza, taught that God was transcendent and immanent and that God's transcendence existed before His immanence.

Van Til overlooks the traditional point that neither transcendence nor immanence has any meaning in God apart from the Creation. As soon as God creates he becomes transcendent over what He has made and at the same time immanent because it is in Him that all things live and move and have their being. It can hardly be maintained that God is transcendent before He is immanent anymore than it can be said that He is immanent before He is transcendent. God is self-existent before He is immanent but transcendence is relative to that which is created, as is immanence. God is simultaneously transcendent and immanent with respect to the created order.

Van Til misses the point of Fairbairn's criticism. Calvin's notion of immanence as sole efficient will is a genuine problem for theology. Fairbairn is aware of it and certainly Spinoza was aware of it. The question is, how can an infinite God be in any kind of relationship to anything else? In fact how can there *be* anything else alongside of something infinite? If God is infinite how can anything exist outside of His infinity? The very concept of finite implies that it exists alongside the infinite, thereby limiting the infinite. If there is something other than the infinite, then the infinite must have some kind of boundary. The infinite is no longer infinite, but limited by the finite. Theologians like Edwards and Hodge have agonized over this problem. Van Til fails to meet the difficulty, being satisfied merely to assert that because Calvin taught transcendence, he was therefore not a pantheist.

But what of Calvin's assertion of sole efficiency? Van Til writes: "The very fact that Calvin has been characterized as a deist and a pantheist is indicative of the fact that he took God's transcendence and immanence equally seriously."[16] But Van Til does not seem to notice that taking these concepts "seriously" does not mean that Calvin was able to meet the objections to taking them seriously. Calvin was very loathe to engage in speculative thought. It is not at all like Calvin to go into any careful theoretical justification of his doctrines. That being the case, it is even less feasible for Van Til simply to cite that Calvin did affirm both transcendence and immanence and therefore was not a pantheist. There is no disputing the fact that Calvin did not claim to be a pantheist. The great question of Fairbairn is, if Calvin maintained that there is only one efficient will in the universe, how could he be anything other than an *implicit* pantheist? Further (we add), if Calvin did maintain (as he certainly did) that God is infinite, how can he theoretically allow any role for the finite? How does he avoid the notion of Christian Science that the finite is unreal since God is all? or the option of Eastern mysticism which interprets everything that appears as illusion (*maya*)?

Van Til gives Calvin credit for avoiding the pitfall into which Plato fell. Plato tried to interpret the world first of all in terms of a sensory "many" and failed because of the ideal "one." When Plato attempted to interpret the many in terms of the one, that also failed because there was diversity in the ideas themselves. Van Til represents Calvin as solving this problem simply by saying that God is transcendent and immanent. Anyone can say this, but making such statements stick is the problem. Plato wrestled with the problem and failed; Calvin did not even wrestle with it, much less conquer it.

Van Til also credits Calvin for solving the problem of the unity of the ideal world by following Augustine's identification of ideas with the nature of God. This is a sound observation with respect to Augustine and to Calvin who followed in his footsteps. The theory would have appealed to Plato also. But he would have said that it is easy to *say* that there is a God whose very nature is the basis of the expression of these various ideas. Nevertheless, saying this and showing it are two different things. We believe that both Augustine and even Calvin did indeed show this, proving it from both natural theology and revealed theology. We think it behooved Van Til to have mentioned this and not simply to have asserted the fact that Calvin did indeed *conceive* of this unity in terms of God and his various harmonious attributes. *Proofs* of that position should have been indicated as well. (We will not discuss here Van Til's definition of the Trinity as, "God is three persons, God is one person," a blatant use of contradiction.)

The significance of this whole discussion of Van Til's theology is its apologetic bearing. As we said, the "self-attesting God" is the center of his whole system of thought. But in his description of this "self-attesting God," we hear contradiction, paradox, confusion, incoherence. His description of the God of Scripture defies comprehension. That which purports to be the foundation of all thought, he says, cannot be thought. He who is the principle of all knowledge cannot, in the most elemental sense of the word, be known. *Deus absconditus* is an understatement. Orthodoxy which has always been known for its clarity is here obscurantism, pure and simple. Granted that all Reformed theologians—even Gordon H. Clark—admit that God is not totally "comprehensible," they nevertheless insist that He is knowable. "I know in part," said the greatest theologian of all time. But how anyone can know even "in part" a God who desires what He does not desire, who gives grace which is not grace, and who is only one person while being three persons, wholly escapes us.

CHAPTER 17

The Internal Testimony of the Holy Spirit

GOD THE FATHER, the self-attesting God, is the heart of presuppositionalist apologetics. God the Son brings apologetics still closer to us by virtue of His incarnation in human nature. But God the Holy Spirit brings it all home to the heart of the individual elect person. The testimony of the Holy Spirit is the heart of the heart of presuppositionalism. The Holy Spirit is the one who convinces inwardly of the truth of the self-attesting God.

TRADITIONAL REFORMED DOCTRINE OF INTERNAL TESTIMONY

The presuppositionalist's understanding and employment of the internal testimony must be viewed against the background of classic, Reformed doctrine. Calvin's famous treatment having already been summarized, we will briefly consider the seventeenth-century doctrine and Jonathan Edwards's later formulation in *The Divine and Supernatural Light*.

The seventeenth-century doctrine was true to Calvin and perhaps even more precise.

> The unconverted can at best appropriate only a theoretical and pure external knowledge of truths of faith. As an animal can quite see the body of a man but not his spirit because it has not one itself, even the unspiritual man may see and understand the letter but not the Spirit of the Scripture.[1]

This is from Heinrich Heppe, who also cites Polanus, Bucanus, and Voetius as denying that the unregenerate have "sanctifying and saving understanding." On the other hand, Voetius allows the unconverted the capacity for a knowledge of Scripture, by which they may be convinced theoretically of the "truth of the Gospel and of other dogmas of faith." This he considers possible "only by a general assistance or a kind of general grace of the illumining and convincing Spirit."[2]

What is implicit in Calvin has become explicit in his successors. Calvin was, no doubt, referring to saving knowledge when he described the knowledge which could only come by the internal testimony. He was, no doubt, not intending to deny that the unregenerate had any (non-saving) knowledge of God or His Word. But as we can see, the Reformed scholastics did not leave these matters to inference.

The same is true also of seventeenth-century Puritanism. John Owen, for example, speaking of theology wrote: "And in this, chiefly, is its nature different from all other sciences: even as the apostle plainly declares that 'the natural man receiveth not the Spirit of God.'"[3] And in the same place:

> That which the human mind may obtain without the special assistance of the Holy Spirit, does not constitute theology properly so-called. . . . We allow, then, that every man with reason and understanding and having the regular use of them, may, *without the saving agency of the Holy Spirit,* according to the measure of his ability, find out the true sense of these propositions and retain their meaning.[4]

Probably the most definitive statement of our doctrine, since Calvin himself, was in Edwards's famous sermon "The Divine and Supernatural Light." Edwards makes clear not only the difference between the two knowledges but their different sources. One was natural or speculative or merely rational, open to all rational minds (of devils as well as unregenerate men). On the other hand, saving knowledge was "the sense of the heart." Mere knowledge of the Bible could be obtained by any unregenerate mind, but only the new heart could perceive the "beauty" of this knowledge, its "divine and supernatural light."

While the unregenerate could have the first knowledge without the second, the regenerate could not have the second without the first. There is never saving knowledge without the rational. While the rational knowledge has no tendency in itself to produce the spiritual knowledge, the latter powerfully affects the former. That is, when one is illumined by the divine and supernatural light, it intensifies one's conviction of the rational, objective truth, removes the sinful opposition to it, and leads one gladly to acquiesce in it.

THE PRESUPPOSITIONALIST DOCTRINE OF INTERNAL TESTIMONY

For the presuppositionalist doctrine of the internal testimony we will note representaive formulations: Van Til, John Frame, and Dooyeweerd.

Van Til

All presuppositionalists recognize a dependence on Abraham Kuyper, the man we regard as the father of the movement. When any of them depart from him at a given point it is usually significant. This is so with respect to Van Til.

After outlining his rejection of Kuyper's logos-speculation[5] and doctrine of formal faith,[6] Van Til makes this general observation:

> The basic difficulty is that neither Kuyper nor Bavinck nor Woltjer, had worked out a Christian conception of logic as implied in the Christian view of man and of fact. These men assume that if you were to engage in reasoning with unbelievers *you must first agree with their view of man, of fact, and of logic.*[7]

Van Til is denying what is essential to the orthodox doctrine, according to which the internal testimony is divine light thrown on ordinary, natural, human knowledge (pertaining to Scripture). But for Van Til this is not so. *It is not only more than but other than and opposite to speculative knowledge.* In this critical passage, Van Til is faulting his fellow presuppositionalists for a lack of thoroughness. He is quite right in showing that they are halting between two opinions—the orthodox and the presuppositionalist—and that if they are going to depart from traditionalism they will have to be more thoroughgoing.

Van Til will have no truck with the common view of "man, of fact, and of logic." We have seen that the traditional view sees natural man as capable of understanding not only the world but the Bible itself. The unregenerate need no supernatural, spiritual, illumination to understand anything of which the human mind is capable. The testimony or illumination of the Spirit enables them to see what the unaided mind cannot see—the beauty and "sweetness" of revealed truth. This comes by a "sense of the heart" concerning biblical data apprehended by the mind. Charles Hodge says that the only reason unconverted people do not see this divine light is that the God of this world has "blinded" them.[8] However, they can quite well see man, fact, and logic if able to see even the natural revelation of God.

When Van Til denies this—as even Abraham Kuyper did not dare—he loses not only the natural but the spiritual world as well. If people cannot understand common facts in and out of the Bible, how can they be illuminated in them by the Spirit? Even Van Til grants that the Spirit does not communicate information, only illumination. If there is no information, how can it be illuminated? If the Holy Spirit testifies, to what does He testify? To be sure, Van Til insists that Christianity is not "unnatural." It must not be taken on "blind faith."[9] What he means is that we know by the encounter that it is the Holy Spirit with whom we have to do. That is the opposite of blind faith—it is immediate awareness. True enough, but how do we know that the experience is of God, inasmuch as the Spirit does not say so or reveal that fact? Orthodoxy, as expressed in the *Westminster Confession of Faith*,[10] finds many arguments that "abundantly evidence" the Bible to be the Word of God while the Spirit brings only *persuasion* of these arguments. The arguments "evidence" and the Holy Spirit "persuades." The arguments do not persuade and the Holy Spirit does not evidence. But there is neither prior proof nor posterior proof of the Bible in Van Til's presuppositionalism. In spite of his protestations to the contrary, his Christianity is unrational and is taken on "blind faith."

John Frame

One of the most consistent and sophisticated presuppositionalists, Frame believes that the internal testimony of the Holy Spirit must be utterly apart from and prior to speculative knowledge and evidence of the inspiration of the Word. Consequently, he gets into the same problems as his mentor, Van Til. In an orthodox fashion, he recognizes that the internal testimony is immediate, internal, and carries its evidence of divinity in itself. But by divorcing this experience from all external evidence that the Bible is the Word of God and can be interpreted correctly without the internal testimony, Frame falls into pure, mystical subjectivism. Consequently, he forfeits (as Charles Hodge, e.g., never did) all possibility of arguing for his doctrine.

If we ask John Frame why the non-Christian cannot see the truth of the doctrine of the internal testimony, Frame would answer because it does not please God to illumine everyone's mind. In that case, we reply, there is no reason for the non-Christian even to read the Bible because unless God wills to illumine his mind, he will not see the wisdom of looking at things the biblical way. Frame would probably urge this person to keep reading it and talking with Christians. But this person may not read the Bible at all, or talk with Christians, either. He may turn the whole thing off because he does not see any wisdom in it.

Before Frame is finished he gets himself into another thicket from which he cannot extricate himself. He addresses himself to the person who is still considering the possibility of going Frame's way. "He must not be allowed to think that he can become a Christian and go on thinking the same old way. He must be told that Christ demands a *total* repentance. . . . He must learn that Christ demands a change in ultimate criteria."[11] In other words, it is not enough for this non-Christian to be illuminated by God and see the wisdom of looking at things the biblical way, he must see them the way Frame sees them. Suppose, for example, he claims that the Spirit has opened his eyes and he sees the Bible to be the Word of God, teaching Arminianism. Though John Frame is a Calvinist and does not believe that Scripture's way is the Arminian way, he would not be prepared to say that this person has not been illumined by God.

Frame is up against a difficult problem. God wills to enable a person to see things Scripture's way. Is that necessarily Calvin's way? Frame would say, "Yes, it is." So would we, but we would give a reason for saying so. We would say to many an interpreter that his interpretation is not consistent with this, that, or some other thing in the Bible. We would argue that indeed the Calvinistic exegesis is the one that is consistent with biblical revelation. If he is convinced of his Arminianism, he will try to show us that it is the Arminian way that is the biblical way. We have, at least, a means of conversation and debate, and the same canons of reason and exegesis as we pore over the pages of Scripture. The point is that we are using good old reason in the process of our debate. We have been "reborn" and thus have a new disposition to follow, rather than flee from the truth, to yield to it, rather than suppress it. Nevertheless, we are both imperfect. Consequently, at any time, either one of us can be guilty of attempting to suppress evidence which he finds difficult to accept. But the other one can point out the fallacy of our reasoning and we are quite capable, rationally, of seeing our error (our dispositions having been changed), acknowledging and correcting it.

But when Frame says that the Calvinistic way is the biblical way, he dare not appeal with the naked reason to rational interpretation, implication, systematic coherence, and so on for obvious reasons. This would be asserting reason as an ultimate criterion against the ultimate criterion of the Bible which Frame says is not a legitimate thing to do. Though we are not for a moment admitting reason as any ultimate criterion, it is certainly a means of ascertaining the ultimate criterion. Frame makes no such distinction, however, and consequently we have to ask on what basis he speaks, argues, contends, and tells other people that they are not allowed to accept their interpretation. His only answer must be that if God illumines them, Calvinism is what they will see. The Arminian says that his eyes are illumined and he does not see that. We can argue with him, but Frame cannot. He can argue with Frame, but Frame will not argue with him. Frame can only tell him that he is in error and that he must change his mind because he, Frame, has been illumined by God to see otherwise. Frame would not be capable of putting it that way, however, without immediately recognizing that it is an untenable approach. So he leaves it buried, implicit. Perhaps he is a little hesitant to think too deeply on this point, lest he see what that clear mind of his could easily detect.

Then comes the grand conclusion: "He must learn that Christ demands a change in ultimate criteria." The "ultimate criteria" is, of course, the Bible and not the reason which the person had been using before discovering that the Bible is the Word of God and the ultimate criteria. But this Arminian and many Calvinists (such as the authors of this book) never considered reason as the ultimate criterion, but only the penultimate, leading to God. But once reason has lead to God, it cannot be given up as the means of interpreting—the ultimate means of interpreting—the ultimate criterion.

But we are in error. John Frame says so. John Frame says so because the Lord tells him so. Proving God is the same as hearing and obeying Him. So the end of the matter is that the converted person does not really see the wisdom of looking at things Scripture's way. He simply hears God speaking. He obeys Him. The wisdom to see and therefore obey would make reason the ultimate criterion. So if the Bible is to be the ultimate criterion, there can be no reason. There must be only hearing and obeying. Evidence is no evidence. Wisdom is no wisdom. It is all a matter of arbitrarily saying that one has heard God's voice because John Frame says that is the way it happens.

When you hear His voice, He speaks in the language of John Calvin. That too cannot be proven by John Frame. It is simply asserted with all the authority of the God Frame insists he hears. Those of us who think we hear God saying something else are mistaken. No reason can be given because that would make reason the ultimate criterion. John Frame is the ultimate criterion. What John Frame says, God says. If we say that there is something wrong with his hearing, he is going to have to deny it. Is it possible that we have hearing as good or even better than his? He is going to have to say: "No, you don't." If we try to argue, he is not going to argue with us because he is not going to succumb to the temptation to make reason the ultimate criterion. The Bible is the ultimate criterion, John Frame will say. Apparently, he does not realize that what he has done is substitute his personal testimony for all rationality. The basic "reason" for believing the Bible, as far as John Frame is concerned, is that John Frame hears God in the Bible. Anybody who thinks he hears God speaking any other way must be mistaken; apparently he does not hear God at all.

"Thus saith John Frame." We know John very well, and know that he does not speak that way at all. He does not even think that way, in a sense. At least, he does not think that he thinks that way. He is low-key, modest, and sounds eminently rational. One cannot imagine him raising his voice, much less shouting dogmatically. Nevertheless, the only evidence he gives that the Spirit witnesses is not evidence, but mere assertions. On mere assertion he rests his whole "case."

At times Frame does defend logic as revealed in the Scripture, and he constantly argues exegetically. How then can we say what has been written above? Our answer is this:

1. Frame and the presuppositionalists generally claim that the Bible teaches logical principles.

2. But they had to use logical principles to learn what the Bible teaches.

3. So not having logical principles before reading the Bible, they could never learn what the Bible teaches about logical principles or anything else.

4. Consequently, their so-called interpretation of the Bible is impossible and all their exegetical labors are futile.

5. Thus we represent John Frame above as, with all other presup-

positionalists, having arbitrarily to assert the Bible teaching. What John Frames says that God says, God says.

Dooyeweerd

According to Dooyeweerd, the Scriptural message at its core cannot be understood without the Holy Spirit.

> The biblical ground motive is not a doctrine that can be theologically elaborated apart from the guidance of God's Spirit. Theology in and of itself cannot uncover the true meaning of the Scriptural ground motive. If it presses that claim, it stands against the work of God and becomes a satanic power. Theology makes God's self-revelation powerless if it reduces the religious ground motivation of revelation to a theoretical system.[12]

This also is subjectivism pure and simple. What prevents a person from saying, "Dooyeweerd, you do not understand the biblical ground motive because you do not have the Holy Spirit"? What prevents that other from saying, "*I* understand. *My* interpretation is correct because *I* have the Holy Spirit"? If Dooyeweerd then tried to prove that the other person does not have the correct interpretation by exegesis or coherence, or something like that, he would not be relying on the Holy Spirit alone. It would be his interpretation proving the presence of the Holy Spirit, rather than the presence of the Holy Spirit proving his interpretation. So he has to rely on a direct claim that the Holy Spirit is moving him to his interpretation and that the Holy Spirit is not moving someone else.

How does he know that the Holy Spirit is not moving someone else? Presumably, because the interpretation of that other person is different from his own. Again, he is inconsistently offering a rational test of the presence or absence of the Holy Spirit. That is, he accepts his interpretation (arbitrarily) of the testimony of the Holy Spirit and no proof of that need be offered. But when someone else makes a counter-claim, that is rejected on rational grounds, presumably that the Holy Spirit would not contradict Himself. How does this differ from the man we saw once in an institution who claimed that his neighbor was *not* Alexander the Great? Why? Because he himself was Philip of Macedon and he ought to recognize his own son! He had no rational evidence for his own identification, but very rational evidence when evaluating his neighbor's.

CHAPTER 18

Presuppositionalism and Verification

THE TITLE OF THIS chapter must seem to be a contradiction in terms. To link presuppositionalism with verification must be the ultimate paradox. Verification is the hallmark of evidentialism and the antithesis of presuppositionalism. One tradition says that seeing is believing; the other, believing is seeing.

Still, there are presuppositionalists who claim to prove or verify their case. They enter the common arena of thought and debate all contenders. Thom Notaro's *Van Til and the Use of Evidence*[1] is devoted to proving that presuppositionalists prove.

Because Notaro's undertaking, if successful, would be refutation of this entire volume, we will devote this chapter to considering this challenge.

Notaro states at the outset that it is time "Van Til be recognized for his appreciation of evidences as they are engaged in a presuppositional apologetic."[2] He cites Montgomery, Buswell, and Pinnock as disagreeing with Van Til, while Carnell, Gordon R. Lewis, Ramm, Gerstner, Schaeffer, and Geisler more or less take other positions.[3] According to Notaro, Van Til supports B. B. Warfield's claim that "'The Christian faith is not a blind faith but is faith based on evidence.' With Warfield and Charles Hodge he [Van Til] maintains that 'Christianity meets every legitimate demand of reason' and 'is not irrational' but 'is capable of rational defense.'"[4]

Again, Van Til states, "I do not reject theistic proofs but merely insist on formulating them in such a way as not to compromise the doctrines of Scripture."[5] But, as we have explained above, what Van Til means by not compromising the doctrine of Scripture is that he does not accept the theistic proofs. Bahnsen is cited as saying, "The Gospel does not cater to *rebellious* man's demand 'for evidences and reason' that will pass a test of *autonomous* scrutiny."[6] This chapter will say that Van Til believes in evidences as Van Til believes in evidences, which, in our opinion, is no belief in evidences at all. Carnell makes the distinction between pre-evangelism and evangelism but Van Til allows for no real distinction between apologetics and witness. John Frame coined the term "perspectival evidences."[7]

Finally, we get a definition of evidences. "In other words evidences are the application of Scripture to controversies primarily of a factual nature."[8] Scripture is arbitrarily (that is, for no reason) accepted here as the Word of God as we have shown earlier. On this nonrational foundation, Scripture is accepted as if it did carry rational weight and when applied to factual matters is called evidence. So still there is no evidence for evidence.

Notaro thinks that it is out of character for apologetes such as Pinnock, Montgomery, or Fineberg to argue that Van Til is against the sinner's knowledge when all that he opposes is their acceptance of it. According to Notaro,

> Van Til enumerates several specific kinds of knowledge of which even the remotest heathen is aware: for example, that God is the Creator of the world, that the world is controlled by God's providence, that the world manifests a non-saving grace of God, that man is responsible for evil, that there is a need for God's special grace, and that man's failure to recognize God results in eternal punishment.[9]

But the point that Notaro misses is that Van Til will not and cannot consistently defend the sinner's knowledge. Van Til's "knowledge" dissipates in paradox. By contrast, the type of knowledge about God that Aquinas in his *Summa* attributes to the unregenerate is far superior to anything that Van Til has envisioned, and more stable. Once again, Notaro notes that Van Til mentions in *My Credo* that sinners have theologically correct or formally correct knowledge about God. But he does not note the nature of this knowledge or its inconsistency with presuppositionalism.

Still trying to explain and defend the "knowledge" Van Til supposedly grants to non-Christians, Notaro quotes Van Til: "Abraham Kuyper located the fundamental problem: '. . . you can receive no knowledge of God when you refuse to *receive* your knowledge of him in absolute dependence on him.' Whereas the Christian's knowledge is self-consciously dependent, the non-Christian's knowledge pretends to be independent of God."[10] But how can knowledge of God be independent of God in a meaningful sense? How can Kuyper say that you receive no knowledge when you refuse to receive your knowledge of Him in absolute dependence? You do have the knowledge but you are not responding in the proper way. It could not be said that you did not respond in the proper way if you did not have the knowledge in the first place. Knowledge and reception of knowledge in a proper way are by no means mutually exclusive propositions; rather, they are mutually dependent. At least, the latter is dependent on the former. Now Notaro gives us the essential Van Til: "What is meant by knowing God in Scripture is *knowing and loving God,* this is true knowledge of God: the other is false."[11] Instead of saying that this is *true* knowledge, Van Til ought to say that this is *saving* knowledge. *We could know nothing unless we know everything.*

Notaro is distinguishing between actual knowledge and knowledge derived from Scripture which requires presuppositions.[12] He does not notice (or care) that no evidence for the Bible is given. Van Til acknowledges natural knowledge only on the basis of the Bible, which is unproven. Then Notaro and Van Til go on to confuse the correct notion that natural men know God but do not love him with the supposition that they do not know Him as He is because they do not love Him.[13]

John Frame also applauds a certain biblical verifiability. This becomes part of Notaro's argument and therefore requires brief notice. Frame holds that religious language is odd or unusual language because it is ethically qualified: people are *obliged* to heed it and believe the biblical system. But, characteristically, no evidence is given by Frame. Christianity is verifiable and conclusively so.

But this verification of truth claims, according to Van Til, is by presuppositionalism alone: "If one really saw that it is necessary to have God in order to understand the grass that grows outside his window, he would certainly come to a saving knowledge of Christ, and to the knowledge of the absolute authority of the Bible."[14] But to Jonathan Edwards, every blade of grass is demonstrative evidence that God is its Creator; but how differently he shows it. And if Van Til's statement were applied to Satan it would make him a believer which, of course, he is not. Here is Frame's crucial statement: "Presuppositions and evidences are one."[15] Notaro brings this chapter to a close by urging all people to acknowledge the Trinity—not for any evidence, but in spite of the lack of evidence.[16]

Pinnock refers to Van Til's apologetics as "a form of irrational fideism."[17] But Notaro thinks that Pinnock's charge is unfair because Van Til is constantly denying that Christianity is irrational. Van Til's point is that the Christian circle of thought can be presented *for what it is,* because it *possesses the power and authority to subdue* what would otherwise be called a vicious circle by nonbelievers.

Notaro notes with disapproval that Pinnock first cites the Bible as error-ridden[18] and then applauds Barth as a powerful ally in the defense of biblical authority. We agree with the inerrancy doctrine of Van Til and Notaro, but we have more respect for the *augmentation effort* of Pinnock, Jack Rogers, and Barth, despite their *unsound reasoning.* The presuppositionalists arrive at a sound conclusion by a wrong method, the others, at an unsound conclusion by a right method.[19]

Notaro himself gives an illustration of Vantillian evidence at work in the case of the apostle Thomas:

> Thus, the value of all the evidence was of significance within a particular framework of understanding. In the passage there is a pronounced shift away from the physical wounds themselves to the self-attesting Christ who was "was pierced through for our transgressions" and "crushed for our iniquities" (Isa. 53:5). The evidence was more than enough, and there is no indication in the text that Thomas ever followed through with his empirical test. Suddenly that had become unnecessary.[20]

Perhaps Thomas never did "follow through with his empirical test" of touching the body of the resurrected Christ. But that would be because at the sight and hearing of Jesus Christ, Thomas had enough genuine "empirical" evidence. One who sees with his eyes and hears with his ears, hardly needs to touch with his fingers. The "self-attesting Christ" attested to His bodily resurrection by his *living bodily* presence after *death*. That is empirical evidence if ever there was empirical evidence.

Discussing Acts 2:14–36, Notaro shows how the resurrection acts as evidence or as presupposition. It seems to do both.[21] Peter treats the resurrection as, in some sense, observable, and as presupposed. Notaro fails to mention that it had been demonstrated by miracles and witnesses that the Resurrection really happened and had not been arbitrarily presupposed. He then concludes that the account lends generous support to Van Til's emphasis upon the Christian system as a unit and his circular method, showing the authority of a self-attesting Lord.

This treatment of Scripture is astonishing. The truth of Christ's resurrection is supposed to be demonstrated by presupposition, while Scripture everywhere is speaking of visible, audible, tangible evidence that anyone could see, hear, or touch, whether knowing the meaning of a presupposition or not.

Van Til would be on our side in this controversy. He would never submit to a translation of plain empirical evidence into presuppositionalism. He would argue that empirical evidence is a contradiction in terms, being neither "empirical" nor "evidence" apart from presupposition. He would bring us back to brute facts, mute facts, and the noetic influence of sin. All of these we have already considered and need not refute again here. Suffice it to say that Van Til puts all his apologetic eggs in one basket—presuppositionalism. Evidence cannot prove God but God must prove the evidence. So Van Til does not use Christian evidences but utterly destroys them. In so doing, he destroys the real evidence of the Christian religion which he loves so much.

Several years ago, Greg Bahnsen wrote an impressive essay attempting to prove that Van Til was no fideist.[22] Reflecting on Clark Pinnock and Daniel Fuller, Bahnsen charges that they "have counterfeited the presuppositional outlook by aligning it with fideistic deductionism over against empirical and inductive methods."[23] Bahnsen supports his defense of Van Til against the charge of fideism simply by citing the fact that Van Til always speaks in favor of induction, claiming that presuppositionalism alone grounded valid induction. We have proven throughout this volume and against Notaro in this chapter, that Van Til's claim, though honest, is specious. Nothing Bahnsen says here, or anything of his that we have read elsewhere, refutes or even addresses our critique. In fact, Bahnsen's own quotation of Van Til ("Such [archaeological] corroboration is not of independent power"[24]) shows that both he and Van Til deny the validity of an empirical approach *apart from* presuppositionalism.

Bahnsen next challenges the proposition that the inductive method is neutral. He asserts that Pinnock and Fuller have their own presuppositions which they "may try to hide" from themselves; they are therefore "*not* the presuppositionless inductivists that they make themselves out to be."[25] But we are here only concerned to see if Bahnsen can clear Van Til of the charge of fideism[26] and the charge of being "against empirical and inductive methods." We think he does not. He claims that the "very use of that [empirical] epistemology commits [any] one to a great deal of unargued philosophical baggage."[27] But he does not support this claim.

In the end, Bahnsen himself falls into the presuppositional, fideistic trap: "Finally, we know that presuppositionless impartiality and neutral reasoning are impossible and undesirable because God's word teaches [otherwise]."[28] God's Word is arbitrarily assumed. It is clear to anyone who will reflect seriously on this question, Bahnsen maintains, that the statements of Scripture *about* Scripture are primary and must determine our attitude toward all the rest.[29] Hence, the unproven Scripture must be the determiner of all truth. This "primary" truth is accepted fideistically.

If the presuppositionalist offers any reason, he ceases to be a presuppositionalist. Bahnsen is too consistent to do that. But a faith in Scripture, or in anything for that matter, that does not rest on reasons, is fideism. Thus, if Van Til or Bahnsen deny that their faith in Scripture is fideistic they will be denying their presuppositionalism. If they admit it, they admit fideism. In short, presuppositionalism is a form of fideism, and this charge cannot be denied without denying presuppositionalism.

CHAPTER 19

Analogical Thinking

HOWEVER WONDERFUL GOD'S knowledge, which begins and ends in Himself, how can it ever come down to earth? However futile human knowledge which begins and ends futilely in autonomy, how can we escape it? What is the bridge over the apparently unbridgeable gulf between God's perfect knowledge and humankind's perfect ignorance? The presuppositional answer is: analogical thinking.

Analogical thought, a key concept in presuppositionalism, is fundamental, in fact, to *all* thought. In this chapter, we will examine the traditional "analogy of being" in medieval and seventeenth-century Reformed scholasticism, then the radical rejection of the *analogia entis* ("analogy of being") by Karl Barth. Finally, we will focus on the distinctive usage of analogical thought by presuppositionalism (which is neither orthodox nor neo-orthodox), as seen in Robert Knudsen, Van Til, and Frame.

According to medieval (especially Thomistic) scholasticism, one may reason backwards from effect to cause, from creation to Creator. It considered three possible conclusions: Univocal or identical knowledge, which implied pantheism, was unthinkable because God is infinite and humans finite. Equivocal knowledge, which implied skepticism, was unthinkable because God is rational and therefore somehow knowable. Analogical knowledge (*analogia entis*), which implied true but limited knowledge, was alone thinkable because it enshrined the Creator's infinity and acknowledged human finitude. God's incomprehensibility and His knowability were simultaneously honored, Christianity was established on a sound epistemological base (as we have shown throughout this text).

Reformed scholasticism also used analogical thought. In spite of strong idealist thought and a tendency toward pantheism in the eight-eenth century, Jonathan Edwards, for example, strongly defended analogical thought.

In the twentieth century, on the other hand, Karl Barth has writ-ten that "the *analogia entis* is the invention of Antichrist."[1] This was because he thought it would infringe on God's sovereignty. By it one would be able to reason to God whether He chose to reveal Himself or not, as if natural revelation were not divine revelation also. Uncon-scious of the inconsistency, Barth did not object to God's giving us, by His Word, the analogy of faith. Brunner defended the analogy of being, accepting it as a revelation of God, insisting, however, that, because of human depravity, it is of no avail for a natural theology.[2] Brunner directly attacked Barth, rightly arguing that the analogy of faith would have to presuppose the analogy of being.[3]

This is one of the strangest theological debates. Barth and Brun-ner agreed on the bottom line—no natural theology—Barth denying the analogy of being on which natural theology rests, Brunner defend-ing analogy of being only to eviscerate it by his view of total depravity. We shall see that presuppositionalism has an approach all its own but comes to rest on the same bottom line: no natural theology and, by implication, no analogy of being.

After commenting on Van Til's view of analogy, Knudsen re-marks, "One of the beginning insights of the philosophy of Vol-lenhoven and Dooyeweerd was that the logical (analytical) is an aspect of the cosmos, dependent for its meaning upon a creative structure of reality which is itself not analytical in character."[4] For the Dooye-weerdians, in other words, the logical is only one aspect of human life. That life, as such, is not, properly speaking, logically qualified. We classicists consider it a deficiency in Van Til that he put so little emphasis on the intellectual. Neo-Dooyeweerdian Vander Stelt attacks Van Til for over-emphasizing the intellectual, however virtually classi-fying him with the Old Princetonians. While Van Til has battled the prevalent notion of the primacy of the intellect, says Knudsen, "nev-ertheless, it must be asked whether Van Til's metaphysical notion of the archetypal intellect does not clash with the more central notion that man in the center of his being is constantly in the act of respond-ing to God in his self-revelation in Christ."[5]

Later Knudsen asks,

> Is it not better to lay aside the notion that our locus of meaning
> resides in the theoretical-logical, and to see the theoretical-logical

as a human activity which is taken up in the law-order of God's creation, an activity which must depend upon this law-order for its possibility and whose final service must be a constant transcendental reflection back on the point transcending itself out of which it lives in terms of which it has its impulse and direction?[6]

To which Van Til gives this revealing and rather peppery reply:

What is my reaction to all this? It is simply and basically that I have *never* held to the idea that "the locus of meaning resides in the theoretical-logical." I have on the contrary *always* opposed this notion in terms of what I learned from the Scriptures. For me "the analytical judgment" is an invention of apostate thought.[7]

Further on in the same context, Van Til is still more clear: "My position is that man should by the logical gifts that he has from his Creator discover the 'law-structures of the universe.' " He concludes, "If, therefore, I really made the 'analytical judgment' a model for my view of the divine mind I would be thinking along the lines of unbelief."[8]

This seems to be fancy academic footwork on Van Til's part. Knudsen is accusing him of making the analytical or analogical judgment the basis of his system of thought. And surely this is true, for Van Til claims to know anything only because God knows everything and allows believers to know after their own mode—*analogically*. To be sure, this does not exhaust the meaning of "human." Nevertheless, it *is* the way by which the universe and God is opened up to humans.

Dooyeweerd, Vollenhoven, Knudsen, and others in that tradition believe that even the opening up of the universe comes by heart rather than the mind, by a kind of healing, rather than by a type of analogical thinking. It seems to us that, in the dispute among Westminster, Toronto, and Amsterdam, the latter two schools do rightly attribute to Van Til a relative intellectualistic strain that they themselves do not possess and that, in not acknowledging this, Van Til is being something less than candid.

Nonetheless, before he is finished, Van Til gets in a deft stroke against Dooyeweerd:

Whereas Kant's limiting concepts pointed to the void, yours point to the depth of the wisdom of God in whom no darkness dwells. They do not point to an origin, whether or not this origin be called "God" (as Dooyeweerd maintains). Concept formation itself must presuppose the Christian world-order if it is to make any intelligible contact with the world at all.[9]

With this remark, Van Til clearly distances himself from Kant, toward whom, undoubtedly, Dooyeweerd has moved.

Concerning the limiting concepts and ideas in Van Til and Kant: Van Til stresses the fact that, for Kant, God is a limiting concept. He is just a pointer toward the void. For Van Til this limiting concept is a pointer from God Himself, indicating the difference between His own omniscience and the merely analogical thinking of the enlightened creature. Certainly there is a real and profound difference between Immanuel Kant and Cornelius Van Til. It is questionable, however, how real that difference actually is in the realm of thought. We return to square one: for Van Til the creature can know nothing, precisely because he is a creature having knowledge merely of brute facts which are mute facts. Van Til's solution is in God who knows everything; for God there are no brute–mute facts.

But how does God communicate this to the creature? According to Van Til, He cannot really communicate it, because omniscience is not a communicable attribute. There is a great gulf fixed between the knowledge which belongs to God alone and ignorance which is characteristic of the creature.

Presuppositionalism's analogical thinking is open to various criticisms. First, the supposed necessity for it is based on a false idealistic supposition, namely, that brute facts are mute facts, that we cannot know the flower in the crannied wall without knowing the world and all.

Second, even if this argument were justified on the idealistic supposition, this knowledge which God has could not be communicated analogically because of that very supposition. For if God has knowledge of the flower in the crannied wall only because He knows the world and all, then the only way God could communicate that knowledge would be by communicating His own incommunicable attributes of infinity and omniscience. If to know the flower you must know all, then God would have to communicate to us the knowledge of all so that we too could know that elusive flower in the crannied wall. But the theologians rightly call infinity and omniscience "incommunicable" attributes. Obviously, God could not communicate infinity without, first, destroying us by destroying our finitude; second, making us infinite (which would be impossible since, besides the fact that there can only be one infinite, we simply were not there before time and space). Omniscience would also be hard for us Johnny-come-latelys to come by. So, if it is true (and its opposite is not conceivable) that God cannot do the inconceivable (not because He is unable, but because it is without meaning), then God cannot communicate "analogically" for the very reason that such communication is deemed necessary by presuppositionalists: because one must know everything in order to know anything.

Third, even if divine knowledge could be communicated analogically, it could not be *received* analogically, because such "knowledge" would fall afoul of the supposition which made it necessary in the first place. Granted that God knows the flower in the crannied wall, suppose the unsupposable—that He could communicate His knowledge of the flower to us creatures. It would still have to come to us as a brute fact. We are not metamorphosed into divinities. We are creatures still who are confined to finite knowledge. So, if God said to us, "I know the flower in the crannied wall because I know the world and all," what would that tell us? That would tell us that God knew the flower in the crannied wall because He knew the world and all. We would wonder why He would be telling us what we knew all along, even before the presuppositionalists told us. While we would be wondering about God bothering to reveal to us the obvious, Van Til would come along and say: "Don't you traditionalists get the good epistemological news? Now *you* too, can know the flower in the crannied wall." We thank him and explain that we had known it all along, but he breaks in and reminds us: "No, you didn't, but now you do!" "O.K.," we say, "suppose we had not known it all along because we wrongly supposed we had heard the mute facts speaking to us of their Creator. How is it that we can now hear them?" "Because," patiently explains the good doctor, "only God knew them. But now he has enabled you to know them." "But Dr. Van Til," we reply, " we still cannot know the world and all which you say is necessary in order to know the flower in the crannied wall." "No," replies Dr. Van Til, "you are not made omniscient, to be sure; but God assures you that since He knows the flower so can you."

Let us turn now to Frame's defense of Van Til's position on analogical thinking. Van Til stresses continuity and discontinuity in thinking God's thoughts after Him. Frame explains that we think God's thoughts (continuity) *after* Him (discontinuity).[10] Our criticism of this is that, according to Van Til, we do not think God's thoughts after Him. To think God's thoughts after Him literally would be univocal thinking, which Van Til denies. We think analogically. But that is not the same thing as thinking God's thoughts after Him. In the presuppositional system, there is no real bridge between God's thought and human thought, even analogically considered. Apparently, Frame is no more conscious of this than is Van Til.

This is not a minor mistake. It is absolutely fatal to the Vantillian system. According to that system, finite knowledge is not knowledge at all. Only infinite knowledge is true knowledge. If one begins on the premise that only infinite knowledge is true knowledge, there is simply no way by which the creature can ever have true knowledge, because there is no way that a finite creature can have infinite knowledge. Van Til thinks that God guarantees or sanctions human knowledge; but this violates his fundamental principle that finite knowledge cannot be true knowledge. He makes God a liar, calling something knowledge which is not knowledge. Van Til is blind to this because he simply assumes at this point, that God can do anything He pleases to do. But God cannot lie. Van Til will say at this point, "Who are you to say that God is lying? If God says that I have knowledge analogically, then I have knowledge analogically. The fact that you or I cannot understand how that is does not change the situation." We reply that it does change the situation in one sense. If God can say that finite knowledge is knowledge, then Van Til can never say that finite knowledge is not knowledge. Van Til's system goes down the drain. He cannot get started because his starting point is that finite knowledge is no knowledge. God Himself, according to Van Til, contradicts Van Til and says finite knowledge may be true knowledge.

Without realizing it, Frame continues and spells out everything that we had been saying: "Thus, just as it is important for us to *agree* with God, so it is equally important to *distinguish* our thoughts from His. God reveals Himself to us, not exhaustively, but 'according to man's ability to receive his revelation.'"[11] If humans have the ability to receive God's special revelation, then presumably we could receive God's natural revelation as well. Frame presumes that humans do not have that ability, being finite creatures who cannot understand comprehensively, and therefore cannot understand. But now God vouchsafes human ability to understand even the special revelation. That understanding must be according to human ability to receive the revelation. If this is true, of course, if makes Van Til's contention that people can receive God's special revelation a valid one, but it makes his original contention that humans cannot receive God's revelation an invalid one.

Frame continues, "We do not know God the same way He knows

Himself." A massive understatement. We do not know God or anything else the same way that God knows Himself or anything else. That inability is presumably our creaturely deficiency that would follow us as long as we remain creatures, that is, forever. It is interesting to notice how the presuppositionalists slip back into traditional thinking quite unconsciously. Traditional thinkers will always say what Frame has just stated, that we do not know God the same way He knows Himself. We admit the difference between our finite and His infinite knowledge, but we do not deny the validity of finite knowledge as Van Til denies it. We affirm it from the very beginning, and continue to maintain its finitude throughout our own everlasting existence. In order to get his system started, Van Til denies finite knowing as the starting point. But once his system is moving, he affirms it in the way in which we have noticed. In other words, traditionalism is consistent throughout, and Van Til is inconsistent.

Frame gets deeper into the mire: "Without such discontinuity, the continuities mentioned earlier would be meaningless, for if we cannot clearly distinguish between our thoughts and God's, how can we regard the latter as authoritative for the former?"[12] We have to have discontinuity in order to have continuity, he argues. That is, we have to be discontinuous in our knowledge in order to recognize that God is continuous in His. Of course, that is perfectly true; however, it also annihilates the earlier proposition about continuity. It is our discontinuity that enables us to recognize God's continuity of knowledge. Our discontinuity, according to Van Til, would preclude the possibility of any continuity. As Frame says, discontinuity is not only essential to knowing continuity, but it essentially destroys the continuity of humans with God as well. Frame continues, "Van Til, therefore, even acknowledges a sense in which man himself is a kind of 'starting point' for thought: He is a proximate 'starting point' while God is the 'ultimate' starting point."[13] Man *is* a starting point in Van Til's system. Indeed, Van Til cannot start anyplace other than with the man Van Til, anymore than any of the rest of us can start anyplace other than with ourselves. He is constantly denying any kind of common starting point. What makes Frame's statement amusing is that he is obliged to recognize a kind of starting point—not a special variety of starting point, just a plain, ordinary starting point; namely, that humankind is finite and therefore cannot have knowledge. If one supposes that infinite knowledge is essential to any kind of knowledge, then humans cannot have *any* kind of knowledge. But anyone can see that, whether he is proceeding from a revelational or nonrevelational viewpoint. Thus, we have a common starting point indeed. But there is no point to calling it "proximate" as over against "ultimate," because the proximate is the ultimate starting point as long as we remain human creatures, which happens to be forever. God's starting point is always His own starting point as along as He remains God, which is also forever.

CHAPTER 20

Circular Reasoning

IN ALL SYSTEMS OF thought except presuppositionalism circular reasoning is considered demonstrative evidence of error. In presuppositionalism, instead of being a vicious circle, it is a sign of intellectual virtue. While neo-orthodoxy could say that "contradiction is the hallmark of truth," presuppositionalist orthodoxy makes circularity the hallmark of truth. This "glorious circle" distinguishes revealed truth presupposed from all other systems which are circular also but ingloriously so.

In this final chapter we will consider a range of presuppositional thinkers on this central notion. After stating the traditional position, we will survey the deviation from it, ranging from Van Til himself to Gordon Clark, including, in between, Rushdoony and Frame. We conclude with a reaffirmation of the inevitable conviction of the mind that a circle gets one nowhere and that even those who travel in these circles either admit this, or are naked fideists.

REASONING IN THE REFORMED TRADITION

In the Reformed tradition the use of reason in theology is perfectly justified. According to Heinrich Heppe,

(1) the true God must be proved to be the author of revelation; (2) theological harmony or the rationality of revealed truths must be set forth; (3) the connection of conclusions resulting from each of them is to be developed, and (4) the entire natural, historical, linguistic, etc., knowledge of theology to be made use of.[1]

Heidegger, for example, says:

Illumined reason is of no contemptible use to theology. And its chief use consists in the fact that forthwith it brings forth from its own treasury arguments on behalf of faith. This happens in four ways. Firstly, reason urged and directed by the Spirit of God through sure and undoubted criteria and signs of divinity discovers that he who reveals the way of salvation, God, is not an imposter, demon or man suspected of falsehood. Secondly, illumined reason puts forth arguments for the principles of Christian faith, by which it shows to the unbelieving of those who embrace it its worthiness of credit, which is not a thing impossible, irrational or contrary to man's uncorrupted nature; and it dissolves subtleties adduced to the contrary by a perverse reason. Thirdly, reason occasionally proceeds in accordance with its own principles by collecting suitable arguments on behalf of faith, in those matters which are known both by faith and by reason; or arguments at least known by faith, which stimulates reason in many, are confirmed by reason. Fourthly, in a word reason, accompanying the use of words and of the things signified by these words, whether natural ideas and reasons which we have of and for the things and which revelation presupposes, has power of judgment on equal terms, i.e., those considered apart from construction or conjunction. Use is the judge in familiar words which are not proper and peculiar to revelation. Faith alone judges on the supernatural construction and conjunction of simple words or terms which belong to revelation alone. *The Spirit alone secures our right use of reason and the propriety of our faith.*[2]

So it continues for the rest of Heppe's first chapter. Nonetheless, Heppe does not do justice to the use of reason in the testing of revelation. On occasion, he even tends to give the opposite impression. According to orthodoxy, once the Bible is recognized as the Word of God, then reason is utterly docile. But classical Reformed theologians recognized that the reason must be satisfied before the Bible can be accepted as the Word of God.

VAN TIL ON CIRCULAR REASONING

From the very beginning of his career in 1932 to the end of the 1960s, Van Til implicitly advocated not a fideistic but a rationalistic type of apologetic. He appealed not to faith but to reason, appealing by his own reasoning to human reason in general. Unless you presuppose God, he argued, you cannot have an "intelligible" world.

How does this differ from traditional apologetics, inasmuch as it does not differ in the autonomous rationality of its approach? As we have said, it is not a fideistic versus a rationalistic approach, at least not apparently. How then does it differ? The traditional approach begins with a creature and the world rather than with God and His world. It claims that every person must begin here—with self and the world. At the outset, he simply does not *know* that there is anything more than himself and that which surrounds him. When he does reflect on himself and that which surrounds him, which he insists he can do (and which Van Til will insist he cannot do without presupposing God), he realizes that the world is not self-explanatory. By various theistic arguments he shows that that transcendent explanation is a being called "God." Traditional thought concludes that unless one does acknowledge that, the person and the world remain unexplained. One may go on knowing himself and the world in that limited, truncated fashion; but he does not understand his own or the world's ultimate nature, source, or destiny. If a person wants to understand himself and the world, he must acknowledge the existence of the divine being who explains, and who alone explains, everything.

Is this Van Til's approach? Because of a deep ineradicable inconsistency in Van Til's whole thought system, the answer is yes and no. The answer is yes in the sense that, in this statement and hundreds of others, Van Til indicates that by observing science, philosophy, and theology, one can see that apart from presupposing the revelation of God, nothing will be ultimately intelligible. That is not essentially different from the traditional way of saying that the world is not explicable except in terms of God. The only difference here is a modal difference, a *way* of arguing, not so much the argument itself. That is, the traditional method tends to follow the five ways of Thomas Aquinas's traditional theistic arguments while presuppositionalism follows a somewhat different path to the same end. Presuppositionalism's way, as we have seen, is to try the different philosophies and theologies of the ages and show that they are, as a matter of fact, inexplicable in terms of themselves. We will examine "way" in more detail below. For now, we will observe in passing that both presuppositionalists and traditionalists are arguing rationally with rational people about rational conclusions which are not arbitrarily asserted but theoretically demonstrated.

The answer is also no because Van Til insists that we must affirm God at the outset. This is his inconsistency. It is fundamental to his thought that one cannot *end* with this observation (though he himself often does), but must *begin* with it.

> It thus appears that we must take the Bible, its conception of sin, its conception of Christ, and its conception of God and all that is involved in these concepts together, or take none of them. So also it makes very little difference whether we begin with the notion of an absolute God or with the notion of an absolute Bible. The one is derived from the other. They are together involved in the Christian view of life. Hence we defend all or we defend none. Only one absolute is possible, and only one absolute can speak to us. Hence it must always be the same voice of the same absolute, even though he seems to speak to us at different places. The Bible must be true because it alone speaks of an absolute God. And equally true is it that we believe in an absolute God because the Bible tells us of one.[3]

Van Til cannot reverse these last two sentences. If we put the second sentence first, we must ask, Why must we believe in an absolute God simply because the Bible speaks of one? A reason would have to be given or the assertion would be arbitrary and obscurantist. The reason is the first sentence: "The Bible must be true because it alone speaks of an absolute God." When we ask why that is so, the answer is the core of Van Til's apologetic: That we cannot know ultimately anything at all unless we presuppose such a God as the Bible alone reveals. If Van Til's apologetic is sound, then he proves rationally at the outset with his autonomous mind to other autonomous minds the necessary assumption that the Bible which alone reveals this God must be true, because this God alone brings rationality.

But Van Til ends in hopeless paradox of which he seems unaware: "The Bible must be true because it alone speaks of an absolute God. And equally true is it that we believe in an absolute God because the Bible tells us of one." So, we believe in the Bible because it tells of an absolute God. Why? Because an absolute God alone enables us to know or predicate. As we say, this is Van Til's ultimate, autonomous criterion. But we are also said to believe in the absolute God because the Bible tells of one. Presumably this means that we believe in the absolute God merely because the Bible tells us of one and not because such an absolute God makes predication possible (which would be an equivalent of the first statement and redundant). Presumably, also, this does not mean that once we have recognized that the Bible is the Word of God (because it alone tells of the God who makes predication possible), we believe the Bible because it is the Word of God. In that case, we would not be believing something merely because the Bible says it but because the Bible that says it proves itself to be the Word of God. Such a statement would be pure circularity going nowhere: The Bible is true because it speaks of an absolute God; an absolute God is true because the Bible speaks of Him.

> To admit one's own presuppositions and to point out the presuppositions of others is therefore to maintain that all reasoning is, in the nature of the case, *circular reasoning*. The starting point, the method, and the conclusions are always involved in one another.[4]

This definition of circular reasoning involves Van Til in the violation of two logical fallacies. The first is the one he readily admits to, the exercise of *petitio principii*—question begging. This fallacy of circular reasoning is defined by Irving Copi:

> In attempting to establish the truth of a proposition, one often casts about for acceptable premises from which the proposition in question can be deduced as conclusion. If one assumes as a premise for his argument the very conclusion he intends to prove, the fallacy committed is that of *petitio principii*, or begging the question.[5]

With respect to the existence of God and the authority of the Bible, presuppositionalists frankly admit to the use of circular reasoning in precisely this sense.

When we move to their justification of this reasoning, a more subtle fallacy emerges. The justification proffered is that objections to circular reasoning are gratuitous because "all reasoning is, in the nature of the case *circular reasoning*." According to Van Til, this universal problem of circular reasoning indicates that "the starting point, the method, and the conclusions are always involved in one another."

It is indeed true that circular reasoning, as a fallacy, is not limited to syllogistic constructions but may also be "hidden" within complex and lengthy systems so as to go undetected:

> Circular definitions are a rather obvious instance of question begging. In its full-blown maturity question begging can go on for volumes, even through whole systems of thought. As can be quessed, the mature fallacy is not easy to handle. There it is, big as the universe (in Hegel, for example), but just how it operates is hard to show in a simple instance.[6]

What Van Til is saying, however, is not that he can demonstrate examples of such hidden and complex forms of circular reasoning in all other human reasoning, but that he can show that all reasoning is circular in the sense that the "starting point, the method, and the conclusions are always involved with one another." This means that if one begins with rationality and reasons consistently, his conclusions will be of a rational sort. One never leaves the "circle" of rationality.

We grant Van Til the premise that if one begins with rationality and reasons consistently, his conclusions will be of a rational sort. But we object to calling this process "circular reasoning" on two counts. The first is that here we detect the subtle fallacy Van Til introduces, namely the fallacy of ambiguity. In responding to the charge of circular reasoning, Van Til changes the meaning of the term "circular reasoning." The circular reasoning of which he is guilty is the sort which violates the *petitio principii* principle. The sort of circular reasoning Van Til pins on all others does not constitute the same violation of logic. Even if Van Til could show that all others indulge in the same kind of circularity, all he would achieve is to show that the reasoning of everyone is as fallacious as his own.

Van Til's ambiguous treatment of circular reasoning is misleading. If our starting point and conclusion are both of a rational sort, this indicates a virtue, not a rational failing. Why use the paradigm of the circle? If we begin rationally with self-consciousness and conclude rationally with the existence of God, we do not end at our starting point. We have made progress. Our thinking has been synthetic, not merely analytical. New information appears in the conclusion which is not analytically contained in the opening. This is not circular reasoning, but linear reasoning—arriving at a destination not found in the point of departure.

"The only alternative to 'circular reasoning' as engaged in by Christians," Van Til writes,

> no matter on what point they speak, is that of reasoning on the basis of isolated facts and isolated minds, with the result that there is no possibility of reasoning at all. Unless as sinners we have an absolutely inspired Bible, we have no absolute God interpreting reality for us and unless we have an absolute God interpreting for us, there is no true interpretation at all.[7]

Here Van Til not only reasserts this principle of circular reasoning, but gives the reason for so doing. We say that circular reasoning is the end of all reasoning and Van Til not only considers it the beginning of all reasoning but he gives a *reason* for the necessity of circular reasoning. This is a circle within a circle. If Van Til can prove that circular reasoning is necessary if there is to be any reasoning at all, he has proven circular reasoning by noncircular reasoning. That is, he is assuming that there is such a thing as reasoning, that is, drawing conclusions on the basis of data. This is what is usually meant by reasoning and Van Til is here trying to show, or at least state, that unless we begin with circular reasoning we cannot move to linear reasoning. So the proof of circular reasoning would be its necessity for linear reasoning. Van Til, of course, would not want to say that. This would be the autonomous thinker beginning, once again, at an autonomous starting-point, calling for linear reasoning and finding that only if he begins with circular reasoning can he end with linear reasoning. Van Til falls back into the vernacular and insists that if we would have linear thinking, we must begin with circular thinking. The conclusion is absurd but the method of arriving at the conclusion—a traditional type of "argument"—is quite normal. Incidentally, it shows that one simply cannot live in circles and think as a rational human being. In order to justify abnormal, antitraditional, irrational patterns of thought (circles), he has to accept normal, traditional patterns of thought.

In the same context, Van Til makes this remarkable statement: "We cannot subject the authoritative pronouncements of Scripture about reality to the scrutiny of reason because it is reason itself that learns of its proper function from Scripture."[8] Reason "learns" of its proper function from Scripture. Reason, therefore, is represented as already existing and functioning. Now it reports to headquarters and gets orders as to *how* it is to function. But we note that it has already been functioning before it reports to headquarters. It has to report there to learn how it ought to function properly. One shows reason that the reasonable thing to do is to report to headquarters in order to learn to function reasonably. Is it not obvious in all of this that reason is at least functioning before it ever reports to headquarters and that it is functioning soundly enough that Van Til can say to it, "It is a reasonable thing for you to report to headquarters to find out how to function perfectly"? Reason is already functioning well enough to make a rational judgment about the need of subordinating its rationality to perfect directions from headquarters.

Van Til does not put it that way, but he is proceeding in an utterly traditional manner. It is exactly what the theist usually says. Reason can be shown by various and sundry considerations that there is a God and that He is the one who made the reason and the laws by which the reason operates. His special revelation, if He chooses to give one, would have to be the perfect standard of truth for reason. Reason would conclude that if it concluded otherwise it was not proceeding in the soundest possible, rational manner. It could then rationally correct its irrational behavior by a standard of full and perfect rationality. This is not circularity, this is linear reasoning consistently following a line of thought to the revelation of the Deity who is the proper standard, source, and inspiration for all thought once His Word is located.

Van Til sometimes prefers to call his circular reasoning "spiral." "Van Til calls this *'spiral reasoning,'*" Bahnsen says,

> because we are not reasoning about and seeking to explain facts by assuming the existence and meaning of certain other facts on the same level of being with the facts we are investigating, and then explaining these facts, in turn by the facts with which we began. We are presupposing *God,* not merely another fact of the universe. This is not circular, it is transcendental. Nor is it autonomous, seeking to establish the groundwork of knowledge by means of a scholarly investigation carried on independently of God's revealed Word. The Christian begins with an interrelated system, a revealed world view, and from *that vantage point* examines all facts, competing systems, and the transcendentals of knowledge. Therefore, we can say that Christian epistemology is revelationaly transcendental in character.[9]

Van Til calls this "spiral" rather than "circular" because God and the world are not on the same level of *being.* But they are on the same level of *knowing.* According to Van Til, to know the world one must know God and knowing God one knows the world. The argument often goes this way, as Bahnsen says, but when it goes this way it is neither circular, nor spiral, but linear. That is, we must begin with the world, and we discover it to be inexplicable apart from God. But that is the transcendental argument, and though Van Til often infers it he never apparently explicitly defends it. If he did, that would be the end, of course, of his *pre*suppositionalism. He insists on *pre*supposing God without *rational compulsion.* Then he moves to the world which can be understood, he argues, if approached presuppositionally. But he cannot *argue,* because that would be proving the *pre*supposition which cannot be proven by autonomous human reason. But the understanding of the world is assumed because the God who explains it is assumed. We cannot get off this theoretical merry-go-round. It cannot move up and down or even spirally, but only in dizzying circles.

We conclude with a glance at Van Til in historical context. Descartes, Locke, and Kant claim that epistemology is prior to philosophy. On the other hand, Spinoza, Hegel, and Whitehead attack the metaphysical problems and adopt the view of knowledge consonant with their metaphysics which, in method, is essentially what Van Til does. Others argue that a metaphysically presuppositionless epistemology is as unattainable as epistemologically presuppositionless metaphysics. This is merely semantic antithesis. Sound epistemology is presuppositional only in the sense of necessary presupposition (that is, one cannot think at all without assuming the validity of logic). Whereas presuppositionalism in Van Til and others is arbitrary (when consistent). If they deny this, they will be denying their whole approach which insists that one cannot *rationally* demonstrate presuppositions because they are necessary for rationality.

Descartes, Spinoza, and Leibniz rely *primarily* on reason as a source of genuine knowledge, whereas the empiricists Locke, Berkeley, and Hume rely *mainly* on experience. It is to be noted that Locke, for example, is not a sensationalist because he admits the use of reflection also. Kant tried to combine both methods and, in a different sense, Scottish Realism also combines both methods. The Scottish Realist, James McCosh, for example, claimed that Aristotle did the same. We would say the same thing of Aquinas and Edwards. So far as we can see, it is the only possible way of knowing in this world. If we rely on reason alone, we could not get started. If we relied on the senses alone, we could not get moving. One thinks of Kant's formally correct statement that sensations without ideas are blind and ideas without sensations are empty. He did not solve the problem in the correct way. But the problem has to be dealt with in a *generally* Kantian way in the sense of recognizing the role of both senses and reason. Presuppositionalism tends to avoid all the problems by a simple arbitrary presupposition of God.

RUSHDOONY ON CIRCULAR REASONING

"It is reason and man that depend on God, not God, His word, or His miracles, that depend on man or reason."[10] This statement is typical of Rushdoony. He is perhaps even more blunt than Van Til.

The statement quoted shows that he simply does not understand the thinkers he is criticizing. He has in mind people like Aquinas, Butler, Hodge, Warfield, and other Christian theists, as well as non-Christian thinkers, theistic and otherwise. It is hardly true of any of them, and it is utterly untrue of Christian theists such as Warfield, for example, that they suppose or imply that God *depends* on human reason. On the contrary, they agree with Rushdoony that reason and the reasoners depend on God and not God and His Word on humans and human reason. We must see the difference between approaching God by means of reason and elevating reason above God. Reason is the apprehending instrument which we have by virtue of being human. It is the only gateway to understanding and experience of the universe which is met at the outset. It is not assumed at the outset that there is or is not a God. The theist certainly does not assume that his reason is supreme and exalted above everything else simply because it is the only instrument he has with which to apprehend what surrounds him. As soon as theists, especially Christian theists such as Butler or Warfield, recognize by the use of their reason that there is a God, they immediately recognize that reason itself is of God and dependent upon God.

As soon as the reason realizes that there is a God, it immediately yields itself to that God, and honors Him as the author of itself, unless the reasoner has a vested interest in suppressing this information, as sinful people do have. We are not arguing whether this approach of Warfield and the others is successful or not. We know that Rushdoony and others do not think that it is. We believe that they are wrong. We believe that Warfield is right. But the question here is not whether the rational approach of Warfield and others can actually be defended. The question is merely this: Does the rational approach imply, by its very nature, that reason is a deity and that the deity which it claims to apprehend by the rational approach is actually inferior to that which apprehends it? No one could conceivably say honestly that people like Warfield think such a thing as that. Why does Rushdoony make such charges? In the sentence which precedes the one quoted, he explains the dreadful conclusion to which he comes: "*What depends on man and his reasonable testimony, is less than man and what depends on God is less than God.*"[11]

But who said that what reason apprehends *depends* on reason? To be apprehended it depends on reason, to be sure. If one must begin with reason to find out the nature of the universe which surrounds the rational creature then, of course, he must depend on his reason to apprehend what surrounds him. But what a vast difference between humans depending on reason as the instrument of apprehension, and representing God who is apprehended thereby as depending on humans and human reason. The difference is so obvious that it is difficult to understand Rushdoony's statement.

Commenting directly on circular reasoning, Rushdoony writes:

> All reasoning is either from God to God-given and God-inter preted fact or from man to man-made interpretation of brute factuality. All reasoning is circular, but man refuses to admit to the circularity of his reasoning because he assumes that an infinite and exhaustive view of things is possible to himself, and can, in other words, reason like God rather than as man.[12]

In the fundamental thinking of both presuppositionalism and traditional apologetics these affirmations are false. That is to say, neither the traditionalist nor the presuppositionalist, in spite of any assertions to the contrary, reasons in a circle, that is, not fundamentally. We would not deny that presuppositionalists and traditionalists both slip on occasion and may actually engage in a circular reasoning; but that is not the basic pattern of either system of thought. We are not denying that presuppositionalists proudly claim to reason in circles and think that they succeed.

Let us first consider the presuppositionalist claim to circular reasoning as Rushdoony gives it in this sentence. He claims to be circular in his reasoning because he moves from God to God-given facts. But is that, in presuppositionalist reasoning, truly circular? Why, we ask, does the presuppositionalist begin with God? Because he has *already* argued that any other starting point is impossible, and that starting with God provides a basis for true knowledge. In other words, whether his argument be good or bad, he is giving a reason for beginning with God. Now, supposing that argument to be sound, we all must begin with God, the presuppositionalist logically concludes. It follows reasonably that the facts we are talking about are fully and exhaustively understood by God alone. That would be what we would call a natural and sound, even obvious, deduction. There is nothing circular about it.

Circular reasoning would be a different matter. One would gratuitously, without reason, say that God alone *can* understand facts. Then he would proceed on the basis of that gratuitous assumption to assert that God *does* understand facts. We call such reasoning circular because one assertion depends on a mere arbitrary assertion, and the deduction from it therefore is also gratuitous because it rests on the gratuitous assumption initially made. One is making no logical progress because the consistent deduction is based on the merely gratuitous. To put the matter another way, to the question, "How do you know that God knows facts?" the answer is, "I just know it." If it is then asked, "How do you know that all facts are indeed interpreted by God?" the answer is again, "Because God by definition is omniscient and knows all facts and is the only one who does know and interprets all facts." That deduction, while sound, has no cogency because it rests on something which has no cogency. It is therefore circular, not moving ahead but around and around, getting nowhere.

But that is not the way the presuppositionalist proceeds. He is as rationalistic, if we may use that term, as any rationalist is. He begins by demonstrating, arguing, that God alone can understand the facts. Apart from Him there is no such thing as understanding the facts. Then the presuppositionalist goes on to this second statement, that God who alone does indeed know the facts must interpret them for humans if we are to know. That is not circular reasoning because the presuppositionalist already has, in his own opinion at least, demonstrated the fact that God alone can be conceived of as knowing the facts, which, it is assumed, must be "intelligible."

The question may occur to the reader why presuppositionalists think they reason in a circle when their reasoning is no more circular than any other thinker's. We suspect it is because these men are sincerely devout Christians and presuppositionalism has a pious ring to it. It creates a sort of intellectual halo. Notice for example, this statement from Rushdoony: "All reasoning is from God to God-given and God-interpreted facts." He is talking about moving from God to God. That, of course, makes it sound like a pious, circular movement. You are not getting out of the sphere of God at all. You are gratuitously assuming God. Presuppositionalists devoutly assume that the facts are God-given and God-interpreted facts. Actually, as we have noticed, the presuppositionalists do not gratuitously assume God any more than traditionalists do. They *argue* that God *must be* assumed. It is a necessary, rationally-demonstrated assumption, not an arbitrary one. The *pre*supposition, according to their own thinking, is a necessary one. The presuppositionalist is charmed by the sound of words. We, on the other hand, have the seemingly impious duty of reminding him that he gives an *argument* for his position as he unconsciously avoids circularity of reasoning.

We next consider the allegation that traditional thinking is circular. Rushdoony is again charmed by language—"from man to man-made interpretation." It sounds utterly arbitrary, even humanistic, for someone to move from man to man-made interpretations while the presuppositionalist piously moves from God to God-made interpretations. But just as truly as the presuppositionalist gives an argument for moving the way in which he does, so does the traditionalist. Whether the argument be sound or unsound is beside the point; the presence of argument ends circularity in either case.

What is the comment of the traditionalist about beginning with man? The argument is as we have been saying constantly—that man must start where man is, that is, with man. The presuppositionalist argues that we must begin with God because only by God can we understand facts. The traditionalist says that we cannot begin with God because we cannot even understand God unless we utilize the laws of logic, such as contradiction, with which we are endowed. We must begin with ourselves. There is no other place from which we can begin. This is not arbitrary, but necessary. It is not circular, but linear. One moves from a sole source of original information to information derived through that source.

JOHN FRAME ON CIRCULAR REASONING

John Frame defends circularity, especially with respect to one's approach to the Bible, by making the observation that "one may not argue for one ultimate criterion by appealing to another."[13] If the Bible is the ultimate criterion one cannot assume at the outset of the investigation that reason is the ultimate criterion. Putting the matter that way leaves no room for argument. Of course, no one should argue for an ultimate criterion by appealing to another ultimate criterion. If one assumes at the outset that he has the ultimate criterion, he is not going to be looking for another ultimate criterion. The fallacy lurking here, however, is the assumption that, by following a rational investigation, one is holding reason as the *ultimate* criterion. But the traditionalist assumes only that reason is the only *available* criterion, the *immediate* criterion. Maybe further investigation will show that it is the ultimate criterion; but one does not assume that. In fact, when he reaches the theistic conclusion (by theistic proofs apprehended by reason), the traditionalist realizes immediately that the God he thereby discovers is the ultimate source and criterion of truth. He even discovers then that it is God who gave him reason as the immediate criterion by means of which he would discover his Maker, the Ultimate Criterion.

It is true that rational observation is here made the basis for concluding that there is a God. But it is "ultimate" only in the sense that it is the *only* criterion we have. Without it we would not come to know that there is a God who is, indeed, the ultimate criterion. One can see how there could easily arise confusion at this point, but it is not easy to see why constant repetition of this by Frame and others never yields the simple observation that reason is not considered the ultimate criterion simply because it is the only criterion at the beginning. It is provisionally ultimate if one wants to put it that way. It might prove to be ultimate, as indeed the rationalists (incorrectly) do think. But its being used as the only criterion for a time certainly does not mean it is the ultimate criterion for all time. For those who become theists, it most certainly is not.

We might liken the situation to a telephone and the telephone company. One may use a phone to contact the telephone company and thus confirm the existence of something more "ultimate" that makes possible the working of the telephone. But whether or not one contacts the telephone company, the telephone continues to be a useful tool.

Frame assumes that because God is indeed the ultimate criterion, we cannot assume that reason is the ultimate criterion (which he wrongly thinks the traditionalists assume). We must rather *begin* with the ultimate criterion if we are ever going to *arrive* at the ultimate criterion. But what meaning is there in talking about arriving at something with which you begin? One must simply say that this is the ultimate criterion and add no reasons for so thinking. Any reason would be fatal in Frame's pattern of thought because that would mean that reason had become the "ultimate" criterion, implicitly superseding God as the ultimate criterion. Therefore, Frame argues, one must assume outright, without any reasons whatever, that the Bible is the ultimate criterion. But what kind of reasoning is it that assumes without any evidence whatever that something is something? This is not even circular reasoning, inasmuch as one does not move at all—not even in a circle. Frame simply stands on the ground of the Bible and says it is the Word of God and dares not give any reason for it whatever. If he did, he would fall afoul of his own indictment of those who seek an ultimate criterion with another ultimate criterion.

Having shown the futility of such an enterprise as Frame would embark upon, let us now notice the enterprise itself. It is really much more sober than the hypothetical analysis we have given. We are not surprised at that because Frame is a sensible person who does not go around making silly remarks. And it is obviously silly to say that one simply accepts an ultimate criterion without any reason whatsoever. But on the surface, this is what must be done within Frame's and Van Til's method. But rationality will out.

Frame says that we should not urge non-Christians to accept the Bible because the Bible says so, since that would be somewhat misleading. Rather, he says something very traditional: "A non-Christian must start from where he is."[14] He then goes on to suggest that perhaps the nonbeliever thinks the Bible is historically reliable and he can start at that particular point to read the Bible. Then, says Frame, he will be confronted with the claims of Scripture about God, about Christ, about humans, about itself. He will compare the biblical way of looking at things with his own way. And, if God wills, he will see the wisdom of looking at things Scripture's way.

Notice that this non-Christian has some reason for reading the Bible, namely, the notion that it is an important source of Christian information. Frame is careful not to make an argument out of that, of course. But at the same time, it cannot be overlooked that there is something less than an absolutely arbitrary acceptance of the Bible without any reason. A person at least has this much reason for reading the Bible, that it is a source of Christian information. More significantly, Frame adds that, "if God wills," this non-Christian will "see wisdom" in looking at things the biblical way. "See wisdom." That is the equivalent of some sort of theistic proof. When the traditionalist examines the evidence in the light of reason, he is looking for the wisdom or the rationality of the matter. The presuppositionalist is saying, in other words, that the non-Christian will be enabled to see reasons for faith in the biblical revelation. John Frame will be tempted to say, "Yes, but the reasons come after the faith, rather than before the faith." There is faith in reasons, not reasons for faith. The non-Christian, if God wills, sees the *wisdom* of looking at things the biblical way. He does not first view things in the biblical way in the sense of arbitrarily accepting its divine authority, and *then* see the wisdom of it. He sees the wisdom of the biblical view and he then very wisely, very rationally, accepts the biblical way of looking at things.

Frame also says that *only if God wills* does this non-Christian come to see the wisdom of looking at things the biblical way. Presumably, if God does not so will, the nonbeliever will never see the wisdom of looking at things the biblical way. Apparently, apart from special illumination of the special revelation, he will never see the wisdom of the biblical way. This is a flat contradiction of the whole thrust of the Vantillian and Framian apologetic. The argument which we have seen repeatedly is that the non-Christian will see, when it is pointed out to him by the presuppositional apologetic, that he cannot even predicate and that if he does indeed accept the biblical way of looking at things, then and only then, will he be able to predicate. Presumably, the non-Christian can be shown this and can see this even though God does not will that he acquiesce in this biblical way. This is a continuing fault in the Vantillian school. The adherents do not elucidate the matter so as to distinguish between a rational recognition of the soundness of biblical principles and the spiritual acquiescence in them. According to traditional apologetics, a non-Christian who is not illumined according to the divine will, can nevertheless understand the wisdom of looking at things the biblical way.

CLARK AND CIRCULAR REASONING

Characteristically, Gordon Clark begins by saying that the word *heart,* which appears 875 times in the Old Testament, refers to the total personality. The heart includes the head. He will not allow for a contrast between head and heart. The contrast is between heart and lips, between thought and expression.

Clark critiques the common distinction between the intellectual element and the volitional element. One *knows* that the chair will hold his weight, he says, only by *choosing* to sit on it. You cannot choose to do something without knowing it in the first place. Neither can you know something or give intellectual assent to it without choosing to act accordingly. "It can be no intellection without volition."[15] Intellectual assent is of itself an act of the will. It is predictable, therefore, that Clark will deny that one can know who Christ is while his will is negative toward Him.

Commenting on the epistle of James, Clark writes: "James does say some intellectual belief is inadequate, to show that some is fruitless, or to show that some is condemnatory, not that true faith is not intellectual.[16] Clark deals with the matter without adequately considering the inseparability of thought and volition. What the devils know is that God is their enemy and they act accordingly—they tremble. Clark tries to show, in other words, that the devils' behavior is *not inconsistent* with what he is saying, though he could actually show that it *is consistent* with what he says, at least as far as he articulates it. As the thought, so goes the choice. Abraham believes God is his friend and so loves and obeys. Satan believes God is his enemy and so hates and trembles.

Further into this same commentary, Clark actually retreats from the primacy of intellect and truth which he means to champion: "The primacy of truth will mean that our voluntary actions ought to conform. Obviously sometimes they do not . . . but the primacy of truth means that we ought to believe the truth and we ought not to believe the lie."[17] Earlier failure to claim the James 2 passage in support of it revealed that Clark was really not fully committed to his own view.

When he says that voluntary responses "sometimes do not" follow the truth before the mind, Clark demonstrates that he does not follow the primacy of truth principle all the way. He believes that truth *ought to be* primary, or *generally* is primary, but not that it *always* is primary. The very illustrations which he cites to prove the exception, prove the rule. The devils, no less than Abraham, follow the primacy of intellect principle. Both chose to act according to their understanding of what is "good" or desirable. Abraham has a regenerate taste and the devils a depraved one; but each acts according to what tastes good or seems good or what his mind judges to be good. This is the inalienable nature of rational beings: be they God, good angels or bad, good men or bad. They choose according to the "last dictate of their (practical) understanding." God's choice is by nature inflexibly virtuous; good angels and just men made perfect are by divine grace made inflexibly virtuous; bad angels and depraved men, not given divine grace, are inflexibly sinful. But all choose according to the last dictate of their mind. That is the universal principle of the primacy of the intellect. It admits of no exceptions.

Consequently, Gordon Clark, though in many ways presuppositionalism's most formidable foe, becomes an unconscious advocate. Abandoning the primacy of intellect principle, the anti-intellectual invades his thought and the door is open to presuppositionalism, a form of the anti-intellectualism which the primacy of the intellect disavows.

Van Til and Clark had a famous debate in which the latter appeared as the champion of rationality. In this debate that was true. But we will show that ultimately Clark was as circular in his reasoning as was Van Til.

Van Til has written that Clark understands the incomprehensibility of God in the Romanist or Arminian way, not in accord with the Reformed view.[18] Opponents of Clark charged him with teaching that Van Til's view that "man can grasp only an analogy of the truth itself" is "pure skepticism."[19]

According to Van Til, the Reformed view of the incomprehensibility of God is this: (1) The essence of God's being is incomprehensible to humans except as God reveals truths concerning His own nature. (2) The manner of God's knowing, an eternal intuition, is impossible for humans. (3) Humans can never know exhaustively and completely God's knowledge of any truth in all its relationships and implications, and since each of these implications in turn has other infinite implications, these must ever, even in heaven, remain inexhaustible for us. Van Til also recognizes that the doctrine of the incomprehensibility of God, as held by Clark, does not mean that a proposition, for example, two times two are four, has one meaning for humans and a qualitatively different meaning for God, or that some truth is conceptual and other truth is nonconceptual in nature.[20]

Van Til then insists that no one can know anything about God except through revelation. But Clark thinks one can know by reason. Clark also makes various claims the revelation system being penetrable by logic, logic that is able to choose among "revelations." Van Til's point here is that if anything can be said about the nature of God apart from revelation, everything can be said. There would be no need for revelation at all.

Whatever faults Clark's own system of thought may have, at the points where it differs from Van Til it seems quite sound. Van Til thinks that if we can know anything apart from revelation we could know everything and no revelation would be necessary. But why would that follow? Suppose, for the sake of argument, that God and humans both know the meaning of two times two. Would that say anything about whether God could or would, save or damn, this arithmetically-minded sinner? Traditional apologists have always maintained that sinners know far more than the value of two times two, yet whether God would save or damn would have to be supernaturally revealed.

Second, Clark seems quite sound in challenging the paradoxicalness of many things Van Til so labels. Specifically, what indeed is the genuine paradox between divine sovereignty and human choices? Most people assume, as Van Til does, that these two concepts are mutually exclusive. But when Clark challenges that commonplace, no refutation is forthcoming. These are not contradictory propositions, though, even if they were shown to be so, Van Til himself would still insist that that is only an appearance of contradiction. He denies that there ever is *real* contradiction. Clark is virtually challenging Van Til on Van Til's own ground that contradictions are never real.

Third, Van Til's own system seems to allow what Clark claims: that the human mind can distinguish and discriminate between rival revelation claims. Van Til is repeatedly arguing that apart from biblical revelation we cannot predicate, whereas, on that presupposition, we can. Is this not a penetrating discrimination of what humans, apart from revelation as a truth-presupposition, are capable of, in both Van Til's and Clark's opinion?

Before we conclude this section we must pitch Clark against Clark. He makes so many telling criticisms of Van Til that it is surprising to find him ultimately fideistic himself. Clark reasons this way: first, traditional arguments for God, though not intrinsically invalid, cannot carry the freight of proof. Second, the Humean and Kantian criticisms against the theistic proofs of causality seem essentially sound. Third, if the Holy Spirit is the author of Scripture, there are no criteria by which such a fact could be proven. So Clark's whole case for Christianity is based on the unsubstantiated claim that the Spirit of God is the author of Scripture.

That is almost fideistic. Why "almost?" Because, in spite of himself, Clark gives a reason for accepting without reason the inspiration of the Bible. There are no criteria above God, so when God says He speaks, the words that He speaks must be accepted without any tests. That sounds fideistic and Clark undoubtedly wants it to sound so, though he probably would not like to be called fideistic.

Clark really is not fideistic because he gives a reason for proceeding fideistically. Rational fideism is a contradiction in terms. But Clark does give a reason for fideism, namely, that when God says He is speaking, one cannot impose tests of His "truth-claims." How does Clark know that God is speaking? Must there not be criteria for that claim? A true fideist will say, "No, it must simply be accepted." But then even this pure fideist is caught in his own rational toils. What he is *arguing* is that the very claim to be God speaking is proof that He is speaking. We all agree that if God is speaking, His Word must be accepted *because He is God* who by very definition, is Truth. But the Clark type of fideist is inferring that we must accept a *claim* to be God speaking because, in the case of God speaking, the claim is the proof and the only proof is the claim. We contend that this is absurd, but what we are here noting is that it is a "rational" absurdity. It is an *absurd* argument, but it is an absurd *argument*. It is not pure fideism, which would simply say, "I accept this claimed Word of God as the Word of God." The absurdity of that need not be pointed out. What needs pointing out is that *that* is the only consistent fideism. By shying away and finding a criterion for believing, Clark is not truly fideistic, though he sounds that way and insists that there can be no criterion by which to test the inspiration of Scripture.

If Clark cannot hold to this most radical form of "presupposi-tionalism" no one can. And Clark cannot hold to it. Therefore, if our premises are demonstratively sound, our conclusion is indisputable: No one can reasonably be a presuppositionalist.

In closing, we will advert to Carl F. H. Henry to show that circular reasoning leads even the most rational apologists into anti-intellectualism and fideism. Henry objects to presuppositionalist theology because, he says, it "exaggerates the noetic consequences of the fall of man."[21] That is true, though an understatement. He admits (though not in his magnum opus[22]) that some statements of presuppositionalism do exaggerate the noetic influence of sin. It is true that there is a difference of *degree* between Van Til's and Clark's and Henry's presuppositionalism. Clark and Henry have always been much more appreciative of the role of reason in the unregenerate. Nevertheless, we said it before and we say it now (after reading Henry's *God, Revelation and Authority*) that Henry's (and, even more obviously, Clark's) apologetic reduces to fideism.

We can understand why Henry does not see his fideism—he puts such great emphasis on the role of reason that he does not see that there is anything important that he does *not* grant.

But there is one important thing he does not grant: the *indispens-able* role of reason. Notice the six items which he lists in the two chapters where he discusses "The Method and Criteria of Theology":

(1) divine revelation is the source of all truth, the truth of Christianity included;

(2) reason is the instrument for recognizing it;

(3) Scripture is its verifying principle;

(4) logical consistency is a negative test for truth and

(5) coherence a subordinate test;

(6) the task of Christian theology is to exhibit the content of Biblical revelation as an orderly whole.[23]

Reason is the "instrument" which recognizes, organizes, and elucidates. But reason does not *verify* revelation; and revelation is the source of *all* truth and its *own* "verifying principle." As an instrument, reason must simply acquiesce in the Bible's claim to be the revelation of God. The Bible is the *axiom* by which reason itself will ultimately be tested. Reason has no independent role. Even the honoring of the indispensability of the law of contradiction is not maintained where *"revelation is the source of all truth."* Clark is inconsistent here and blatant about it. Henry is inconsistent here but not so blatant.

In this chapter, we began with circular reasoning, endemic to all presuppositionalism though stressed more in some forms than others. We have tried to show that instead of being a "glorious circle" it leads inevitably to anti-intellectualism and ultimate fideism even in the most "rational" presuppositionalists.

The Emperor of the Land of Presuppositionalism where Van Til, Frame, Clark, Henry, and others live, has no clothes. Van Til is embarrassed. Frame is more embarrassed and is always trying to pin something on the Emperor's bare skin. Clark does not blush so easily, and Henry doesn't notice the nakedness. Classical apologetics, with its horror of circularity, is the little child who embarrasses everybody by pointing out the obvious.

Notes

CHAPTER 1

[1]Harvey Cox, *The Secular City* (New York: MacMillan, 1965), 18–21.

[2]Alexander P. D. Mourelatos, ed., *The Pre-Socratics* (Garden City: Anchor Press/Doubleday, 1974), 67.

CHAPTER 2

[1]Henry Dodwell, Jr., *Christianity Not Founded on Argument and the True Principle of Gospel Evidence Designed: In a Letter to A Young Gentleman at Oxford*, 3rd ed. (printed for M. Cooper, 1743), 160–65. The book had to be published anonymously.

[2]Dodwell's work antagonized both Christianity and Deism and was the first great strike toward skepticism. For an excellent summary, see John Orr, *English Deism, Its Roots and Its Fruits* (Grand Rapids: Eerdmans, 1934).

[3]Alan Richardson, *Christian Apologetics* (London: SCM, 1947).

[4]Karl Barth, *The Doctrine of the Word of God*, vol. 1, part 1, trans. G. T. T. Thomson (Edinburgh: T. & T. Clark, 1960), 18.

[5]William Barrett, *Irrational Man: A Study in Existential Philosophy* (Garden City: Doubleday, 1958).

[6]H. L. Stewart, "The Reverent Agnosticism of Karl Barth," *Harvard Theological Review*, no. 3 (July 1950): 215–32.

[7]Ibid. Stewart concluded "that the reverent agnosticism inculcated by Karl Barth may in others remain agnosticism while losing its reverence" (p. 232).

[8]Reinhold Niebuhr, *Nature and Destiny of Man*, 2 vols. (New York: Scribner, 1941–43), 2:86.

[9]This is evident throughout Kierkegaard's works, but see especially *Concluding Unscientific Postscript*, trans. David F. Swenson (Princeton: Princeton University Press, 1944).

[10]Emil Brunner, *Revelation and Reason*, trans. Olive Wyon (Philadelphia: Westminster, 1946), 166.

[11] C. I. Lewis, *Mind and World Order* (New York: Scribner, 1929), 306.

¹²Herbert Braun, *Jesus of Nazareth,* trans. E. R. Kalin (Philadelphia: Fortress, 1979), 2.

¹³Ibid.

¹⁴See Norman Perrin, *What is Redaction Criticism?* (Philadelphia: Fortress, 1974), vii–viii.

¹⁵John Locke, *The Reasonableness of Christianity,* ed. I. T. Ramsey (Stanford: Stanford University Press, 1958), 2.

¹⁶See *The Many-Faced Argument,* ed. John Hick and Arthur C. McGill (New York: MacMillan, 1967).

¹⁷Cf. Paul Tillich, *My Search for Absolutes* (New York: Simon and Shuster, 1967); also: Robert Ross, *The Non-Existence of God* (New York: Edwin Mellen, 1978); Leonard Wheat, *Paul Tillich's Dialectical Humanism* (Baltimore: Johns Hopkins University Press, 1970).

¹⁸Georg Bertram, ἔργον, in *Theological Dictionary of the New Testament,* ed. Gerhard Kittel, trans. G. W. Bromiley (Grand Rapids: Eerdmans, 1964), 2:635–54.

¹⁹*A Greek-English Lexicon of the New Testament,* 4th ed. (Chicago: University of Chicago Press, 1952), 307.

²⁰Ibid.

²¹J. K. S. Reid, *Christian Apologetics* (Grand Rapids: Eerdmans, 1969), 17.

CHAPTER 3

¹G. C. Berkouwer, *A Half Century of Theology: Movements and Motives,* ed. and trans. Lewis B. Smedes (Grand Rapids: Eerdmans, 1977), 35.

²Hans Küng, *Does God Exist? An Answer for Today,* trans. Edward Quinn (New York: Random House, 1981), 24–25.

³Ibid., 512.

⁴A. M. Fairweather, ed., *Nature and Grace: Selections from the Summa Theologica of Thomas Aquinas, Library of Christian Classics* (Philadelphia: Westminster, 1954), 11:137–39.

⁵Quoted in Etienne Gilson, *Reason and Revelation in the Middle Ages* (New York: Scribner, 1938), 10.

⁶Frederick Copleston, *A History of Philosophy: Vol. 3, Late Medieval and Renaissance Philosophy,* Part I, *Ockham to the Speculative Mystics* (Garden City: Doubleday, 1963), 23.

⁷Ibid., 24.

⁸In *Nothing is Known* (1581), Sanche attacked Aristotle as an enemy of the Christian faith.

⁹James Collins, *God in Modern Philosophy* (Chicago: Regnery, 1959), 40.

¹⁰Ibid., 41.

¹¹Ibid., 42.

¹²Ibid., 46.

¹³See Immanuel Kant, *Critique of Pure Reason,* trans. F. Max Miller, Anchor edition (New York: MacMillan, 1966), 410–18.

¹⁴See Jaroslav Pelikan, *From Luther to Kierkegaard* (St. Louis: Concordia, 1950).

¹⁵Roger Scruton, *From Descartes to Wittgenstein: A Short History of Modern Philosophy* (San Francisco: Harper and Row, 1982), 167.

[16]John B. Cobb, Jr., *Living Options in Protestant Theology: A Survey of Methods* (Philadelphia: Westminster, 1962), 31. Cobb notes, "Hegelian philosophy of religion as such cannot be understood as a natural theology, since it sought to supercede theology rather than to provide it a basis" (p. 29).

[17]Hugh Ross Macintosh, *Types of Modern Theology: Schleiermacher to Barth* (New York: Scribners, 1937), 152.

[18]See G. C. Berkouwer's discussion of this in *De Algemene Openbaring: Dogmatische Studien* (Kampen: Kok, 1951), 27–37. Berkouwer cites Paul Althaus's evaluation of Barth's treatment of Romans 1 and 2, calling Barth's exegesis an "act of pure despair" (*reiner Verzweiflungsakt*) (p. 37).

[19]Barth never rescinded his famous No, but he did temper it by sending Brunner a kindly note while Brunner was on his deathbed. The note was carried by Brunner's pastor Peter Vogelsanger: "If he is still alive and it is possible, tell him I commend him to *our* God. And tell him the time when I thought I should say No to him is long since past, and we all live only by the fact that a great and merciful God speaks his gracious Yes to all of us." Karl Barth, *Letters: 1961–1968*, ed. Jurgen Fangmeir and Hinrich Stoevesandt, trans. Geoffrey W. Bromiley (Grand Rapids: Eerdmans, 1981), 202.

[20]Karl Barth, *Epistle to the Romans*, 6th ed., trans. Edwyn C. Hoskyns (London: Oxford University Press, 1933), 38–39. Dr. John Gerstner relates an anecdote told in class by his former professor Julius Seelye Bixler. Bixler, seeing a book entitled *The Reasonableness of Christianity* on Barth's desk, asked Barth what he thought of the book. Barth replied, "It is no good." Barth admitted that he had not read the book but said, "I read the first sentence in which the author says that he is going to show the reasonableness of Christianity. From that I know the book could not be any good."

[21]G. C. Berkouwer, *A Half Century of Theology*, 164, citing Pannenberg.

[22]Clyde L. Manschreck, *A History of Christianity*, 2 vols. (Grand Rapids: Baker, 1964), 2:220.

[23]Ibid., 225.

[24]Ibid.

[25]Aquinas, in *Nature and Grace*, ed. A. M. Fairweather, 53.

[26]Cornelius Van Til, *The Defense of the Faith* (Philadelphia: Presbyterian and Reformed, 1955), 262.

[27]Ibid., 264.

[28]Ibid., 265.

CHAPTER 4

[1]See R. C. Sproul *If There Is a God, Why Are There Atheists?* (Minneapolis: Bethany, 1974).

[2]John Murray, *The Epistle to the Romans*, The New International Commentary on the New Testament, 2 vols. (Grand Rapids: Eerdmans, 1959), 1:36.

[3]Werner Foerster, "ἀσεβής," in *Theological Dictionary of the New Testament*, ed. Gerhard Kittel and Gerhard Friedrich, trans. Geoffrey W. Bromiley (Grand Rapids: Eerdmans, 1971), 8:190.

[4]J. H. Bavinck, *The Church Between Temple and Mosque* (Grand Rapids: Eerdmans, n.d.), 118–19.

[5]Some confusion may exist about the use of the term "immediate" here. When the word immediate is used in ordinary language it usually has reference to time. We think

of things happening immediately, meaning there is little or no time gap between them. When theologians use the term immediate with respect to general revelation, however, they are not speaking in terms of time but in terms of medium.

[6]G. C. Berkouwer, *De Algemene Openbaring: Dogmatische Studien* (Kampen: Kok, 1951), 50.

[7]Ibid.

[8]Ibid.

[9]See John Calvin, *Institutes of the Christian Religion,* trans. Henry Beveridge (Grand Rapids: Eerdmans, 1964), and *Calvin's Commentaries: The Epistles of Paul the Apostle to the Romans and to the Thessalonians,* trans. Ross MacKenzie (Grand Rapids: Eerdmans, 1960).

[10]H. C. G. Moule, *The Epistle to the Romans* (London: Pickering and Inglis, n.d.), 44.

[11]C. K. Barrett, *A Commentary on the Epistle to the Romans* (New York: Harper and Row, 1957), 35.

[12]Murray, *Epistle to the Romans,* 38–39.

[13]Charles Hodge, *The Epistle to the Romans* (London: Banner of Truth, 1972), 37.

[14]John Calvin, *Institutes of the Christian Religion* 1.5.8.

[15]Bavinck, *The Church Between Temple and Mosque,* passim.

[16]Berkouwer, *De Algemene Openbaring,* 121.

[17]Ibid., 123.

[18]Ibid.

[19]Rudolf Bultmann, "γινώσκω," in *Theological Dictionary of the New Testament* 1:689–714.

[20]George Bertram, "μωρός," in *Theological Dictionary of the New Testament* 4:832.

[21]Murray, *The Epistle to the Romans,* 1:41.

[22]Mircea Eliade, *The Sacred and Profane,* trans. William R. Trask (New York: Harper and Row, 1957), 122–23.

[23]Ibid.

[24]Karl Barth, *The Epistle to the Romans,* 6th ed., trans. Edwyn C. Hoskyns (London: Oxford University Press, 1933), 51.

[25]Wilhelm Pauck, ed., *Luther: Lectures on Romans,* vol. 15, *The Library of Christian Classics,* ed. John Baille, John T. McNeil, and Henry P. Van Ausen (Philadelphia: Westminster, 1961), 33.

[26]See Yehezkel Kaufmann, *The Religion of Israel,* trans. Moshe Greenberg (Chicago: Chicago University Press, 1960). See also Leviticus 18:22–30; 20:13.

[27]This theme of moral consciousness is more fully developed by the Apostle in Romans 2.

[28]Murray, *The Epistle to the Romans,* 1:53.

[29]*Webster's New Collegiate Dictionary,* 8th ed., s.v. "trauma."

[30]John Calvin, *Istitutes,* 1.1.2.

[31]Bavinck, *The Church Between Temple and Mosque,* 121.

[32]Ibid., 122.

[33]Ibid.

[34]Helmut Gollwitzer, *The Existence of God as Confessed by Faith,* trans. James W. Leitch (Philadelphia: Westminster, 1965), 89–90.

[35]Baruch Spinoza, *The Philosophy of Spinoza* (New York: Carlton, 1927), 25.

CHAPTER 5

[1]*Creative Minds in Contemporary Theology,* ed. Philip Edgcumbe Hughes (Grand Rapids: Eerdmans, 1966), 9.

[2]*Claude Debussy: His Greatest Piano Solos, A Comprehensive Collection of His World Famous Works,* comp. Alexander Shealy (Carlstadt, N.J.: Copa, 1971), 3.

[3]See the comparative systems and innovations in logic proffered by men like De Morgan, Boole, Carnap, Schroder, Pierce, Russell, and Whitehead in Hans Reichenbach, *Elements of Symbolic Logic* (New York: The Free Press, 1947), passim, especially v–ix, 38, 137–138. Cf. David Mitchell, *An Introduction to Logic* (Garden City: Anchor, 1970), 40, and Julius R. Weinberg and Keith E. Yandell, *Theory of Knowledge: Problems in Philosophical Inquiry* (New York: Holt, Rinehart and Winston, 1971), 1:52–54.

[4]*The Altizer-Montgomery Dialogue* (Chicago: InterVarsity, 1967), 21.

[5]*Aristotle Selections,* ed. W. D. Ross (New York: Scribner, 1927), 56.

[6]Ronald H. Nash, *The Word of God and the Mind of Man* (Grand Rapids: Zondervan, 1982), 105.

[7]Gordon H. Clark, *Language and Theology* (Phillipsburg, N.J.: Presbyterian and Reformed, 1980), 12–24.

[8]Helmut Gollwitzer, *The Existence of God as Confessed by Faith,* trans. James W. Leitch (Philadelphia: Westminster, 1965), 47.

[9]Nash, 95.

[10]Ibid., 99.

[11]*The Philosophy of Gordon H. Clark,* ed. Ronald H. Nash (Philadelphia: Presbyterian and Reformed, 1968), 67.

[12]Ibid.

[13]Ibid.

[14]Gerhard von Rad and Gerhard Kittel, "δοκέιν," in *Theological Dictionary of the New Testament,* ed. Gerhard Kittel, trans. G. W. Bromiley (Grand Rapids: Eerdmans, 1964), 2:232–33. The root of this word was used in the early church to designate the heretical position of Docetism, the notion that Jesus only "appeared" or "seemed" to have a physical body, denying the reality of incarnation.

[15]*Webster's New Twentieth Century Dictionary,* 2d ed., s.v., "paradox."

[16]From a private conversation with Gordon Clark.

[17]See Paul's use of "mystery" in Colossians 1:25–27.

[18]See G. Bornkamm, "μυστήριον," in *Theological Dictionary of the New Testament* 4:817–27.

[19]Francis A. Schaeffer, *The God Who is There* (Chicago: InterVarsity, 1968), 73.

[20]Nash, *The Philosophy of Gordon H. Clark,* 70.

[21]Emil Brunner, *The Divine-Human Encounter,* trans. Amandus W. Loos (Philadelphia: Westminster, 1943), 173–74.

[22]David Hume, *An Enquiry Concerning Human Understanding,* in *The Empiricists,* ed. Richard Taylor (Garden City: Anchor, 1974), 349–64.

[23]*Philosophy: A Contemporary Perspective,* ed. Robert Hoffman and Sidney Gendin (Belmont, Calif.: Wadsworth, 1975), 83.

[24]We agree with the summary of causality offered by Charles Hodge who followed the thought of the Scottish Realists Thomas Reid and James McCosh "(1) A cause is something. It has a real existence. It is not merely a name for a certain relation. It is a

real entity, a substance. This is plain because a non-entity cannot act. If that which does not exist can be a cause, then nothing can produce something, which is a contradiction. (2) A cause must not only be something real, but it must have power or efficiency. There must be something in nature to account for the effects which it produces. (3) This efficiency must be adequate; that is, sufficient and appropriate to the effect. (4) All men assume that every effect has an antecedent to whose efficiency it is due. They never regard mere antecedence, however uniform in the past, or however certain in the future, as constituting a causal relation. The succession of the seasons has been uniform in the past . . . yet no man says that winter is the cause of summer. Every one is conscious that cause expresses an entirely different relation from that of mere antecedence. . . . The belief is not that one thing must always go before another thing; but that nothing can occur, that no change can be produced, without the exercise of power or efficiency somewhere; otherwise, something could come out of nothing." Charles Hodge, *Systematic Theology* (Grand Rapids: Eerdmans, n.d.), 1:209.

[25]Irving M. Copi, *Introduction to Logic,* 4th ed. (New York: MacMillan, 1972), 82.

[26]Ibid., 369–70.

[27]γάρ is defined as a conjunction used to express cause, inference, continuation, or to explain. See Arndt and Gingrich, *A Greek-English Lexicon of the New Testament.*

[28]Karl Heinrich Renzstorf, "σημεῖον," in *Theological Dictionary of the New Testament,* 7:200–261.

[29]Ibid.

[30]Walter Kaufmann, *Philosophic Classics: Thales to St. Thomas* (Englewood Cliffs, N.J.: Prentice Hall, 1963), 1:128–31.

CHAPTER 6

[1]G. C. Berkouwer, *De Persoon van Christus: Dogmatische Studien* (Kampen: Kok, 1952), 242.

[2]G. C. Berkouwer, *De Sacramenten: Dogmatische Studien* (Kampen: Kok, 1954), 297.

[3]*Cassell's New Latin Dictionary,* ed. D. P. Simpson (New York: Funk & Wagnalls, 1959).

[4]Heinrich Heppe, *Reformed Dogmatics,* ed. Ernst Bizer, trans. G. T. Thomson (Grand Rapids: Baker, 1978), 52.

[5]Seward D. Morris in his *Theology of the Westminster Schools* (Columbus: Champlin, 1900) was surprised that the compilers of the Westminster Confession of Faith did not appeal more to miracles and Christ in support of the inspiration of the Scripture. We are too. On the other hand, it should be noted that all that they did appeal to which did "abundantly evidence" the Bible to be the "Word of God" was essentially miraculous. "We may be moved and induced by the testimony of the Church to an high and reverent esteem of the Holy Scripture, and the heavenliness of the matter, the efficacy of the doctrine, the majesty of the style, the consent of all the parts, the scope of the whole (which is to give all glory to God), the full discovery it makes of the only way of man's salvation, the many other incomparable excellencies, and the entire perfection thereof."

[6]Jaroslav Pelikan, *From Luther to Kierkegaard* (St. Louis: Concordia, 1963), 98.

[7]Heinrich Ott, *God.* trans. Iain and Ute Nicol (Richmond: John Knox, 1974), 33.

[8]Jurgen Moltmann, *The Crucified Knowable God,* trans. R. W. Wilson and J. Bowden (New York: Harper & Row, 1974), passim.

[9]Karl Rahner, *Theological Investigations* (Baltimore: Silicon, 1966), 4:113.

[10]Ibid.

[11]H. P. Owen, *The Christian Knowledge of God* (London: Athaline, 1969), vi.

[12]*St. Anselm: Proslogium; Monologium; An Appendix in Behalf of the Fool by Gaunilon; and Cur Deus Homo,* trans. Sidney Norton Deane (LaSalle, Ill.: Open Court, 1959).

[13]Immanuel Kant, *Critique of Pure Reason,* trans. F. Max Muller (Garden City: Doubleday, 1966), 399.

[14]Malcolm Diamond, *Contemporary Philosophy and Religious Thought: An Introduction to the Philosophy of Religion* (New York: McGraw Hill, 1974), 268. Here Diamond cites Norman Malcolm's defense of Anselm, adding the charge of "glaring contradiction" to the skeptic.

[15]Normal Malcolm, "Malcolm's Statement of Anselm's Ontological Argument" in *The Ontological Argument: From St. Anselm to Contemporary Philosophers,* ed. Alvin Plantinga (Garden City: Anchor, 1965), 155–56.

[16]Rene Descartes, *Discourse on Method and Mediations,* trans. Laurence J. Lafluer (New York: Bobbs-Merrill, 1960), 99.

[17]Ibid., 102.

[18]Ibid., 122.

[19]Ibid., 123.

[20]*The Ontological Argument,* ed. Plantinga, 146.

[21]Ibid., 171.

[22]Jonathan Edwards, *Freedom of the Will,* ed. Paul Ramsey (New Haven: Yale University Press, 1957), 186.

[23]W. G. T. Shedd, *Dogmatic Theology* (New York: Scribner, 1888–94), 1–224.

[24]Ibid., 224.

[25]Ibid.

[26]Ibid., 226.

[27]Ibid., 227.

[28]Ibid.

[29]Ibid.

CHAPTER 7

[1]Jonathan Edwards, *Freedom of the Will,* ed. Paul Ramsey (New Haven: Yale University Press, 1959), 180–81.

[2]James Collins, *God in Modern Philosophy* (Chicago: Regnery, 1959), 153.

[3]*A Modern Introduction to Philosophy,* ed. Paul Edwards and Arthur Pap (New York: Free Press, 1957), 478.

[4]Ibid., 479–80.

[5]William L. Rowe, *The Cosmological Argument* (Princeton: Princeton University Press, 1975), 268.

[6]Ibid.

[7]Immanuel Kant, *Critique of Pure Reason,* trans. F. Max Muller (Garden City: Doubleday, 1966), 414–15.

[8]Ibid., 416.

[9]John Warwick Montgomery, *The Shape of the Past* (Ann Arbor: Edward, 1962), 140.

[10]Clark H. Pinnock, *Set Forth Your Case: Studies in Christian Apologetics* (Nutley, N.J.: Craig, 1968), 41.

[11]Montgomery, *The Shape of the Past*, 140.

[12]Kant, *Critique of Pure Reason*.

[13]In *The Cosmological Argument*, ed. Donald Burrill (Garden City: Doubleday, 1967), 199–207.

CHAPTER 8

[1]John Calvin, *Institutes*, 1.8.2.

[2]Ibid., 1.10.9.

[3]Westminster Confession of Faith, 1.5.

[4]James Martin, *The Reliability of the Gospels* (London: Hodder and Stoughton, 1959).

[5]F. F. Bruce, *The New Testament Documents: Are They Reliable?* (Chicago: Inter-Varsity, 1960).

[6]F. F. Bruce, *The Defense of the Gospel in the New Testament* (Grand Rapids: Eerdmans, 1959).

[7]Ernst Kasemann, *New Testament Questions of Today* (Philadelphia: Fortress, 1969), 49.

[8]Joachim Jeremias, *New Testament Theology: The Proclamation of Jesus,* trans. John Bowden (New York: Scribner, 1971), 3f.

[9]W. F. Albright and C. S. Mann, *Matthew: Introduction, Translation, and Notes* (Garden City: Doubleday, 1971), v–vi.

[10]In a lecture delivered at De Paul University in 1969.

[11]Ibid.

[12]Ibid.

[13]Ibid.

[14]Lessing expresses this idea throughout his writings, but see especially "The Education of the Human Race" (1780); "G. E. Lessing" in J. M. Creed and J. S. Boys Smith, *Religious Thought in the Eighteenth Century* (Cambridge: Cambridge University Press, 1934).

[15]Albert Schweitzer, *The Quest of the Historical Jesus*, 3rd ed. (London: Adam and Charles Black, 1954).

[16]Ibid., 345.

[17]S. V. McCasland, *By the Finger of God* (New York: MacMillan, 1951), 222–26.

[18]This is a record of John Gerstner's personal experience under Pfeiffer.

[19]David Hume, *Inquiry Concerning Human Understanding*, Selby-Bigge edition (Oxford: Oxford University Press, 1975), 116.

[20]J. C. A. Gaskin, *Hume's Philosophy of Religion* (New York: Barnes & Noble, 1978), 122. Gaskin appropriately remarks in this *Of Miracles* citation that this is "an incipient mistake. The word 'unalterable,' although possibly justifiable on some account of the laws of nature, is not justifiable on Hume's."

[21]C. H. Dodd, *The Authority of the Bible* (New York: Harper, 1960), 222–23.

[22]Emil Brunner, *The Mediator*, trans. Olive Wyon (Philadelphia: Westminster, 1948), 368.

23Emil Brunner, *Religionsphilosophie* (München, 1927), 77–78; cited by Paul King Jewett in *Inspiration and Interpretation,* ed. John F. Walvoord (Grand Rapids: Eerdmans, 1957), 211.

24See Aquinas, *Summa Theologica,* Part 3, Question 27; see also Bonaventura, III *Sent.* D3.

CHAPTER 9

1John Calvin, *Institutes of the Christian Religion,* trans. Henry Beveridge, 2 vols. (Grand Rapids: Eerdmans, 1964), 1:72.

2Reference to New American Standard Bible marginal note to Romans 10:17.

3*Biblical Authority,* ed. Jack Rogers (Waco: Word, 1977).

4*The Foundation of Biblical Authority,* ed. James M. Boice (Grand Rapids: Zondervan, 1978).

5Jack Rogers and Donald McKim, *The Authority and Interpretation of the Bible: An Historical Approach* (New York: Harper and Row, 1979).

6John D. Woodbridge, *Biblical Authority: A Critique of the Rogers/McKim Proposal* (Grand Rapids: Zondervan, 1982).

7Lake wrote: "It is a mistake often made by educated persons who happen to have but little knowledge of historical theology, to suppose that fundamentalism is a new and strange form of thought. It is nothing of the kind; it is the partial and uneducated survival of a theology which was once universally held by all Christians. How many were there, for instance, in Christian churches in the eighteenth century who doubted the infallible inspiration of all Scripture? A few, perhaps, but very few. No, the fundamentalist may be wrong; I think that he is. But it is we who have departed from the tradition, not he, and I am sorry for the fate of anyone who tries to argue with a fundamentalist on the basis of authority. The Bible and the *corpus theologicum* of the church is on the fundamentalist side." *The Religion of Yesterday and Tomorrow* (Boston: Houghton, 1926), 61.

8See Hans Küng, *Infallible? An Inquiry,* trans. Edward Quinn (Garden City: Doubleday, 1971).

9For a fuller discussion of inerrancy, see R. C. Sproul, "The Case for Inerrancy: A Methodological Analysis," in *God's Inerrant Word,* ed. John Warwick Montgomery (Minneapolis: Bethany, 1974), 258–59. See also extensive definition of inerrancy in the International Congress on Biblical Inerrancy Summit I "Articles of Affirmation and Denial" in *Inerrancy,* ed. Norman Geisler (Grand Rapids: Zondervan, 1979), 494–97.

CHAPTER 10

1E. R. Geehan, ed., *Jerusalem and Athens* (Presbyterian and Reformed, 1971).

2Mark Hanna, *Crucial Questions in Apologetics* (Grand Rapids: Baker, 1981).

3Gordon H. Clark, *Language and Theology* (Presbyterian and Reformed, 1980).

4Jonathan Edwards, *Freedom of the Will* (1754 edition), II, III. Italics ours.

5Paul Ramsey, ed., in the introduction to Jonathan Edwards, *Freedom of the Will* (New Haven: Yale University Press, 1957), 2.

CHAPTER 11

[1]See Robert Cushman, *Faith Seeking Understanding* (Durham: Duke University Press, 1981), chap. 1, "Faith and Reason in the Thought of St. Augustine." His first subsection is on the priority of faith. Nowhere does he discuss the priority of reason. In one passage he suggests this possibility: "If we are to understand Augustine's insistence upon the priority of faith, we must not assume that he was urging upon the pagan reason a sort of blind acquiescence to authority as the condition of understanding" (p. 10). However, he does not develop this at all. In "Authority and Reason, Faith and Understanding in the thought of Augustine," *Augustinian Studies* vol. 4 (1975), Frederick Van Fleteren does recognize the priority of reason but gives it very little discussion. Commenting on a quote from Epistle 120 he says: "In essence, this is but a restatement of Augustine's position in the Cassiciacum dialogues, that it is reasonable to accept authority prior to a pursuit of rational understanding. There is a priority both of reason and of faith" (p. 69).

[2]J. H. S. Burleigh, ed., *Augustine: Earlier Writings*, Library of Christian Classics, (Philadelphia: Westminster, 1953), 6:292.

[3]Augustine, *Confessions* 6.5.7 in *Nicene and Post Nicene Fathers* (Grand Rapids: Eerdmans, 1974), 1:93.

[4]*Augustine: Earlier Writings*, 307.

[5]Augustine says, "But as it happens that he who has tried a bad physician fears to trust himself with a good one, so it was with the health of my soul" (*Confessions*, 92).

[6]Ibid. He seems to be referring here to Ambrose's allegorical interpretation.

[7]*Augustine: Earlier Writings*, 305.

[8]Ibid., 247.

[9]Ibid.

[10]Ibid., 248.

[11]Epistle 119 in *Saint Augustine Letters* in *The Fathers of the Church* (New York: CVA, 1953), 294–300.

[12]Ibid., 295.

[13]In Epistle 120 Augustine says: "God forbid that He should hate us that faculty by which He made us superior to all other living things." Ibid., 302.

[14]Ibid.

[15]Augustine, *On the Predestination of the Saints*, in *Nicene and Post Nicene Fathers*, 5:499: "For who cannot see that thinking is prior to believing? For no one believes anything unless he has first thought that it is to be believed."

[16]*Augustine: Earlier Writings*, 318.

[17]Augustine, *The City of God*, in *Nicene and Post Nicene Fathers*, 2:482.

[18]Ibid., 484–85.

[19]Ibid., 483.

[20]Ibid., 482.

[21]Ibid., 484.

[22]See *City of God*, Book 22.

[23]Augustine, *The Catholic and Manichean Ways of Life (Demoribus Ecclesiae Catholicae)* in *The Fathers of the Church* (New York: CVA, 1953) 56:25–46, esp. 39.

[24]Augustine, Epistle 118(32), *Nicene and Post Nicene Fathers*, 1:292: "Those who are weak are encouraged to enter the citadel of authority and then their defense may be maintained with the most strenuous use of reason."

[25]Ibid.

[26]*Ancient Christian Writers* (Baltimore: Newman, 1950), 12:150.

[27]Augustine, *On Order* 2.5.15–16, cited in Van Fleteren, "Authority and Reason, Faith and Understanding in the Thought of Augustine," 46.

[28]Ibid., 49–50.

[29]Augustine, *The Catholic and Manichean Ways of Life,* 11.

[30]For further study on Augustine's view of faith, reason and authority see J. J. O'Meara, "St. Augustine's View of Authority and Reason in A.D. 386," *Irish Theological Quarterly,* 18 (1951): 338–46; R. O'Connell, *St. Augustine's Early Theory of Man* (Cambridge, Mass.: Belknap, 1968), 227–57; B. B. Warfield, *Calvin and Augustine* (Presbyterian and Reformed, 1974), 387–477; John A. Mourant, "Augustine on Miracles" in *Augustinian Studies,* vol. 4 (1973): 103–27.

[31]B. A. Gerrish, *Grace and Reason: A Study in the Theology of Luther* (Oxford: Clarendon, 1962), 1 (W.A. 275.17; 344.23; 362.15, 22; 365.18)

[32]Ibid., 1–2.

[33]Ibid., 27, 70.

[34]Ibid., 4.

[35]See Luther's *Works* T.R. 6.345.28, V.A. 44.704.15

[36]W.A. 42.408.34

[37]T.R. 5.155.1

[38]W.A. 1.226.10

[39]Gerrish, *Grace and Reason,* 135.

[40]John Calvin, *Institutes of the Christian Religion,* ed. John T. McNeil, trans. Ford Lewis Battles in The Library of Christian Classics (Philadelphia: Westminster, 1960), 1.5.1.

[41]See Edward Dowey, *The Knowledge of God in Calvin's Theology* (New York: Columbia University Press, 1952), 50–51.

[42]John Calvin, *Commentary on the Book of Psalms* (Grand Rapids: Eerdmans, 1963), 317.

[43]Wilhelm Niesel, *The Theology of Calvin* (London: Lutterworth, 1956), 43; Dowey, in *The Knowledge of God in Calvin's Theology,* p. 132, note 414, makes an interesting comment on the way Niesel structures his work. Niesel is so eager to show a Christological starting point in Calvin that he begins his discussion of the "theology of Calvin" with a discussion of Calvin and Scripture rather than following Calvin's order by discussing the knowledge of God in the creation. Dowey comments, "The question remains as to why Calvin, from whom Niesel gets the references, did not arrange his book like Niesel's."

[44]T. H. L. Parker, *Calvin's Doctrine of the Knowledge of God* (Grand Rapids: Eerdmans, 1952) 2–27.

[45]John Calvin, *Calvin's New Testament Commentaries* (reprint ed., Grand Rapids: Eerdmans, 1976) 8:31–32.

[46]B. B. Warfield, *Calvin and Augustine* (Presbyterian and Reformed, 1974), 41–42.

[47]Parker, *Calvin's Doctrine of the Knowledge of God,* p. 9, n. 1.

[48]Ibid.

[49]Dowey, 73.

[50]Ibid.

[51]Bernard Ramm, *The Witness of the Spirit* (Grand Rapids: Eerdmans, 1959), 13.

⁵²John Calvin, *Commentary on Daniel* (Grand Rapids: Eerdmans, 1948), 1:237.

⁵³John Calvin, *Commentary on the Harmony of the Pentateuch* (Grand Rapids: Eerdmans, 1948), 1:87–88.

⁵⁴Roy Clouser, "Religious Language: A New Look at an Old Problem" in the Conference Papers for *Rationality in the Calvinian Tradition* held at the Institute for Christian Studies, Toronto, Ontario, p. 20; we are indebted to the comments of Dr. Alvin Plantiga on this paper for insight into this question.

⁵⁵E. Hirsh, *Geschichte Der Neuern Evangelischen Theologie*, 2d ed. (Gütersloh: Gerd Mohn, 1960), 308.

⁵⁶Heinrich Heppe, *Reformed Dogmatics*, 1–11.

⁵⁷J. D. Nelson, "The Rise of the Princeton Theology" (Ph.D. diss., Yale University, 1935), 1–11.

⁵⁸W. D. Livingston, "The Princeton Apologetic . . . B. B. Warfield and J. B. Machen" (Ph.D. Diss., Yale University, 1948).

⁵⁹B. B. Warfield, *The Inspiration and Authority of the Bible* (Philadelphia: Presbyterian and Reformed, 1948), 25.

⁶⁰H. J. D. Denzinger, *The Sources of Catholic Dogma*, trans. R. J. Deferrai, 30th ed. (St. Louis: Herder, 1957), 410, 411.

CHAPTER 12

¹See Charles Hodge, *Systematic Theology* (Grand Rapids: Eerdmans, n.d.), 1:49–50.

²See Cornelius Van Til, *Jerusalem and Athens*, ed. E. R. Geehan (Presbyterian and Reformed, 1971), 349–50, 392, 426–27.

³See *The Philosophy of Gordon H. Clark*, ed. Ronald H. Nash (Philadelphia: Presbyterian and Reformed, 1968).

⁴Cornelius Van Til, *The Defense of the Faith* (Philadelphia: Presbyterian and Reformed, 1955), 296.

⁵Cornelius Van Til, *A Survey of Christian Epistemology* (Den Dulk Foundation, 1969), 226.

⁶Van Til, *Jerusalem and Athens*, 16.

⁷Ibid., 369.

⁸Cornelius Van Til, "An Introduction to Systematic Theology" (Classroom Syllabus, 1949), 9.

⁹Van Til, *A Survey of Christian Epistemology*, 120.

¹⁰Cornelius Van Til, *Psychology of Religion* (Phillipsburg, N.J.: Presbyterian and Reformed, 1971), 3.

¹¹Ibid.

¹²*The Defense of the Faith*, 91.

¹³Van Til, *Jerusalem and Athens*, 16.

¹⁴Thom Notaro, *Van Til and the Use of Evidence* (Phillipsburg, N.J.: Presbyterian and Reformed, 1971), 199.

¹⁵Ibid.

¹⁶Cornelius Van Til, *The Reformed Pastor and Modern Thought* (Philadelphia: Presbyterian and Reformed, 1971), 199.

¹⁷Van Til, *The Defense of the Faith*, 109.

¹⁸Ibid., 17.

[19]Van Til's system requires that he use the expression "fruitful exercise of the human intellect" to mean that the unregenerate are quite capable of cogent and meaningful thinking. Of course, nothing that the unregenerate ever do is "fruitful" in the sense of virtuous or meritorious. In that sense of the phrase Van Til's expression is unobjectionable. But Van Til will have it that the unregenerate are incapable of "fruitful," that is cogent and meaningful, thinking, to say nothing of their inability to grasp "the totality view granted us in Scripture."

[20]Van Til, *Survey of Christian Epistemology,* 4.

[21]Ibid., xi.

[22]See Ronald H. Nash, *Dooyeweerd and the Amsterdam Philosophy* (Grand Rapids: Zondervan, 1962), chap. 6, "The Archimedean Point of Philosophy."

[23]Van Til, *Jerusalem and Athens,* 107.

[24]Rousas John Rushdoony, *By What Standard?* (Philadelphia: Presbyterian and Reformed, 1959), 6.

[25]Ibid., 11.

[26]Karl Barth, *The Doctrine of the Word of God, Church Dogmatics* I./1, trans. G. T. Thomson (Edinburgh: T. & T. Clark, 1936), 273.

[27]Van Til, *Introduction to Systematic Theology,* 156.

[28]Gordon H. Clark, "The Primacy of the Intellect," *Westminster Theological Journal* 5 (1945): 190.

[29]Notaro, 52.

[30]Quoted in Van Til's *Jerusalem and Athens,* 292.

CHAPTER 13

[1]John Calvin, *Institutes of the Christian Religion,* trans. Henry Beveridge (Grand Rapids: Eerdmans, 1964), 1:74–75.

[2]Ibid., 77.

[3]Ibid., 79.

[4]Ibid., 82.

[5]Ibid., 83.

[6]Ibid.

[7]Voetius, quoted in Heinrich Heppe's *Reformed Dogmatics,* ed. Ernst Bizer, trans. G. T. Thomson (Grand Rapids: Baker, 1950), 7; italics ours.

[8]Ibid., 7–8.

[9]From John H. Gerstner, "Jonathan Edwards and the Bible," *Tenth : An Evangelical Quarterly* 9 (Oct. 1979): 1–9.

[10]John E. Smith, *Review of Metaphysics* 30 (Dec. 1976): 306.

[11]Gerstner, "Jonathan Edwards and the Bible," 16–22.

[12]Van Til, *Jerusalem and Athens,* 385.

[13]Cornelius Van Til, *The God of Hope* (Philadelphia: Presbyterian and Reformed, 1978), 199.

[14]*Foundations of Christian Scholarship,* ed. Gary North (Vallecito, Calif.: Ross House, 1976), 223.

[15]Ibid., 209.

[16]Ibid., 210.

[17]Ibid.

[18]Ibid., 235.

[19]Rushdoony, *By What Standard?*, 13.

[20]Ronald H. Nash, *Dooyeweerd and the Amsterdam Philosophy*, iv.

[21]David Hugh Freeman, *Recent Studies in Philosophy and Theology* (Philadelphia: Presbyterian and Reformed, 1962), 38f.

[22]Van Til, *Jerusalem and Athens*, 92.

[23]Ibid., 89.

[24]Ibid., 98.

[25]Ibid., 98–99.

[26]H. Evan Runner, *Scriptural Religion and Political Task* (Toronto: Wedge, 1974), 46.

[27]Ibid.

[28]Ibid., passim.

[29]Ibid., 48.

[30]Published London, 1732.

[31]The terminus of this line of thinking may be seen in John C. Vander Stelt's treatment of the testimony of the Holy Spirit. See his *Philosophy and Scripture: A Study in Old Princeton and Westminster Theology* (Marlton, N.J.: Mack, 1978).

CHAPTER 14

[1]Cornelius Van Til, *Immanuel Kant and Protestantism*. Unpublished Syllabus, p. 1.

[2]J. W. N. Sullivan, *The Limitations of Science* (New York: Mentor, 1957).

[3]Van Til, *Immanuel Kant and Protestantism*, 4.

[4]Ibid., 14.

[5]Ibid., 18.

[6]Ibid., 22.

[7]Ibid.

[8]Emil Brunner, *Revelation and Reason*, 361.

[9]Cf. L. Harold De Wolf, *Present Trends in Christian Thought* (New York: Association, 1960) 44–46.

[10]Van Til, *Survey of Christian Epistemology*, viii.

[11]Benjamin Breckinridge Warfield, *Calvin and Augustine*, ed. Samuel G. Craig (Philadelphia: Presbyterian and Reformed, 1956), 143.

[12]Van Til, *Survey of Christian Epistemology*, 251.

[13]Van Til, *Introduction to Systematic Theology*, 58.

[14]Van Til, *The Defense of the Faith*, 121–22.

[15]Rushdoony, *By What Standard?*, 43–44.

[16]Van Til, *Survey of Christian Epistemology*, 106.

[17]Gary North's defense of natural revelation is virtually traditional. He writes: "The second section of Deuteronomy 28 reverses these blessings. Nature can and will become intensely malevolent to God's people. Everything men put their hands to, will fail (vs. 20). The pestilence comes, sickness comes, along with mildew, drought and war (21–24). What could be plainer? The laws of nature are fixed, like the stars supposedly are, but they are ethically based, and shifts in men's ethical status will cause shifts in nature's regularities. The laws of nature are indeed regular, but not in a mechanical sense. They are fixed in an ethical sense. They are man-oriented. They exist for the sake of man's testing. They are part of the dominion covenant." *An Introduction to Christian Economics* (Nutley, N.J.: Craig, 1973), 214ff.

18Van Til, *Survey of Christian Epistemology*, 63.

19Ibid., 60.

20Ibid., vii.

21Van Til, *Introduction to Systematic Theology*, 244.

22Van Til, *Survey of Christian Epistemology*, iii.

23Van Til, *Introduction to Systematic Theology*, 156.

24Ibid.

25Wilbur Smith, *Therefore Stand* (Boston: Wilde, 1945).

26Gordon H. Clark, "Primacy of the Intellect," *Westminster Theological Journal* 5 (1945).

27Van Til, *Jerusalem and Athens*, 15.

28Ibid., 15–16.

29Van Til, *Jerusalem and Athens*, 16.

30Ibid., 18.

31Gordon H. Clark, *Religion, Reason, and Revelation* (Philadelphia: Presbyterian and Reformed, 1961), 36.

32Ibid., 37.

33Ibid.

34Ibid.

35Ibid.

36Ibid.

37Ibid., 38.

38Ibid., 40.

39Ibid., 42.

40Ibid.

41Ibid., 43.

42Ibid.

43Ibid.

44Ibid., 58.

45Ibid.

46Van Til, *Jerusalem and Athens*, 291.

CHAPTER 15

1Cornelius Van Til, *Survey of Christian Epistemology*, 12.

2Van Til, *The Defense of the Faith*, 176–77.

3*Introduction to Systematic Theology*, 185.

4Rushdoony, *By What Standard?*, 17.

5Cornelius Van Til, *Christian Theistic Evidences* (Philadelphia: Presbyterian and Reformed, 1976), 63.

6Cornelius Van Til, *Systematic Theology* (Philadelphia: Presbyterian and Reformed, 1974), 3.

7*Hearing and Doing: Philosophical Essays Dedicated to H. Evan Runner*, ed. John Kraay and Anthony Tol (Toronto: Wedge, 1979), 67.

8Karl Barth, *The Doctrine of the Word of God, Church Dogmatics*, I./1. trans. G. T. Thomson (Edinburgh: T. & T. Clark, 1936), 119–20.

CHAPTER 16

[1]Cornelius Van Til, *Common Grace and the Gospel* (Philadelphia: Presbyterian and Reformed, 1973).
[2]Ibid., 146.
[3]Ibid., 138.
[4]Ibid.
[5]Ibid.
[6]Ibid., 138–39.
[7]Ibid., 140.
[8]Ibid.
[9]Ibid.
[10]Ibid., 141.
[11]Ibid., 141–42.
[12]Ibid., 132.
[13]Ibid., 134.
[14]Ibid.
[15]Van Til, *Survey of Christian Epistemology*, 99.
[16]Ibid., 100.

CHAPTER 17

[1]Heinrich Heppe, *Reformed Dogmatics*, ed. Ernst Bizer, trans. G. T. Thomson (Grand Rapids: Baker, 1950), 33.
[2]Ibid.
[3]*The Works of John Owen*, ed. William H. Goold, vol. 3, 1 (Philadelphia: Leighton, 1860), 259.
[4]Ibid., 260.
[5]Van Til, *Jerusalem and Athens*, 239.
[6]Ibid., 243.
[7]Ibid.
[8]Charles Hodge, *Systematic Theology*, 2:69.
[9]Van Til, *Common Grace and the Gospel*, 184.
[10]Westminster Confession of Faith, chap. 1.
[11]John Frame, "Scripture Speaks for Itself," in *God's Inerrant Word*, 179.
[12]Herman Dooyeweerd, *Roots of Western Culture: Pagan, Secular and Christian Options,* trans. John Kraay, ed. Mark V. P. Vennen and Bernard Zylstra (Toronto: Wedge, 1979), 12.

CHAPTER 18

[1]Thom Notaro, *Van Til and The Use of Evidence* (Phillipsburg: Presbyterian and Reformed, 1980).
[2]Ibid., 8.
[3]Ibid., 13.
[4]Ibid., 16.
[5]Van Til, *The Defense of the Faith*, 197.
[6]Notaro, *Van Til and the Use of Evidence*, 17.

[7]Ibid., 26.

[8]Ibid., 28.

[9]Ibid., 34.

[10]Ibid., 37.

[11]Ibid., 38.

[12]Ibid., 40.

[13]For more detail of Notaro's examination of Van Til's critique of verification, see Notaro, 65–66.

[14]Ibid., 90.

[15]Ibid., 92.

[16]Ibid., 95.

[17]Ibid., 97.

[18]Ibid., 103.

[19]Ibid., 105.

[20]Ibid., 111.

[21]Ibid., 114–17.

[22]Greg L. Bahnsen, "Inductionism, Inerrancy, and Presuppositionalism," *Journal of the Evangelical Theological Society* 20 (Dec. 1977).

[23]Ibid., 289.

[24]Ibid., 294.

[25]Ibid., 299.

[26]Ibid., 293.

[27]Ibid., 299.

[28]Ibid., 300

[29]Ibid., 301.

CHAPTER 19

[1]Quoted by Henri Bouillard in *The Knowledge of God* (New York: Herder and Herder, 1967), 12–13.

[2]Emil Brunner, *Revelation and Reason*, 80.

[3]Ibid.

[4]Quoted by Van Til in his *Jerusalem and Athens*, 294.

[5]Ibid., 294–95.

[6]Ibid., 297.

[7]Ibid., 299.

[8]Ibid., 300.

[9]Ibid., 302–3.

[10]John Frame, "The Problem of Theological Paradox" in *Foundations of Christian Scholarship*, ed. Gary North, 313.

[11]Ibid.

[12]Ibid.

[13]Ibid.

CHAPTER 20

[1]Heinrich Heppe, *Reformed Dogmatics*, trans. G. T. Thomson, ed. Ernst Bizer (Grand Rapids: Baker, 1978), 9.

[2]Quoted by Heinrich Heppe in *Reformed Dogmatics*, 9–10.

[3]Van Til, *Survey of Christian Epistemology*, 12.

[4]Van Til, *The Defense of the Faith*, 118.

[5]Irving M. Copi, *Introduction to Logic*, 4th ed. (New York: MacMillan, 1972), 83.

[6]W. Ward Fearnside and William B. Hoether, *Fallacy: The Counterfeit of Argument* (Englewood Cliffs, N.Y.: Prentice-Hall, 1959), 166.

[7]Van Til, *Systematic Theology*, (Classroom Syllabus, 1949), 142.

[8]Van Til, *The Defense of the Faith*, 125.

[9]*Foundations of Christian Scholarship*, 290.

[10]Rushdoony, *By What Standard?*, 15.

[11]Ibid.

[12]Ibid., 29.

[13]John Frame, "Scripture Speaks for Itself" in *God's Inerrant Word*, 178f.

[14]Ibid.

[15]Gordon H. Clark, *Religion, Reason and Revelation* (Philadelphia: Presbyterian and Reformed, 1961), 98.

[16]Ibid., 102.

[17]Ibid., 105f.

[18]Van Til, *Introduction to Systematic Theology*, 162.

[19]Ibid., 163.

[20]Ibid.

[21]Carl F. H. Henry, *God, Revelation and Authority: God Who Speaks and Shows* (Waco: Word, 1976), 1:226.

[22]Ibid.

[23]Ibid., 213–45.

Index